Correctional Facility Planning and Design

Correctional Facility Planning and Design

Second Edition

Jay Farbstein

VNR VAN NOSTRAND REINHOLD COMPANY
New York

Copyright © 1986 by Van Nostrand Reinhold Company Inc.
Library of Congress Catalog Card Number: 86-6393
ISBN: 0-442-22619-5

Printed in the United States of America.

Van Nostrand Reinhold Company Inc.
115 Fifth Avenue
New York, New York 10003

Van Nostrand Reinhold Company Limited
Molly Millars Lane
Wokingham, Berkshire RG11 2PY, England

Van Nostrand Reinhold
480 LaTrobe Street
Melbourne, Victoria 3000, Australia

Macmillan of Canada
Division of Canada Publishing Corporation
164 Commander Boulevard
Agincourt, Ontario MIS 3C7, Canada

16 15 14 13 12 11 10 9 8 7 6 5 4 3 2 1

Library of Congress Cataloging-in-Publication Data
Farbstein, Jay.
   Correctional facility planning and design.

   Includes index.
   1. Correctional institutions—Planning.   2. Correc-
tional institutions—Design and construction.   3. Jails—
Planning.   4. Jails—Design and construction.   I. Title.
HV8805.F37   1986   365'.5   86-6393
ISBN 0-442-22619-5

Contents

Acknowledgments

While credited to a single author, this book is the result of many people's efforts. The original edition, five separate handbooks with the overall title "Corrections Planning Handbooks," was prepared by Farbstein/Williams & Associates under a contract with the California Board of Corrections. Jay Farbstein was the project director, principal author, and editor. Mark Goldman was project manager and wrote several chapters. Gregory Williams, John Heiss, and Herbert Sigurdson also wrote several chapters. Other authors included Larry Barone and David Dupree. Richard Wener coauthored a paper that provided the basis for one of the chapters. Linda Farbstein provided graphic design, and she and Andy Wheeler prepared the illustrations. Marlene Goldman was editor for the original, while Richard Schmidt and Brian Schermer helped edit the final. Nancy Hirschfeld and Dorothy Pike typed the original version, and Nell Whaley, Jolie Lucas, and Margaret Castro assisted with the final.

Considerable credit must be given to the California Board of Corrections for their contributions to the book. They have kindly given permission to republish this revised and expanded edition. Even more than this, they offered guidance and support in the book's conception and realization. Board staff who must be thanked include Mark O. Morris, who served as project director, Norma Phillips Lammers, Executive Officer, Edgar A. Smith, Assistant Executive Officer, Karen L. Rosa, Verne L. Speirs, J. W. Pederson, E. P. Williams, and R. Neil Zinn. In addition, the board convened a broadly representative advisory committee that gave generously of its time. Thomas V. A. Wornham was the chair; Other members included Connie Carter, Susan Berk Cohen, Tom Finley, Clyde Gould, Richard Kenyon, Ron Koenig, Don Lunsford, Jan Marinissen, Raul Ramos, Maxine Singer, Cecil Steppe, Hon. Peter Stone, Betty Trotter, and Steve Zehner. David Voorhis was consultant to the board. Funding for the original edition was provided in part by a grant from the Law Enforcement Assistance Administration and the California Office of Criminal Justice Planning.

The National Institute of Corrections Jail Center also provided considerable assistance with the project. A significant proportion of the material in the original edition was developed for NIC's Planning of New Institutions program. Specific thanks are due to John Milosovich and to the staff of the NIC National Information Center.

The following individuals reviewed one or more drafts of the book and provided valuable comments: David Bennett, David Burright, Susan Cohen, Gerald Davis, Gail Elias, Michael Feerer, Bill Ferguson, Robin Ford, Min Kantrowitz, Dennis Kimme, Carol Kizziah, John McGough, Paula Menkin, Susan Stanton, Michael Stonebreaker, Ron Taylor, Betty Trotter, Marion Varner, Don Voth, and Ed Zimmerman. Of course, the reviewers are not responsible for any shortcomings that may exist in the final version.

In addition, certain of the techniques presented in the text were field-tested in California jails. Butte County Sheriff's Office, San Luis Obispo County Sheriff's Department, Santa Clara County Sheriff's Office, and Solano County Sheriff's Office kindly cooperated in this testing.

Foreword

This volume represents a most important work for corrections. As new facilities continue to be built to accommodate rapidly increasing jail and prison populations, we are only just starting to study seriously our incarceration needs in light of societal intent, humane incapacitation requirements, and costs to the state and local taxpayer.

This document has been compiled with the excruciating detail needed to assess and plan for a community's incarceration needs. It provides detailed step-by-step guidance to local officials who are planning new construction or major renovation of jail facilities. It addresses each aspect of the planning and forethought that should go into reasoned decisions about a community's jailing needs. Such factors as population analysis and projection, alternatives to incarceration, the use of multijurisdictional facilities, and inmate programs and services are all considered. The impact of relevant court decisions on the local jurisdiction is analyzed.

In recent years, many new jails and prisons have been constructed and opened only to exhibit inadequate planning. The planning process detailed in this book takes into account the myriad factors associated with building a correctional facility that will function efficiently, safely, fairly, and humanely. There are no easy or quick solutions to planning a highly functional, secure facility. The process requires the broad-based involvement and thinking of all of the main participants in the state or local criminal justice system, as well as the public.

The correctional facilities we build today are likely still to be operational fifty years from now. Construction dollars are only the down payment when operating expenses over future decades are considered. The management of these facilities, the programming opportunities they permit, the security they afford, and the flexibility required to meet present needs and adapt to future ones all will be shaped to a great extent by the structure itself.

I would highly recommend that this document be carefully studied by those who have responsible roles in jail capacity planning and construction. The decision to build and expand jail capacity must be a carefully weighed policy decision based on input and determinations that reflect the community's real detention needs and an informed understanding of the issues.

ALLEN F. BREED, DIRECTOR
NATIONAL INSTITUTE OF CORRECTIONS

Foreword
to the
Original Edition

These jail planning handbooks were commissioned by the Board of Corrections to help counties decide whether to build a new jail. In addition, the handbooks chart a course that encourages clear and careful thinking about what to build in those counties that have already decided that they must build.

California's jails face a crisis. Many jails are overcrowded, many are outdated. Almost all face challenges in the courts. The Board of Corrections seeks, in these handbooks, to encourage thoughtful planning. When the need for replacement or renovation is urgent, there is a danger that some counties will rush to build without having a clear, long-term view of the best and most cost-effective correctional options. The procedures outlined in the handbooks are time-consuming, but they are worth the time invested because they help counties discover the best long-term solutions to their jail problems.

The handbooks reflect the board's belief that jail planning should involve broad-based participation by all segments of county government and the public. Of course, sheriffs and jail commanders must be centrally involved. For the long-term support of corrections activities, it is crucial that other officials and citizenry also take part in the jail planning project.

In addition to describing special planning tasks, issues, and methods, the handbooks recommend a framework for planning, involving an advisory committee, and various task forces and planning groups.

To supplement these handbooks, the Board of Corrections will provide a number of technical assistance and training resources. Interested counties should contact the Board of Corrections for further information.

These handbooks do not represent board policy or thinking in every particular, but the board does urge county officials to study and use them. They contain excellent guides to the difficult, but invaluable, process of thinking carefully about a county's jail requirements.

HOWARD WAY
Chairman
Board of Corrections

Part 1.
Learning about Corrections and Correctional Facilities

1. Introduction

Purpose

Correctional Facility Planning and Design is intended for a wide range of purposes. While the primary audience consists of counties that are planning jails, architects, citizens, and others may find it useful as well. Since jails are operated and built by counties, we address "the county" in the text. The book can·

- Help counties identify and define correctional problems and find solutions to such difficult problems as an overcrowded jail; an old, inefficient, or unsafe facility; limited resources.
- Aid the county in defining a planning process in which important questions are asked and critical information collected prior to entering a building program.
- Encourage consideration of planning alternatives (programs, operations, facility approaches) that may be less costly but equally beneficial.
- Simplify and help organize the planning process.
- Help avoid costly mistakes by reviewing other counties' experiences.

The book presents a "model" corrections planning process consisting of valid, tested methods. The process is flexible so that your county as well as counties with differing needs can apply it to a variety of situations. Not every county will need to complete each step or use all the information provided. To help find your own and your county's way through the process, refer to the sections below on "Options for Counties with Differing Needs" and "Introductions for Each Participant."

Why This Is a "How-to-Do-It" Book

Planning for corrections can be a long and complex process. Because of the effort required, many counties simply do not bother to plan as carefully as they might. Thus they do not benefit from possibly better, more cost-effective solutions that are often discovered during the planning process. To encourage counties to plan carefully, this book provides a step-by-step process and guide to the many skills you can tap from county agencies, community organizations, and interested citizens.

Each step in the planning process is spelled out in terms of **what** is to be done, **who** can or should do it, **how long** it will take, and what the end **product** will be like. Forms are provided for collecting and analyzing information, and questions are suggested to help interpret the results. Examples and illustrations are given throughout. Each chapter or part identifies its intended primary and secondary users.

Crime, Corrections, and the Jail

The jail is only a part of the entire criminal justice system. Unfortunately, it is often regarded as the poor relation, even the receptacle, of the rest of the system, with detainees "dumped on the doorstep" and left. The question to be answered is: How and for whom does your county wish to use the scarce and expensive resource of the jail?

Corrections planning too often focuses entirely on a "concrete" end product— the jail facility. Sometimes the assumption that a new or expanded jail will solve a county's problems with crime (or even with the existing jail) is so strong that it is never questioned or tested. However, you must examine **who** is currently held in custody and for how long. Before adding jail beds, the necessity for detention must be compared to its cost. A jail is extremely expensive to build and operate, costing about forty dollars per day to house one inmate. Yet considerable evidence indicates that jails are "capacity driven": the more jail space available, the more it will be used by law enforcement, prosecution, and the judiciary.

While many communities do need to construct or renovate jail space, others may find different solutions to their problems. These alternatives can include changing policies and practices concerning who is detained (and for how long) before trial, or employing sentences such as restitution or community service. The problem for corrections planning is to satisfy the increasing public demand for security and protection while minimizing the costs of incarceration—both to the community that pays for the jail and to the individuals who are held in it.

"4567811302 HAS BEEN PAROLED? HEY, THAT'S GREAT NEWS, WARDEN! IF YOU HAVE A NEW PRISONER WHO'S 5'6", NOT OVER 110 POUNDS, WITH FLAT EARS AND SMALL FEET, I THINK WE CAN FIT HIM INTO THE VACANCY"

By permission of Etta Hulme.

This book will help you examine the purpose of jailing in your county and whether jailing is achieving those goals. By studying who is incarcerated, for how long, how they are released, and so forth, your county can consider options for dealing with alleged and sentenced offenders in the near and more distant future. At the same time, the character and potential of your county detention and corrections facilities can be studied in light of predicted future needs. With all these considerations, it is to be hoped you will be able to avoid the costs of overbuilding or underbuilding to meet your county's needs.

Variations among Jurisdictions and in Terminology

Many aspects of correctional practice vary from state to state. Variations are found in the laws that define criminal behavior and set sentences for those convicted. Standards for correctional facility design and operation also vary widely among the states—though most states now have established such standards. Some states —Alaska, Connecticut, Delaware, Hawaii, Rhode Island, and Vermont—do not even have county-level corrections but choose to operate integrated statewide systems. To plan effectively, you must become aware of the legal and organizational basis for corrections in your state and be knowledgeable about your state's standards.

Various states and counties also use different terms to describe the same people and places. Within these first few pages, we have already used a variety of terms, some of which have similar meanings. Throughout the book, we have attempted to use the terms most commonly used. To clarify our use of terms, the following brief definitions may be helpful.

People who are locked up in jail may be called **detainees, inmates,** or **prisoners** once they are booked into the jail, **arrestees** before. They are **defendants** before conviction, **offenders** afterward.

Regarding their status, inmates are referred to as **pretrial** before the court has ruled on their guilt or innocence, **presentenced** before sentence is passed, and **sentenced** thereafter.

The person responsible for operating the jail in most counties is the sheriff. While we will use the term **sheriff** for this role, it could also be filled by a director of corrections, chief of police, or chief probation officer. In most cases, a subordinate is designated as **facility manager** and runs the jail on a day-to-day basis.

In most states a county's primary governing body is called the **board of commissioners.** However, they are called **supervisors** in California, **freeholders** in New Jersey, **police juries** in Louisiana, **county courts** in Texas, and other names in other states. Since "board of commissioners" is most common, it is used hereafter.

Finally, the **jail** itself. We use this term loosely to denote any secure place where people are detained. It is important to remember, however, that there can be a wide range of specialized detention (or **corrections**) facilities, including:

- Intake (or short-term holding) facilities
- Pretrial detention centers
- Sentenced facilities of various security levels, such as honor farms or camps
- Women's facilities
- Special mental health or substance-abuse units
- Prerelease facilities
- Multifunctional jails

Overview of the Corrections Planning Process: Five Phases

We have organized the planning process into five major phases that correspond to the five parts of this book, as described below.

Phase One: Learning about Correctional Planning Issues

The first step for most participants in the planning process is to acquaint themselves with the major issues involved in corrections. Phase One presents an overview of many of these issues. It involves:

- Learning how the corrections and justice systems work
- Understanding the demands made by correctional standards and other legal requirements
- Becoming acquainted with recent trends in corrections operations and facility design
- Becoming aware of the significant costs involved in building and operating correctional facilities and of the role of planning in controlling those costs
- Finding out about sources of information and help

Phase Two: The First Planning Steps

Phase Two includes the activities necessary to begin the planning process. These activities involve:

- Setting up a participatory planning structure
- Reviewing the history of the project and identifying current problems
- Setting goals and objectives for corrections
- Preparing "action" plans for solving problems
- Selecting a planning consultant, if one will be used in the next phase

Phase Three: Gathering, Analyzing, and Interpreting Data

Phase Three involves finding out what has happened in your correctional facility in the past—for example, who has been jailed, why, and for how long—and projecting what is likely to occur and what your county wants to occur in the future. Data gathering and analysis are technical tasks that will be done by experts (county staff or consultants). On the other hand, many critical policy decisions concerning how the jail is to be used and which kinds of programs and alternatives may be acceptable or desirable for your county will have to be weighed by citizens and elected officials. Phase Three tasks involve:

- Developing a profile of your county's jail population and programs
- Documenting the operation of the justice system in your county (crime, law enforcement, prosecution, courts, probation, etc.)
- Identifying key issues in terms of how justice system operations affect the county jail
- Considering a range of alternative programs other than incarceration that may be desirable or necessary in your county
- Documenting the trends in population growth, crime, and incarceration rates that will affect your county's future need for jail beds and other programs
- Projecting needed jail beds and programs for the next five, ten, and twenty years

By the end of Phase Three, your county will have developed a clear picture of its future correctional needs.

Phase Four: Feasibility Study

In Phase Four, corrections needs are translated into facility requirements, ways of satisfying those requirements are considered, and a feasible approach is identified. Like Phase Three, these tasks are done in part by specialists and in part by citizens and elected officials. Phase Four tasks include:

- Establishing a preliminary estimate of facility needs
- Evaluating the potential of existing facilities for continued and future use
- Developing a range of options for facility development
- Considering the possibility of sharing a consolidated or regional facility with other jurisdictions
- Calculating the construction and operating costs of proposed facilities
- Exploring potential funding sources for facility construction
- Selecting the best—and most feasible—facility option

Phase Five: Facility Development

In Phase Five, you will be involved in designing and constructing (or renovating) a correctional facility, if the earlier phases showed it to be both needed and feasible. Some of the focus will shift to the facility operators; however, input, review, and approval from citizens and elected officials will still be required. Phase Five activities include:

- Overview of the facility development process
- Information on human factors in jail design
- Facility programming and design
- How to estimate staffing requirements
- Site selection
- Selecting and working with an architect
- On-going project review and coordination

Options for Counties with Differing Needs

Each county has special needs depending on its size, its particular problems, and its available expertise and resources. Because of these variations, your county may use some sections of this book and skip others. Thus, there are a number of options in the planning process, depending upon your county's starting point and where it is heading.

Option 1: Little Change or Expansion Anticipated

You may intend to make only minor changes or slight additions to your current facility and therefore think that a full-scale needs assessment is unnecessary. However, you should review the reasons given earlier for doing a needs assessment. Some may well apply to your county. The process outlined in this book is designed to help you develop much useful information about, and considerable local support for, your jail.

Option 2: Recently Completed Needs Assessment Study

If your county has completed a corrections-system needs assessment study within recent years and is considering whether to update it, compare each of the phases and steps presented here with the kind and quality of information you already have. You will need to evaluate whether the information is still valid. If more work is needed, follow the steps as indicated.

Option 3: Immediate Fire and Life Safety Problems

If your jail faces certain immediate problems, such as fire and life safety deficiencies, overcrowding, or court order, turn to Chapter 23 for help in evaluating your facility. Once the current problem is resolved, start the planning process at the beginning.

Option 4: Possibility of Shared Facility

For certain counties, particularly small ones, and for certain special groups of prisoners (mentally disturbed, sentenced, women, and others), it may make sense to consider a regional or shared facility. If such a possibility exists, your county should explore it at once since many tasks will need to be coordinated between jurisdictions. Read Chapter 25 before starting other tasks, even though you will not have all the information you need to make a final decision until much later. Be sure that other potential cooperating counties or cities also embark on the needs assessment process and that you establish a means of coordinating your efforts.

Participants in the Planning Process

Many people—each with his or her own particular interest, expertise, and level of involvement—will be involved in the planning process at one stage or another. The overall organization and specific roles of various participants and groups are detailed in "Participatory Planning." Some people will follow the sequence of steps from beginning to end. Some will have an overview with less direct involvement. Others will be called upon from time to time to perform particular tasks or advise on particular issues. The following brief descriptions are intended to help each participant start the process with a basic understanding or what is expected.

Board of Commissioners

The board of commissioners plays a crucial role in local corrections planning. The board represents the interests of county citizens, and as such sees that local law enforcement and detention services are adequately funded. At the same time, the board must make certain that the services are provided in a cost-effective way by the sheriff directly responsible for detention and corrections.

Specific duties of the board in the needs assessment process include:

- Establishing an advisory committee and selecting its members
- Issuing a directive to county staff to carry out the planning study (or to hire a consultant)
- Funding the project manager (and perhaps other staff positions) as well as other project expenses
- Supplying input to and reviewing policy issues as they develop
- Reviewing and approving major reports produced in the process
- Ratifying selection of and contracts with any consultants used in the process
- Authorizing capital and operating costs for detention facilities and programs

Sheriff and Corrections Staff

With his immediate responsibility for detention and corrections, the sheriff plays a critically important role in the planning process. The sheriff is in a sensitive position, particularly when others question the way things have been done in the past and suggest how to do them in the future. The difficulty of his position can be aggravated by inviting comments from the community and other agencies, not to mention having to gather and digest extensive data. The process can succeed only with the sheriff's support and active involvement from beginning to end. Sheriffs who have not used the techniques outlined here before have been surprised to find that justification and support for their difficult work became stronger than ever before.

Corrections staffers also have a great deal to contribute, both in time and ideas. Staff will carry out the results of the process much more enthusiastically if they have been involved in their development. A corrections staff person should be assigned full-time to this project, perhaps as project manager, to provide liaison with the jail and the rest of the department. In addition, other corrections staffers should be involved in detailed operations and facility planning.

The Project Manager

The project manager will be a pivot of the entire project—a person who will always know what is going on. The project manager will attend all group meetings, will convene the planning team, and be part of the staff of the advisory committee. He or she should also sit in on all task force meetings. Duties will include coordinating and scheduling activities, serving as contact and spokesperson, and documenting the results of each planning activity.

The Planning Team

Made up of individuals with corrections, justice, and general planning experience, the planning team will carry out most tasks detailed below. Specialized tasks such as data collection or site analysis may be delegated to a task force or be accomplished by the team as a whole. The team will report to the advisory committee and the board of commissioners.

The Advisory Committee

While some advisory committee members will already be familiar with correctional planning issues, others will be invited to participate because of their particular concerns or because they represent important community interests. Broad participation in planning is important because the jail belongs to the community it serves, not just to the sheriff or jailers. The kind of jail your county builds and the way it is used (that is, who is held there and for what reasons) is as much a reflection of community values as it is of state or federal law.

The planning process is rather long and involved, yet rewarding when it produces effective results. A great deal will be asked of advisory committee members in terms of time and thought, especially of unpaid representatives of the public or community-based organizations. It will, however, be a worthwhile investment in learning about corrections and in contribution to the community.

Representatives of Criminal Justice Agencies

Justice agency representatives will be asked to serve on the advisory committee or planning team. Since each justice agency has a significant impact on corrections, this input and expertise will be of great value in the planning process. Police, courts, prosecutors, defense attorneys, and probation departments all make myriad decisions that influence who goes to jail and for how long. Thus the representatives' ability to speak for their agencies is very important.

Consultants

Some counties will hire consultants to help with certain tasks. Chapter 12 provides guidance in their selection and in how to work with them. A variety of consultants may be considered, but the major ones are corrections planners (for early steps) and architects/engineers/construction managers (for later steps). Consultants may have minor or major roles. In any case, the county and its corrections staff must control the planning process. Whether or not consultants are used, the **process** will be the same and will require considerable involvement from the county.

Special Task Forces

Task force members will have special duties at various points in the corrections planning process. More detailed information on the functions they may fulfill can be found in the chapters dealing with each subject.

Special task forces can be involved with such activities as consultant and architect selection, data gathering and analysis, facility evaluation, cost analysis, site selection, and fund raising.

Planning to Plan: Allocating Time and Resources

Two conflicting conditions of corrections planning must be reconciled:

- Good corrections planning takes time.
- You do not have that kind of time.

Time pressures on correctional planning can be great. They may range from severe operating problems (such as life safety deficiencies or overcrowding) to court orders, deadlines for filing grant applications, or anticipated inflation in construction costs that can mean as much as a 10 percent or even an 18 percent erosion in what a dollar will buy from year to year.

Thus it is easy to understand why once the planning process has started people will be very anxious to proceed. However, after too-hasty beginnings, many counties have had to start over. Good planning and organization at this stage will save time later.

How much time does corrections planning take? From the start of planning to the ribbon-cutting ceremony, a new facility can take from three to six years to complete. While much of this time is spent in architectural design and construction, the preplanning phase is also quite time-consuming. It is important to note that certain phases and steps can be carried out concurrently. Here are reasonable time frames for each planning phase.

Table 1-1. Planning Timetable

Phase I (Issues):	1 month (Concurrent with Phase II)
Phase II (First steps):	1–5 months
Phase III (Needs):	4–12 months (Start during Phase II)
Phase IV (Feasibility):	2–6 months (Start during Phase III)
Phase V (Architectural design): (Construction):	4–12 months 9 months–3 years

The time required by your county's project will depend on its scope and complexity, your ability to overlap tasks, the level of controversy within county government and in the community at large, and the number and length of delays you may encounter for any reason. Finally, the amount of time, attention, and number of resources devoted to the project will have a major effect on how long it will take.

Range of Time Requirements

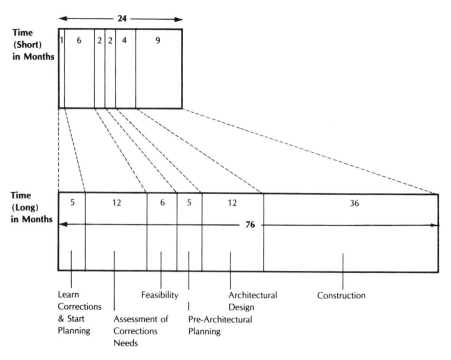

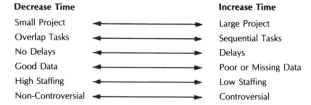

The county should be prepared to appoint a full-time project manager and sufficient staff to carry out the planning tasks.

To control the progress of the project, the project manager should at the outset establish a schedule that is realistic in terms of providing sufficient review and decision-making time. It may need to be revised periodically as the actual completion time of tasks become known. Experience suggests that schedules are only revised in one direction: longer!

We hope that you will find the information presented here to be of help in your community.

Thus, as your county begins this exciting and difficult planning project, we wish all of you: **GOOD LUCK!**

2. Corrections and the Justice System

Who Will Use This Chapter

Primary Users
Advisory committee
Planning committee

Secondary Users
Board of commissioners
Justice and corrections agency representatives

Description of the Criminal Justice System

The criminal justice system is a complex mechanism charged with minimizing criminal behavior—and dealing with it when it occurs. It encompasses all levels of government and is comprised of three major divisions: law enforcement, the courts, and corrections.

Variations among States

States vary both in the criminal justice process itself and in the terms used for parts of that process. This chapter describes, in nationally recognized terms, practices common to California and points out where major variations are likely to be found among the states.

Governmental Responsibility

Criminal justice functions are performed at all four levels of government: city (or town), county, state, and federal. We will focus on those that are the province of the county and, secondarily, those that concern the city and state.

Law Enforcement. On the local level, law enforcement is undertaken by city police and county sheriffs' departments, which are primarily responsible for investigating offenses and apprehending suspects. These suspects may be detained temporarily before transfer to a county facility.

Corrections. Local corrections involves detaining pretrial defendants and enforcing sentences, such as incarceration, probation, community treatment, or restitution. Corrections' personnel includes police and sheriffs' department detention staff, probation and parole officers, and work furlough and community treatment staff.

Courts. Although the names vary, all states have several kinds of local courts. Usually, a lower court is primarily responsible for misdemeanors and a higher one for most felonies. Responsibilities center around setting bail, hearing motions, holding trials, determining guilt or innocence, and sentencing convicted offenders.

Routes through the System

There are numerous possible routes for defendants and convicted offenders within the criminal justice system. The route taken and the speed of travel depend upon many variables. These include the type and severity of the offense, personal characteristics of the offender, available pretrial programs, and available sentencing options for those convicted. Numerous officials—including police, booking officers, district attorneys, judges, and probation officers—take part in determining an individual's route.

Many offenses take the defendant along a route through more than one governmental sector. For example, a city patrol officer may apprehend a felony suspect who may be detained and tried in county facilities but sentenced to a state correctional facility.

To explain the justice system more fully, the next sections discuss its goals and the means through which it tries to achieve them.

The Justice System, and Correctional Goals and Objectives

There are many goals and intentions of the justice system. Some of these are:

- To **protect** people from being victimized
- To **deter,** reduce, and prevent criminal activity; to discourage people from violating the law; to lower the incidence of crime
- To **apprehend** and (when necessary) **detain** suspects
- To **carry out justice;** to be fair to all parties (victims, alleged offenders, society)
- To **determine innocence or guilt** of defendants
- To determine and **carry out appropriate measures** to deal with convicted offenders, including incarceration, probation, fines, community service, or restitution

Looking specifically at detention and corrections, some often-stated goals are:

- To assure that accused offenders **appear in court**
- To **punish** convicted offenders ("revenge")
- To **rehabilitate,** reform, educate, reintegrate, or "correct" convicted offenders
- To **deter crime** through providing **undesirable consequences** such as incarceration that potential criminals may wish to avoid, and by **immobilizing** potential criminals ("keeping them off the street")
- To **exact restitution or repayment** to society and individuals who have been harmed

(Correctional goals and objectives are developed in Chapter 10.)

The Criminal Justice Process

The criminal justice process varies according to type of offense and decisions made by the local agencies. The accompanying chart showing the criminal justice process uses fifteen steps to graphically illustrate the major routes. For simplification, a generalized version is presented.

Major law enforcement and court activities are indicated in the middle column and generally are chronological. Opportunities for temporary or permanent release are indicated by arrows pointing to the right column ("out of custody"). Activities requiring detention and corrections facilities are shown in the left column ("in custody").

1. **Offense Is Committed and Reported.** An individual becomes involved with the criminal justice system in three ways. One, a law enforcement officer observes an offense being committed. Two, a victim, witness, or other interested party reports an occurrence, and a warrant for the suspect's arrest is issued. Three, an investigation by law enforcement or the district attorney points to the alleged offender, and a warrant is issued.

2. **Initial Contact.** When law enforcement officers come into contact with a suspect, they may take one of several possible actions.

If the offense is not considered serious or the officer believes prosecution is unlikely (and if a warrant has not been sworn out), the officer may **warn and release** the suspect.

An officer may issue a **field citation or summons** to an alleged offender. This charges him or her with an offense without arrest and booking, but requires that he or she appear in court and/or pay a fine. Field citations are used for a variety of infractions and misdemeanors.

An officer may bring a suspect to the police station or sheriff's office, where a **station house citation** may be issued. Like a field citation, a station house citation is frequently used for alleged misdemeanants and results in releasing the defendant upon his or her signing a promise to appear in court.

Officers may refer a suspect to a **diversion program** if one is available, or to outside services and resources such as substance abuse programs. Some counties have detoxification centers for this purpose. (Late in the process, prosecutors and judges can also refer defendants to diversion programs.)

Officers may **arrest** a suspect and take him or her into custody to insure appearance in court.

3. **Booking.** Upon arrest a suspect is escorted to the city or county jail (depending

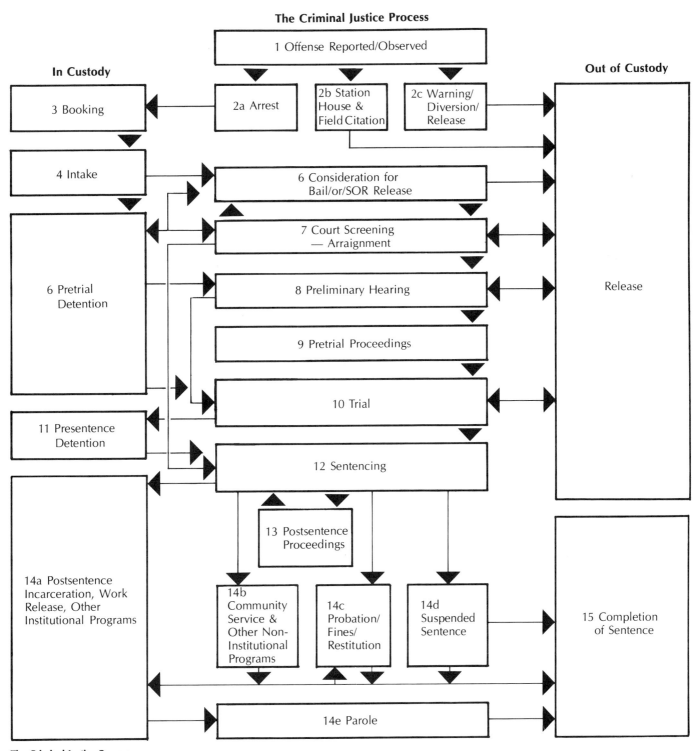

The Criminal Justice Process

The Criminal Justice Process

upon offense and jurisdiction) and booked. Booking consists of the police or sheriff's department recording the defendant's name and alleged offense; checking criminal records; and fingerprinting, photographing, interviewing, and holding the defendant. After booking, the booking officer may issue a citation release or move the prisoner on to intake.

4. **Intake.** In the detention facility, the accused is classified, screened, evaluated, and may be medically examined and diagnosed. This process determines whether

the suspect should be detained, and, if so, where he or she should be housed and whether immediate medical attention is required. The detainee's clothes and possessions are usually taken and institutional clothing issued.

5. **Consideration for Bail or Release on Own Recognizance (OR).** An arrestee may be released from detention until his or her court appearance on bail or on an own recognizance release program. Release on OR is based on the probability of the defendant appearing in court. As no relationship has been shown between success on OR and type of offense, OR programs should be charge-blind except for several capital offenses. The primary selection criteria usually include prior criminal history, stability and ties in the community, and employment at the time of arrest. Some OR programs referred to as "supervised OR" are more structured and may require reporting to a court official, counseling, or engaging in other activities that help insure that defendants appear in court.

There are several variations of release on bail or bond. A person charged with a misdemeanor or felony may post the entire amount or, as is most often the case, pay a bonding company a nonrefundable percent of the bail while the bonding company guarantees the entire amount. An arrestee charged with a misdemeanor may participate in a bail program that requires a deposit of 10 percent of the bail with the court. When the defendant appears in court, almost all of this money is returned. The amount of bail is intended to be commensurate with the seriousness of the offense and the defendant's likelihood of appearing in court. Failure to appear may result in forfeiting bail.

6. **Pretrial Detention.** Following intake, offenders who are not likely to be released within a relatively short period of time are assigned and escorted to pretrial detention quarters.

7. **Court Screening and Arraignment.** The prosecuting attorney reviews the case to determine whether charges should be pressed. This process may involve reading police reports, interviewing arresting officers, and speaking with witnesses and victims. Armed with pertinent case information, the prosecutor decides to prosecute, defer the case, or drop charges.

If charges are deferred, the defendant is released but may be required to enter a diversion program consisting of some combination of counseling, psychological treatment, job training, or restitution. In general, successful completion of the diversion program is necessary for charges to be dropped.

If the case will be pursued by the prosecutor, the accused is brought before a magistrate who scrutinizes the legality of the arrest and insures that the defendant understands his or her rights.

If bail or OR release has not already been achieved, these release options may be considered in court. A defendant who is not released by a station citation, OR, or bail is detained in a county detention facility. (The accused chooses a defense attorney or is assigned a public defender. Complaints are taken to the local municipal or justice courts, where arraignment is conducted by a judge or magistrate.)

In a **misdemeanor** case, the arresting officer and prosecutor appear with the accused before a judge. The judge clarifies the rights of the accused and reads the formal charges. Next, the judge calls for a plea. If the accused pleads guilty, the judge may sentence him or her immediately. If the accused pleads not guilty, a trial date is assigned.

In a **felony** case, a municipal or justice court judge determines whether the accused is to be released or detained. Preliminary hearings are ordered, bail is set, and the case may be bound over to the superior court.

8. **Preliminary Hearing.** The purpose of the preliminary hearing is to determine whether there is sufficient evidence to proceed with adjudication of the charges. After examining the evidence to establish probable cause, the judge, or in some cases the grand jury, has four options:

- The judge can hold a defendant for trial. If a misdemeanant pleads guilty, sentencing dates are set that allow time for presentence investigations. If the accused pleads not guilty, the case moves toward trial.

- If an accused felon pleads not guilty, he or she is bound over to superior court for arraignment and trial.

- A judge can reduce charges and request a plea to the reduced charge.
- A judge can dismiss charges and release the defendant.

9. **Pretrial Proceedings.** Prior to the trial, possible legal proceedings are numerous.

Motions initiate or challenge procedural steps. They can be entertained before or during a trial. There are many kinds of motions, including those to suppress involuntary confessions, to ask for a new trial, to adjourn or postpone a case, to sever a codefendant, to change venue (move trial to another county), to seek a competency hearing, and discovery motions (for disclosures of information by one party).

Pretrial hearings serve to clarify issues and stipulate facts, by scrutinizing records such as medical reports. As a result of this information review, a case may move in one of three directions. One, the prosecutor may discover that there is not sufficient cause to prosecute, and drop charges. Two, the defendant and defense attorney may realize that there is an overwhelming likelihood of being found guilty and decide to plead guilty or to plea bargain. Three, the pretrial hearings may not affect the direction of the case, and it may continue on course.

Negotiation/plea bargaining may occur anytime after arrest. The defense and prosecution try to reach a compromise. The defense attempts to have the charges reduced in seriousness and number. The prosecution attempts to secure a conviction by agreeing to press a lesser charge if the accused will plead guilty to it. Generally, the result is that the accused does plead guilty to the lesser charge.

10. **Trial.** If charges have not been dropped and if the defendant has not pleaded guilty to the original or negotiated charges, the case is heard. The defendant can choose to be tried by a judge alone or with a jury.

Trials begin with both attorneys making opening statements concerning the issues of law that they intend to prove. Evidence is presented; witnesses are heard, and motions may be submitted. Finally, the judge or jury deliberates and decides whether the defendant is guilty as charged. Before the judge or jury reaches a verdict, a motion for acquittal may be filed.

11. **Presentence Reports.** Most convicted defendants remain free on bail or on own recognizance release until they are sentenced. It is assumed that good risks before trial continue to be good risks until sentenced.

For all cases awaiting sentencing in superior court, a presentence investigation report is prepared by the probation officer. In the lower courts the judge or the defendant may request a presentence report. The probation officer interviews the defendant, persons close to him or her, neighbors and employers, and other collateral sources. The defendant's criminal history is reviewed and a comprehensive report and sentencing recommendation is submitted to the court.

12. **Sentencing.** The judge (in some cases with, or assisted by, the jury) determines the sentence. States vary in prescribing sentences, with a few having "determinant sentence" laws (as California). Others set parameters for a given crime while leaving the judge some discretion to lighten or increase the sentence based on factors such as criminal history and circumstances (e.g., use of a gun). Greater discretion may be possible for misdemeanors and less serious felonies.

Probation—with or without jail time—is the most commonly given sentence. Recently, only about one-quarter of felons convicted in California were sentenced to state prison. Judges also sentence offenders to serve time in jail or to alternative programs within or outside of institutions. Sentences—or their imposition—may also be suspended under certain circumstances. (See "Wider Variety of Consequences and Alternatives" later in this chapter as well as Chapters 15 through 17).

13. **Postsentence Proceedings.** After the defendant is sentenced, several legal options remain. Motions may be filed for a new trial or reduction of the sentence. A judge can deny posttrial motions, leaving the defendant the option to appeal the conviction.

To appeal, the aggrieved party files a notice of appeal with the lowest applicable appellate court. Then, attorneys for both sides file and exchange briefs and orally present arguments to a panel of appellate court judges. Judges discuss the case, reach a decision, and issue an opinion.

While a misdemeanant convicted in municipal courts or justice courts may

Dispositions of Felony Arrests

DISPOSITIONS OF ADULT FELONY ARRESTS, 1980
"SYSTEM FALLOUT"

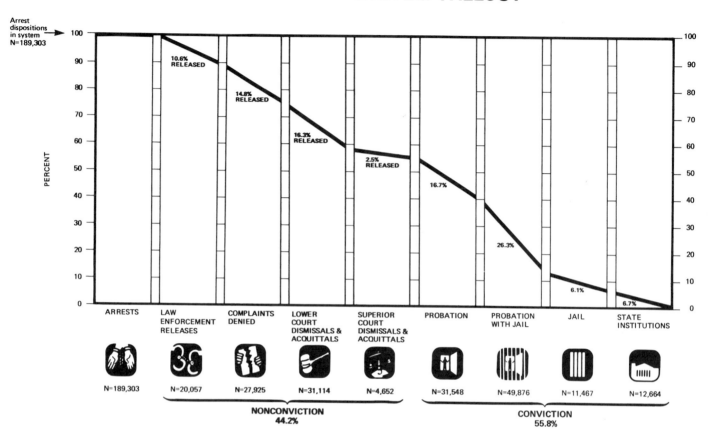

Arrest dispositions in system
N=189,303

PERCENT

ARRESTS	LAW ENFORCEMENT RELEASES	COMPLAINTS DENIED	LOWER COURT DISMISSALS & ACQUITTALS	SUPERIOR COURT DISMISSALS & ACQUITTALS	PROBATION	PROBATION WITH JAIL	JAIL	STATE INSTITUTIONS
	10.6% RELEASED	14.8% RELEASED	16.3% RELEASED	2.5% RELEASED	16.7%	26.3%	6.1%	6.7%
N=189,303	N=20,057	N=27,925	N=31,114	N=4,652	N=31,548	N=49,876	N=11,467	N=12,664

NONCONVICTION 44.2%

CONVICTION 55.8%

Notes: Probation includes straight probation, fine, and other (no sentence given and sentence suspended).
State institutions are comprised of prison, Youth Authority, California Rehabilitation Center, and state hospitals (mentally disordered sex offenders).
Prison includes 24 death penalty sentences.

State of California
Department of Justice
Division of Law Enforcement
Criminal Identification and Information Branch
Bureau of Criminal Statistics and Special Services
8/81

By permission of: California Bureau of Criminal Statistics and Special Services. From: **Adult Felony Arrest Dispositions,** August, 1981.

appeal his or her case in the county superior court, the appellate process is used more often in felonies. State courts of appeal hear appeals of felony convictions. The final appeal options for convicted felons is the state supreme court and then the United States Supreme Court if a matter of federal law is presumed.

14. **Serving Sentence.** A person convicted of a misdemeanor or a minor felony may be sentenced to a county detention facility, usually for less than one year. A person sentenced for a major felony remains in a county facility until transferred to a state correctional facility. A felon appealing a conviction may remain in a county detention facility until the case is reheard. One who receives probation and violates its terms may have it revoked and serve the remainder of the sentence. Similarly, one who receives a suspended sentence and violates its conditions may have the original sentence activated.

15. **After Completion of Sentence.** Upon completion of sentence, the offender is processed out of detention, probation, or an alternative program, and has no further obligation to the criminal justice system. He or she returns to the community.

It is widely recognized that many ex-offenders have a difficult time "making it" and consequently revert to criminal ways. An ex-offender is most likely to commit a new crime during the twelve months following the completion of a sentence. He or she may return to find home, family, friends, and job gone. The ex-offender may need job training, employment, housing, and help in solving personal and family problems. Assistance in these areas may be provided by county mental health, housing, and education departments, but too often the ex-offender is not aware of these services. In some instances help is available through the sheriff's department, probation, or county corrections department. In addition, private nonprofit ex-offender programs such as California's Project JOVE and Friends Outside provide assistance during this often difficult transitional period.

One issue facing society is whether there is a benefit or a duty to provide more extensive re-entry assistance. There is a point of view that such re-entry assistance could make significant inroads in the cycle of arrest, incarceration, and rearrest.

Problems and Trends in Criminal Justice and Corrections

Crime Patterns

Crime patterns change regularly and are difficult to anticipate or predict. In fact, it is difficult even to measure crime accurately. Typical measures include reported crimes (as reflected in the FBI's Uniform Crime Reports), arrest rates, and victimization rates. Each gives a different picture of crime patterns.

Reported Crime. Crimes reported to police agencies do not reflect all the crimes that take place. Nationally, it is believed only about one-third to one-half of property crimes and one-half to three-quarters of violent crimes are reported. Many individuals do not bother to report crimes of which they have been the victims for a variety of reasons, including a low expectation of effective response. Nonwhites tend to report fewer property crimes, while whites report fewer violent crimes (U.S. Department of Justice 1983a). Overall, it would seem that the level of reporting rises as awareness of crime grows and as expectations of police service increase. Thus statistics on reported crime are criticized as reflecting society's attitudes toward crime and law enforcement as much as actual crime rates.

In any case, crime rates in the United States have risen steadily from about two crimes per hundred people in the early 1960s to slightly less than six per hundred in the 1980s —a threefold increase (U.S. Department of Justice 1983a). About 10 percent of these are violent crimes and the other 90 percent are crimes against property. Looking in more detail at recent trends, reported crimes declined somewhat in the first half of 1982 after a four-year rise to a peak in 1980 and 1981. Violent crimes decreased 3 percent and the more numerous property crimes decreased 6 percent (California Telegram-Tribune 1982).

It is difficult to interpret either the long-term increase or recent decrease in reported crime, although some commentators suggest that the great rise in the number of people in jail and prison is serving to incapacitate criminals, keeping them off the streets. Some criminologists argue that the crime rate is not increasing. They claim that crime rates appear higher because of an increase in reporting due to more and better law enforcement and improved mandatory record-keeping systems. Others argue that if the crime rate is rising, it may be temporary, cyclical, and due to the economy or the "baby boom" (Doleschal 1979).

Victimization. Nationally, more than 24 million households—almost one out of every three—are touched by crime each year. Most prevalent are property crimes, such as theft. The percentage of victimized households has declined slightly since 1975 when similar statistics were first collected (U.S. Department of Justice 1981a and 1983b). Interestingly, this measure of crime contradicts the increased rates reported to the police.

While we cannot predict whether the crime rate will stabilize or escalate, we can be fairly certain that the incidence of crimes against people and property is likely to continue to be high.

Who Is Incarcerated

In planning a jail facility, it is critical to consider which persons and how many of them are incarcerated. These issues are often matters of fundamental social justice and public policy so farreaching that they cannot be significantly influenced by decision-makers in one county. For example, criminologists have stressed that so-called white collar criminals are less likely than other offenders to be apprehended and incarcerated. Differential access to legal assistance results in jail populations disproportionately constituted of poor and minorities.

It is beyond a jail's responsibility and capability to resolve whether such outcomes are just, let alone to correct them when they are deemed unjust. Yet consideration of these issues may influence the programs and services planned for a jail and may affect other policies through which county officials determine who goes to jail.

Of all Western industrial nations, the United States incarcerates the highest percentage of its population (Herbers 1980). In 1977, for example, the U.S. imprisonment rate was 244 per 100,000 people, while most other Western countries had rates below 100. The incarceration rate in Scandinavia was as low as 18 per 100,000 (Doleschal 1979).

Although the average stay in prison is considerably longer than in jails, far more people spend some time in city and county jails. In the mid-seventies, jails held between three and four million people annually, as much as 35 times the number entering all state and federal prisons (Goldfarb 1976).

In 1978, there were 158,394 inmates, or 76 per 100,000 people, in this country's 3,493 jails. In California, the jail incarceration rate was considerably higher: 26,206 inmates, or 120 of every 100,000 were in the state's 135 jails on an average day. The District of Columbia had the highest jail incarceration rate, with 208 per 100,000. Overall the West and the South had the highest rates (at about 100) and the Northeast and North Central had the lowest (at about 50) (U.S. Department of Justice 1983c).

There was an astounding increase in the U.S. jail population to 209,582 in mid-1982. Even before this rise, some criminologists believed that U.S. incarceration rates were unnecessarily high. They point out that more than two-thirds of prisoners in jails are detained for nondangerous and nonassaultive crimes and argue that such offenders could be incarcerated at a far lower rate (National Council on Crime and Delinquency 1978).

In fact, as jail populations swell, there is a tendency for less serious offenders to be released first, leaving the more serious ones to make up the balance. Perhaps as a result, there appear to be increasing levels of violence in jails and prisons. Opinions differ about the causes and scope of this violence. Some believe the offender entering jails and prisons today is more prone to violence than in the past. Others argue that crowded conditions and other problems in the jails stimulate violence and hostility.

Regardless of who commits crime, some characteristics of jail populations remain virtually the same as in the past. Overwhelmingly, they are poor and/or minorities. Many badly need social services that are unavailable or difficult to find—until a crime is committed (Doleschal 1979).

One especially significant trend in jail populations is that a larger portion is prone to mental illness. This may be largely due to the trend in mental health toward deinstitutionalization—removing people from mental hospitals and placing them in community treatment facilities or discharging them with insufficient support. Consequently many receive inadequate treatment, and many are arrested for crimes symptomatic of their illnesses. The end result is that many of the mentally ill are "criminalized"; they have moved from the mental health system to the corrections system. Mental health and corrections professionals strongly agree that jails are poorly suited to treat the mentally ill. Yet with the mentally ill, as with chronic public inebriates and substance abusers, the jail tends to become the placement of last resort because other resources are limited.

Growing Public Awareness and Demands for Change

The news media reports frequently and often sensationally on crime and problems in correctional institutions. Thus most people are acutely aware of crime, whether they experience it directly or not. In fact, some criminologists contend that the perceived amount of crime far exceeds the actual level of crime because of this exposure.

The degree to which citizens worry about crime varies from locale to locale. A

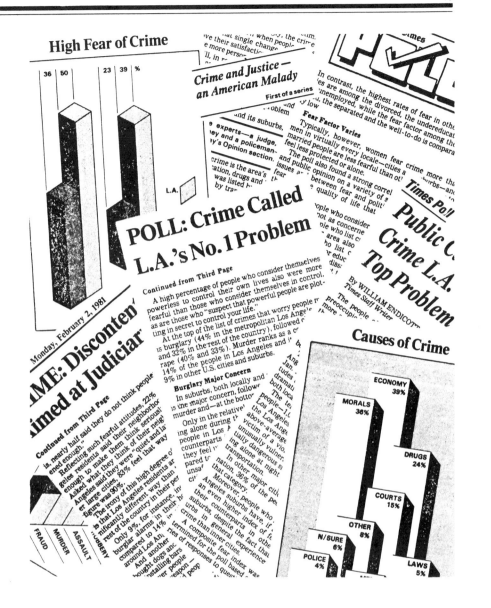

U.S. Department of Housing and Urban Development 1978 survey found that 72 percent of urban dwellers believe crime is a "severe problem," a higher percentage than for any other problem examined. However, only about 20 percent of suburban residents and about 15 percent of inhabitants of towns and rural communities considered crime to be a severe problem (U.S. Department of Housing and Urban Development 1978).

Whatever people's perceptions of crime, there is disagreement about how society should respond. While many citizens and criminologists advocate harsher penalties including longer sentences, others are pushing for lighter punishments. Citing research that indicates that there is no relationship between length of imprisonment and recidivism, some criminologists advocate short sentences. They believe resources should be allocated to attacking the root causes of crime: poverty, racial discrimination, lack of education, broken homes, and unemployment (Gilliam 1977).

Wide Variety of Consequences and Alternatives

In the search for more effective and economical solutions to crime, alternatives to many traditional criminal justice system practices have been tried recently to expedite justice, reduce costs, and lower recidivism. Some alternative programs are briefly described below. These and others are discussed in greater detail in Chapters 15 through 17.

At **initial contact,** besides the traditional methods of arrest or issuance of field and station house citations, specially trained law enforcement officers may **mediate.** For example, when neighbors report a domestic disturbance, officers can talk with the parties involved and work out conditions acceptable to both. This method keeps persons who commit minor crimes out of the correctional system, at least temporarily.

In addition to release on **bail,** programs such as **own recognizance (OR), supervised OR, reduced percentage bail,** and other liberalized bail programs may be considered.

Various types of **pretrial diversion** programs are often available, including **mediation centers** and other nonprosecution alternatives to arrest.

Other approaches to diverting offenders from the judicial process include **temporarily suspending prosecution** for defendants charged with certain types of offenses who agree to participate in a program such as counseling or vocational assistance. Dismissal of charges is contingent on the successful completion of the program. One objection sometimes raised about this approach is that, in a sense, people are sentenced without having been tried.

Using a similar method of handling cases outside of the courts, some counties have experimented with **"unofficial probation."** Juvenile delinquents who admitted guilt were placed on probation without adjudication (Greenberg, p. 114). Like temporarily suspended prosecution, unofficial probation has been criticized for possibly violating people's rights.

The greatest number of both traditional and innovative alternatives within the corrections process come at **sentencing.** Offenders can receive **suspended sentences;** these specify imprisonment for a specific length of time only if terms are violated, for example, by committing another crime.

Although **probation** per se is not new, there are now a number of variations, including more intensive versions and those that incorporate educational programs.

As part of probation, offenders may be sentenced to pay **fines** to the county and/or **restitution** to the victim. Some jurisdictions have established restitution centers that are similar to work release centers, except that a portion of the money that the offender earns goes to the victim. Restitution to victims has been proven to be far less costly and more effective than imprisonment for most nonviolent offenders (National Council on Crime and Delinquency 1978).

Offenders charged with nonserious and nonassaultive offenses can also be sentenced to **community service** programs.

Another sentencing alternative outside of correctional institutions is the **community-based program.** These range from all day every day, to an hour or so a week. Some are designed for a particular problem (such as alcoholism), while others are geared to a particular type of offender (such as first offenders) or offense (such as driving violations). In some counties successful work-oriented community service programs operate through nonprofit health and welfare agencies (National Council on Crime and Delinquency 1978).

Even with determinate sentences, judges have some discretion over the **length of sentences to institutions** for many offense types. Since longer sentences tend to mean more crowded jails and prisons and therefore greater public expense, it is important for counties to be clear about their purposes for incarceration. Studies that relate length of incarceration with postrelease outcomes should be reviewed (Kassebaum, Ward, and Wilner 1971; Kolodney et al. 1970).

Judges also have discretion over types of sentences to institutions; they can sentence certain individuals to serve **weekend sentences,** or **"days only."** Judges can also recommend (but not sentence) offenders to **work release programs.**

For offenders who apparently need to be confined or closely supervised but for whom jail seems inappropriate, judges may use **alternative institutions.** Offenders who suffer from a common malady such as drug addiction could be sentenced to a halfway house for narcotics addicts. Other institutions can serve prereleasees, work releasees, those in restitution centers, first-time misdemeanants, and so forth. To date such programs have been most often used for juveniles and young adult offenders, who may be sent to minimum security forestry camps and inner city community treatment centers.

Correctional programs within local correctional facilities vary widely; still, most convicted offenders have minimal exposure to them. Such programs are less common in local correctional facilities than in state and federal correctional facilities, largely because of the philosophy that less can be learned during shorter sentences and that constant turnover of inmates makes it difficult to offer medium- or long-term programs. Institutional programs may include academic schooling or vocational education that may involve work for the jail, such as cooking. Counseling programs may include individual, group, prerelease, self-help, religious, problem-oriented (such as alcoholism, drug abuse, criminal behavior) counseling. The programs may be led by staff, inmates, staff from other agencies (such as mental health) or volunteers (for example, Alcoholics Anonymous).

County parole is similar to probation but is administered by the sheriff. If allowed by your state laws, county parole can be structured to serve the particular needs and objectives of your county.

Although **re-entry programs** are recognized by criminologists as among the most important in the criminal justice system, they are often inadequate or nonexistent. Releasees from prisons and jails are often in dire need of assistance to "get back on their feet." Many need help with housing, employment, education, and a wide array of personal and family problems. However, ex-offenders in many areas experience difficulty obtaining help during this crucial period. Since lack of assistance during re-entry is one factor that affects recidivism, it may be cost-effective for jurisdictions to develop or expand re-entry programs.

Alternatives to incarceration have been—and will continue to be—controversial. On the one hand, alternatives can help control incarceration levels and reduce pressures for costly jail construction and operation. In addition, the alternatives create a wider variety of sanctions and greater flexibility of response to criminal convictions. On the other hand, alternatives often "widen the net" without actually reducing jail populations; they can create new forms of control over persons who previously had limited contact with the criminal justice system.

Thus careful attention should be given in jail planning to the intended consequences of alternatives and to the avoidance of the pitfalls of unintended—and costly—consequences. Once implemented, ongoing monitoring of alternatives is crucial to ensuring that their impact is as intended.

Pressure for Constitutional and Humane Treatment of Inmates

Studies of local correctional facilities indicate that conditions and treatment affect inmates. For example, overcrowding has been shown to increase stress seriously and to affect health and behavior. Conditions in institutions have been related to inmate disturbances, violent incidents, and other antisocial behaviors (see Chapter 31).

Armed with these studies, organizations such as the Committee Against More Prisons (CAMP) and the American Friends Service Committee (AFSC) have long criticized correctional systems and facilities. They have been instrumental in rousing public awareness of such institutional problems as overcrowding.

Other segments of our society, including the courts, are seeking better treatment of offenders from arrest to discharge. Often class action suits instigated by inmates at one facility affect inmates at all facilities within the state or other states. At one time or another many jails and more than half of all the states' penal systems have been ruled unconstitutional by the courts because of overcrowding, double celling, and inhumane conditions. The legal issues and directions required by standards are treated in more depth in Chapter 3.

Re-evaluation of Punishment and Rehabilitation

Inevitably, those involved in jail-planning efforts become involved in discussions of the merits of "punishment vs. rehabilitation." This is a perennial and perhaps unresolvable issue. During the past couple of decades, rehabilitation or "correction" of offenders was a much-stressed objective for both correctional institutions and alternatives to incarceration.

Recently the pendulum appears to have swung back toward punishment. The California Legislature, for example, changed the Penal Code in the late 1970s to state directly that the purpose of imprisonment is punishment.

What constitutes "punishment"? To remain consistent with professional, humanitarian, and legal requirements, loss of liberty—in and of itself—is punishment. Further deprivation or degradation could be expected to embitter prisoners, almost all of whom will return to society.

And what about "rehabilitation"? Although currently out of vogue, some argue that rehabilitation has never been tried with the kind of resources needed to test it. Others point to programs that seem to work for some offenders.

Your county should look at its own special needs and circumstances, planning for programs and facilities that will allow the best response now and in the future—when the pendulum may swing back.

Spiraling Costs of Corrections

In recent years the costs of building, maintaining and operating correctional programs and facilities have skyrocketed. Furthermore, the rising cost of borrowing money has made the effective cost of building much higher. Unionization among corrections staff and court orders requiring more staff have driven up the number of employees, their salaries and benefits (see Chapter 5).

References

Bazelon, David L. "No, Not Tougher Sentencing." **The New York Times.** 15 February 1977.

Berecochea, J. E., and G. E. Sing. 1971. "The Effectiveness of a Halfway House for Civilly Committed Narcotics Addicts." Report No. 42. Sacramento: California Department of Corrections.

California Department of Justice, Division of Law Enforcement. 1980. **Adult Felony Arrest Disposition in California.** Sacramento: California Department of Justice.

"Crime Rate Drops After Four-Year Rise." **California Telegram-Tribune.** 20 October 1982.

Doleschal, Eugene. 1979. "Crime: Some Popular Beliefs." **Crime & Delinquency** 20 (1): 1–8.

Gilliam, Jerry. "Prison Term Limit of 5 Years Suggested." **Los Angeles Times.** 12 April 1977.

Goldfarb, Ronald. 1976. **Jails: The Ultimate Ghetto of the Criminal Justice System.** Garden City, NY: Anchor Books.

Greenberg, David F., ed. 1977. **Corrections and Punishment.** Beverly Hills, CA: Sage Publications.

Herbers, John. "The Growing Number of Prisoner Lawsuits." **San Francisco Chronicle.** 18 June 1980.

Kassebaum, G., D. A. Ward, and D. M. Wilner. 1971. **Prison Treatment and Parole Survival.** New York: John Wiley.

Kerle, Kenneth, and Francis Ford. 1982. **The State of Our Nation's Jails—1982.** Washington, DC: National Sheriffs' Association.

Kolodney, S., P. Patterson, D. Daetz, and R. L. Marx. 1970. **A Study of the Characteristics and Recidivism Experience of California Prisoners.** San Jose, CA: Public Systems, Inc.

National Council on Crime and Delinquency. 1978. "Prisons: The Price We Pay." Washington, DC: Government Printing Office.

"Prisoners Can Be Rehabilitated—NOW." 1976. **Psychology Today.** October 1976: 129–34.

United States Department of Housing and Urban Development, Office of Policy Development and Research. 1978. **The 1978 HUD Survey on the Quality of Community Life.** Washington, DC.

United States Department of Justice, Bureau of Justice Statistics. 1981a. **The Prevalence of Crime.** Washington, DC: Government Printing Office.

———. 1981b. **Sourcebook of Criminal Justice Statistics—1980.** Washington, DC: Government Printing Office.

———. 1983a. **Report to the Nation on Crime and Justice: The Data.** Washington, DC: Government Printing Office.

———. 1983b. **Sourcebook of Criminal Justice Statistics—1982.** Washington, DC: Government Printing Office.

———. 1983c. **Jail Inmates—1982.** Washington, DC: Government Printing Office.

Venezia, P.S., and W. A. McConnell. 1972. **The Effect of Vocational Upgrading Upon Probationer Recidivism: A One-year Evaluation of the Singer/Graflex Monroe County Pilot Probation Project.** Davis, CA: National Council on Crime and Delinquency.

"When Will It Happen Again?" **Newsweek.** 18 February 1980: 68–76.

3. Correctional Standards and Legal Requirements

Who Will Use This Chapter

Primary Users
Advisory committee
Board of commissioners
Sheriff

Secondary Users
Corrections professionals
Facility evaluation task force

Introduction

The sheriff or director of corrections of your county is responsible for caring for and protecting the rights of every prisoner in your jail. This means providing for such basic needs as safety, shelter, food, and medical care, as well as attempting to respond to the sometimes more difficult guarantees of the U.S. and state constitutions to certain rights such as privacy. A number of specific standards, legal requirements, and regulations also apply to the operation of a jail. As with all matters of law, the county should confer with its legal counsel. This chapter, however, provides an overview of the issues involved.

Standards include a range of guidelines for how correctional facilities should be designed and operated. These have been developed by state and federal agencies as well as professional groups to improve correctional practices. While not legally binding, they often form the basis for court judgments or governmental funding decisions. **Legal** (or constitutional) **requirements** refer to legally binding state statutes and case-law definitions of constitutionally mandated rights of the inmates to particular conditions or treatment.

There is a reciprocal relationship between standards and legal requirements. The development of standards has been stimulated by court action, and, as standards have evolved, the courts have referred to them in making their judgments. Standards and legal requirements change as society changes or, as one court case put it, according to "the evolving standards of decency that mark the progress of a maturing society" (**Trop v. Dulles,** 1957).

It is the legal responsibility of your county sheriff and board of commissioners—both as county officials and also as private individuals—to comply with a wide range of requirements. Compliance with standards is the best protection against suits. Failure to comply could expose the county and its officials to unacceptable liability. In the event of a suit in federal court, elected officials do not enjoy the same immunities they have in state court and they may be liable for personal damages.

Thus one of the issues to consider when determining your county's need for new or renovated jail facilities is whether your existing facility does—or can—meet standards. The question of compliance of your existing jail is dealt with specifically in "Evaluating Existing Facilities" (Chapter 23).

For a new, renovated, or expanded facility, you must understand which standards you are required to meet and which you may want to meet for other reasons, such as the desire for a professional corrections system, out of ethical considerations, or to avoid potential legal liability. All of these topics are dealt with later in this chapter.

Standards, Problems, and Goals

Two of the early activities of the advisory committee are identifying problems and setting goals for the corrections system (Chapters 9 and 10). Before engaging in these activities, it is helpful to understand the issues surrounding compliance with standards and other legal requirements. This knowledge may inform the discussion of problems and goals.

National and State Standards

Keep in mind that many standards—although some people feel they are high—are intended to set **minimum** levels of compliance. Thus while meeting standards clearly requires the expenditure of effort and resources, they are not unattainable or utopian. Rather, standards help identify and solve corrections problems and form a foundation for establishing goals.

Typical physical factors addressed by standards include:

- Natural light, especially in living areas
- Privacy in toilet and shower areas
- Fire safety regulations
- Health and sanitation regulations
- Single occupancy cells for certain inmates
- Staff and inmate safety (the ability to summon immediate help)
- Heating and cooling requirements for comfort and energy conservation

Obviously, the design and operation of correctional facilities require considerable special expertise. To provide guidance to corrections specialists, several agencies and organizations have undertaken the development of standards for the planning, design, operation, and administration of jails and prisons.

The United Nations issues a set of international standards for jails and prisons. These standards, like their national (and many state) counterparts, are advisory in nature. They are guidelines, rather than law.

National Standards

National standards are promulgated by the following bodies:

- Commission on Accreditation of the American Correctional Association (CAC)
- American Medical Association (AMA)
- American Public Health Association (APHA)
- American Bar Association (ABA)
- U.S. Department of Justice (DOJ)

The CAC standards, which incorporate many recommended by the AMA, are the most widely recognized of the national standards. They form the benchmark for accreditation by the CAC as well as for the National Sheriffs' Association Jail Audit System. DOJ standards affect potential federal funding of jails and serve as guidelines for Justice Department litigation.

A Brief Guide to the CAC Standards for Adult Local Detention Facilities, 1981 Edition

While CAC standards are directly applicable only to jails that wish to be accredited, they should be of interest to all jails. The standards vary somewhat between those for existing and for planned facilities. They cover many aspects of jail operation—administration, fiscal management, personnel, training, inmate records, safety, security, food services, sanitation, inmate rights and rules, admission and release, and classification. While many of these indirectly effect design, others are explicit about physical plant. Here is an overview of the physical plant standards for new facilities (CAC reference numbers in parentheses).

The intake/booking and release area shall be separate from inmate living areas and within the security perimeter. It shall contain a sally port, booking area, access to drinking water, shower facilities, inmate storage, telephones, interview area, holding rooms with seating, and toilet and sinks (2-5109).

Cells shall be designed for single occupancy, shall hold no more than one inmate (2-5110), and shall have at least 70 square feet (2-5138). Cells shall have

STANDARDS
for
Adult Local Detention Facilities

Second Edition

In cooperation with the
**COMMISSION ON ACCREDITATION
FOR CORRECTIONS**

Funded by the Standards Program Management Team, Office of
Criminal Justice Programs, Law Enforcement Assistance Administration,
United States Department of Justice

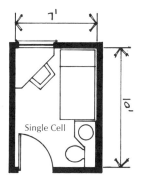

Single Cell

access to sinks, showers, hot and cold running water, a bed above floor level, a writing surface, hooks or closet space, a chair or stool, natural light, and, without staff assistance needed for its use, a toilet available 24 hours a day. In addition, they shall receive certain minimum amounts of natural light specified by the standards, have adequate circulation area, be of comfortable temperatures, and not be noisy (2-5112).

Living spaces. There shall be **dayrooms** for each living unit with at least 35 square feet per inmate (2-5144). There shall be at least one **multipurpose** room for inmate activities (2-5128). If the capacity is less than 100, indoor and outdoor **exercise areas** shall provide at least 15 square feet per inmate (2-5145). If the capacity is greater than 100, each indoor and outdoor exercise area shall be at least 30 feet by 50 feet (2-5146).

Segregation rooms shall provide living conditions approximate to those of the general population, including at least 70 square feet in single cells (2-5115) and shall permit inmates to talk with and be observed by staff (2-5116).

Security provisions. The facility perimeter shall be secured (2-5121). There shall be sally ports between inmate areas and public areas (2-5123). The facility shall maintain a control center (2-5164). Chemical agents and security equipment shall be securely stored (2-5122).

Fire safety provisions. There shall be at least two identifiable emergency exits in each inmate housing area (2-5120). Interior finishing materials shall meet national fire safety codes (2-5136).

Storage space shall be provided for clothing, bedding, and supplies (2-5131). Space shall be provided for the secure storage of inmates' personal property (2-5132). A space with a sink shall be provided for the storage of cleaning supplies and equipment (2-5130).

Males and females shall be provided visually and acoustically separate sleeping quarters (2-5118). If both males and females are held, space shall be available to provide equal opportunities for participation in programs and services (2-5129).

Other provisions include at least one single **infirmary room** for seriously ill, mentally disordered, injured, or nonambulatory inmates (2-5117). The **kitchen,** if any, shall contain at least 200 square feet (2-5126). Space shall be provided for **administrative,** professional, and clerical staff, including conference rooms, employee lounge, jail records, storage room, lobby, and toilet facilities (2-5127).

The facility shall be **geographically accessible** to criminal justice agencies, community agencies, and inmates' lawyers, families, and friends (2-5140).

The facility shall provide for the safety and security of **handicapped** inmates, integrating them with the general population, and making programs and activities accessible to them (2-5142). All public parts of the facility shall be handicapped accessible (2-5143).

State Standards

Many states have developed their own standards for local detention facilities. They usually have a mechanism for inspection and compliance built into them, although the standards themselves may be either advisory in nature (like California's) or mandatory (like Texas's). In general, state standards are somewhat less detailed and demanding than the national standards, although this is not always true. Major areas of divergence between state and national standards include provisions for staffing, operations, and space.

Significant differences for physical requirements might include space provision in cells or dorms (requirements for a single cell can range from forty-eight to seventy square feet, for example). Single occupancy cells may be required for all pretrial detainees or only for a few.

Other State Regulations That Affect Jail Planning

Besides the state and national standards, there are a number of other state regulations that can affect local corrections. While the title and location of these regulations will vary from state to state, typically laws will be contained in the following documents.

The **state constitution** may specify rights of prisoners (see "Legal Issues").

The **penal code** may define release programs, the separation of women from men and juveniles from adults, work and educational furlough, bail, confinement of state prisoners in transit, the use of city facilities or facilities of other counties, and so forth.

The **health and safety code** and **building code** will include fire safety and health standards.

The **education code** may allow for the education of detainees.

A **labor code** would be concerned with workplace safety.

A **government code** might pertain to county departments of corrections, rehabilitation programs, intergovernmental contracts, and inmate work.

A **welfare and institutions code** or other law may detail special provisions for juvenile detainees.

Building Codes That Affect Local Correctional Facilities

In building and renovating correctional facilities, state and local building codes must be followed. Generally, one of the national building codes will be adopted or modified for local use. The three major building codes are the **Uniform Building Code** (of the International Congress of Building Officials), the **Basic Building Code** (of the Building Officials, Code Administrators), and the **Standard Building Code** (of the Southern Building Code Congress). The **Life Safety Code,** which may or may not be required in your jurisdiction, has special chapters on correctional facilities. The codes require fire-resistant building materials and furnishings; adequate exits, light, and ventilation; and a workable evacuation plan. Your architect should be aware of all codes that apply in your area.

The Relationship between Standards and Legal Issues

Standards do not define legal or constitutional mandates for the jail—which may be higher or lower than standards suggest. Meeting standards does not guarantee that inmates' legal or constitutional rights are being met, although compliance is clearly a step in the right direction. Many courts use state or Commission on Accreditation standards in evaluating conditions and ordering changes. Sometimes they will go well beyond standards in their orders.

Failure to meet state standards—if they exist—may suggest a lack of concern (or perhaps, lack of professionalism) on the part of jail administrators and probably would leave an unfavorable impression in court if an action were brought against the jail. Lack of resources to meet standards is not normally accepted by the courts as grounds for denying constitutional treatment to prisoners. Although corrections depends on county government for most of its funding, the failure of the board of commissioners to provide for needed improvements or the failure of a bond issue would not prevent a judge from ordering that those improvements be made.

Avoidance of legal liability is a somewhat negative way of stating what should be a positive goal for the jail: providing humane and constitutional conditions for inmates. The questions are: How have these conditions been defined by the courts? How can the county anticipate directions in which the definitions will evolve?

Legal and Constitutional Issues for the Jail

Until relatively recently, the courts were reluctant to become involved on behalf of prisoners. This so-called hands off attitude lasted until the late 1960s, when the courts actively began to apply Eighth Amendment protections against cruel and unusual punishment and other constitutional guarantees.

Prior to that time, it was held that prisoners lost their rights upon incarceration (**Price v. Johnson,** 1948) or that even terrible conditions were acceptable if they were beyond the resources of the jail to correct (**Pickens v. Alaska,** 1951). And these were very bad conditions:

> Pickens, along with 40 other prisoners, 36 of whom were being held for trial, was confined to a room 27 feet square, heated by an ancient coal stove, with fewer than 20 bunks, virtually no ventilation and one unsanitary latrine.

Subsequent cases gradually redefined the courts' ability to apply constitutional guarantees to prisoners. In 1961, **Monroe v. Pape** held that Section 1893 of the federal Civil Rights Act, which gives people the right to seek remedy against anyone who deprives them of their rights, also applies to inmates. The Supreme Court confirmed this in 1964 (**Cooper v. Pate**). Early cases dealt with freedom of religion, brutality, and access to the courts.

Nineteen seventy-one was a key year for court action affecting prisoners. The court began to distinguish between conditions acceptable for pretrial detainees compared to those for convicted prisoners. In **Hamilton v. Love,** the court held that the Fourteenth Amendment guarantee of equal protection required that conditions for pretrial detainees (who are presumed innocent) be superior to those permitted for convicted prisoners. Detention should be in the least restrictive manner possible, according to that decision. This was confirmed in **Anderson v. Nossen,** in which

> plaintiffs were arrested for parading without a permit. After arrest, they were transported over 200 miles to the Mississippi State Penitentiary where they were forced to strip naked, consume a laxative, and were then confined eight men to a cell for up to 36 hours.... The bunks In each cell were without mattresses or bedding of any kind; neither towels nor soap were provided.

Another important 1971 case, **Holt v. Sarver,** held that the "totality of conditions" of incarceration could be considered as cruel and unusual punishment. In other words, while no single condition might be a violation in and of itself, many small problems could be collectively considered as a whole.

Since that time a great deal of litigation has concerned conditions of incarceration, in a continuing process of defining both what makes a "constitutional jail" and what the court's role should be in developing that definition. The courts have ruled upon many conditions, including the following.

- Space provision, overcrowding, single- versus multiple-occupancy cells
- Sanitation
- Fire safety
- Diet and exercise
- Medical and mental health care
- Protection from violence
- Access to visitation, correspondence, and telephone calls
- Classification and privileges

It is difficult to measure the overall impact the courts have had on jails. In the opinion of Norman A. Carlson, director of the Federal Bureau of Prisons, "The courts have done more to improve conditions in our nation's prisons and jails than any other individual, organization or branch of government" (Carlson 1983).

Litigation, of course, is an adversarial process. The courts can bring judgment only in particular cases, and these must be judged each upon its own merits. Thus court involvement in the specification of jail conditions moves sporadically and not always in a single or clear direction.

The U.S. Supreme Court may be moving away from its prior willingness to intervene. Recent cases, including **Bell v. Wolfish** (1979) and **Rhodes v. Chapman** (1981), indicate a narrowing of the scope of court involvement. In the Wolfish decision concerning conditions in the modern, highly advanced Federal Metropolitan Correctional Center (MCC) in New York City, the Supreme Court reversed a lower court's finding that among other things double celling was not permissible. The high court held that courts should not get involved in "the minutiae of prison operations" but should leave such issues to administrators and confine themselves to broad constitutional questions.

In addition, the court appeared to draw back from the **Hamilton v. Love** protections for pretrial detainees, stating that the presumption of innocence "has no application to a determination of the rights of a pretrial detainee during confinement." It is now unclear what rights and standards for pretrial detention the federal courts will uphold.

In **Rhodes v. Chapman,** the Supreme Court ruled on the extent to which Eighth Amendment guarantees apply to prison conditions. It held that double celling at the Southern Ohio Correctional Facility at Lucasville did not constitute "cruel and unusual punishment." While the opinion was careful to leave open a different interpretation under other circumstances, the court found that in this "unquestionably . . . top-flight, first-class facility," double celling did not inflict "unnecessary or wanton pain."

Some jurisdictions might interpret these findings as making double celling constitutional. However, keep in mind that there are very few jails in the country that provide a "totality of conditions" as high in quality as that of the New York MCC or the Ohio prison. The concurring opinion in the Rhodes case even stated that the "decision should in no way be construed as a retreat from the careful judicial scrutiny of prison conditions."

Avoiding Legal Liability

Although there is no official tally, as many as half of the counties in California may have suits pending, have had court orders, or are about to have suits filed concerning their jails. These include all of the state's largest counties where inmates have won serious cases. Other states are probably experiencing similar levels of litigation. In some states, all jails have been sued concurrently or have felt the impact of a single suit (Louisiana, Mississippi). In Texas, the Commission on Jail Standards has been sued concerning its enforcement of standards in the state's 254 counties (Taft).

Since the future of corrections litigation is uncertain, what steps may a county take now to minimize the likelihood of losing court cases in the future?

Strategies that hold some promise of success—although no guarantee—include keeping informed about current trends in corrections, meeting state and national standards, and making "good faith" efforts to insure the rights of the incarcerated.

References

Current Major Standards

American Bar Association Standing Committee on Standards for Criminal Justice, **Legal Status of Prisoners,** 1800 M Street, N.W., Washington, DC: 1980. This covers many aspects of the treatment of prisoners, including those affected by the facility such as availability of programs, medical care, visitation, physical security, and maintenance of institutions.

The National Sheriffs' Association, which does not have its own standards, has developed a jail audit system employing standards that generally follow the Commission on Accreditations. The audit system includes an initial portion for jail staff followed by a visit from trained auditors who evaluate the jail's compliance with standards and make practical remedial recommendations.

American Medical Association, Pilot Program to Improve Medical Care and Health Services in Correctional Institutions, **Standards for the Accreditation of Medical Care and Health Services in Jails,** 555 N. Dearborn Street, Chicago, IL 60610: 1978 (draft). These are the most widely accepted standards for health care and facilities in jails and form the basis for the Commission on Accreditation and Department of Justice standards. The AMA also provides a helpful booklet "Practical Guide to the AMA Standards . . . "

American Public Health Association, Jails and Prisons Task Force, **Standards for Health Services in Correctional Institutions,** 1015 Eighteenth Street, N.W., Washington, DC: 1976. Another useful guide on medical care standards.

The Commission on Accreditation for Corrections (of the American Correctional Association), **Manual of Standards for Adult Local Detention Facilities,** 6110 Executive Boulevard, Rockville, MD 20852: 1981. These voluntary professional standards are widely regarded as the leading edge of correctional practice. The current goal of the California Department of Corrections is for all state facilities (e.g., prisons) to be accredited by meeting these standards in the relatively near future. All new construction is planned in compliance.

Department of Justice, Attorney General's Office, **Federal Standards for Prisons and Jails,** Washington, DC: 1980. Modeled on Commission on Accreditation (CAC) standards, these apply to federal facilities and local jails that contract with the Bureau of Prisons to hold federal prisoners. They will also be used to administer potential Department of Justice financial assistance (see "Funding Sources and Strategies," Chapter 27) as well as providing guidance to its litigation divisions. While compliance with these standards cannot be a guarantee against lawsuits brought by others, the Justice Department does not intend to bring suit where substantial compliance or a good faith effort to comply is demonstrated.

Legal Issues

"Carlson Praises Courts, Pushes Guidelines." 1983. **On The Line** (published by the American Correctional Association), 6(5):1.

Collins, William C. 1979. **An Administrator's Guide to Conditions of Confinement Litigation.** College Park, MD: American Correctional Association. This very readable guide to the current state of "conditions of confinement" litigation relates what may happen during a lawsuit from the point of view of the corrections administrator.

Jail and Prison Law Bulletin. Published monthly by Americans for Effective Law Enforcement, Inc., 501 Grandview Drive, Suite 209, South San Francisco, CA 94080. (tel. 415-877-0731). This bulletin reviews litigation affecting jails and prisons.

National Association of Attorneys General, Corrections and Institutional Confinement Committee. 1979. **Prison Conditions: an Outline of Cases.** Raleigh, NC: National Association of Attorneys General Foundation. A brief synopsis of cases is presented.

Rudovsky, David, et al. 1977. **The Rights of Prisoners. The Basic ACLU Guide to a Prisoner's Rights.** New York: Avon. This includes a useful review of the range of issues that have led to lawsuits and judgments, mostly from the point of view of the inmate who may consider bringing suit. It is written in an easy-to-read, question-and-answer format but is somewhat outdated.

Sensenich, Ila Jeanne. 1979. **Compendium of the Law on Prisoners' Rights.** Washington, DC: Federal Judicial Center. (Available from the Government Printing Office.) This compendium is an encyclopedic listing of rights and cases.

Taft, Philip B., Jr. 1983. "Jail Litigation: Winning in Court is Only Half the Battle." **Corrections Magazine** 9(3):23–31.

Note: If they are needed, full case citations can be found in the above publications. In addition, the state attorney general or public defender may be able to provide up-to-date information on litigation in your state courts.

4. Recent Developments in Jail Operation and Design

Who Will Use This Chapter

Primary Users

Advisory committee members
Planning committee members
Corrections staff

Secondary Users

Members of the facility programming and design task force
Board of commissioners
Other interested participants

Introduction

Pan-Opticon Plan

The physical environment is important to the organizations and people who use it. The design of **any** building can have considerable impact on people's experience, activities, and health, on operating efficiency, energy use, and of course costs.

In a correctional setting, the physical environment is particularly important, primarily because of the very specific mission of incarceration. The physical environment must be secure, safe, and meet physical and social needs. Thus correctional philosophy, operations, and environment all work together to create a successful—or unsuccessful—correctional milieu.

Correctional facility design has always sought to reinforce correctional philosophy and practice. One historical example is the eighteenth-century "pan-opticon" design that featured small private cells (to encourage contemplation, prayer, and self-reform). A single jailkeeper in the center of the building simultaneously observed all inmates (to maximize efficient staffing).

Presentday correctional practitioners also see the potential in using the physical environment as a tool for implementing correctional programs. As correctional philosophy, programs, costs, and available technology have evolved, so have jail design and operations also changed. This chapter traces some of the pressures that have caused the changes and reviews current practices in jail operations and design.

Pressures and Opportunities for Change

A number of forces press for change in correctional systems. Issues such as changing public attitudes toward crime and the criminal, spiraling costs, and increased numbers of inmates and services were discussed in Chapter 2. In Chapter 3, we discussed pressures for compliance with evolving correctional standards and legal requirements. In addition, new technologies and materials are now available that influence operational and design responses to these pressures. The impact of each of these factors is briefly reviewed here.

New Attitudes and Philosophies: New Environments

The 1960s were characterized by a general liberalism and the questioning of past practices. The first major court involvement with the jails came at the end of the decade and forced some substantial changes. In other social service fields, such as mental health, movements toward "deinstitutionalization" and "normalization" developed. Many of these factors contributed to the design of the first "humane" or "normalized" jail facilities built by the federal government—the metropolitan correctional centers.

Increased Numbers of Inmates: More Jails Being Built

The tolerant attitudes of the idealistic sixties and seventies have yielded to a period of increasing crime, along with higher rates of more incarceration and a much harder public attitude toward the criminal. With more people in jail, overcrowded conditions are becoming all too common. Although more attention than in the past is directed to incarceration alternatives, more jails are also being built.

The considerable amount of new jail construction in recent years has provided opportunities to try out new ideas. New concepts have been tested and modified.

New Standards and Legal Requirements

As detailed elsewhere in this book, court involvement in the jails and the development of state and professional correctional standards have been major causes of change in jail operations and design.

Court orders have covered such operational issues as inmate mail, searches, visiting, access to the courts, provision of meaningful programs, medical services, and many others. Individual courts have also ruled on the conditions of incarceration, space requirements, crowding, access to recreation, lighting, and more. Professional standards set targets of performance in these and many other areas, often at higher levels than the courts are willing to impose.

Spiraling Costs: More Efficient Designs and Operations

In times of rapid inflation, the costs of staffing, operating, and constructing jails rise rapidly. Current cost surveys reveal that over the thirty-year life of a jail, the operating costs may be eight to nine times higher than the first costs of construction. These operating costs are inescapable. The dilemma arises of how to **afford** secure and safe detention for more prisoners while at the same time satisfying court demands and standards for more space, more staff, and better facilities. Alternatives to incarceration that reduce the demand for jail space are one response to rising costs. More efficient design and operations are another.

New Materials and Technologies

New systems and materials are now available for use in jail design, thanks partly to space and defense technology. These include security and surveillance systems, remote sensors, communications, and computers, as well as glazing materials such as polycarbonate plastic, and, more recently, multilayered plastic and glass laminates.

Some communities have built new facilities at lower costs than comparable "traditional" jails by incorporating some of these materials and systems into their designs (National Clearinghouse for Criminal Justice Planning and Architecture 1978). This may mean replacing steel bars with glass and plastic glazing, replacing traditional jail furnishings and fixtures with less expensive ones of wood or porcelain, or using new security systems to reduce direct staff surveillance of little-used areas such as corridors or sallyports. When used appropriately, these applications make jails more flexible, less oppressive, and less costly to build. They have not, however, reduced overall staff requirements.

In response to these pressures and opportunities, new trends in jail design and operations have emerged.

Changes in Correctional Operations

Services and Security

Newer design approaches to detention facilities tend to encourage greater flexibility in the use of space and in operations than before. We see multiuse program areas for education or counseling, dayrooms in residential clusters for dining or recreation, and so on. Yet the newer jail must be able to be locked down in the event of an emergency and run as securely as its predecessors. In part, this is achieved through smaller living-unit levels that nonetheless continue to offer essential services to inmates.

The jail is also becoming more of an instrument in the delivery of services than it

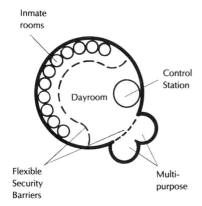

Inmate rooms

Control Station

Dayroom

Flexible Security Barriers

Multi-purpose

was in the past. This change has meant more contact with programs offered by staff within the jail or agencies outside (pretrial diversion, work furlough, education, alcohol and drug abuse counseling, and so on). In order to accommodate the program staff, a somewhat more open facility design is necessary.

The security of new jails is not necessarily compromised by their open character. In some cases it is strengthened by the increased contact between staff and inmates. Many correctional personnel find that such increased contact helps to reduce tension and to control inmates.

Most jails now have more services to offer inmates than in the past, some provided by other agencies, interns, or volunteers. As a result, there is often increased movement of inmates, staff, and other users within the building. The relative inflexibility of traditional structures has proven to be a limiting factor for some programs.

Intake Screening

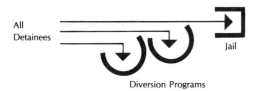

All Detainees

Jail

Diversion Programs

Pretrial release and diversion programs emphasize limiting the number who are detained or incarcerated by screening people entering the jail. To accommodate this new function, intake areas are usually situated near the offices of pretrial release or diversion programs so that those services can be provided at the time of booking. If the volume of cases warrants, the intake and screening functions may be physically removed from longer-term detention areas, thus creating the intake service center as an entity apart from the jail.

Booking, records searches, and processing of inmates can now be accomplished electronically. Computers can perform a number of operations to aid in processing people through the jail. To name a few applications, they can accept and file booking data; they can quickly search a central data system for prior arrest records; and they can keep track of inmate property or court schedules.

Other booking improvements include the use of Polaroid-type cameras, those with self-developing film. This equipment eliminates elaborate camera and lighting requirements and reduces the need for expensive darkroom space and equipment.

Classification and Housing Assignments

Probably the greatest operational changes are occurring in the living areas of jails. These changes are a response to several pressures. There is the need to separate various categories of prisoners according to behavior, type of offense, security requirements, age, sex, adjudicatory status, and other requirements. This separation protects one group from another while responding to differing needs in different settings.

In attempting to achieve this rather fine level of subdivision of inmate population, many jails cannot adequately use all of their facilities. They may have to overutilize one area and underutilize another.

In newer facilities, inmates are often housed in single-occupancy cells grouped in units of varying sizes. These units usually have direct access to dayroom and dining spaces as well as to program, activity, and recreation areas. Such units grant the flexibility necessary to operate facilities with various classifications of inmates, each requiring a defined degree of separation from others while still needing access to similar services and programs.

This "unit management" concept of operations has the advantage of concentrating various services close to the inmates, thereby reducing movement between areas and requiring less staff supervision of that movement. By contrast, inmate movement within the unit is much less restricted. Thus inmates have more freedom to use recreational facilities, attend a counseling session, or remain in their room, all without requiring the involvement of staff to move them. This leaves correctional officers free to perform other duties or to assist in the delivery of jail programs and services. Since staff typically increases when a new jail is built, such flexibility can help minimize those increases.

Because freedom of choice offered by a system of differential privileges and rewards seems to motivate some inmates toward positive behavior, it provides a basis for incentive-oriented correctional programs. In this model, varying residen-

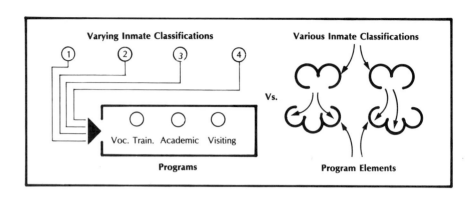

tial units have increasing degrees of freedom or privileges associated with them. Inmates who desire those relative freedoms strive to be assigned to particular living units by assuming increasingly more responsibility.

Support Services

Operational changes in jail **support** functions are also occurring. Medical and dental services are provided through contract services, the county health department, or staff medical personnel. They are typically available to all inmates and, whenever possible, are provided in dedicated clinic areas of the facilities. For minor complaints, larger jails may hold a daily sick call in residential unit facilities rather than move inmates to a central exam room.

Food preparation and dining services are also changing. Some jurisdictions find it more economical to contract for food preparation and service rather than to invest in outfitting and operating a kitchen. Most large facilities, however, still prepare food on site. The airline method of quick-chill preparation has been introduced in some newer facilities, in which food is prepared in the traditional manner but undercooked by about 20 percent. It is then quick-chilled in blast refrigerators and held for final delivery. Deliveries are made to the dining areas for reheating and serving.

Other new approaches to support functions include microwave and convection ovens, kitchens in living spaces for meal preparation, and individual washer/dryer installations in certain inmate groups' living units.

Changes in Facility Design

Historical Legacy

It sometimes seems that more attention is focused on the changing appearance of correctional facilities than on operational changes. This is perhaps because we are seeing the first real changes in the appearance of these buildings in many years. The great majority of jails built in this country prior to 1970 were modeled on structures built about 200 years ago—the so-called Pennsylvania or Auburn plan buildings.

Auburn and Pennsylvania Plans

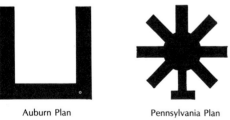

Auburn Plan   Pennsylvania Plan

These traditional buildings provided correctional environments that may have represented advanced thinking for their times, but they offer an inappropriate response to today's correctional ideals. They presented a relatively secure, highly inflexible physical plant that created an extremely oppressive environment. Generally providing little program space and few opportunities for positive staff-inmate interaction, these facilities are characterized as the "warehousing" approach to corrections.

Correctional practitioners evaluating these facilities realized that operations and correctional philosophy were severely limited by facility design.

New Directions

In response to the criticism of warehousing and the attendant desire to experiment with new approaches, the design of new jails has changed substantially in the last ten years. More attention is now focused on architecture's potential to make a positive contribution to the correctional program.

The shift in physical design concentrates on two aspects. The first is to improve operational efficiency so that the facility can be efficiently operated by custody staff and be built and maintained at a lower cost. The second is to achieve a more normal or humane environment for inmates and staff, thus lessening the noise, boredom, stress, and violence of the traditional jail.

Design for Effective Staffing

Both older and newer jails rely heavily on proper staffing patterns to operate effectively. Since staffing represents such a large proportion of operating costs, design features that minimize staff requirements without sacrificing security or program objectives are widely sought.

Circulation and surveillance are two critical functions greatly affected by design. In terms of surveillance and the layout of living units, the issue involves the number of areas that can be seen from a staff station. Since staff-inmate interaction may also be an objective, the design must balance the number of inmate areas that a staff member can observe with the number of inmates he or she can effectively serve or control. Stationing staff **within** the living unit rather than in a secure control booth is being tried in some jails in order to make effective observation possible even with limited staff and to promote staff-inmate interaction. Although some tradition-minded corrections officers may find this approach hard to accept at first, it has been shown to work in a variety of jails (Wener, Frazier, and Farbstein 1985; Miller 1985; Sigurdson, 1985). In units accommodating appropriately classified inmates, staff safety need not be compromised. Ray Nelson, ex-director of the National Institute of Corrections Jail Center, has also pointed out that the challenge of managing a unit from the inside builds a more professional corrections staff (Nelson 1983). See also Chapter 33 on staffing.

Nonobtrusive Security

Combined with effective staffing, new technologies are also contributing to achieving nonobtrusive security. Audiovisual or closed-circuit TV monitors are now widely used in jails. They are appropriate primarily for little-used areas such as corridors, service yards, or sallyports. Do not rely too heavily upon these technologies: they are easy to ignore, can malfunction, and can give a false sense of security. As every correctional officer knows, cameras do not respond to a situation—people do.

With the use of mass sensors and other electronic devices for perimeter security, you can achieve a greater degree of control over potential escape or intrusion while frequently avoiding the cagelike appearance of barbed wire (Benton, 1973).

Normalized Physical Environment

The "normal" physical environment is noninstitutional in character, similar to other buildings in use elsewhere, and has a scale that is neither overwhelming nor oppressive.

The physical appearance of a space creates its image and indicates its degree of closeness to normal life. This image is a combination of elements such as size, shape, color, light, view, furnishings, and symbols. An individual's reaction to image and space will depend upon his or her past experiences and reason for being there. We recognize what type of place it is and then develop expectations of how we may be treated and what may happen there. Thus the space or building itself serves as a medium of communication between its operators or designers and its users.

A more normal-seeming correctional environment—one with fewer symbols of incarceration—can have a positive impact upon staff and inmates by reducing some of the tensions normally associated with the loss of freedom. This concept was carried out in the design of the Federal Metropolitan Correctional Centers in New York, Chicago, and San Diego. They are not traditional in appearance, yet they still provide a secure detention environment. Features such as exterior windows, comfortable furniture, carpeting, and bright interior colors reduce the trauma of incarceration and encourage inmates to care for their living areas.

There is some evidence that these more normal environments do indeed achieve their objective of having a positive impact on inmates and staff. In an evaluation of the Metropolitan Correctional Centers, Wener and Olsen (1978) concluded that positive inmate and staff attitudes were definitely achieved by the normalized environment. Both inmates and staff clearly perceived their environment to be more attractive and less institutional than in traditional facilities. Inmates were more active, felt there was less violence and vandalism, and had a more favorable attitude toward the institution.

Summary of Recent Design Characteristics

Design techniques for achieving a more normal environment include using natural light and offering views; the use of bright, stimulating colors, textured materials such as wood, tile, brick, and carpet; limiting the size and volume of spaces; and providing spatial variety. These methods are combined with other details (appropriate to the level of security), such as doors in place of grill gates, noninstitutional furniture, and security glazing in place of bars. They result in facilities that are secure, yet humane in appearance.

The following summarizes some characteristics of recent jail design. **Elements that impart "human scale" or a normalized physical environment.** These include the use of bright colors, graphics, or materials such as brick and wood where appropriate. Large, undifferentiated spaces are avoided; areas are tailored to specific uses.

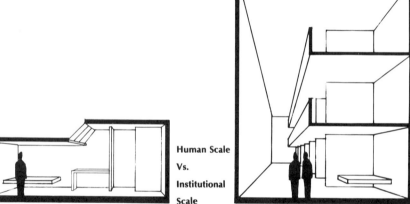

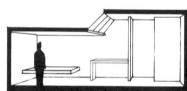

Human Scale Vs. Institutional Scale

Surveillance

Unobtrusive surveillance/observation of inmates. Living and activity areas, for example, are arranged so that they may be observed easily from a central point rather than encircling them with guard walks. Facilities can accommodate inmate movement without constant escort. There is judicious use of closed-circuit television monitoring.

Preference for single-occupancy cells. Single-occupancy cells are frequently preferred because they allow inmate privacy and protection and may help to diminish tension (Farbstein & Associates 1983). They are not intended as forced segregation. Many standards require seventy square feet in single-occupancy cells.

Incorporation of program areas into residential units. These provide inmates with somewhat more internal freedom of movement without escort than in earlier designs, make program areas more accessible, and provide opportunities for correctional staff to offer programs such as counseling, education, or job training.

Greater overall building area. Space provided per inmate ranges from 350 to 450 gross square feet. The increase over past practices results from the inclusion of single cells and additional program and service elements. Most of the last are required by the changing role of the jail as it becomes more service-oriented and not merely a place for detention.

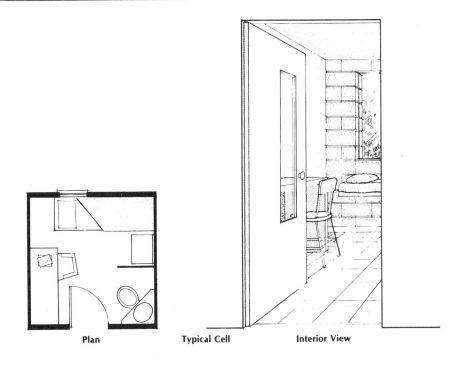

Plan   **Typical Cell**   **Interior View**

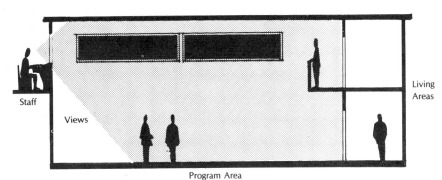

Staff

Views

Program Area

Living
Areas

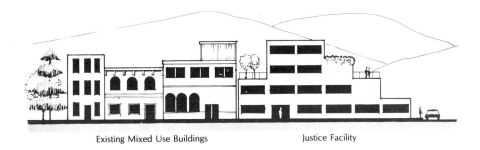

Existing Mixed Use Buildings   Justice Facility

Sensitivity to the context of community and environs. The contemporary jail attempts to reduce barriers to community acceptance and participation. It is designed to conform to the scale and appearance of its surrounding areas without compromising the need for security. Its goal is to project an appropriate image for a detention facility while being a good neighbor to the community.

Summary of Operational and Design Changes

Operational and design changes in new jails have responded to two types of pressure. New attitudes and operations have been stimulated by the courts, professional standards and practices, and community attitudes concerning incarceration. These have led to new practices such as inmate classification, program offerings, and increased visiting and telephone privileges. They have also meant higher-quality jail buildings that provide more humane environments for inmates and staff.

The second stimulus for change comes from evolving technology, which has had a considerable influence on correctional design. New methods of surveillance, types of security systems, means of information processing, and new techniques for providing services such as food preparation are developing rapidly. It is worth remembering, however, that not all of the recent experiments have worked out well. While valuable experience has been gained, much remains to be learned. The "state of the art" in operations and design is changing almost daily as technology responds to evolving needs. An update and review of new developments will familiarize you with current options when you plan your facility.

Jails to Visit

Tours of other counties' jails are essentially for sound planning. The operational and design characteristics of newer jails are best understood when observed first hand. While on site, you have the opportunity to ask questions of staff, administrators, and inmates concerning how various design and operational features work in practice. You can also observe wear and tear of materials and systems. Surprisingly, it can be valuable to visit facilities that are experiencing problems and may not be entirely successful (though none of these is intentionally included here). You may learn much about **what not to do** and thereby avoid costly mistakes.

It has been somewhat difficult to prepare an adequate list of suggested jails to visit around the country. We have not made nationwide visits, and new facilities are continually being designed and built. Therefore, while we have included three kinds of facilities, you should make an effort to identify those of interest in your area.

The first list is of National Institute of Corrections **Area Resource Centers.** These have been selected by NIC as having areas of strength (including operations and at least some aspects of physical design) and are geared to hosting and helping visitors.

The second is a compilation of all jails included in recent **exhibitions** and catalogs of the American Institute of Architects' Committee on Architecture for Justice (in conjunction with the American Correctional Association). Each of these was found by a jury of architects and corrections administrators to be worthy of inclusion in the exhibit. Some of these facilities are still under construction and have not yet proven their qualities in practice, but they would probably be worth a visit in any case.

Finally, information about **selected jails in the Western states** is provided in somewhat greater detail. These are facilities that we have visited and know to have at least some interesting aspects.

Inclusion on any of these lists does not constitute an endorsement of a facility design or its operation. It simply suggests that you may be able to gain exposure to a range of recent ideas by visiting these facilities.

National Institute of Corrections' Area Resource Centers

The list below was compiled in 1983. For more recent Area Resource Centers, contact the NIC Jail Center at (303) 497-6700.

Boulder County Corrections Center, Boulder, Colorado (detailed information in Western Jails below). Phone (303) 441-3671.

Contra Costa County Detention Facility, Martinez, California (detailed information in Western jails below). Phone (415) 372-4647.

Minnesota Jail Resource Center, Saint Paul, Minnesota. Phone (612) 296-3969.

Montgomery County Department of Correction & Rehabilitation, Rockville, Maryland. Phone (301) 251-7545.

New Haven Community Correctional Center, New Haven, Connecticut. Phone (203) 789-6980.
Southeast Kansas Regional Correctional Center, Fort Scott, Kansas. Phone (316) 223-2380/2050.

Facilities Exhibited by the American Institute of Architects' Committee on Architecture for Justice and the American Correctional Association

Each year the American Institute of Architects' (AIA) Committee on Architecture for Justice, and the American Correctional Association, sponsor an exhibit of recent justice facility projects. These are selected by a jury of architects and corrections professionals. Each facility is illustrated with plans and photos and described in a booklet, recent editions of which may be available from the AIA. The following list contains all local correctional facilities included in the exhibits from 1974 to 1984. A booklet listing all facilities exhibited since 1974 is available from the Committee on Architecture for Justice, the American Institute of Architects, 1735 New York Avenue, N.W., Washington, DC 20006. Note that some of these facilities also appear elsewhere in this section.

Alabama
Jefferson County Region III Corrections Center (1974), Birmingham
Shelby County Jail (1976), Columbiana

Alaska
South Central Correctional Institution (1980), Anchorage

Arizona
Federal Correctional Institution (1984), Phoenix
Maricopa County Presentenced Facility (1982), Phoenix
Pima County Correctional Facility (1981), Tucson
Pima County Jail—Medium Security Addition (1984), Tucson
Pima County Work Release Center (1981), Tucson

Arkansas
Pulaski County Community Correctional Center (1978), Little Rock

California
Alameda County Criminal Justice Facilities (1979), Oakland
Contra Costa County Detention Facility (1978), Martinez
Metropolitan Correctional Center (1974), San Diego
Pretrial Detention Facility—Main Jail (1983), Ventura
Sacramento County Main Jail (1983), Sacramento
Santa Cruz Pretrial Detention Facility (1982), Santa Cruz
Shasta County Justice Center (1981), Redding
South Bay Regional Center (1979), Chula Vista

Colorado
Larimer County Detention Facility (1982), Fort Collins
Pitkin County Jail (1984), Aspen

Delaware
Multipurpose Criminal Justice Facility (Gander Hill) (1982), Wilmington

Florida
Alachua County Corrections Center (1974), Gainesville
Bay County Detention Facility (1977), Panama City
Broward County Jail (1981), Fort Lauderdale
Central Booking and Processing Facility (1984), Orange County
Collier County Justice Center Expansion (1983), Naples
Dade County Stockade Expansion (1984), Miami
Orange County Correctional Center (1979), Orlando
Orange County Minimum Security Housing Complex (1982), Orlando

Georgia
Richmond County Law Enforcement Facility (1983), Augusta

Hawaii
Oahu Intake Service/Community Correctional Center (1976), Honolulu

Illinois

Champaign County Correctional Center/Courts Building (1977), Urbana
Lasalle County Criminal Justice Center (1977), Ottawa
Peoria County Juvenile Detention Center (1976), Peoria
Program Services Center (1979), Lincoln

Indiana

Kosciusko County Justice Building 1983), Warsaw
Marion County Jail Addition (1983), Indianapolis

Iowa

Community Corrections Residential Facility (1984), Dubuque
Lee County Correctional Center (1982), Fort Madison

Louisiana

Lincoln Parish Detention Center (1984), Ruston
St. Bernard Parish Jail Addition (1984), Chalmette

Maryland

Baltimore County Jail (1978), Towson Frederick County Courthouse and
    Multiservice Center (1981), Frederick
Montgomery County Detention Center Expansion (1984), Rockville
Washington County Detention Center (1982), Hagerstown

Massachusetts

Suffolk County Detention Facility (1980), Boston

Michigan

Arenac County Detention Facility (1981), Standish
Berrien County Jail (1980), St. Joseph
County Law Enforcement/Adult Detention Center (1979), Monroe
Ingham County Jail Addition (1982), Mason
Washtenaw County Corrections/Law Enforcement Center (1976), Ann Arbor

Minnesota

Ramsey County Adult Detention Center (1976), St. Paul
St. Paul Ramsey Hospital, Security Treatment Facility (1976), St. Paul
Work/Study Release Residence (1983), Plymouth

Mississippi

Jefferson Davis County Jail (1984), Prentiss

Missouri

Jackson County Detention and Courts Facility (1984), Kansas City

Montana

Lewis and Clark Criminal Justice Facility (1984), Helena

Nebraska

Douglas County Correctional Center (1980), Omaha
Omaha Correctional Center (1982), Omaha

Nevada

Clark County Detention Center (1982), Las Vegas

New Jersey

Camden County Correctional Center (1984), Camden
Gloucester County Justice Center (1981), Woodbury
Hunterdon County Jail (1981), Flemington
Monmouth County Correctional Institution (1982), Freehold
Warren County Correctional Center (1982), Belvedere

New Mexico

Bernalillo County Detention Center, Additions and Alterations (1982),
    Albuquerque
Metro Corrections/Bernalillo County Detention Center (1979), Albuquerque

New York

Dutchess County Jail and Sheriff's Department (1981), Poughkeepsie
Manhattan House of Detention for Men, Addition and Renovation (1980),
    New York City
Onondaga County Correctional Facility (1982), Jamesville

Rockland County Jail (1984), New City
Westchester County Correctional Center (1981), Valhalla
Westchester County Correctional Medical Facility (1976), Valhalla

North Carolina
Southern Correctional Center (1981), Troy

Ohio
Clermont County Law Enforcement and Corrections Center (1982), Batavia
Cuyahoga County Justice Center (1978), Cleveland
Dayton Forensic Psychiatric Unit, Dayton Mental Health and
    Developmental Center (1982), Dayton
Hamilton County Justice Center (1981), Cincinnati
Justice Center (1979), South Euclid
Lake County Sheriff's Offices and Detention Facility (1984), Painesville
Ottawa County Detention Facility (1981), Port Clinton
Wayne County-Wooster Justice Center (1976), Wooster

Oklahoma
City Criminal Justice Center (1981), Oklahoma City

Oregon
Jackson County Justice Building (1978), Medford
Justice Center (1984), Portland
Northeast Oregon Regional Youth Center (1974), Pendleton

Pennsylvania
House of Correction, Maximum-Security Housing—Fifty Women (1984),
    Philadelphia
House of Correction Work Release Housing (1979), Philadelphia
Huntingdon County Jail (1979), Huntingdon
Luzerne County Prison (1982), Wilkes-Barre
Lycoming County Prison (1983), Williamsport
Schuylkill County Prison Expansion (1984), Pottsville
Warren County Jail (1979), Warren
Wyoming County Jail (1984), Tunkhannock
York County Prison (1980), York

South Dakota
Public Safety Center (1978), Sioux Falls

Texas
Jefferson County Courthouse, Additions and Alterations (1983), Beaumont
Lew Sterrett Justice Center (1984), Dallas
McLennan County Correctional Center (1979), Waco

Virginia
Fairfax County Detention Center (19830, Fairfax
Pittsylvania County Jail (1982), Chatham
Roanoke County—Salem Jail Facility (1979), Salem

Washington
Benton County Justice Center (1984), Prosser
Clark County Law Enforcement Center (1983), Vancouver
Kitsap Work/Training Release Facility (1984), Port Orchard
Lewis County Jail (1983), Chehalis
New Correctional Facilities for King County (1982), Seattle
Pierce County Detention and Corrections Center (1982), Tacoma
Skagit County jail (1982), Mount Vernon
Spokane County Correction/Detention Facility (1983), Spokane
Whitman County Correctional Facility (1983), Colfax

Wisconsin
Racine County Law Enforcement Center (1979), Racine

Canada

Alberta
Province Correctional Centre (1981), Lethbridge

Province Remand Centre (1981), Edmonton
West Calgary Remand Centre (1983), Spy Hill

Ontario

Metro Toronto West Regional Detention Centre (1980), Etobicoke
Metropolitan Toronto East Regional Detention Centre (1982), Scarborough

Quebec

Drummond Institution (1984), Drummondville
La Macaza Correctional Institution (1984), La Macaza

Selected Western Jails

Alameda County Detention Center
Hellmuth, Obata & Kassabaum Architects, Engineers &
Planners

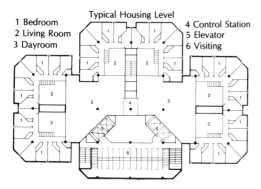

Note that staffing figures, where provided, include all jail staff, not just correctional officers.

Alameda County Detention Center, Oakland, California. The Alameda County Detention Center is designed to hold 576 male and female detainees under minimum, medium, and maximum security conditions. It consists of self-contained living units with decentralized services. Each housing unit is split level with two 48-bed units clustered around a central dayroom. A single officer-control station per floor supervises all activity areas and observes the door to each sleeping room. All services, including visiting, occur in the housing units in an effort to minimize inmate circulation. Housing units have visiting stations on upper floors, classrooms and medical office on lower floors. The center is connected to adjacent municipal courts by exterior bridges.

Benton County Regional Corrections Center, Corvallis, Oregon. Currently, this 27-bed facility houses male and female, pretrial and sentenced inmates, but in five years will hold only pretrial detainees. Located in the city of Covallis, it is attached to the courthouse. All rooms are single occupancy. The security system and hardware have a maximum-security potential, but the program currently runs at a medium level. The facility replaced an 18-bed jail with dormitories and multiple-occupancy rooms. There were no staff members permanently assigned to the old jail. Fourteen permanent staff members presently run the facility with a projected need for an additional 4.5 members. In 1980 operating costs approximated $700,000, which—after five years of operation—approach initial construction costs.

Boulder County Corrections Center, Boulder, Colorado (NIC Area Resource Center). Located on the fringe of the city of Boulder, this 100-bed facility houses male and female, sentenced and pretrial inmates. The correctional facility is of one-story modular design built around a central courtyard and attached to a two-story justice center.

The staff consisted of 66 persons with a projected need for 92 (NIC assessment). The operating budget for this facility was approximately $1.25 million in 1980. Plans called for an addition to the jails in 1984, which is currently underway.

By comparison, the facility's predecessor in 1961 contained 80 beds in four-man cells and employed some 20 staff members. Before moving into the current facility, the staff was increased to 40 during a five-month transition and training period.

Contra Costa County Detention Facility, Martinez, California (NIC Area Resource Center). This facility in downtown Martinez houses 383 residents, most in medium security but with one maximum-security housing unit. A four-level design with nine housing clusters of about 48 rooms each, it is a good example of grouping residential areas around common, double-height dayroom/dining areas. Each colorful and carpeted dayroom includes lounges, visiting rooms, and direct access to a secure courtyard. Correctional staff are stationed within the living unit, rather than in a secure control booth. Unique to this facility is the separate visitor circulation corridor, which allows visiting to take place at the housing cluster. The facility also contains courtrooms and judicial support space for arraignment and pretrial procedures.

Lane County Adult Correctional Facility, Eugene, Oregon. Currently a 116-bed facility, this downtown low rise includes all the core facilities needed to add three double-height housing areas above the present roof. Ultimate capacity is projected at 404 beds. The facility is of concrete and masonry construction in a cluster

Lane County Correctional Facility
Lutes/Sanetel/Architects

Mendocino County Rehabilitation Center
Kaplan/McLaughlin Architects/Planners

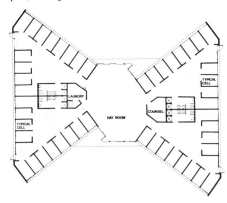

arrangement. Sixty-eight of the current cells are single occupancy with the remaining 48 beds in four 16-person dorms.

Mendocino County Rehabilitation Center, Ukiah, California. This 125-resident facility for sentenced male and female misdemeanants is located in a primarily residential area, necessitating a great deal of sensitivity to the community. Its design is simple and of an appropriate scale to surrounding houses. Four wood-exterior buildings are situated in a minicampus arrangement and house primarily minimum-security inmates.

Metropolitan Correctional Center, San Diego, California. This 455-bed facility was the first of three Metropolitan Correctional Centers (MCC) to be opened by the federal government. It began operation in 1974 and was followed a year later by facilities in Chicago and New York. The MCCs house federal unsentenced prisoners and short-term sentenced offenders in areas where local facilities cannot provide sufficient beds.

The downtown San Diego facility is a highrise building that provides 70- to 80-square-foot private rooms for each inmate. Each room has a narrow window with an exterior view and is furnished with toilet, lavatory, bed, and combination counter and cabinet storage space. The general floor arrangement clusters two levels of inmate rooms around dayrooms and dining/activity areas. These are grouped around elevators that provide for most movement of people and materials.

Other MCCs, based upon similar programs, are located in New York City, Chicago, and Miami, with another one planned for Los Angeles.

Metro Corrections/Detention Center, Bernalillo County, Albuquerque, New Mexico. A 288-bed jail for male and female inmates, this facility houses both pretrial and sentenced prisoners. It is located on a downtown site close to courts and community services. The housing consists of single rooms clustered in groups of 12 around small dayrooms that combine to form 48-bed living units. These are stacked vertically and are served by a central elevator system. Most services—dining, visiting, indoor recreation, sick call, attorney consultation—are provided at the living unit. A single security station on each floor monitors all activities. Administration, central kitchen, infirmary, and staff services are on the ground level and outdoor recreation is accommodated on the roof.

Ventura County Pretrial Detention Facility/Main Jail, Ventura, California. This pretrial detention facility, designed to hold 436 male and female inmates, is a component of a county administrative complex. It contains patrol, central dispatch, sheriff's administrative and fiscal offices, as well as detention areas. Three hundred forty-eight single rooms are located in eight 48-person quads including one quad

Ventura County
Pretrial Detention Facility/Main Jail
John Carl Warnecke & Associates in association with
Daniel L. Dworsky, F.A.I.A. & Associates Architects

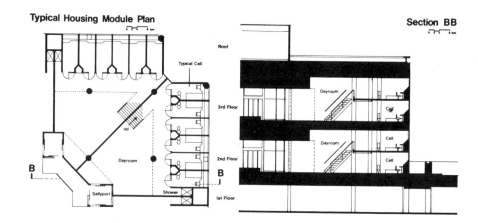

Typical Housing Module Plan

Section BB

for females. Additional special housing, medical, and disciplinary segregation rooms bring the total to 436 beds.

The five-level steel structure is clad in precast concrete panels. Two levels of housing each contain four quads that are divided into 12-room clusters. Six rooms are located on one level with six above sharing a day room area. Each cell has a concrete slab bed and seat. All services are brought to inmates and occur in the dayrooms, shared recreation, program, and visiting areas on each level. Each quad has a central control booth with a central control area for every four quads. The 220,000-square-foot facility was built at a cost of approximately $55,000 per cell. The current staff numbers 161 persons.

References

American Correctional Association and National Institute of Corrections. 1983. **Design Guide for Secure Adult Correctional Facilities.** American Correctional Association, College Park, MD.

American Institute of Architects, Committee on Architecture for Justice. **Architecture for Justice Exhibition.** Washington, DC. Booklets for several individual years may be available.

Benton F. Warren, and Robert Obenland. 1973. **Prison and Jail Security.** National Clearinghouse for Criminal Justice Planning and Architecture. Urbana, IL: University of Illinois.

California Department of Corrections, Program Planning Project. 1978. **Report on the Colloquium on Correctional Facilities Planning.** Sacramento, CA: Department of Corrections.

Farbstein, Jay, & Associates. 1983. **Housing Pretrial Inmates: the Costs and Benefits of Single Cells, Multiple Cells and Dormitories.** A report prepared for Sacramento County and the California Board of Corrections.

Farbstein, Jay, William Frazier, and Richard Wener. 1985. "Three Generations of Evaluation and Design of Correctional Facilities." **Environment and Behavior** 17 (1):71–95.

Farbstein, Jay, Richard Wener, and Patricia Gomez. 1979–80. **Evaluation of Correctional Environments.** San Luis Obispo, CA: Jay Farbstein & Associates. Five reports on jail evaluation methods and results.

Miller, Robert L. 1985. "New Generation Justice Facilities: The Case for Direct Supervision." **Architectural Technology** 3(4):12–21.

Nagel, William G. 1973. **The New Red Barn: A Critical Look at the Modern American Prison.** New York: Walker.

National Clearinghouse for Criminal Justice Planning and Architecture. 1978. **The High Cost of Building Unconstitutional Jails.** Urbana, IL: University of Illinois.

Nelson, William "Ray." 1983. "New Generation Jails." **Corrections Today** 45:108-12.

Sigurdson, Herbert R. 1985. **The Manhattan House of Detention: A Study of Podular Direct Supervison.** Boulder, CO:U.S. Department of Justice, National Institute of Corrections.

Wener, Richard, and Richard Olsen. 1978. **A User Based Assessment of the Federal Metropolitan Corrections Centers: Final Report.** Brooklyn, NY: Polytechnic Institute of New York.

5. The Cost of Building and Operating Correctional Facilities

Who Will Use This Chapter

Primary Users
Advisory committee
Planning team
Board of commissioners
Sheriff and corrections staff
Project manager

Secondary Users
Criminal justice agency representatives
Task force members

Introduction

Correctional facilities are among the most expensive of all buildings to construct, particularly if they are built for maximum security. But construction is only a relatively small percentage of the total cost of keeping people in jail, even without taking into account the social costs of lost productivity, welfare support, and so forth. Operating costs, especially staffing, will far outstrip construction in a very short time.

Thus the costs of building and operating the jail will be one of the most crucial considerations throughout the planning process. While ideally the county should build and operate the facilities and programs it wants, in the real world, goals and policies will be tempered by the affordability—and cost-effectiveness—of various options.

Three types of costs are associated with construction and operation of correctional facilities:

- **First costs** or **project costs** to construct the jail
- **Operating costs** or the recurrent costs associated with running the jail
- **Life-cycle costs** or the net result of all costs and benefits measured over the economic life of the jail

The components and current ranges of each type of cost is discussed below. Methods for estimating costs—and strategies for limiting them—are discussed in Chapter 26.

Components of Cost

The cost of building correctional facilities is very high when compared to other buildings, perhaps two to three times that of residential or commercial space in the same geographic area. Many counties see the **first cost** as prohibitive but resolve to "bite the bullet" and fund a project at substantial expense. Unfortunately they all too often find that they have overlooked the burden of ongoing **operating costs.** These can be as much as eight to ten times greater than first costs over the estimated thirty-year economic life of a correctional facility. An assessment of **life-cycle costs** gives a truer picture of the financial commitment the county must make to construct, operate, and maintain a correctional facility.

A national survey looked at construction costs of thirty-four recently built jails that were designed to conform to current standards and operational philosophies (as described in Chapters 3 and 4). From this survey, the Center for Justice Planning estimated average first costs of correctional facilities at $36,000 per bed (as of January 1, 1980).

Adjusted for California and other higher construction cost markets, average costs were about $40,250 per bed. When adjusted for inflation in construction costs and projected to a future bid date, average per bed first costs will soon exceed

$50,000 with a range from $35,000 to $70,000. In 1981, recently completed jails in higher cost areas are estimated to cost up to $77,000 for maximum-security beds and $25,000 to $42,350 for minimum-security beds.

However, when the per bed cost is multiplied by the total number of beds (capacity) and then by an anticipated thirty-year operational budget of eight to ten times first costs, the results are staggering. A hundred-bed facility in 1981 may require an initial investment of $5,500,000 plus an additional $45 million to operate and maintain it until the year 2013.

The implications of this mathematics are both simple and powerful. The people with fiscal responsibility for the county must understand what the **total** costs of building and operating correctional facilities will be before committing to a project.

The next sections discuss each type of cost—first, operating, and life cycle— and its components.

First Costs

First cost is also referred to as "project cost," "construction cost," or "initial cost." However, the term "first cost" is most accurate because it represents the cost of constructing the building including land, professional fees, permit fees, and other associated costs—the amount of money you pay to open the door of your facility. First costs do not include staff, utilities, ongoing plant maintenance, services such as food and medical care, and other recurrent costs associated with running the facility.

The first costs typically receive more attention than the operating costs, perhaps because they represent a tangible product—steel and concrete on a piece of land.

Components of First Costs

First costs are considerable, with current estimates ranging from $35,000 to $60,000 per bed space for the entire facility. Cost per square foot depends on many factors, including security level, types of systems and equipment, and quality of finishes. Per bed costs depend upon these factors as well as programs, services, and overall capacity (two factors important in determining operating and life-cycle costs). To some extent, limiting first costs can help reduce operating costs if the savings are due to reduced capacity. If corners are cut on construction quality, however, operating costs are likely to increase.

The basic components of first costs are shown in the following table in ascending order of their contribution to the total first cost. Note that the cost of the building itself comprises a large part of the first costs (60 percent).

Table 5-1. Components of First Costs

2%	Special equipment systems (fire detection, CCTV, sprinklers)
4	Site preparation
7	Architect/engineer fees
7	Jail equipment, locking systems, etc.
10	Plumbing and electrical
10	Heating, ventilation, air conditioning systems
60	General construction work (basic building)
100%	Total First Costs (not including land acquisition)

Range of First Costs for Various Types of Facilities

Although first costs may range from $35,000 to $70,000 or more per bed for the overall facility, more specific examples may help you understand how these vary. Table 5-2 supplies such information about three recently built jails. The costs in these examples have been adjusted to reflect a July 1981 construction date. They illustrate a range affected by location, capacity, and number of floors. By using a multiplier equivalent to the rate of construction inflation (recently about 10 percent per year) times the elapsed time since July 1981, these figures may be modified to show today's cost. This may be helpful as a reference when estimating the cost of your project.

Table 5-2. Comparison of First Costs

Capacity	Location	High/Low Rise	Area per Bed (GSF)	First Cost	Cost per SF	Cost per Bed
1. 586 beds	Downtown	High	400	$32.9 million	$140.77	$56,300
2. 382 beds	Downtown	Mid	474	$25.3 million	$139.69	$66,223
3. 189 beds	Rural	Low	350	$7.33 million	$110.85	$38,796

Estimating First Costs

Cost estimates are prepared by an architect, often with the aid of a professional estimator. Such estimates vary in accuracy depending on when they are done in the planning process. As more becomes known about the project, cost estimates can be made more accurate. They are generally compiled during five periods, as follows.

During **planning** it is usually necessary to rely on rather rough figures based upon **cost per bed** for a given security level.

During **programming** much more information will be available about the facility, including estimated total square footage, desired security hardware, and systems. This will allow a more accurate estimate of the **cost per square foot.** The site may also have been selected, and acquisition and development costs (e.g., for utilities) can be estimated.

During **design** several cost estimates will be produced. By now, the actual area of the building will be known, structural and mechanical systems will be defined, and materials will be selected. At this point, detailed estimates will be prepared based upon **quantity take-offs and unit prices** for each aspect of the building. Only at this period can a reasonable degree of accuracy be expected from an estimate.

At **bidding,** bonafide offers will be received to construct the building as described in the plans and specifications ("bid documents") at a **specified price.** Their range is generally somewhat above and below the cost estimates. The lowest bid will establish the cost of the project.

However, during **construction** the cost may change because of alterations in the project. These will be reflected in **change orders** that will increase, or occasionally decrease, the accepted bid price. Thus the only point at which the first cost of the facility can be determined with complete accuracy is after construction is completed. At that time, all change orders can be accounted for and added to (or subtracted from) the bid price.

Operating Costs

The initial shock of first costs for a correctional facility is relatively mild compared to the bill you will get to operate it. The above-cited survey of recently constructed jails confirms other estimates. Operating costs are projected at approximately **ten times** more than first costs over the thirty-year economic life of these facilities. This means that, for every one million dollars invested in a facility's first cost in 1981, you will need another $10 million 1981 dollars to see you through to the year 2011.

Unfortunately, the higher operating costs of detention facilities are frequently overlooked during planning. They do not seem to appear until a budget appropriation session just before the move to the new jail.

The major component of operating costs is the expense of staffing the facility. Staffing may account for as much as 70 percent of operating costs. Since the jail operates 24 hours a day, seven days per week, each staff post (such as a control center) requires approximately five persons to operate it (three shifts daily, days off, vacation, training time).

Thus a facility having seven 24-hour posts would need 35 security staff members. Fifteen others might be required for functions that are not 24-hour posts (administration, programs, food service, maintenance), for a total complement of 50. In terms of possible savings resulting from design choices, the elimination of one control station could free up five staff for other duties.

The round-the-clock operation of the jail is also a key factor in its high operating costs. Wear and tear on the building and its mechanical systems is accelerated; maintenance costs are increased; and lighting, heating, and air-conditioning systems require energy for nonstop operation. These recurring costs are estimated to account for about 20 percent of total operating costs.

Provisions for inmate needs are generally the smallest component of operating costs. These are estimated to be about 10 percent of the total operating costs and include items such as food service, commissary supplies, telephone usage, and miscellaneous supplies. Despite their relatively small percentage, they are usually the figures cited when inquiries are made about the costs of jail operation.

Estimating Operating Costs

Like first costs, estimates of operating costs can be developed at increasing levels of accuracy as planning and design progress. In the early stages of planning, estimates of operating costs must be of a general nature. Until a facility is planned, programmed, and designed, it is difficult to estimate accurately the staff required to operate it. On the other hand, since planning and design will have a great impact on operating costs, it is imperative that they be factored into decision making. Thus in subsequent parts of this book methods are presented for estimating staffing and operating costs (Chapters 19, 26, and 32).

A broad indication of operating costs may be developed by using the categories previously discussed and comparing them to first costs. The example given in the graph illustrating the comparison of first and operating costs applies this very general formula to a hypothetical hundred-bed jail costing $5.5 million in 1981 dollars to build.

Comparison of First Costs and Operating Costs

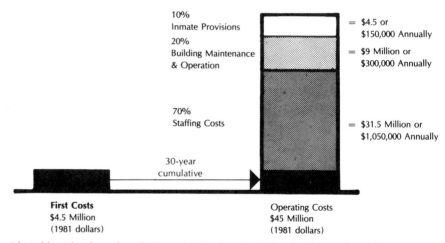

First Costs
$4.5 Million
(1981 dollars)

Operating Costs
$45 Million
(1981 dollars)

Adapted from data from Alameda County jail developed by Hellmuth, Obata and Kassabaum.

Life-Cycle Costs

Life-cycle costing is a technique that takes into account all of the costs incurred during the various stages of a project. These range from the capital investment in land, construction, and financing, to the eventual costs of salvage and disposal of the building. In other words, the costs spread over a period that corresponds to the economic life cycle of the building. Life cycles differ from one building type to another and also change with time and technological succession. Currently, detention facilities are assumed to have a thirty-year economic life. This is a generalization that includes both many older jails still in use and ten- or twenty-year-old jails that have been abandoned.

The value of life-cycle costing is that it allows the "weighing" of trade-offs in building construction and operation. For example, the specification of a cheaper material may reduce first costs but require greater maintenance, earlier replacement, and more operating personnel during the facility's life cycle. Life-cycle costing can help balance out the long-term economic consequences of these immediate decisions.

A life-cycle cost analysis should weigh both economic and noneconomic consequences of alternatives. In this way the analysis is used as a tool to compare the economic consequences of various alternatives. These consequences are then combined with the noneconomic consequences (such as effect on the community's attitude regarding detention facilities, the need to meet standards, or the desire to maintain a humane environment) to reach a final decision. This notion is illustrated in the accompanying figure.

The Use of Life Cycle Cost Analysis in Decision-making

Adapted from American Institute of Architects, 1977.

The proper timing of the life-cycle cost analysis is extremely important to its effective use. It may be used initially to determine the feasibility of corrections solutions other than construction, such as more efficient management or organization of space. If some type of building modification is necessary, the analysis may be used again to assess such options as building, renovating, or renting space.

When a decision is made to build a new jail, the life-cycle cost analysis deals with issues such as the level of amenities desired, project timing, site constraints, configuration (for example, location of control or surveillance points), building systems (structural, mechanical, and electrical), and the exterior building enclosure.

It is important to note that as the project progresses, each succeeding set of decisions tends to have a smaller impact upon total project cost. The decisions of major consequence are made in the early stages of the project and consequently should receive the most attention. This progressive reduction in impact is illustrated in the graph.

Decision Makers' Influence on Total Facility Costs

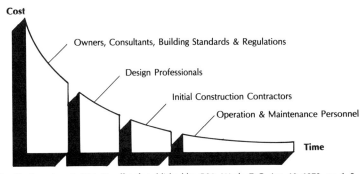

Adapted from **Value Engineering: A GSA Handbook** published by GSA, Wash. D.C., Jan. 12, 1972, pg. 1–8. Source **AIA Life Cycle Cost Analysis—A Guide for Architects.**

Calculating Life-Cycle Costs

Because life-cycle costs depend upon a large number of factors, it is not possible to give any rule of thumb figures. In fact, it is not prudent to think in terms of "standard" life-cycle costs. Rather, life-cycle cost analysis provides a technique for comparing alternatives or assessing the feasibility of an option.

Depending on the objective of the analysis, different cost categories may be used. They may include the full range of first costs and operating costs (or a more narrow range) considered over a project's life cycle. The following categories may be considered.

- Initial capital investment costs
- Financing costs
- Maintenance and operations costs
- Repair and replacement costs
- Alteration and improvement costs
- Personnel costs
- Salvage costs

Some of these are one-time nonrecurring costs and others are ongoing or recurring costs. Those that recur should be examined in more detail to determine what factors may cause a change in the cost. (This is discussed in Chapter 26 on cost analysis.) The result of the analysis is a measure of life-cycle costs in "equivalent uniform annual cost"—a way of converting current and future dollar values into a uniform annual cost for each year in the life cycle.

Summary and Conclusion

It is easy to see that the costs of building and operating correctional facilities are quite high. While first costs and operating costs can be controlled independently, they are highly interdependent. That is, when first costs are trimmed, operating costs often are higher. Sometimes spending more on first costs can effect considerable savings over the long run, thus making cycle costing a valuable tool in the decision-making process. It allows us to study the effects of diminished first costs on the longer term consequence of operating costs. By using this technique, we can make better decisions about the short- and long-term economic consequences of project development.

References

American Institute of Architects. 1977. **Life Cycle Cost Analysis: A Guide for Architects.** Washington, DC: American Institute of Architects. A guide to the basic components, techniques, and uses of life-cycle costing. Includes remarks from the Harvard Graduate School of Design 1975 conference "Long-Term Economy: The Real Cost of Buildings."

Center for Justice Planning. 1980. **Costs of a New County Jail: Pay Now and Pay Later.** Champaign, IL: Center for Justice Planning. Discusses construction and operating costs determined in a 1980 survey of thirty-four recently built jail facilities throughout the U.S.

Dell'isola, Alphonse and Stephen Kirk. 1981. **Life-Cycle Costing for Design Professionals.** New York: McGraw-Hill.

Department of Justice, Law Enforcement Assistance Administration, National Criminal Justice Information and Statistics Service. 1978. **Expenditures and Employment Data for the Criminal Justice System.** Washington, DC: Government Printing Office.

Haviland, David S. 1978. **Life-Cycle Cost Analysis 2: Using it in Practice.** Washington, DC: American Institute of Architects. Contains numerous practical examples of how to actually carry out life cycle analysis.

Kirk, Stephen J. 1979. "Life-Cycle Costing: Increasingly Popular Route to Design Value." **Architectural Record,** December 1979, 63–67.

6. Sources and Resources: Where to Find Information and Help

Who Will Use This Chapter

Primary User
Project manager

Secondary Users
Corrections staff
Task forces
Advisory committee

Introduction

There are many sources of information and help for individuals and agencies involved in studying or planning for local corrections. Much of this help is free to the user and offered to improve the quality of our justice system and jails. While the help is available, you need to know **where to find it** and **who to ask for it.**

The purpose of this chapter is to provide you with an overview of the kinds of resources that are available. Many more specific references are listed at the end of each chapter or part to which they apply. Two main kinds of resources are listed here. One, agencies that offer **help** in the form of advice, counseling, or technical assistance. Two, sources of printed or other **information.**

Agencies Offering Technical Assistance

INFORMATION

A variety of governmental, professional, and charitable organizations offer technical assistance and other less formal kinds of help to county jails. Some of these services are paid for by taxes, charity, or membership dues. There may be a small fee for others, generally nominal in relation to the services performed.

Department of Corrections

Most states have a department or agency that oversees local detention facilities throughout the state. Frequently this state agency is a major resource to counties involved in the process of needs assessment. The department most likely is familiar with your jail as a result of inspections. (The reports prepared by the jail inspector are also a valuable source of information about the performance and problems of your jail.)

While this book is designed for you to use on your own, your state local corrections agency may be able to help with the various steps involved in the correctional planning process, including answering questions about data gathering and analysis. This agency may also be able to provide examples of other counties and how they have handled problems similar to those your county may face. It should be able to recommend contacts who are willing to share their experience with you.

Your state's local corrections department or a separate agency may collect and dispense criminal justice statistics. It may also provide a criminal justice profile with detailed information about arrests and dispositions in your county.

NIC Jail Center

1790-30th Street
Suite 140
Boulder, Colorado 80301
(303) 497-6700

The National Institute of Corrections Jail Center (NIC) in Boulder, Colorado, is a branch of the federal Bureau of Prisons (Department of Justice). The institute's mission is to provide training and technical assistance to corrections systems around the country.

NIC will respond to specific requests for assistance and may provide small grants for certain purposes. (Requests must come from a county supervisor or jail official.) In addition, NIC offers several training programs that may help your county considerably in its planning effort. The most notable is called Planning of New Institutions—or PONI for short. Much of the material contained in this book was originally developed for the PONI program.

PONI. The Planning of New Institutions program consists of two phases. The first is an intensive two-day meeting in your community with many of the people who would comprise your advisory committee. An overview of jail planning issues is combined with initially identifying—and making a commitment to solving— some of the problems with your jail. The second phase, often held in Boulder, involves a week-long working session for three to five county representatives to help them learn in greater depth how to follow through on the facility planning and development process.

Other NIC Programs. Other training programs that may be of interest include County and Corrections, which focuses on the county's role in providing correctional services; Management Training, which covers techniques of achieving effective jail organizations; and Legal Issues, which explores in much greater depth the topics dealt with in Chapter 3.

Commission on Accreditation for Corrections

American Correctional Association
6110 Executive Boulevard
Suite 750
Rockville, Maryland 20852
(301) 770-3097

The American Correctional Association's Commission on Accreditation for Corrections, in addition to promulgating standards for local corrections, offers an accreditation system for those jails or other institutions that wish to document their success in meeting standards.

National Sheriffs' Association

1250 Connecticut Avenue, N.W.
Washington, D.C. 20036
(202) 872-0422

The National Sheriffs' Association audit system can help you evaluate your jail facility in terms of operation and design. Compliance with ACA standards is stressed. Methods are suggested for organizing your effort to solve problems, and practical suggestions for improvement offered if technical assistance is requested.

Pretrial Services Resource Center

918 F Street, N.W.
Suite 500
Washington, D.C. 20004
(202) 638-3080

The Pretrial Services Resource Center, funded by the Law Enforcement Assistance Administration (LEAA), provides a number of services that could be useful to your county as it examines its own pretrial practices and considers alternatives to incarceration (Part 2 activities). Services include references, publications, technical assistance, and training.

Sources of Information

The following agencies are valuable sources of information on a variety of subjects related to corrections and criminal justice. The range of topics and services is indicated for each source.

American Bar Association (ABA)

1800 M Street
Washington, D.C. 20036
(202) 331-2295

The ABA publishes the association's standards as well as booklets reporting ABA studies on the costs of alternative programs and other topics.

American Correctional Association (ACA)

4321 Hartwick Road, Suite L-208
College Park, Maryland 20740
(301) 864-1070

The ACA publishes directories of correctional agencies and a variety of other documents on corrections topics.

American Institute of Architects (AIA)

Committee on Architecture for Justice
1735 New York Avenue
Washington, D.C. 20006
(202) 626-7300

The committee occasionally publishes documents on jail and justice facility design. One of these, **The 1980 Design Resource File: Planning Justice Facilities,** is a particularly valuable reference. Documents are available through the AIA Publications Office, which also offers other publications on facility development.

American Justice Institute (AJI)

1007 Seventh Street
Sacramento, California 95814
(916) 444-3096

AJI has conducted research and development on a wide range of topics of interest to local corrections. Of particular note are its reports on projects concerning jail classification, overcrowding, and alternatives to incarceration.

National Association of Counties

Criminal Justice Program
1735 New York Avenue
Washington, D.C. 20006
(202) 785-9577

The National Association of Counties has published a series of pamphlets on correctional and criminal justice issues reflecting the viewpoint of county citizens and governments.

National Council on Crime and Delinquency (NCCD)

Continental Plaza
411 Hackensack Avenue
Hackensack, New Jersey 07601
(201) 488-0400

NCCD publishes pamphlets and reports emphasizing the high cost of building and operating jails and prisons and stressing the use of alternatives to incarceration.

National Criminal Justice Reference Service (NCJRS)

User Services
Box 6000
Rockville, Maryland 20850
(301) 251-5500

Sponsored by the National Institute of Justice, the NCJRS publishes the monthly "Selective Notification of Information." If you want to keep abreast of a variety of criminal justice topics as information becomes available, the publication is available on request. NCJRS will also conduct literature searches and supply abstracts of books and articles on particular subjects. (There may be a fee for the latter service.)

National Fire Protection Association (NFPA)

Battery Marsh Park
Quincy, Massachusetts 02269
(617) 328-9290

The NFPA publishes the **Life Safety Code,** covering all aspects of building design for fire safety. It includes a special section on penal institutions. NFPA also provides information and training on fire safety for corrections.

National Institute of Corrections/National Information Center

1790-30th Street
Room 314
Boulder, Colorado 80301
(303) 444-1101

The NIC National Information Center maintains a comprehensive collection of documents on all facets of corrections. The center will usually help you find information on a specific topic and provide a copy of materials, other than books.

National Institute of Law Enforcement and Criminal Justice

U.S. Department of Justice
Law Enforcement Assistance Administration
Washington, D.C. 20531
(202) 633-2000

The National Institute of Law Enforcement and Criminal Justice publishes reports of studies that it has sponsored, many of which concern corrections and criminal justice.

National Sheriffs' Association

1250 Connecticut Avenue, N.W.
Washington, D.C. 20036
(202) 872-0422

The National Sheriffs' Association publishes a series of pamphlets on jail management, one on jail architecture, and a more recent one on guidelines for planning a detention facility.

Unitarian Universalist Service Committee

National Moratorium on Prison Construction
Branches throughout the country.

As the name suggests, this group opposes the use of incarceration (and therefore the construction of jails) for most detainees and prisoners. It publishes pamphlets that argue this case and encourage the maximum use of alternatives.

Other Counties

Finally, an invaluable source of information and help for your county can be found in other counties. Most corrections systems and county governments will be happy to share their experiences with you. This help may range from hints on organizing your planning effort to specific suggestions on design features or materials to use or avoid. Your state corrections department may be able to suggest a county or individual who can help you with your particular needs.

Part 2.
Starting the Corrections Planning Process

7. Introduction

Part 2 shows your county how to carry out the first steps in the corrections planning process. It includes the following five steps:

- The first step in corrections planning: **form and use an advisory committee** (Chapter 8).
- The second step: **identify corrections system and facility problems** (Chapter 9).
- The third step: **set goals for corrections and develop a mission statement** (Chapter 10).
- The fourth step: **develop action plans** to solve problems and achieve goals (Chapter 11).
- The fifth step: **select a planning consultant** if you need one (Chapter 12).

The planning process begins when your county recognizes that it faces a corrections problem and begins mobilizing an organization to deal with it. Primary responsibility lies with the **sheriff** and/or **corrections administrators** to recognize problems with jail populations, programs or facilities and to inform the **board of commissioners.** The commissioners, in turn, will organize the **planning team** and **advisory committee** and establish their responsibilities. Chapter 8 on participatory planning will explain how to organize these committees and help them carry out their first tasks.

The second step is for the planning team and advisory committee to identify and carefully define the problems faced by the corrections system (Chapter 9). Only in this way can the planning process yield solutions to these problems.

In the third step, the advisory committee establishes the community's goals for its detention and corrections functions and records these in a "mission statement" (Chapter 10). These goals, which need to be revised periodically, give direction to the planning process and guide decisions made along the way.

As the fourth step, the planning team and advisory committee organize specific action plans to solve problems and achieve goals (Chapter 11). Action plans develop timetables and assign responsibilities for achieving the tasks that need to be carried out in order to find solutions. The plans will be reformulated as necessary throughout the planning process.

The fifth and final step is to consider the need for a planning consultant, and if needed to select one and contract for services (Chapter 12). The chapter also explains how to select other types of consultants, such as architects, who may be needed later in the project.

Each of the subsequent chapters first introduces the general concepts needed to understand why the step is necessary and then shows how to achieve each part of it.

8. Step 1: Set Up a Participatory Planning Structure

Who Will Use This Chapter

Primary Users
Board of commissioners
Advisory committee
Project manager
Planning team
Task forces

Introduction to Step 1

Step 1 in the planning process is to organize the people and lines of communication that will be used for your correctional planning project. This chapter explains the processes involved in participatory planning and the reasons for their existence. As it builds a case for participation, the chapter also shows how to organize and set up a participatory planning structure for the project and, more important, how to make it work. The model of participation presented here is a general one, and we fully expect that your county will modify that model to fit your particular needs and circumstances.

Participatory planning is considered essential for projects of the size and importance of most jail renovation or construction. Such involvement does not necessarily imply smooth sailing through a participatory process. Indeed, it is quite likely that divergent points of view will crop up from time to time and may be troublesome to resolve.

While some communities feel that participation adds precious time to the planning process, many who have tried to proceed without participation have had the project backfire in one way or another—by failing to pass a bond issue or by building a facility that did not meet community expectations or legal mandates. Participation is well worth the time it takes.

Participation Defined

Participation in the context of this book refers to activities organized and carried out by those not formally empowered to make decisions, yet whose contributions influence the decisions of those with authority. This definition excludes situations in which government officials formulate policy based on their own beliefs and values without the benefit of alternative ideas, beliefs, and values from organized interest groups and or influential community leaders.

Thus participatory planning refers to interaction between organized citizen groups and governmental decision makers. The purpose of this interaction is to improve the quality of the planning product and social policies adopted by those making and carrying out decisions.

The quality of the final plan is enriched by including in the planning process a broad and often diverse spectrum of vested-interest groups from the community. Social science literature consistently finds that group decisions are superior to individual decisions. In matters that have profound and lasting socio-economic implications for the community such as planning new jail facilities or programs, it logically follows that the scope, depth, and diversity of community participation will contribute to the quality of the planning process, the planned product, and ultimately the formulation of social policy. Participatory planning involves citizens by giving them a voice in decisions that affect the community at large and an opportunity to debate and resolve divergent points of view.

Importance of Participation

Participation in the planning process is important for three reasons.

First, citizen participation is a valued goal in our democratic form of government; we expect individuals and interest groups to have some influence over social policies that affect them.

Second, participatory planning provides a practical and viable opportunity to educate the community at large regarding the constitutional, legal, and social importance of allocating scarce resources to the construction and operation of a jail facility. Throughout this process, participatory planning integrates a broad base of beliefs, values, and information. Ultimately this combination leads to superior planning and decision making.

Third, widespread participation in the planning process increases the likelihood that decisions will be effectively carried out. People tend to "own" and support that which they help create. This implies an organized strategy for disseminating information about the problems faced in planning as well as the progress being made. An informed and involved citizenry is likely to support available means of publicly financing the construction and operation of a new jail facility (see the section on selling the project in Chapter 27).

Organization Climate and Conditions for Participatory Planning

The technical complexity of corrections planning, construction, and operation would seem to imply that professional planners, architects, engineers, penologists, and other specialists should carry out the planning function. Why then should nonspecialists representing community interest groups be invited to participate in this complex enterprise?

American history testifies to the fact that crucial matters of social responsibility can be decided by nonspecialists. In the administration of justice, for example, the innocence or guilt of a person is determined by a jury of twelve individuals considered peers of the accused. Similarly, the planning of a jail is a crucial matter of social responsibility, creating important roles for nonspecialist involvement.

By and large, however, government fails to involve citizens in the planning of programs of social consequence. Instead, when any necessary public hearings are held, officials tend to defend previous decisions. If public opinion is rejected, the backlash can mean serious political consequences for those involved and financial hardship for programs that are little understood by the public.

Participatory planning provides an alternative leadership approach particularly suited to "unpopular" projects such as jail construction. This alternative recognizes the benefits that can accrue from taking into account many points of view, from responding flexibly to new ideas, and from sharing planning and decision-making power with a large number of community representatives.

Participation in Various Levels of Planning

Participation serves different purposes and functions at different levels of planning. Three levels are considered here: long-range planning, strategic and middle-range planning, and operational or more immediate planning.

Long-range planning is concerned with **what ought to be and why.** Jail planning falls into this framework because the planning process is long-range in nature and involves questions concerning values. Those involved undertake commitments of consequence for perhaps thirty years. The social responsibility of such an undertaking quite clearly suggests the need for wide community involvement along with the technical expertise of qualified specialists and the experience of professionals.

Strategic or **middle-range** planning is concerned with **what we can do and how** to do it for the next three to five years. Again, because of the social responsibility factor, what we can do is an issue decided by widespread community participation. The "how" question, on the other hand, requires considerable input from specialists.

Operations planning, on the other hand, is concerned with **what we will do and when.** Issues and concerns of operations planning, by their increasingly technical nature, call mainly for the input of professionals and specialists. On the other hand, because line staff is conversant with the daily operations of the jail, it is important to include their practical input into operations planning.

In summary, successful corrections planning requires a judicious mix of nonspecialists and specialists in a dynamic participatory process.

Conceptual Model for Participatory Planning

An important basic principle of planning holds that the planning structure should follow its desired function. Thus, understanding the functions of normative, strategic, and operations planning helps provide a basis for considering the appropriate structure for each of these planning levels.

Planning associated with establishing major policy directions (perhaps including facility construction) has been defined above as a normative planning activity. Thus its planning structure ideally requires widespread community involvement. However, the definition of "widespread involvement" will vary from one county to another. Consequently there is no single model of participation that is universally valid.

To provide you with a frame of reference, we present below an "ideal" model for participatory planning. Subsequent sections offer suggestions regarding membership considerations for various planning groups along with their respective roles and responsibilities.

Participatory Planning Model

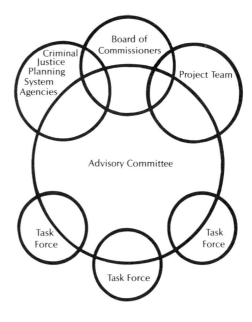

Roles, Responsibilities, and Membership of Planning Groups

Board of Commissioners

The board of commissioners is made up of elected officials representing the citizens of the county. The board has the responsibility and authority to evaluate and approve staff recommendations regarding the corrections planning structure, roles, and responsibilities as your county will interpret them from the ideal planning model. The board makes the final selection of members for the planning team and the advisory committee.

Usually these decisions are made in consultation with the sheriff or jail administrator, who will be responsible for operating new programs or facilities. Because of familiarity with criminal justice system agencies, the sheriff also helps the board select appropriate representation to the planning team and advisory committee from law enforcement, the courts, and corrections agencies. The membership and responsibilities of these groups will vary from county to county depending on three factors. One, the personalities on the board of commissioners; two, the status and influence of the sheriff; and three, the confidence that the supervisors and the sheriff have in county administrative staff.

The board will also define the roles and responsibilities of the planning team and will monitor its activities and progress. (The advisory committee and planning team can set up certain task forces on their own, while others should be approved by the board.) Any planning decisions that have impact on county laws, fiscal commitments, or operations policies must ultimately be approved by the board of commissioners. Thus, as the planning process unfolds, the efforts of the planning team, the advisory committee, and task forces are presented to the board of commissioners for official approval.

Sheriff and Corrections Staff

The sheriff (or director of corrections) has direct responsibility for the jail and thus must be intimately involved in corrections planning.

While participating in several planning groups, the sheriff also has specific responsibilities. He must take an active role in defining policy direction for both law enforcement and correctional functions. He must give access to the jail's facility and records, ensuring that staff cooperates fully in data-collection phases.

As physical planning begins, a task force of corrections staff and administrators should participate in defining operations and space needs as well as in reviewing architectural plans.

The sheriff, as head of the primary user agency, should approve each major planning product.

Project Manager

The project manager is the pivot point for the entire planning project. He or she is responsible for planning, organizing, scheduling, and controlling all aspects of the work on the county's behalf. The different phases of the project, and the specific duties called for in each phase, are given below.

Planning Phase

- Orient the planning team and advisory committee to the project.
- Coordinate the consultant selection process.
- Provide liaison among the planning team and advisory committee, the local funding authority, criminal justice agencies, and the consultant.
- Supervise all in-house data collection and analysis activities.
- Assist in the development of the corrections master plan and the functional program for the new facility.
- Oversee the feasibility analysis.
- Monitor the project timetable.

Design Phase

Provide liaison among the planning team and advisory committee, the local funding authority and the architect.

- Coordinate user agency review in the preparation of the design and construction documents, bidding, and selection of the construction contractor.
- Supervise the development of the fixed and movable equipment lists.
- Monitor the project timetable.

Construction Phase

Provide liaison among the planning team and advisory committee, the local funding authority, and the architect and contractor.

- Conduct on-site inspections of construction activities to determine conformance of the work, materials, and equipment with the construction documents (may also employ a clerk of the works).
- Assist the purchasing agent in the acquisition of fixed and movable equipment.
- Coordinate all local, state, and federal agency inspections of the project. Obtain all necessary certifications and licenses.
- Obtain and maintain all project records, architectural and "as-built" drawings, and equipment user manuals.
- Assist in developing written documentation of all change orders.
- Monitor the project timetable.
- Review and approve all applications for payment submitted by the contractor (after review by the architect).
- Represent the facility owners in the identification of construction deficiencies ("punch list"). Review and approve the correction of all deficiencies.
- Orient and serve as a resource to all individuals involved in the transition process.

Planning Team

The size of the planning team will depend on the size and complexity of the planning problem, but it should be small enough to be workable—generally about six members. The team may be smaller if consultants are heavily relied on. Planning team members may be drawn from the following areas of expertise:

- Corrections planners or other staff
- County and, if appropriate, city planners and administrative analysts
- Public works personnel
- Fiscal managers
- Technically qualified community volunteers (corporate planners from private industry or loan executives or retired professional planners)

The project manager is the leader of the planning team, with direct responsibility for coordination and communication as indicated in the job description given earlier.

The planning team is responsible for carrying out or overseeing the needs assessment and feasibility study tasks. Policy matters and findings are submitted to the advisory committee. Ultimately, the team is responsible to the board of commissioners, keeping it informed as the planning process unfolds and seeking board approval at each major planning step. Thus the planning staff has two equally important responsibilities:

- The coordination of **people**
- The coordination of **tasks**

Certain skills will help the members of the planning team and particularly the project manager carry out their tasks in coordination with the other participants. These individuals should be:

- Technically competent in planning
- Task-oriented and willing to take charge
- Good managers of people, time, and resources
- Innovative and creative
- Skillful in working with groups (board of commissioners, community advisory committee, task forces, and so on)
- Skillful at conflict management
- Enthusiastic/energetic pacesetters
- Politically astute.

If the county does not have qualified planning staff available, the board of commissioners may choose to contract out certain tasks to jail-planning consultants. The project manager, however, should certainly be a county staff member, since continuity over the planning cycle is critical to the coordination and success of the project. If consultants are hired, they will serve as staff to the project manager.

Advisory Committee

The advisory committee is essential to any participatory planning effort. In general terms, its role includes:

- Receiving reports prepared by the planning team
- Studying and evaluating recommendations and their factual background
- Studying, formulating, and recommending policy

Thus the advisory committee provides input to the planning process and evaluation and feedback to the planning team, and endorses recommendations for board of commissioners approval.

If carefully selected, committee members can greatly contribute to the planning process and help to ensure implementation of the product—the corrections plan. Members should be chosen for their willingness to work on and become involved in the project. Representatives in a position to speak for the following groups or agencies **should be included** on the advisory committee:

- Board of commissioners
- Sheriff and corrections staff

- The judiciary (presiding judges of the municipal and superior courts)
- District attorney
- Public defender
- County administration
- Public works staff or county architect
- Probation
- Municipal law enforcement
- Alcohol, other substance abuse, and mental health programs
- The public (who may be represented by individuals listed below)

In addition, representatives of the following groups **may be considered for inclusion:**

- Elected officials from city governments
- County grand jury
- County bar association
- League of Women Voters
- Church groups (ministerial association or interfaith council)
- Community service clubs or civic organizations
- Minority or public interest groups
- Inmate support groups such as Friends Outside
- American Civil Liberties Union or other prisoner rights advocates
- Media
- Other community groups whose support is important to the jail construction plan

The advisory committee should consist of about fifteen to twenty persons. To maintain a manageable number yet provide for widespread community representation, attempt to identify individuals who occupy prominent roles in more than one community interest group. An existing corrections or criminal justice advisory group could form the basis for the advisory committee. Larger counties may require broader membership. If this is the case, organize subgroups to perform specific tasks.

Once established, both the planning team and the advisory committee will follow the steps defined in this and subsequent parts of this book. First tasks involve reviewing and discussing the issues defined in earlier chapters. These groups then identify correctional system and facility problems and develop goals and a mission statement for county corrections. Later tasks involve data collection and analysis and evaluation of options for facility development.

A corrections-needs assessment is a major undertaking. To help the planning team and advisory committee collect and process information, certain tasks are assigned to so-called task forces.

Task Forces

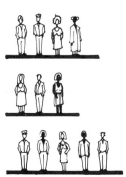

Task forces are small groups of three to five persons who receive specific assignments and a timetable for reporting back to the planning team and advisory committee. Any number of task forces can be organized over the life of the planning process and several task forces may work simultaneously. They may include community representatives or specialists who are not formal members of the planning team or advisory committee.

Task force assignments may include:

- Gathering and analyzing data
- Studying alternatives to incarceration
- Analyzing inmate service needs
- Evaluating existing facilities
- Assessing facility consolidation
- Cost or funding analysis
- Site selection

- Selection of a consultant/architect
- Facility programming and design review

Task forces can address some of these issues without staff support. However, as a general principle it is recommended that professional staff from the planning team be assigned to each task force to help to schedule meetings, gather pertinent information, and prepare task force reports. The project manager monitors the operations of each task force, either as a working or ex-officio member.

Each task force is organized to perform a specific task within a specific time. Task forces report their findings and recommendations to the advisory committee. After evaluation, clarification, and any necessary revisions, the advisory committee forwards task force reports to the board of commissioners.

The Media

The media can be an invaluable ally in corrections planning—or the undoing of the entire project. An independent force, it can nonetheless spread the word about problems facing corrections, the jail, and the planning process. The only way to build community support for the project is to keep the people informed, and the media can do this best. A continuous effort should be made to find human interest value in the jail planning project.

Although it is desirable to include representatives of the media on the advisory committee (at least as observers), this is not sufficient community relations. The project manager should use the sheriff and members of the board of commissioners and advisory committee to present the project to the media in your community. A task force or subcommittee might serve as the effective link.

Participatory Role Relationships

The participatory planning model presented earlier provides for maximum communication and interaction among the board of commissioners, planning team, advisory committee and task forces. Note the overlapping areas on the diagram which identify situations where individuals are members of at least two of the formal groups.

For example, the planning team acts as staff to the board of commissioners, the advisory committee, and the task forces. In addition, one or more members of the board of commissioners also serves on the advisory committee. Their overlapping memberships or "linking pins" facilitate both formal and informal communication among what might otherwise be separate units. The linking-pin concept provides the vehicle for open exchange of ideas in planning.

To extend the sphere of involvement even further, open all planning meetings to the public and make minutes of meetings available to anyone interested. Each person involved in the corrections planning process will probably have informal or formal associations with a wide range of community-interest groups. It is possible to provide additional opportunities for community involvement by arranging for participants at all levels to keep their respective community-interest groups systematically informed about problems being confronted and the progress being made in the planning process.

Participation: An Effective Approach to Correctional Planning

To summarize the importance of participatory planning for corrections, a comparison is made on the following table between effective and ineffective planning experiences. Effective correctional planning refers to projects that experienced a minimum number of problems throughout the needs assessment process, architectural design, and construction. Moreover, these projects resulted in jails that met legal imperatives and national and local standards. Ineffective corrections projects experienced many problems throughout the life cycle of the planning and construction phases and were sometimes rejected by the community. The ones that reached construction sometimes conflicted with legal imperatives or national and local standards from the day they opened.

Table 8-1. Effective and Ineffective Corrections Planning

Aspect of Planning	Effective Corrections Planning	Ineffective Corrections Planning
Planning Structure	Widespread community involvement	Primarily professionals and politicians
Planning Method	Needs assessment and planning highly structured	Ad hoc planning, little formal structure
Planning Meetings	Scheduled—open to public, minutes available, media invited	Unscheduled—no notice to public or media
Leadership	Stable throughout life of project	Multiple changes throughout life of project
Conflict	Openly addressed, resolved, or defused	Avoided at all costs
Project Control Over Needs Assessment, Feasibility Study, and Design	Highly controlled by board of commissioners, corrections, advisory committee, and planning team	Largely controlled by planners or architect (by default)
Approval Authorities	Endorsed by advisory committee, planning team, and board of commissioners on a step-by-step basis	Endorsed by board of commissioners at the end of the planning process, with input limited to professionals

Examples of effective community-based participatory planning can be found in the following counties:

Alachua County, Gainsville, Florida

Boulder County, Boulder, Colorado

Contra Costa County, Martinez, California

Jackson County, Kansas City, Missouri

Kane County (near Chicago), Illinois

Benton County, Corvallis, Oregon

Linn County, Albany, Oregon

Contra Costa County, California, is an example of a county that initially spent a large amount of money and experienced many problems at least in part because it failed to provide for community involvement. The county scrapped its first set of architectural plans, returned to basic planning, and provided for widespread community involvement to generate the support needed to build its present facility.

The lesson to be learned from these experiences is that community-based participatory planning may not take you precisely where you think you want to go, but without it you may not be going anywhere at all.

References

Burns, Jim. 1979. **Connections: Ways to Discover and Realize Community Potentials.** Stroudsburg, PA: Hutchinson Ross. While oriented toward urban design projects, this book provides valuable methods for any community based planning.

Glass, James. 1979. "Citizen Participation in Planning: The Relationship between Objectives and Techniques." **American Planning Association Journal** 45 (2). Reviews a number of participatory techniques in terms of when they are applicable.

Likert, Rensis. 1966. **New Patterns of Management.** New York: McGraw-Hill. Reports on ten years of research on the impact of involving employees in setting organization goals and the means for achieving them. This participation led to an acceptance of the goals and commitment to insuring their achievement.

McGregor, Douglas. 1960. **The Professional Manager.** New York: McGraw-Hill. Contrasts the relative merits of autocratic versus participative management styles and concludes that the contemporary organization is made up of creative, sophisticated personnel wanting to have a voice in planning the direction and work effort of their organization.

Sanoff, Henry. 1978. **Designing with Community Participation.** Stroudsburg, PA: Hutchinson Ross. Stresses the need for sharing information and expertise between designers and those affected by environmental change.

9.   Step 2: Identify Correctional System Problems

Who Will Use This Chapter

Primary Users
Planning team
Advisory committee
Task forces

Problem Identification: A Prerequisite to Achieving Goals

This chapter provides techniques for identifying corrections system and facility problems and developing solutions to these problems in an organized and democratic manner. However trite it may sound, you must clearly **identify** problems before they can be **solved.** This is no easy task, because of the almost universal tendency of people to think in terms of solutions rather than to try to specify the scope and nature of the problem. Beginning with a solution statement may lock you into that solution.

For example, if you ask, "What is the major problem confronting the administration of our jail?" it is likely that you will hear: "We need more recreation, a library, substance-abuse counseling, and leisuretime activities." When you think about it, this can be recognized as a statement of a solution to the problem, not a statement of what the problem is.

The problem statement might sound more like this: "Enforced idleness is a problem in our jail. Inmates spend 85 percent of their waking hours locked in their cells with little or nothing of a constructive nature to occupy their time. Out of anger, hostility, and sheer boredom, they resort to their own leisuretime devices. They harass the corrections officers, create unbearable noise, and engage in a host of other unpleasant and counterproductive activities. Last year our malicious damage costs were up 22 percent over the previous year. We experienced forty-two physical confrontations between inmates (up 10 percent over the previous year), and our inmate escape statistics were up 6 percent over the previous year with a total of fifty-three escapees."

Another example of a solution statement rather than a problem statement might be "We need tighter key control." Whenever a problem statement begins with "We need" you can expect a solution statement to follow rather than a problem statement. With respect to key control, the problem statement might sound something like this: "One of our master keys has been missing for the past two months. We all know what would happen if it got into the hands of the inmate population. In addition, in the shift reports over the past six months, corrections officers reported on twelve occasions that they couldn't get access to needed supplies and equipment because of missing keys." From this problem statement, a number of alternatives could be generated to solve the problem, including tighter key control.

The Nominal Group Process

Once problem statements have been distinguished from solution statements, corrections planning requires a systematic and practical means of identifying the wide range of problems confronting those involved in the process. When the problems surface and are clarified, the planning process can move to the formulation of responsive, realistic, and appropriate action plans. The Nominal Group Process

NGP

(NGP) is one efficient and effective method for this purpose. NGP is designed to do the following:

Obtain problem definitions from groups of individuals with common concerns yet diverse backgrounds and frames of reference.

Involve every individual in the group to a maximum degree. Socially shy or retiring members of the group can easily and systematically become involved in the process. Often the contemplative, quiet members of a group have some of the most profound contributions to make. Planning groups can ill afford to lose this talent.

Capture individual perceptions of problems without being influenced by superiors or persons who occupy positions of power and authority in the community. Everyone's contribution is worthwhile and relevant. Members of the group may take an apparently trivial idea and develop it into a significant problem statement.

Enable the group to establish a common ranking of problem statements so that individual members are not influenced by superiors or powerful community leaders.

Enhance creativity and interest in identifying problems including those which pertain to corrections planning.

NGP is easy to understand and use without extensive training. Because the process is relatively easy to learn, participants involved in jail-planning projects can use it immediately. In addition, the method can be applied to problem identification in a wide variety of other formal and informal organizations.

To initiate NGP, a group facilitator (for example, a member of the planning team who has studied NGP) divides the participants at an advisory committee planning meeting into small groups of five to eight persons and asks each group to move to one of several small tables that have been set up in the room before the meeting. The facilitator then distributes to each member a previously printed Nominal Group Problem Identification Form, which includes questions pertaining to substantive areas of specific concern to the jail-planning process. For example, the form may contain one of the following questions:

"As planning proceeds, what problems will we need to address regarding the use of alternatives to incarceration?"

"What problems will we need to address regarding programs and services in our new jail?"

The group facilitator illustrates for group members how to write problem statements rather than solution statements. The examples used above (or others) can be used for illustration purposes. Alternatively, if the planning group is concerned with exploring potential solutions, they are asked to suggest ideas to solve a specified problem. (See Chapter 11 on solving problems).

Carefully follow the steps outlined below during problem-identification sessions.

Task 1. Silent Generation of Problem Statements

The facilitator and the group read the substantive question on the Nominal Group Problem Identification Form, providing clarification if needed. The facilitator then asks each group member to list privately the problems that relate to the substantive question.

Task 2. Problem Statements Recorded on Flip Chart Using Round Robin Approach

The facilitator writes on the flip chart or newsprint one problem statement at a time from each group member, using a round robin approach. Commenting or editing is not permitted at this point. For ease of reference, each problem statement is given a code number.

Task 3. Clarification of Problem Statements

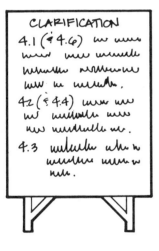

The facilitator and the group clarify each problem statement for common understanding. This is important because some people tend to think in shorthand, while others may not clearly understand the implication of a problem statement or the meaning behind it. At this juncture in the NGP, group members may merge problem statements that seem essentially the same. In addition, if it has not occurred spontaneously the facilitator asks group members if the discussion and clarification process has stimulated further problem statements. If so, these added problem statements are written on the flip chart and discussed for clarification.

Task 4. Ranking Problem Statements: Setting Priorities

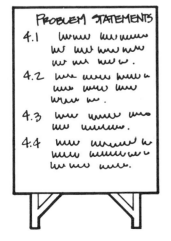

The facilitator gives each group member a 3 × 5 card and asks each to select the five most critical problems recorded on the flip chart. The code numbers corresponding to each problem can be used for this purpose, eliminating the time it would take for each group member to rewrite the five problem statements. When this process is complete, the facilitator asks each group member to rank privately and independently the five problem statements, assigning a 5 to their perception of the most important problem statement, 4 to the second most important, and so on.

Task 5. Establishing Nominal Group Priorities

5 PROBLEMS	RANK
2	III
4	I
5	II
7	V
7	IV

During the period when group members are privately ranking priorities, the facilitator prepares a tally sheet on the flip chart. As each group member finishes ranking the five most critical problems, the facilitator writes the weighted values (from the ranking discussed above) adjacent to the corresponding problem statement number on the tally sheet. The tally sheet is then totaled. The group may choose to comment generally on the outcome.

A sample tally sheet is presented in table 9-1, illustrating how a group of five persons might develop their priorities.

Task 6. Feedback and Evaluation

After each small group has established a list of priorities in substantive areas assigned to them, results are presented to the total advisory committee for evaluation and discussion. This stimulates small groups to be conscientious regarding their assignments and to perform as well as they can. In addition, the advisory committee gets a total perspective of the planning problems with which it must deal. If for any reason two or more small groups happen to generate problem statements pertaining to the same areas, they should meet as one group and repeat the NGP from Tasks 4 through 6.

Table 9-1. Nominal Group Problem Priorities

Problems (by Code Number)	Greg	Sandi	Mary	Carol	Scott	Total	Overall Group Priorities
1							
2	5	4	1	5		15	II
3							
4	2	3	3	5	4	17	I
5	4	5	2	3	2	16	II
6							
7		2	5	1		8	V
8				4		4	
9	3	1	4	2		10	IV
10					3	3	
11	1				1	2	
12							

(NOTE: The overall group priorities are written in Roman numerals (I to V) in the last column. It is not unusual to find group rankings in clusters as indicated above even though each member individually developed his or her own rank order. The pattern simply implies a high level of agreement on the top five priorities. Frequently, the ranking of problem statements below the first five or six tends to spread out, suggesting less agreement among group members over these issues.)

After each NGP session, the planning team organizes the substantive problem statements in priority order and sends results to advisory group members. Minutes of these meetings go to the board of commissioners as well, both for information and for any necessary action.

The planning team must eventually address each identified problem even if it is not included in the higher priority rankings. Additional meetings may be necessary to rank problem statements that failed to surface during the first NGP meeting.

However, if the remaining problem statements seem approximately equal in importance, the planning team may simply rank them arbitrarily.

When used to identify planning problems on a number of issues, NGP serves as an important point of departure. It provides the baseline information upon which you can conduct problem-solving action planning meetings.

Applications of NGP

The NGP has a wide range of applications in problem identification generally and for jail planning in particular. The meeting format presented above is suggested for involving key individuals or groups in each planning phase. These should include:

- Clients (consumers or users) and first-line staff for problem identification and exploration
- External resource people and specialists for exploring knowledge or possible approaches
- Key administrators and decision makers for developing priorities
- Organizational staff for developing program proposals
- All of the above participants for final approval and evaluation.

Thus the format can productively be used to identify problems, explore alternatives, establish problem and program priorities, and in general involve a large constituency in any aspect of the planning enterprise.

The procedure for using NGP in any of its applications can begin with task forces, the advisory committee, or the planning team. Ultimately, however, the board of commissioners must endorse final solutions or products.

Summary and Conclusions

Identifying correctional system problems is serious business, requiring considerable thought and input. The NGP provides an efficient and effective means of uncovering system problems that influence jail planning and construction. Moreover, it does this in a manner that involves all participants in the process.

Identifying the nature of problems faced by your system provides a firm foundation for the next step—developing goals and objectives for the direction you want to pursue.

References

Delbecq, André, and Andrew Ven De Ven. 1971. "A Group Process Model for Problem Identification and Program Planning." **Journal of Applied Behavioral Science** 7(4). Provides an understandable and practical explanation of the nominal group process, including a description of the research on which it is based.

Schein, Edgar. 1972. **Organization Psychology.** Englewood Cliffs, NJ: Prentice-Hall. Focuses on how an organization can productively use its human resources through effective management. Examines problems of organizational integration that arise because an organization is composed of many informal as well as formal groups.

10. Step 3: Develop Corrections Mission Statement and Goals

Who Will Use This Chapter

Primary Users
Advisory committee
Planning team

Secondary Users
Sheriff
Board of commissioners
Corrections staff

The advisory committee is responsible for developing the mission statement, and the planning team is responsible for correctional goals. Drafts of these materials should be reviewed and approved by the sheriff and board of commissioners.

Introduction

For many communities, the opportunity to effect significant change within the local correctional facility comes only once in a lifetime. Major policy decisions regarding the facility must therefore meet both the immediate and long-range needs of the community as well as of the jail staff and inmates. For this reason, the development and documentation of the mission statement and goals for corrections are critical initial steps in the needs-assessment and facility-planning process. Together, these documents define in general terms the nature of the philosophical and operational changes to be achieved through planning. They are essential reference documents that provide focus, direction, and consistency to the myriad of activities which will be undertaken to improve local corrections.

Because each community is unique with respect to its incarceration needs, there is neither a "model" mission statement nor model correctional goals that apply universally to all communities. This chapter is designed to help individuals responsible for the development of the mission statement and correctional goals to clearly define and document your county's approach to and expectations for corrections.

The Mission Statement

Definition

A mission statement is a broad general statement describing the philosophy by which the correctional system and facilities will be operated. Specifically, a mission statement defines the purpose of the correctional facility; the facility's responsibilities to its inmate population and other major constituencies (such as local government, the local criminal justice system, governmental and community agencies that provide services and programs for the facility, and the public); and the philosophical direction of the correctional facility. In essence, a mission statement reflects the ideal correctional facility for a particular community.

Key Issues

In the development of a mission statement, give serious consideration to three key issues: purpose, responsibilities, and philosophical direction.

Purpose. The purposes of the correctional facility include the legal mandate for operating the facility; the role of the correctional facility in the local criminal justice system; the types of inmates who will be incarcerated (such as pretrial and/or sentenced, male and/or female, and adult and/or juvenile inmates); and, in general terms, the role that incarceration plays in the community. To determine the purpose of the correctional facility, the following questions should be addressed:

- Is the operation of the correctional facility mandated by state and/or local statutes?
- Who is ultimately responsible for operating the facility?
- What law enforcement agencies and courts are served by the facility, and how does the facility help them accomplish their responsibilities?
- Who will be incarcerated in the facility, and why should they be incarcerated?

Responsibilities. The mission statement must define the correctional facility's primary responsibilities to the county or community, its inmate population, and other major constituencies. In the broadest sense, those responsibilities are:

- **Security:** making sure that individuals remain incarcerated until legally released.
- **Safety:** making sure that the staff, inmates, and visitors are not subjected to physical, emotional, or psychological abuse or danger while in the facility.
- **Service:** providing for the basic human needs of the inmate population and providing program opportunities for those inmates who choose to participate.

The **3 S's**

How these terms are actually defined and their relative importance to the overall mission of the facility will vary from community to community. The definition of the term "service" is particularly critical because of its cost implications. The mission statement should therefore include a general description of the types of services and programs that will be offered in the facility. In defining all three terms, it is essential that your state's jail standards, if any, and recent corrections-related court decisions be carefully reviewed to determine what, at a minimum, are the correctional facility's responsibilities (refer to Chapter 3 on standards and legal requirements).

The correctional facility, however, has other major responsibilities to its various constituencies. As an example, local government must operate the correctional facility in a cost-effective manner. Thus it is important to identify and reflect in the mission statement all of the correctional facility's major responsibilities.

Philosophical Direction. Determining the philosophical direction of the correctional facility requires putting aside current perceptions regarding the mission of the facility and trying to conceptualize its mission five, ten, or twenty years in the future.

A number of quite different correctional philosophies can be identified, including the so-called Five R's.

The **5 R's**

- **Revenge.** The mission of a correctional facility is to punish inmates in order to repay their "debt to society" and to deter future criminal activity.
- **Reform.** A correctional facility exists to provide inmates with vocational and educational skills and instill in them contemporary community standards, thus making them productive members of society upon release.
- **Rehabilitation.** The mission of a correctional facility is to treat the inmates' social and psychological problems and change their attitudes so that they can "cope" with society upon release.
- **Reintegration.** A correctional facility is responsible for developing a cooperative relationship between the inmates and the community in order to reduce the stigma of criminality and enhance the inmates' ability to successfully re-enter the community upon release.
- **Restraint.** A correctional facility must operate in a smooth and efficient manner and must tightly control the behavior of inmates through the use of rewards and punishments in order to maintain a calm environment in the facility. This philosophy assumes that attempts to reform, rehabilitate, or reintegrate inmates are futile because people change only if they want to.

In terms of the operation of a correctional facility, all these approaches have their advantages and disadvantages. As a result, most communities recognize that the philosophical direction established for the jail will be a combination of two or more of the models. Regardless of the direction chosen, it must be based on the community's expectations for the correctional facility, current correctional standards and court decisions, and the needs of the staff and inmate population of the facility.

Developing the Mission Statement

The most difficult task in the development of a mission statement is thinking through the issues that must be addressed. Once consensus is achieved on the issues, writing the document becomes a relatively simple process.

Substantial community input should be solicited to develop a mission statement. Appropriate representatives of local government, the local criminal justice system, governmental and community agencies, and the public should be actively encouraged to participate in the statement's development because they all have a stake in the success or failure of the correctional facility. For most communities, the advisory committee is the appropriate body to take responsibility for the development of the mission statement because its membership reflects a cross-section of professional, political, and community interests.

As the community's technical experts in the field of corrections, the sheriff and corrections administrator must take a leadership role in development of the mission statement. That leadership role ranges from organizing meetings, to researching the professional standards and court decisions, to actually drafting the statement.

Assuming a leadership role, however, does not mean dominating the process. Everyone involved in the development of the mission statement must be allowed input, regardless of his or her expertise in corrections or personal philosophies.

Involving a diverse group of individuals in the development of a mission statement is a major task. Each person will have his or her own opinion on almost every issue that must be addressed. Regardless of the differences of opinion that may exist, group consensus on the issues is essential. Even if everyone cannot agree that the position taken on a particular issue is the best possible course of action, the group must at least agree to give it a try.

Reaching even this level of consensus may require numerous discussions of the issues. In all probability some compromises will have to be made to arrive at positions that both satisfy the community and comply with professional and constitutional standards. (Help with techniques for group decision making can be found in Chapters 9 and 11.) Once agreement is reached on all issues to be addressed, an initial draft of the mission statement can be developed.

Criteria for Mission Statement Draft

While there is no set format for a mission statement, the draft should meet certain criteria and reflect the characteristics that follow.

Broad Focus. The mission statement should definitively address every major issue regarding the operation of the correctional facility. It should not, however, attempt to address the details of how the facility will operate. Those details should be addressed in other documents, such as the corrections master plan, the functional and architectural programs for the facility, and the operational policy and procedures manual.

Concise. The mission statement should be written as simply and concisely as possible. It should not be more than one or two pages long. If it is any longer, there is a very good chance that it will never be read no matter how well written.

Clear and Unmistakable. The mission statement should be understandable even to those individuals who have little or no knowledge of correctional facilities. Corrections jargon should be avoided.

Realistic and Attainable. While the mission statement should reflect the ideal correctional facility for your county, those responsible for its development must feel certain that, with effort, its ideals can be achieved. A mission statement that includes "pie-in-the-sky" concepts that can never be implemented is worthless.

Positive. Because the mission statement defines the future course of corrections in the community, it must focus on what will be done, rather than on what will not or cannot be done.

Review of Draft

The completed draft of the mission statement should be reviewed and formally approved by the advisory committee, the sheriff, and the board of commissioners. In some instances changes in wording will be necessary before all can approve the draft. But major changes in the content of the mission statement will be unnecessary at this point if agreement on the issues has been achieved.

Correctional Goals Development

Definition

A correctional goal is a brief statement that defines in general terms an end result to be achieved in the operation of the correctional program or facility.

Like the mission statement, a correctional goal reflects an ideal toward which the correctional facility should be striving. A correctional goal differs from a mission statement in that it relates to a specific aspect of operations and is therefore narrower in focus.

A correctional goal also differs from an objective in that a goal defines an end result while an objective describes an activity or group of activities required to achieve an end result. An objective has fixed time parameters and is measurable. Because a goal reflects an ideal, these criteria are not usually applicable. Objectives and their development are discussed in detail in the next section.

Identifying Correctional Goal Topics

The number of goals established for the correctional facility will vary greatly from community to community depending on the size and type of facility and the complexity of its operations. However, at a minimum correctional goals should be established for the broad operational areas of administration, support services, programs, and security.

To determine the actual topics for which correctional goals will be developed, first develop a list of all the functions and activities which must be performed in the facility. Then, rank-order the list, giving highest priority to those functions and activities essential to the mission of the facility. Develop goals for only the highest priority items.

Developing the Correctional Goals

The process for developing correctional goals is basically the same as the mission-statement development process. Consensus on the end result defined in each goal is absolutely essential.

The content of the correctional goals should reflect both the philosophy established for the jail and current professional and constitutional standards. For this reason, the mission statement, applicable jail standards, and recent court decisions are primary references in developing correctional goals. The task of developing the goals should only be tackled after the initial draft of the mission statement has been reviewed and approved.

Like the mission statement, correctional goals should be concise. One or two sentences are usually adequate to define the end result to be achieved. The goals must also be positively stated, clear and unmistakable in meaning, and realistically attainable. In addition, goals should meet certain criteria. They are described below.

Goals Should Be Stated in General Terms

While each correctional goal focuses on a specific aspect of facility operation, the ideal end result is stated in general terms. The specific details of how to achieve that end result will be stated in other documents. A desired end result is stated first too specifically and then in a correctly general way in the following example:

Too Specific. To prepare three hot meals per day in-house and serve each inmate in his or her living unit, with no more than fourteen hours between the evening and breakfast meals. Meals will be prepared conventionally and transported in bulk to the living units.

Correct Level of Generality. To provide meals to the inmate population that meet the recommended daily nutritional allowances established by the National Academy of Sciences.

The first example is actually an objective that describes several activities required to achieve the end result reflected in the second, more properly stated, example. The advantage of stating general correctional goals is that they allow more flexibility in the planning process, making it possible to explore all available options.

Goals Should Be Consistent with the Mission Statement

Each correctional goal developed for the facility must be consistent with the purpose, responsibilities, and philosophical direction established in the mission statement. It is particularly important that the correctional goals are philosophically consistent with the mission statement. If they are not, there is a very good chance that those responsible for implementing the goals will receive a mixed message regarding what they should be trying to accomplish.

Upon reaching team consensus and completion the initial draft of the correctional goals is submitted to the advisory committee, the sheriff, and the board of commissioners for review and approval.

Review and Revision of the Mission Statement and Correctional Goals

It is important to remember that the initial drafts of the mission statement and correctional goals may not represent the final products. Once data about the inmate population and local criminal justice system are collected and analyzed, the drafts should be reevaluated to determine whether the positions expressed in these documents are consistent with your new knowledge.

For example, a position taken on the provision of vocational training programs may be inconsistent with data that indicates that inmates do not stay in the facility long enough to benefit from such programs. If inconsistencies are found, the mission statement and correctional goals should be revised to reflect the findings of the data. Once this update is completed, the final forms of both documents should again be reviewed and approved by the advisory committee and board of commissioners.

Because the planning and construction of a new jail will for most communities take place over a period of from three to five years, the mission statement and correctional goals need to be reviewed on an annual basis to determine whether they remain consistent with professional and constitutional standards. If major changes have occurred, these documents should be revised.

Summary and Conclusion

While the mission statement and correctional goals may appear on the surface to be relatively simple documents, do not take their development lightly. Give careful thought to the major philosophical and operational decisions reflected in both documents. They will provide direction to the needs-assessment and facility-planning processes and ultimately determine the success or failure of the correctional facility.

Once the initial drafts of the mission statement and correctional goals are approved, the next major task is the development of an action plan to determine how to accomplish the changes they call for.

References

O'Leary, Vincent, n.d. **Correctional Policy Inventory: A Survey of Correctional Philosophy and Characteristic Methods of Dealing with Offenders.** Hackensack, NJ: National Council on Crime and Delinquency. A questionnaire to help you examine and assess current policy.

Peña, William, William Caudill, and John Focke, 1977. **Problem Seeking: An Architectural Programming Primer.** Boston: Cahners Book. Provides good discussion of goal development and the distinction between goals and objectives.

11.   Step 4: Develop Action Plans for Solving Problems

Who Will Use This Chapter

Primary Users
Planning team
Advisory committee

Secondary Users
Task forces

Introduction

The scope and complexity of corrections planning require many hours of meetings. It is therefore essential to ensure that meetings are well organized, scheduled for a purpose, and structured to result in specific results. This chapter provides techniques for developing solutions to correctional problems in an organized and democratic manner. These techniques may be used by any of the groups identified in Chapter 8: the advisory committee, planning team, or task forces.

"Problem solving" is a process by which individuals or groups discover a method for correcting an unacceptable or undesirable situation. "Action planning," the problem-solving process proposed here, adds specificity with respect to **who** will be responsible for each step required to solve the problem and **the date** by which each activity will be completed. This structure helps you pinpoint responsibility within agreed-upon time periods. It is applicable to finding ways to reach desired goals as well as to solving problems.

How to Run Effective Action-Planning Meetings

Action planning can be time consuming. Conservative estimates indicate that 50 percent of managers' and community leaders' time is spent in meetings (in groups, one-on-one, or by phone). Yet when managers and community leaders describe how they feel about the meetings they have attended, the response is invariably negative. The words they use include "frustrated," "bored," "impatient," "no structure," "no agenda," "no purpose," and so on.

The single most frequent cause for unproductive meetings is poor planning. Even the most skillful leader cannot conduct an effective meeting without a sound plan that involves the participants in a dynamic, creative exchange of ideas. Social science research informs us that the most effective means of gaining commitment, involvement, and action-oriented results is to create opportunities for others to participate in developing plans that affect them.

The NGP (described in Chapter 9) is designed to help identify relevant planning problems. Beyond this, a structured leadership procedure can maximize participation through the organized exchange of ideas in a process geared toward action-oriented results. The approach requires careful planning by the group leader (generally the project manager, depending upon which group is involved) prior to convening the meeting.

The eight steps or tasks involved in action planning are:

- Task 1: State the problem.
- Task 2: State the meeting objective.
- Task 3: State the starting question.
- Task 4: Develop a list of potential solutions.

- Task 5: Meeting break.
- Task 6: Decide on solutions.
- Task 7: Develop and agree on the action agenda.
- Task 8: Critique the process.

The example below—problems with inmate behavior—will clarify how the process works.

Task 1. State the Problem

The person running the meeting writes the problem statement on a flip chart prior to the advisory committee meeting. The problem statement can be taken from previously conducted NGP meetings. The group then clarifies the problem by examining what currently happens and how it affects people.

What Currently Happens?

Indicate the impact this problem has on the organization and its operation.

Example. The "enforced idleness" problem included a statement regarding the impact this problem has on the organization and its operations. The problem statement concluded as follows: "They [inmates] harass the correction officers, create unbearable noise, and engage in a host of other unpleasant and counterproductive activities. Last year our malicious damage costs were up 22 percent over the previous years. We experienced forty-two physical confrontations between inmates, up 10 percent over the previous year, and our inmate escape statistics were up 6 percent over the previous year with a total of fifty-three escapees." Clearly, these data were collected from jail records prior to the meeting.

How Does This Affect People?

How does this problem affect personnel, emotionally and psychologically?

Example. Jail personnel are frustrated and disillusioned. They can intellectually understand why the inmates behave the way they do but they simply cannot do anything about it. Every year they are required to do more work with fewer resources. They simply do not know where it will stop. We treat the animals in the zoo better than we treat our inmates. Some want to quit this hopeless job, but they do not know what else they would do. They need to support their own families and feel that they are trapped.

Clarify the Problem

Return to the problem statement, underlining key words as you explain the meaning and to ensure that all group members have a common understanding of the problem.

Cause Unknown: If the cause is unknown, you will want the group to examine possible causes. (Enforced idleness was already identified as the cause of this problem.)

Cause Known: If the cause is known, the group needs to examine what can be done about the problem.

Task 2. State the Meeting Objective

The meeting leader writes a concise statement of what he or she wants to happen as a result of this meeting.

Example. "I want this meeting to provide a strategy that will enable the jail to eliminate enforced idleness."

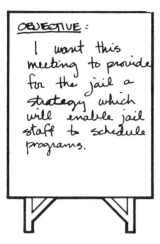

OBJECTIVE:

I want this meeting to provide for the jail a strategy which will enable jail staff to schedule programs.

Task 3. State the Starting Question

State the initial question so that it stimulates brainstorming in the group. Be sure that the starting question relates back to the meeting objective.

Example: The basic cause of inmate idleness is fairly clear. Therefore the starting question might be: "How can we develop a strategy that will enable jail staff to schedule programs and services that occupy at least 60 percent of inmates' waking hours?" Or more specifically: "Would you please think of possible programs and services that would be interesting and beneficial to inmates in the jail? For each contribution, suggest how the jail can obtain these programs and services."

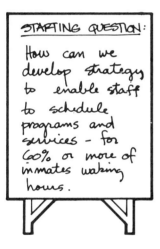

STARTING QUESTION:

How can we develop strategy to enable staff to schedule programs and services - for 60% or more of inmates waking hours.

Task 4. Develop a List of Potential Solutions

You may use the NGP to develop a list of potential solutions to the stated starting question. The leader may wish to have another person record committee members' ideas on a flip chart, so that he or she may actively participate.

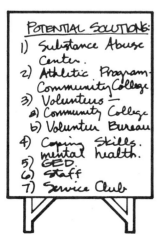

POTENTIAL SOLUTIONS:
1) Substance Abuse Center.
2) Athletic Program Community College
3) Volunteers -
   a) Community College
   b) Volunteer Bureau
4) Coping Skills. mental health.
5) GED.
6) Staff
7) Service Club

Possible Responses

Some possible responses to the question above might include:

"We need to know more about inmate interests, needs, and so on."

"The substance abuse center could run groups for inmates with these kinds of problems."

"Our community college has an excellent athletic program; it should be approached about providing interns to offer recreation programs."

"Students in criminal justice, criminology, sociology, and psychology could also be used as volunteers."

"We have a volunteer bureau and a clearing house for community volunteers. They should be of help."

"The mental health department runs group meetings called Coping Skills in the 80's. Perhaps they could make these sessions available in the jail."

"The school district is legally responsible for running the educational program. The district should provide the educational program for jail inmates."

"The board of commissioners should provide the jail with a staff person to coordinate programs and services."

"A service club may be interested in supplying recreation equipment or quiet games for the jail."

Task 5. Meeting Break

The leader may want the group to take a break after collecting responses to the starting question. This will provide time for the leader to organize the responses in preparation for deciding on solutions to pursue and for preparing the action plan.

Task 6. Decide on Solutions

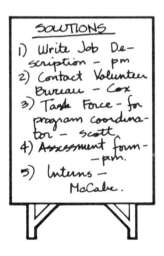

The group determines which of the proposed solutions seem effective and feasible. Consensus is required in achieving a solution—this may take time but the investment will pay off. At this point individuals should commit themselves to specific actions needed to pursue the solutions.

Example. These are action statements that might be made by individual committee members.

Project Manager: "I will write a job description for a jail program and inmate services coordinator."

Mrs. Cox: "I will arrange for a member of the advisory committee to contact the volunteer bureau to determine whether it can supply the jail with a volunteer program coordinator who would provide staff assistance in planning and scheduling programs and services in the jail, and other possible volunteers."

Judge Scott: "I will enlist a task force of the advisory committee as a support group in presenting the request for a program coordinator to the sheriff and then the board of commissioners."

Project Manager: "When volunteers or interns have been screened and assigned to the jail, I will have them design an inmate needs and interests assessment form and collect data for future programming."

Mr. McCabe: "I will contact the office that handles intern assignments at the community college and work with them to organize an intern program for the jail."

Undersheriff Gregory: "I will ask the advisory committee to outline a standard presentation for a speakers bureau. The speakers bureau will be responsible for scheduling presentations to service clubs, church groups, and other community groups. The objective of this activity will be to educate the community about problems in our jail and to request their help either as volunteers or through sponsoring athletics and leisuretime activities by purchasing equipment for the jail."

Mr. McCabe: "When community groups agree to buy equipment and leisuretime games, I will contact the director of athletics of the community college and ask for interns or volunteer students to help us run our recreation program."

Project Manager: "When the program coordinator has been hired and volunteers or interns have learned the routines and responsibilities in the jail, I will work with the coordinator to initiate substance abuse programs, initiate coping skills training, and an educational program."

In this example of a structured meeting, the leader has organized the group members' ideas into action statements that can be organized in a logical sequence of events.

Task 7. Develop and Agree on the Action Agenda

The next task in action planning is to establish an action agenda that fixes responsibility for the activities generated from the meeting and sets a schedule for progress reports and completion.

The action agenda cannot be completed in the absence of the advisory committee because the group leader does not have the authority to assign tasks to other persons. The responsible person is accountable at reporting times and when the activity is supposed to be completed. Moreover, it is important to involve the advisory committee in adopting the final action agenda, thus giving the committee "ownership" in the activities, assignments, and due dates. A sample action agenda is shown in Table 11-1.

Table 11-1. Sample Action Agenda

Who Is Responsible	Actions/Activities	Reporting Schedule	Completion Date
Group leader/Project Manager	Write jail program-coordinator job description	Next meeting, (Jan. 25)	Next meeting, (Jan. 25)
Advisory committee member (Mrs. Cox, League of Women Voters)	Contact Volunteer Bureau for volunteers	Jan. 25	Jan. 25
Advisory Committee member (Judge Scott)	Chair an advisory committee task force to work with planning team. Request program coordinator position from sheriff and board of supervisors.	Jan. 25	Feb. 25
Advisory committee member (Mr. McCabe, Superintendent of schools)	Arrange a meeting with Professor Higgins and planning team staff to discuss reassignment of interns.	Monthly, beginning Jan. 25	June 25
Group leader/Project manager	Work with volunteers on inmate service needs assessment.	Monthly, beginning Feb. 25	June 25
Advisory committee chairperson (Undersheriff Gregory)	Chair a task force of advisory committee members in planning and scheduling speakers' bureau.	Each advisory committee meeting	Ongoing

Since the later items in the preliminary plan were so speculative, the committee decided to postpone the action agenda for these items for ninety days. Those items will be placed on the meeting agenda for April.

Task 8. Critique the Process

At the conclusion of the advisory committee meeting, the group leader reviews for the members those aspects of the meeting that he or she felt were "well done" and asks the group members to provide feedback regarding what they felt he or she did well. Similarly, the group leader states his or her perception of "opportunities for improvement" and asks the group for its feedback in this regard. The critique provides the opportunity for improving the quality of future meetings.

Having developed the action plan, it is critical for the committee to monitor the resulting tasks. The responsible party should be queried at subsequent meetings on the progress of the work and should report at the appointed time.

Applications of Action Planning

To illustrate its utility in the context of a fairly complex problem-solving procedure, action planning has been presented here in the context of a formal advisory committee meeting. However, it should be viewed as a versatile tool having a wide range of applications, including planning team and task force issues.

For example, the project manager and the planning team can establish action agendas covering the total scope of jail planning. The action agenda in this context fixes staff responsibility for data collection and analysis, library research, preliminary document drafting, and so forth. To be sure, the project manager and planning team members need to coordinate their action-planning activities with the advisory committee and the board of commissioners, but the procedure provides a structure for ensuring that each task gets addressed at the appropriate time.

Summary and Conclusions

The problem-solving meeting illustrated above provides for rich involvement of community representatives and professional planners. More importantly, such a meeting concludes with an action plan that structures problem-solving activities in a logical manner, fixes responsibilities for each activity, and establishes a timetable for the completion of assignments. However, bear in mind that your meetings may not be as simple as the illustration.

Action-planning schedules that result should be made available to the advisory committee, the board of commissioners, and the planning team members. In this way all members of the planning process can help monitor the progress. In addition, the board of commissioners should be asked to endorse action-planning activities as major milestones are completed.

Action planning requires the allocation of time and resources. Some counties may assert that they do not have the luxury of "front-end" planning. However, it is a curious phenomenon of organizations that we can always find time to clean up the mistakes made because of deficient planning. Experience tells us that in the long run it is far cheaper to minimize these mistakes by investing in front-end planning. Do not shortchange yourself in this regard.

References

Bradford, Leland P. n.d. **Making Meetings Work.** La Jolla, CA: University Associates.

Doyle, Michael, and David Straus. 1976. **How to Make Meetings Work.** New York: Playboy Press.

Jorgensen, James D. and Timothy F. Foutsko. 1981. **Solving Problems in Meetings.** Chicago: Nelson-Hall. Provides guidance, structure, and alternatives for planning and running decision-making meetings.

Jorgensen, James D. and Timothy F. Foutsko. 1978. **Quid.** New York: Walker. Presents a "force-field analysis" approach in which planners evaluate the relative merits of one choice over another.

Meeting Leadership Skills: A Prescriptive Package. 1976. Boulder, CO: Training Systems Design, Inc. A more detailed exposition of the methods described in this chapter.

Schindler-Rainman, Eva, and Ronald Lippitt. n.d. **Taking Your Meetings out of the Doldrums.** Columbus, OH: Association of Professional Directors.

12. Step 5: Select
Needed Consultants

Who Will Use This Chapter

Primary Users

Planning team
Consultant selection
  Task Force
Board of commissioners
Project manager

Secondary Users

County counsel
Contract officer

Introduction

This chapter discusses the need for consultants, the various types of consultants, the methods for soliciting their services and selecting them, and hints to help you when contracting for and working with a consultant.

You may complete many of the needs-assessment and feasibility-study tasks without the aid of a consultant, but some agencies will want assistance with these tasks. Further, almost all counties that proceed with developing a building will hire an architect. Thus the chapter deals with the selection of both planning and architectural consultants, although the latter will not be needed until later on in the process.

Do You Need a Consultant?

Deciding when to select an architect or other consultant is not the simple procedure that some may think. You cannot just hire some person or firm and expect them to develop solutions without any substantial involvement from you, their client. First, you must develop a thorough understanding of your own problems and needs so that you can better decide what type of consultant you require, what services you expect the consultant to perform, how much you can afford to pay for those services, and how much time is necessary—or available—to complete the job. Once you have analyzed your situation, you can convey the necessary information to your consultant.

After your preliminary assessment of the problem, you will have a basic idea of whether consultation is necessary and what its focus should be. It may be as broad as providing the corrections-needs assessment study or as specific as assessing the potential impact of health-care service standards on your jail.

A frequent reason for hiring consultants is that in-house capabilities do not measure up to the task at hand. Not many agencies can support the specialized staff required for justice system planning and design. It is often impractical to establish permanent positions for these functions. Unless there is long-term demand for these people and their expertise, the dollar savings probably lies with the shorter-term consultant.

If your county has in-house facility planners who might be able to conduct your jail study, consider these questions before automatically turning the job over to them:

Does the county have sufficient qualified staff available to meet your schedule or will delay be inevitable? Will the product from in-house staff be well received by persons who must use or approve it? Will the work be of the required caliber?

If the answer to any of these questions is no, you must decide how much flexibility you can afford with the schedule or the product. A consultant may be the solution if the availability or credibility of in-house staff does not measure up.

If you have decided to retain a consultant, you should double-check your decision against three basic questions:

One, can you identify the **symptoms** of the problem (for example, overcrowded jail or no recreation space)?

Two, are the **causes** of the problem undetermined (for example, why the jail is overcrowded)?

Three, are the immediately **available solutions** undesirable (for example, spending money on poorly defined facilities or studying causes without benefit of expertise)?

The process of thinking through the symptoms, causes, and solutions will provide a good basis for establishing the scope of the consultant's work. A thorough description of existing conditions, previous work, and anticipated changes will help both you the client and your consultant to understand what needs to be done now. When you determine your own needs and limitations, you can help your consultant structure his or her work in a manner that will create the most effective product.

What Type of Consultant?

A Close Fit Between County Needs and Consultants

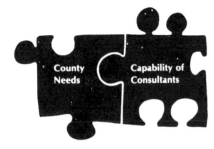

County Needs

Capability of Consultants

The range of consultant types used by justice agencies is wide. However, two basic types are involved in needs assessment, planning, design, and construction of justice facilities. These are corrections planners, and architects. Your choice of either of these, of course, depends on the particular work to be performed. Both types work out of firms and organizations ranging from single-person operations with a specific area of expertise to large multidiscipline firms that combine both planning and architectural services. It is important that you match experience and qualifications to the type of job for which you are contracting.

Clearly, not all consultants possess the same expertise. You should expect specialized knowledge or advice and imaginative solutions from consultants. However, unless consultants are familiar with your particular type of problem, often they will hire consultants of their own with the necessary expertise to deal with your situation.

Selection Criteria

Satisfy some basic criteria before you contract with any consultant. The criteria must be refined by those who develop the "request for proposals" (RFP), but here are some suggested topics to include.

- Are the skills matched to the job (architecture, planning, organizational development, to name three)?
- Does the firm have experience with this type of job? If not, do their consultants?
- Will the consultant give you the time and attention necessary to develop solutions to your problems, or will you get something "off the shelf"?
- Is it the "right"-sized firm to do the work? Make sure the first is not so small that supplemental staff hired for this job would present a problem. Also make sure that a large firm would give your job the attention it requires.
- Is the firm located in an area that will allow the consultants to spend enough time in your community?
- Can you afford them? Is their fee compatible with your budget?
- What do their references say about them:
    Was the product satisfactory?
    Were schedules kept?
    Did they solicit or accept client input?
    Were they responsive to the client?
    Have they been available for followup?
    Were billing practices fair?
    Would the reference rehire them?

Even these criteria have their limitations: they will be of little value if you personally cannot work with the consultant you have selected. Consequently the selection process is extremely important. That is the time to find out how the consultant would approach the job, how he or she would use your county's existing expertise, whether he or she would solicit the involvement of other critical participants, and what his or her previous work record shows. Technique and approach are so significant that it is difficult to overstress their importance. The best technical skills are only as good as the consultant's ability to employ them. If the consultant cannot establish rapport with you, the client, the consultant cannot effectively use his or her skills to serve you.

Methods of Selection

Consultant Selection Process

```
┌──────────────────────┐
│  Assess Problems &   │
│  Need for Consultant │
└──────────────────────┘
          ▼
┌──────────────────────┐
│   Allocate Time &    │
│ Money for Consultants│
└──────────────────────┘
          ▼
┌──────────────────────┐
│ Develop Criteria for │
│ Selecting Consultants│
└──────────────────────┘
          ▼
┌──────────────────────┐
│   Issue Requests     │
│   for Proposals      │
└──────────────────────┘
          ▼
┌──────────────────────┐
│     Review &         │
│ Evaluate Proposals   │
└──────────────────────┘
          ▼
┌──────────────────────┐
│   Select Top Firms   │
└──────────────────────┘
          ▼
┌──────────────────────┐
│ Interview Top Firms  │
└──────────────────────┘
          ▼
┌──────────────────────┐
│  Select & Notify Firm│
└──────────────────────┘
```

An architect or consultant is rarely hired without the formal release of a request for proposals (RFP) and an objective review of responses before the final selection is made. By contrast, the "sole-source" method of selection does not allow the same degree of objectivity and fairness as the open process. Consequently government agencies that must guarantee unbiased selection of consultants rarely use the sole-source method.

More common methods used to select consultants are the **open RFP** and the **invitational RFP.** A design **competition** is much less common (and more time-consuming) and is reserved primarily for the selection of architects for major or prototypical projects.

The open RFP solicits responses from all qualified firms. The county establishes basic minimum criteria for consultant selection and then accepts proposals from anyone meeting those criteria. The RFP can be published in local newspapers, trade journals, professional publications, or any medium likely to reach qualified firms. One example of an open RFP is a request for submissions from any licensed architect to design and construct a jail. This might be further limited to any licensed architect in your state, or even to those with offices in your county.

The invitational RFP is distributed to a limited number of consultants who have been previously selected as qualified to submit proposals. Such a selection requires the prior assessment of each firm to determine which will receive the invitation to submit. The assessment is usually based on certain criteria such as correctional experience, previous work within the county, or inclusion on a county-maintained list of qualified consultants. The distribution of invitations should conform with county or funding agency guidelines for fair hiring practices.

Architect selection is sometimes accomplished through design competitions. These may follow the general RFP format in that they may be either open or invitational competitions. In both cases, some cash award to competitors is customary. Open competitions usually award the best two or three solutions, whereas invitational competitions grant a small cash award to each firm agreeing to participate. The final award is the anticipated contract.

Competitions require that you, the client, supply a building program document and appoint a qualified jury to judge submissions and to make final awards. More information is available in "The Use of Design Competitions," a pamphlet available from the American Institute of Architects (AIA # B 451).

The Request for Proposals

The RFP should be clear, complete, and specific. This allows those who respond to focus on substantive issues and to present comparable information. Because the major issues addressed by correctional projects are often diffuse and completeness of the RFP is so important, task forces are frequently formed to assist

**Request for Proposals to Prequalify Firms
Interested in Providing Architectural Services
for County Justice Facility**

"Any County" is presently completing preliminary planning for construction of a justice facility. The resulting master plan, feasibility study, and facility program will define the scope and location of the project. It may include a new jail of 90 to 100 beds, a court facility with six courtrooms, and offices for related justice agencies.

The county will use a three-stage selection process, starting with prequalification statements that are solicited at this time. On the basis of these statements, a number of firms will be invited to submit full proposals; of this group up to six will be interviewed by a panel of county staff. This panel will then recommend one firm to the board of commissioners.

Firms or associations of firms are invited to submit prequalification statements addressing the following:

(1) Experience with the design of local correctional facilities, courts, and related justice agency offices.

(2) Experience in master planning of governmental facilities.

(3) Experience with construction management.

(4) Design approach and philosophy.

(5) Other relevant experience and information.

Architectural firms located outside of the state may wish to indicate association with a local architectural firm, although this is not essential at this stage of the process.

Submissions consisting of ten bound copies of the prequalification statement should be sent by recognized carrier, postmarked no later than September 5, 19--, to Mr. John Doe, Administrative Officer, Any County, P.O. Box 100. Inquiries should be directed to Mr. Joe Doaks, Project Coordinator, at 999-999-9999, Any Town, Any State 99999.

in drafting the RFP. Such a group may consist of county officials, corrections personnel, attorneys, and members of the public. A representative from your state's local corrections agency might be available to review the RFP or proposals.

If a task force writes the RFP, at least some of its members should also participate in the selection process. The RFP should include the following items:

- Name and location of contracting agency
- Name and phone number of contact person
- Background information on project
- Statement of the problem
- Scope of work to be performed
- Time limitations on work to be performed
- Time deadline and location for submissions; number of copies required (usually one for each member of the selection committee)
- Time and location of "preproposal conference" (if offered) to orient bidders and answer questions
- Anticipated budget for construction (if known)
- Basis for establishing consultant fees (such as percentage of construction cost for architects or fixed fee for planning consultants)
- Request for a statement of understanding and approach to the project
- Request for information concerning the responding firm and key personnel who will be assigned to the job
- Request for the firm's references
- Other legally required or desirable statements or disclaimers (seek the advice of your county counsel)

For architectural services, the RFP would not normally include requests for sketches, cost estimates, or suggested compensation to the architect. However, it could well ask for examples of previous buildings.

One individual (probably the project manager) should be responsible for distributing the RFP, responding to questions regarding it, and notifying all competitors of the final selection. The same person may appropriately coordinate the work of the consultant with the agency during the job. It is important to establish this position in the early stages of the project and continue to use it as a conduit for communications between the client agencies and the consultant.

Reviewing Proposals

Review and ranking of proposals require a considerable amount of time. Individuals reviewing proposals must understand the criteria for review and selection and apply the criteria to each submission. The submissions may be reviewed by the group as a whole or individually by the members of the group.

Proposals should be reviewed in light of the criteria discussed above and any others developed for the specific job. The criteria may be variably weighted. (For example, the size of a firm would be worth fewer points than its references.) Another rating method is to assign competing firms relative scores for each category. In the case of five firms, for example, each category would be ranked one through five, assigned according to the rank of the firms in that category.

Some instances might require different evaluations for various categories of the proposal. For example, this could occur when some specific technical expertise is required to evaluate a projection methodology.

Consultant Evaluation Sheet

Consultant Evaluation Sheet

Firm Name: Ca. Kitchen Consultants
Reviewer: J.S.   Date: 11-16

Criteria	Weight of Criteria	Score	Comments
Experience & Skills: General &	Max. 5	5	many hotels, restaurants of similar size.
Corrections	7	2	only one jail.
Cost Basis (cost of services) Amount of service offered; Amount of on-site work	10	5	per hour - $50/hr - no max. number of hours - although they think it will take 30-50 hrs. ($1500-2500)
References —satisfaction with: Amount of involvement during design development;	3	2	always involve key staff throughout process - but doesn't always listen well.
Sensitivity to local ideas;	4	2	one former client felt all clients get same product.
Reliability;	4	4	highly reliable.
Meeting deadlines;	4	3	generally within a few weeks.
Individual staff experiences.	3	2	mostly positive - one felt they only care about management.
Would rehire?	2	2	unanimous - yes.
Office organization.	5	5	small - (6) - large enough to get job done on time.
Interest in Project.	4	4	enthused.
Current commitments/ workloads; Availability of staff.	4	4	available now.
Other comments, General comments & Overall assessment.			impressive - major concern, however is that they have little experience in correctional facilities.
Total	55	40	

You can incorporate subjective (opinion) criteria as well as objective (factual) criteria into the reviews. Subjective criteria might be appropriate to assess how well the consultant works with clients. This type of review should be well-documented, as all rankings should be, and may emerge from open discussion among those responsible for reviewing the proposals.

Develop a uniform format for each reviewer to use in recording responses to proposals and ranking them. The sample Consultant Evaluation Sheet contains room for information about the firm, a list of criteria and their weights, plus space for scores and comments to be entered.

Narrowing the Field, Interviewing, Selection, and Notification

The method of selection should be determined early in the process and committee members should understand how it works. Typically the process will include both a review of the proposals and a personal interview for the top firms. In any case, the committee members need adequate time to review the proposals prior to discussing them. At the review meeting, the project manager should be responsible for tabulating selection process results, recording them, and maintaining them for future reference.

If the number of apparently qualified respondents is large, a "short list" of the most-qualified firms may be culled for interviews. The development of the short list or prequalification may be the responsibility of the project manager, the board of commissioners, or the task force. Depending on the number of qualified firms, from two to six may be selected for interview.

The number should be considered rather carefully. Interviewing can be time-consuming since each firm should be allotted at least one hour. It may be difficult to assemble the selection task force for the entire day necessary to interview even six firms. If you screen more carefully beforehand, you can limit the interviews to only the most qualified and highly recommended firms.

The importance of the interview cannot be overstated. The interview gives members of the selection task force the opportunity to meet key members of the consultant team and to get a sense of who they will be working with. One useful caution is to make sure that the same people who appear for the interview will indeed be assigned to the job and that the county understands what their responsibilities will be.

Interviews should be carefully planned. The ground rules should be understood both by the committee and the consulting firms. It is best to balance structure and fairness with some freedom for individual expression. All interviews should be allotted the same amount of time. Generally some time is reserved for the consultant to make a presentation, with the balance available for discussion and questions. Facilities should be available to show slides or display drawings. The minimum time for each firm should be forty-five minutes; an hour would be more appropriate. It is very important to allow ten to twenty minutes between interviews for the committee members to record their responses and perhaps to discuss the strengths and weaknesses of the last firm before going on to the next.

Occasionally a county may send a delegation to visit some buildings designed by the top contenders. Such visits are beneficial also because they allow you to speak firsthand to staff, administrators, and others about their experiences with the consultant, their satisfaction with the product, and what they would change the next time. In all fairness, remember that not all aspects of a building are the result of a consultant's expertise or lack of it. On occasion an unyielding client may have insisted on a feature that did not work out well.

One individual, usually the project manager, should be designated to inform all proposers of the result of each stage of the selection process. This should always be done in writing, although the selected firms may also be telephoned to give them added preparation time for the next phase.

Whichever sequence is followed, all stages of the selection should be well documented both for the protection of the county and so that inquiring firms understand how decisions were made.

Contract Issues

Methods of Compensating Consultants

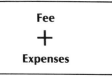

Fee
+
Expenses

$/ hr. or day

% of costs

X x Direct Personnel Expense

The scope of services required from the consultant should be clearly defined before selection so that it need only be refined when negotiating the contract. For architects, the work may include preliminary programming in addition to basic services such as schematic design, design development, construction documents, bidding/negotiations, and administration of the construction contract.

Additional services might be considered beyond the standard architectural scope. These may include financial feasibility studies, planning surveys, detailed estimates, and interior design. Each of these items is negotiated above and beyond the basic architectural fee.

It may be advantageous to define the consultants' key personnel in the contract as well as any subconsultants assigned to various phases of the job. You can request prior notification of any changes in these and the right to approve them.

In the contract, specify key progress dates for presentation or review as well as time required for approval. A requirement for authorization to proceed to the next phase of work Is generally Included as part of the client review and signoff.

Methods of compensating consultants vary. They depend on such variables as the scope of services, the type of contract, and the financial limitations on the contracting agency. Some of the more common methods are the following.

- **Professional fee plus expenses:** Agreed on lump-sum fee for professional services plus compensation for actual job expenses such as travel or printing.
- **Per diem or hourly rate:** Usually used for services involving consultation, reports, opinions, and similar items. Time spent is billed at an agreed per diem or hourly rate. The upper limit for billed time and expenses may be set, with prior written approval required to exceed that limit.
- **Percentage of project construction costs:** Compensation for basic architectural services based on an established percentage of the construction cost of the project. The percentage may vary from 5 to 10 percent or more, depending on the size and complexity of the project. Payments are keyed to the phase of work and are cumulative so that 15 percent has been paid through schematic design, 35 percent through design development, 75 percent through construction documents, 80 percent through bidding and negotiation, and 100 percent at the end of construction.
- **Multiple of direct personnel expense:** Used on projects whose scope is difficult to define or those without a fixed construction budget. The advantage of this method is that it does not require distinction between basic and additional services. Compensation is based on the amount of time required to accomplish project services; payroll costs are multiplied by a factor to cover overhead and profit. The owner may specify an upper limit that cannot be exceeded without authorization.

You may require a consultant to execute a truth-in-negotiation certificate that states that wage rates and other unit costs supporting a fee are accurate, complete, and current at time of contracting. This is appropriate in fee structures based on multiples of personnel expense.

You will want to retain the right to cancel negotiations if a fair and reasonable price cannot be negotiated. In such a case, negotiations can then proceed with the second most-qualified firm.

While many counties choose to create their own consultant contract forms, it may be worthwhile to refer to the American Institute of Architects' "Standard Agreement Between Owner and Architect" (AIA form B-141) as a basis for discussion.

Working with Consultants

The client agency designates the project manager to serve as a communications link between the consultants and the client. (See Chapter 8, which defines the role of the project manager and his or her relationship to the consultant.) He or she also arranges for meetings at which the consultants are introduced, the job scope and schedule discussed, and the working methods of the consultant identified so that all participants may contribute.

The project may be scheduled and tracked in a variety of ways. Two common means used by architects, planners, and construction managers are the Critical Path Method (CPM) and the Project Evaluation and Review Technique (PERT). Both methods identify key progress dates and illustrate the results of meeting them or the consequences of failure. Regular presentations by the consultant are scheduled so that key groups in the county are aware of the project's progress. This also ensures early identification of problems by those participants who may be able to correct them.

It should be evident to the county that any proposed solution must be sensitive to the particulars of its situation. One means of encouraging a responsive product is to begin with a well-defined statement of need. Then make sure that a consultant's methods and approach will, in fact, suit your project. Do not accept stereotyped solutions or "off-the-shelf" plans, if they are offered. Beware of needs-assessment studies conducted by consultants who may derive fee benefits from proposed building solutions; in that case, the consultant could benefit from increase in size or cost of the facility. Use your task force and advisory committee to confirm and endorse appropriate solutions to problems. Some analysis of proposed solutions may be available to you from your state's local corrections agency.

Summary and Conclusion

To get the maximum benefit from a consultant, you must clearly define your needs. Then you can determine what type of consultant you require, what criteria and methods will best suit the selection of the consultant, and what issues should be addressed in the work of the project. Clear responsibility for communicating with potential consultants and the one finally selected should be assigned to the project manager. That person should also insure that methods of selection are objective and well-documented.

Be prepared to devote time, personnel, and expense to choosing the best consultant you can get and to working closely with the one you select. These are the best investments you, as a client, can make in your project.

References

American Institute of Architects. 1974. **How to Find, Evaluate, Select, Negotiate with an Architect.** Washington, DC: American Institute of Architects. A booklet introducing types of selection processes, methods of compensation, and a bibliography to AIA documents on related subjects.

———. 1963. **The Selection of An Architect.** Washington, DC: American Institute of Architects. Description of various means of architect selection.

———. 1971. **Statement of the Architect's Services.** Washington, DC: American Institute of Architects. Discusses architectural services, compensation, and categories of building types.

———. 1978. **You and Your Architect.** Washington, DC. Brief discussion of how to define your need for architectural services, how to select and hire, and client responsibilities.

Craig, Lois. 1978. "Competitions in Search of Quality." **Architectural Record.** Examples of recent competitions for the design of federal GSA projects.

Frankenhuis, Jean Pierre. 1977. "How to Get a Good Consultant." **Harvard Business Review,** November–December 1977, 133–39. A discussion of the right time to seek consultants and how to manage the process of soliciting, hiring, and supervising them.

Part 3.
Assessing Current and Future Corrections Needs

13. Introduction

Who Will Use Part 3

Primary Users
Project manager
Data collection/analysis
  task force
Planning team
Board of commissioners
Policy makers

Secondary Users
Advisory committee
Justice agency representatives

Purpose

The purpose of Part 3 is to provide counties with methods to analyze how existing detention facilities are used, evaluate criminal justice system functions that affect population levels in those facilities, and rationally to project both facility and program requirements for future years.

Part 3 provides detailed guidelines for counties to follow in accomplishing the needs assessment. The process has been broken down into component steps with detailed instructions for each one. Data collection forms, analytical questions, and suggested formats for presenting results are provided.

Virtually all of the techniques and processes have been tested and modified as a result of local corrections planning experience. They have worked for others and, with some commitment of thought and effort, they can provide your county with an excellent basis for making some tough decisions.

Determination of a county's needs for correctional programs and facilities involves input and decision making by individuals from many levels of county government and the community. It is a process that requires "nitty-gritty" data collection and analysis; formulation and testing of various policies based on that analysis; and, ultimately, policy decisions regarding program direction and facility development. These decisions will have a major impact on the county's long-term capital commitment for construction and program operation. Because of this, the methods described in Part 3 will involve people from virtually all levels of county government. Their roles are described below.

Roles of Major Participants

Policy Makers

The ultimate users of the products developed in Part 3 will be county policy makers—members of the board of commissioners, top county management, and key members of the local criminal justice system. Employing data developed by using this section, they will establish priorities for the types of facilities and programs required to meet the county's corrections-system needs over the coming years; they will have as well long-term responsibility for implementing those decisions.

It is therefore important that policy makers understand the data collection and analysis process outlined in the pages that follow. While other people will undoubtedly collect and analyze the data, policy makers should be involved in setting the goals for data collection and in reviewing procedures and assumptions. In this way they will be prepared to make decisions based on issues raised by the analysis.

Planning Team and Data Collection/Analysis Task Force

The primary audience for Part 3 is made up of the project manager and county staff members who are responsible for collecting and analyzing the data required for the needs assessment. Depending on how your county organizes the data collection and planning effort, these individuals may include staff and selected managers of criminal justice agencies, staff analysts from the county administrative office, or consultants. Organizing and staffing a data collection task force is discussed later in this chapter, where the role of the project manager is spelled out.

The Advisory Committee

The advisory committee serves as a link between policy makers and the data collection team. A key task described in Part 3 involves evaluating trade-offs between constructing facilities or providing alternatives for individuals involved in the criminal justice system. Virtually all of these options have advantages and disadvantages from the perspectives of cost, effectiveness, and public safety. An integral part of the planning process will be analyzing these trade offs and determining which choices best suit your county's needs.

Because it represents both community and justice agency interests, the advisory committee provides the proper forum for evaluating trade-offs and for making policy recommendations to the board of commissioners. To do this effectively, it is important that advisory committee members have a broad understanding of the analytical techniques, questions, and decision-making processes covered in this section.

Goals for Data Collection and Analysis

Goal 1: Establish and Maintain Control Over the County's Criminal Justice System

It is often said that a county has little control over its detention facility needs. As population grows and the composition of the community changes, crime may increase. While county government has little immediate impact on the societal forces that result in crime, arrest, sentencing, and therefore jail population, a county can exercise significant control over the scope and type of detention services and facilities required to meet criminal justice system needs.

The county can affect both jail population and jail facility needs through four major areas:

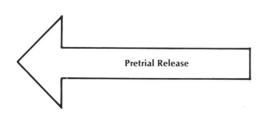

- Its approach toward development and implementation of **pretrial release programs.**

- The **classification of inmates** who are housed in local detention facilities.

Male			Female			Total
Pre-sent.	Sent.	Prob.	Pre-sent.	Sent.	Prob.	
40	60	15	14	18	8	155

- The effective and **timely functioning of the county court system.**

	M	Tu	W	Th	F	Sa	Su
Arraignment	S.	S.	Mc.	Mc.	Mc.	Mc.	S.
Prel. Hear.	J.	J.	J.	K.	K.		
Pretrial Hear.	K.	K.	K.	J.	J.		
Trial	R./St.	R./St.	R./St.	R./St.	R./St.		

- **Sentencing alternatives** for individuals who will serve time in the county.

To help the county gain (or maintain) this control, analysis procedures are designed to:

- Assist counties in documenting and evaluating current performance in each of these critical areas.
- Consider the potential impact of alternative courses of action.
- Assess the costs and benefits of implementing or expanding alternative programs and, when each of these analytical questions has been resolved, to:
- Project detention facility needs.

Goal 2: Evaluate the Impact of Criminal Justice Programs on Jail Capacity Needs

Too frequently, correctional facility planning decisions are based only on past practices. Current jail populations are projected into the future and construction is begun. Such an approach fails to consider other activities and programs that a county could undertake to moderate expensive jail construction and operation. With drastic revenue limitations facing most counties and jail construction costs up to $70,000 per maximum-security bed, it is prudent before building plans are formulated to consider any alternative programs that might reduce the jail population.

Goal 3: Define a Correctional Strategy Based on Facts

The fundamental factors that need to be understood in correctional facility planning are the characteristics of the population that will be dealt with, in the criminal justice system in general and in correction and detention facilities in particular. Without such understanding, too large, too small, or the wrong type of facility may be built.

To avoid building mistaken correctional facilities you must be thoroughly familiar with the type of offenders in your community. Such information will help to ensure that planning provides:

- facilities with security levels consistent with population characteristics
- an assessment of the risk to public safety if certain alleged offenders are granted pretrial release
- an understanding of inmates' specific service and program requirements

Goal 4: Help Each County Find Its Own Best Solutions

Each county has its own population characteristics, crime problems, community concerns, and attitudes toward the criminal justice system. The correctional philosophy defined by the county should reflect each of these unique components. (See Chapter 10 on the mission statement.) The purpose of Part 3 is not to impose a specific correctional philosophy on a county, but rather to assist the county in documenting the effects of its current philosophy. Once the implications of current philosophy are understood, adjustments in that philosophy can be considered and the mission statement revised, if necessary. Only then will it be appropriate to develop a correctional facility program plan.

Overview of the Data Gathering and Analysis Process

Why Gather Information?

As you review the data collection and analysis steps described in the pages that follow, you may ask: "Why do we have to go through such a time-consuming exercise? Why can't we simply use readily available data provided by state criminal justice agencies to estimate our current and long-range needs?"

The principal problem with most readily available data (such as raw statistics about county criminal justice and correction systems) is that such data are too general to answer many key questions related to practical correctional facilities planning. In addition, they are often based on partial or faulty information.

Generalized data available from your state or county, the FBI, and other agencies provide valuable indicators of overall criminal justice system activity in the county or state. But they fail to provide any information about the specific characteristics of jail populations or of individuals who are passing through the criminal justice system. Similarly, such statistics are virtually unusable for evaluating the potential impact of alternative programs on facility needs. Better information must be available before your county can make informed planning decisions.

As you review the data requirements for the needs assessment, you may conclude that some information is not readily available from existing records and files. For example, you may find it difficult to develop a portrait of the behavior characteristics and service needs of the incarcerated population. Or it may be difficult to determine what proportion of those individuals who are granted pretrial releases fail to appear at required court appearances.

Such gaps raise questions about the usefulness of available data not only for planning purposes but also over the longer range, to manage and assess the performance of your county's criminal justice and corrections system. Thus as you collect and analyze data, be attuned to their potential long-range usefulness. A byproduct of the needs-assessment study will be an improvement in your county's detention and correction system records for management purposes.

Major Components of the Data Collection and Analysis Process

The chart, "Data Collection, Analysis, and Projection Sequence," shows how the data gathering and analysis steps fit together, indicates how data produced in each step fit into the analysis in subsequent steps, and outlines the sequence in which the steps are accomplished.

Step 1: Profile the Jail Population in sufficient detail to identify and test program and facility alternatives in subsequent steps. This involves documenting the criminal history characteristics, length of stay, service needs, and behavior of jail inmates. The information is employed to answer such questions as:

- What are the security characteristics of the existing jail population?
- Are security levels of current facilities appropriate for these inmates? Do they provide safety and security for both staff and inmates?
- What proportion of the jail population could be safely released if release and service programs were improved?
- Would there be a risk to public safety if some of these individuals were provided pretrial release?

Profile data also provide important input to each of the subsequent planning steps.

Step 2: Profile Existing Correctional Facility Programs. Develop a thorough picture of the services and programs provided within the walls of the jail and other detention facilities as well as programs available in the criminal justice system and elsewhere in the community. A major product of Step 2 will be identification of gaps between existing services and the needs of the inmate population.

Step 3: Document Current Criminal Justice System Functions and assess the impact of current programs, practices, and operations on correctional facility needs. This step involves understanding how the county criminal justice system functions and how well it relates to inmate needs through the operation of pretrial release programs, court services, and the availability of sentencing programs and alternatives.

Step 4: Consider and Evaluate Alternatives to Incarceration. This is a critical point in the overall assessment process. The planning team, advisory committee, and policy makers are asked to take a detailed look at what the county is doing now

Data Collection, Analysis and Projection Sequence

Step 1. Profile Detention Population

Step 2. Profile Existing Correctional Facility Progams

- Document Programs & Services
- Survey Inmate Needs
- Identify Community Resources

Then

- Identify Service Gaps
- Formulate Service Plans

Step 3. Document Current Criminal Justice Operations

- Evaluate Pretrial Release Programs & Decisions
- Analyze Court System Processing Performance
- Evaluate Alternative Sentencing Programs

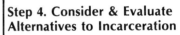

Step 5. Document Trends & Project Future Volumes

- Document & Analyze Historic Trends
- Develop Projection Assumptions
- Select Projection Method
- Project Populations Based on Existing Incarceration Strategies
- Project Populations Incorporating Program Expansions & Adjustments

Step 4. Consider & Evaluate Alternatives to Incarceration

- Define Scope & Cost of Program Adjustment
- Estimate impact on Current Facility Operation

Then

- Select Program Adustments to be Implemented

Step 6. Convert Projections to Capacity & Program Needs

- Determine Facility Needs by Bedspace Type
- Select Alternative & In-Facility Programs

Step 7. Document Results in a Final Report

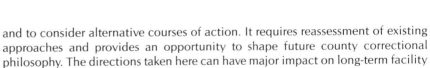

and to consider alternative courses of action. It requires reassessment of existing approaches and provides an opportunity to shape future county correctional philosophy. The directions taken here can have major impact on long-term facility and capital requirements.

Step 5: Document Trends in Justice System and Correction Facility Populations and Project Future Levels. This step gives shape to the evaluation of policy alternatives considered above. It translates existing policies—and potential revisions of those policies—into inmate population projections and clarifies the financial and service impacts of alternative programs.

Step 6: Convert Projections to Capacity and Program Needs. The last step consists of revising forecasts of short- and long-term facility and program needs. It involves refining and selecting program strategies, defining facility requirements over the planning period, and estimating costs of programs and facilities.

As you accomplish each of these steps, remember that data collection is not an end in itself. Be creative in analyzing the data to determine what they say about incarceration strategies in your county. Similarly, take care not to get bogged down in data collection—be selective when data are not readily available; find an alternative source or move on to the next item. Common sense is an important element in both data collection and analysis.

Organizing and Staffing the Data Collection and Analysis Task Force

Do's and Don'ts

The data collection and analysis sequence described here is a considerable undertaking. To successfully analyze and document detention system needs, careful planning and project management are required.

Don't assign project management responsibilities to an individual who cannot devote a significant amount of time managing **and** participating in project work activities. For example, the sheriff or district attorney should not be project managers since they are both already occupied full time.

Do assign project management responsibilities to a staff member who can spend **at least** half-time on the project and can get involved in actual data collection activities. It is important that the project manager get directly involved with the data so that he or she can accurately analyze and interpret it.

Don't "farm out" main data collection and analysis tasks to clerical staff (such as to records clerks in the jail) and expect these tasks to be completed properly unless close supervision and quality control are provided.

Do assign data collection as a major (as opposed to a minor, subordinate, or part-time) responsibility to staff members who will be involved in the effort.

Don't assume that one group can collect data for another group to analyze. Keep the same team involved in subsequent steps.

Selecting a Project Manager

The project manager is the critical person in the data collection and analysis procedures. He or she should meet the following criteria:

- Be available to devote at least half-time to data collection and analysis over the course of the project. The project manager must have adequate time available to become deeply involved in each component of the effort.
- Understand how the criminal justice system functions.
- Possess some quantitative skills. While sophisticated mathematical experience is not required, the project manager should be comfortable with data collection and elementary statistical analysis.
- Have reasonably good writing skills.
- Possess organizational skills and experience including work planning and scheduling, directing staff, and quality-controlling the work of others.

If such an individual is not readily available for the day-to-day management of the planning and analysis effort, consider contracting with a consultant to serve as project manager and to direct the activities of in-house staff who perform the major data collection and analysis tasks. If possible, this should be a long-term contract so that the project manager's experience is retained through later phases.

Assigning Responsibility for Data Collection

Staff assigned to the task force should be available for substantial portions of their working hours. It is more effective to assign responsibility for data collection and analysis to a small number of people than for a large number of people to collect and interpret small, specific amounts of information. Having too many people involved presents many dangers, including greater difficulty in controlling the validity and accuracy of the data and the greater likelihood that their day-to-day job responsibilities will dominate, causing schedules to slip.

Depending on the magnitude of the task, an effective course of action might involve designating a half-time or full-time project manager and hiring interns or students to assist with data collection and analysis. Such an approach, which has been used successfully in a number of counties, minimizes any schedule conflicts of the county staff.

Relationship between the Project Manager and the Advisory Committee

The project manager is responsible to the advisory committee or planning team. A project schedule should be developed to provide milestones for presentation of information to the advisory committee and designate when major analysis, evaluation, and interpretation will be required of the committee. It is the project manager's responsibility to "bring the advisory committee along," educating them as the data are collected. He or she should use the committee as a forum for interpreting and evaluating the data and the alternative courses of action which the data suggest.

Cautions in Analyzing Correctional System Data

Caution

Be cautious as you interpret the data and develop projections for future facility requirements. The experience of counties across the United States has repeatedly shown that corrections tends to be a capacity-driven system—when detention beds are built, they are often immediately filled. The overcrowding they were meant to alleviate simply continues.

While not a formal criterion, judges may choose sentencing options based on their knowledge of and attitudes toward the quality and capacity of local detention facilities. If the jail is overcrowded or deteriorated, judges often use options other than the jail, such as probation or restitution. When facility problems are resolved, judicial decision-making may change in favor of the jail.

Similarly, pretrial-release decisions may reflect conditions in facilities. If they are overcrowded, officials may be inclined to grant releases. If beds are available, release decisions may become more restrictive. Police arrest decisions may follow the same pattern.

Factors outside the county's control also can have major impact. Changes in state law, for example, significantly influence facility population levels.

These factors combine to complicate your task, especially in projecting facility populations. They suggest that:

- No projection is infallible.
- Projections and facility plans need to be flexible and anticipate probable future change.
- Projections need to be periodically reviewed and revised as conditions change.
- Since the success of the planning effort depends on implementation of program and policy commitments, mechanisms must be established to make key criminal justice system officials accountable for decisions that affect jail population.

The next chapters detail the data gathering, analysis, and projection sequence.

14. Step 1: Profile the Jail Population

Why Profile the Jail Population?

Most available statistics do not tell you anything about the people who are, will be, or should be incarcerated. They will tell you, in aggregate, how many have been arrested, how many held, and perhaps what charges have been levied against them. But they will not tell you many things you need to know to answer corrections facility planning questions. For example, they will not show you how long people are held or by what means they are released—information you need in order to consider such critical issues as which detainees might be eligible for a pretrial release program or an alternative sentence. The profile will provide this kind of information.

Questions This Chapter Will Help You to Answer

Development of the jail population profile will provide information that can be used to evaluate existing pretrial and postsentence programs that affect jail population. It will help you analyze other criminal justice system processes that influence inmates' length of stay in jail, and can also be used to consider specific inmate characteristics that bear on the scope and nature of facilities that may be required. Subsequent chapters suggest a variety of analytical questions that must be answered to resolve planning issues. Results of the jail population profile provide important input to answering these questions.

A Note on Terminology

The profile of the jail population described in this chapter is intended to include inmates held at any and all of the facilities that the county may be considering for the purposes of this study. For simplicity, only the term "jail" is used.

What is a Jail Population Profile?

A jail population profile consists of information that describes the county's incarcerated population in terms of a number of personal, behavior indicator, legal status, and offense characteristics.

Major Components of a Population Profile

The major elements contained in a population profile are summarized in Table 14-1. The figure shows the kinds of data that comprise the population profile and how each type is used in the analysis. As you approach the data collection and analysis tasks, you will find that some issues apply to your county and others do not. As an aid to your analysis effort, data requirements listed in this chapter, analytical questions proposed in subsequent chapters, and data collection and analysis forms have been classified as follows:

Basic: Data that must be collected and analyses that must be conducted to satisfy essential needs assessment requirements.

Secondary: Discretionary data that would be valuable to collect or analyses that would be valuable to conduct if data are available in your county and if issues answered by the analysis are relevant to your county's situation. The amount of staff time available will also contribute to the decision about whether to conduct secondary activities.

Table 14-1. Key Characteristics of the Jail Population

Characteristic to Be Documented (Priority*)	Use in Analyzing Detention System Issues and Needs
Sentence status of jail population on an average day. (B)	Proportion of sentenced versus unsentenced should be used to: (1) analyze extent to which pretrial policies can influence facility populations and future space needs; (2) determine types of facilities needed to handle various population components—e.g., segregation of sentenced and unsentenced inmates and housing both population components consistent with applicable jail standards.
Length of stay for each unsentenced inmate. (B)	Analyze impact of current pretrial release policies and procedures on detention system population. Explore impact of court procedures on jail and other detention facility populations. Consider program and service needs of unsentenced population.
Length of stay for each sentenced inmate. (B)	Evaluate program and service needs of sentenced population. The length of stay characteristics of the population should be closely reviewed to determine the types of in-facility rehabilitative or other service programs which can be provided to sentenced inmates.
Charges levied against unsentenced inmates. (B)	Determine if there are opportunities to revise law enforcement agency arrest and booking practices to expand use of the citation release mechanism authorized under your state's penal code. Analyze results of current pretrial release policies (citation release; 10% bail; bail bond schedule and policies; release on own recognizance; supervised release) on jail population. Answer such questions as "To what extent do individuals charged with serious felony offenses make up the unsentenced jail population?" Provide input to the analysis of the security characteristics of the unsentenced/pretrial population.
Security and known behavior characteristics of sentenced and unsentenced inmates. (S)	Evaluate type of housing by security level, required to deal with both the sentenced and unsentenced population.
Criminal history of unsentenced inmates. (B)	Evaluate pretrial programs from perspective of one indicator of security risk associated with individuals held in pretrial custody.
Warrant or hold status of unsentenced inmates. (B)	Identify barriers to granting pretrial release beyond the direct control of the county. Identify proportion of the unsentenced population in county jail and detention facilities being held for other jurisdictions.
Appearance history of unsentenced inmates on previous pretrial releases. (S)	Evaluate current pretrial release programs and policies by analyzing characteristics of inmates not accorded pretrial release.
Personal characteristics of unsentenced inmates to include presence of medical problems, mental health problems, drug and/or alcohol abuse problems. (S)	Identify in-facility service needs of jail and other detention facility populations. Analyze personal characteristics of unsentenced inmates to assess relationship between those characteristics and pretrial incarceration.

*Key

B = Basic

S = Secondary

Jail Population Profile

While large, sophisticated jail systems may choose to design their own surveys, this chapter offers an approach that any county can use to construct a jail population profile.

The **snapshot profile** method describes the jail population at a specific time. It is a two-step process, the first part of which portrays key characteristics of the jail population. The second part samples releases from the jail over a representative period to provide information on average length of stay and release mechanisms.

The snapshot profile provides an opportunity to document personal and behavior characteristics of inmates based on their own responses or the direct knowledge of custodial staff (if formal classification documents are unavailable).

However, this approach requires a second data collection process to document length of stay and release performance. This means managing and coordinating two separate sets of data.

The analyst must also make assumptions about links between population characteristics (such as length of stay up to the profile date) and criminal justice system functions that affect jail population (such as court processing and time to trial). If the jail population fluctuates seasonally, especially in terms of its composition, results of the snapshot profile will be biased if an unrepresentative period is selected for the study.

Constructing a Snapshot Jail Profile

The snapshot approach includes two separate data collection and analysis exercises.

- Part 1: Develop and analyze a profile of the characteristics of the jail population at one point in time.
- Part 2: Survey and analyze jail releases over a period of time.

The sections that follow explain how to accomplish both parts.

How to Gather Information for Part 1 of the Snapshot Jail Profile: Inmate Characteristics

The Snapshot Profile Data Form in Appendix A provides a model for use in collecting jail population profile data. You may use it as is or modify it to fit your needs. Each of the data elements on the form has been annotated to indicate whether it is basic or secondary in terms of the priorities discussed earlier.

The process for collecting and recording Part 1 of the snapshot profile data involves seven main tasks.

Task 1: Develop a Profile Data Form. Familiarize yourself with how jail records are structured, maintained, and filed. Use Appendix B, "Suggested Sources for Snapshot Profile Data," as a guide in evaluating potential sources for each item on the data form and for determining where alternative sources will have to be employed. Based on the results of this review, develop a data collection form or modify the sample form shown in Appendix A.

Task 2: Select a Period to Profile the Jail. Review jail population data for the last six to twelve months. Identify days of the week when facility populations are at peak volume or low points. Pick the appropriate day(s) to construct the population profile(s).

At a minimum, construct a population profile based on midnight or late evening on Sunday—generally the period when jail populations are at their peak.

If facility populations fluctuate significantly (15 to 20 percent difference between peak and low), you should also construct a profile that reflects a low population day, usually a midweek day such as Tuesday or Wednesday. Such fluctuations occur in most counties, and a two-snapshot minimum will be advisable. Again, take the profile as of midnight or late evening when inmates are back from court and bookings have peaked.

If multiple snapshots are taken, study them in two steps:

- Analyze them separately and identify differences in population characteristics and composition.
- Then merge the two snapshots into a cumulative population and conduct the balance of the analysis based on the total profile.

Task 3: Determine Sample Size. Your next major decision is to determine whether the profile will be based on all jail inmates incarcerated at the time the profile is constructed or a sample of the larger population. General rules of thumb to employ in deciding whether or not to sample include the following:

- If the jail population is relatively limited (less than about 200), the entire population should be profiled. That is, each inmate should be included in the profile.
- Substantial samples should be taken from populations of about 200 to 500. These samples should be designed using accepted sampling techniques. Appendix C provides sampling guidelines.

Task 4: Estimate Time Requirements. Estimate the time (calendar and staff) required to develop the basic data as indicated on the Snapshot Profile Data Form. If data sources are readily available, a trained and experienced data collector can complete from five to ten forms per hour. If multiple data sources external to the jail or sheriff's department must be employed to complete data sheets, hourly productivity drops sharply. For example:

- If a supplementary inmate questionnaire is required, at least eight to twelve person days will be needed to develop the questionnaire, test it, administer it to inmates, and transfer results to tally sheets.

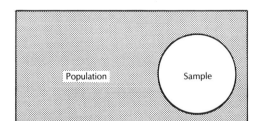

Population   Sample

• If court records must be used in order to develop data on adjudicatory status or history, pending cases, or the like, time requirements can vary substantially depending on court filing systems, document location, and accessibility. A general rule of thumb is two to four person days per hundred inmates for court file analysis.

• Warrant, criminal history, and incarceration data drawn from automated criminal justice information printouts or criminal history documents can be analyzed and transferred to tally sheets at the rate of approximately five to eight per person hour.

• Depending on how documents are organized and filed, classification, medical, or substance-abuse data can be transferred from existing documents at the rate of about ten inmate cases per hour. If these data are not available from existing documents and must be constructed through interviews with jail or medical staff, a comparable level of output can be expected.

• Data available from booking sheets can be tallied at the rate of about fifteen per hour.

• Given the above, Appendix D, "Estimated Time Requirements for Snapshot Profile," presents guidelines that can be used to estimate time requirements to tally data per hundred inmates. Note that these estimates relate to data collection only; processing and analysis will require significant additional time. Since the scope of the analysis and the time needed for manual or computer tabulation can vary so widely, it is impossible to provide valid guidelines for the later activities.

Task 5: Select and Train Data Collectors. Once data collectors are selected, you will have to train them how to complete the profile form and show them the organization and content of records they will be using. Clearly point out the location of each item in the records, review each code and its meaning, and have each collector complete at least one data form in your presence.

Especially if you use several data collectors, conduct random audits during the data collection period to ensure that procedures are uniform among the collectors and that data are being accurately transferred.

Task 6: Photocopy Booking Sheets. On the day that data are to be collected, at the selected time either photocopy all booking sheets or, if booking sheets are not used by the jail, develop a list of every inmate in the jail (name and identification number) and use this number to coordinate data on each inmate from the various information sources employed.

Task 7: Transfer Data to Profile Forms. Starting with the booking sheet copies or their equivalent, transfer data to the profile data forms. After these are entered, use other sources to complete the forms, if required in your situation.

How to Gather Information for Part 2 of the Inmate Profile: Sample of Releases

The inmate profile requires some additional data to develop information about inmates' lengths of stay. These data are developed by completing the following four tasks.

Task 1: Review Release Volumes. Review jail documents to determine the average (or typical) number of inmates released on a daily basis. Analyze several months to get a "feeling" for release volume.

Task 2: Determine Release Sample. Decide how many releases should be analyzed. Use the sampling guidelines in Appendix B to determine this number. Depending on the number required, select a period for the sample that can be expected to produce that number of releases. Be sure that special groups that may be released as a whole (such as weekenders or those sentenced to state facilities) do not create an atypical pattern. You should ensure that your sample covers at least one week.

Task 3: Develop Release Data Form. Review jail records and identify the sources that will provide the required release data. Based on your review, develop a release data form, instructions for data collectors, and a data collection schedule. Appendix E, "Inmate Release Data Form," contains a sample tally sheet for recording release data.

Task 4: Arrange to Hold and Tally Records of Releasees. Make arrangements with jail records personnel to hold custody files of inmates released each day. This is an important step. If files are stored and must subsequently be extracted from archives, the process will be much more complicated and time-consuming. To avoid hampering jail record-processing activities, tally the releases daily.

As with the first part of the profile, care should be taken that release data are tallied accurately and that the necessary releases are collected on a regular, timely basis. To ensure that the data are accurately tallied, the project manager should conduct random audits to check completed work.

Once data have been collected, the next step is to analyze results in order to identify jail program and/or facility planning issues.

Analyzing Profile Data

Even with relatively small jail population or booking samples, analyzing profile data can be a time-consuming task—more so than collecting the data. You face a choice between two methods of analysis—a manual method of analysis or the use of an existing computer data processing package. The sections that follow introduce the scope of the analysis.

An Overview of the Analysis: Two Levels

Profile analysis examines relationships among the characteristics of the jail population. These characteristics have been recorded for each inmate. However, at this point, you are not concerned about individual inmates; rather, you wish to examine aspects of the overall jail population or of specific subgroups (such as felons) to draw general conclusions about the jail as a whole.

The analysis is accomplished at two levels: preliminary and refined. The preliminary level looks at one or two characteristics (or variables) at a time. For example, the first level might begin with charges against inmates. To start, these might simply be listed as **frequencies;** that is, what percent of inmates face which charges. The preliminary level would take this one step further, developing **tables** that allow a look at two characteristics at once, such as the difference in charges between those in the jail pretrial and those who are sentenced. The refined level of analysis breaks this down further, looking at three or more variables at a time. Thus you could look at the number of male or female inmates facing various charges who were pretrial or sentenced.

The following sections elaborate upon the two levels of analysis and give examples of each.

Preliminary Analysis. The preliminary analysis portrays the population by comparing two variables at once. This requires extracting the data on these two characteristics from the total profile and displaying them in a table similar to the one shown below.

Table 14-2. Sample Table from Snapshot Profile

Inmates By Charge and Sentence Status		
Charge	Pretrial	Sentenced
Felony		
Murder		
Other Violent Anti-person		
Misdemeanor		

Refined Analysis. Subsequent analysis examines specific subcomponents of the population and thus refines existing data further. For example, you may want to explore the effect of an expansion of current pretrial release criteria on jail population levels. You would use the population profile in the manner described below to conduct this more intensive analysis.

First, select those inmate characteristics for which you want to test pretrial release decision making. For example, you might select criminal conviction history, current charge, and previous appearance history.

Second, for each inmate characteristic selected, pick those specific data elements or variables that you want to associate with the expansion of pretrial release. To illustrate, assume that you select conviction history (no more than two previous felony convictions), current charge (nonassaultive felony), and previous appearance performance (no previous failures to appear).

Third, use these criteria to identify the percentage of inmates from the population profile who would be eligible for release if these criteria were put into effect.

The purpose of the examples is to provide a sense of how the jail profile can be used as part of the needs assessment and to help you weigh the relative merits of manual versus computerized analysis. Subsequent portions of this chapter and later chapters provide more extensive examples of analytical sequences that you can use to interpret the profile data.

Choosing Between Manual and Computerized Data Analysis

There are two approaches to analyzing the profile data: manual tabulation, or computerized analysis using a commonly available set of statistical programs, such as the Statistical Package for the Social Sciences (SPSS; Nie et al.) or another statistical package. After reading the sections that follow on both approaches and assessing their implications for your situation, decide which is most appropriate for your county.

Manual Tabulation

Once data collection and tallying activities are complete, you will have a variety of data available to analyze. Even with a small sample, the many variables for each inmate make all except the simplest manual tabulation a very time-consuming exercise. Consider Table 14-3, which displays length of stay for unsentenced males according to their booking charge.

Table 14-3. Length of Stay for Unsentenced Inmates by Booking Charge

Booking Charges	Booking Day	Length of Stay Since Booking in Days											
		1	2	3	4	5	6	7	8–14	15–21	22–28	28–56	57+
Felony													
Murder													
Other Violent Anti-Person													

To construct this table manually, the following tasks must be completed.

Task 1. Data from the individual data forms are transferred to a master coding sheet as shown in the example of a master coding sheet.

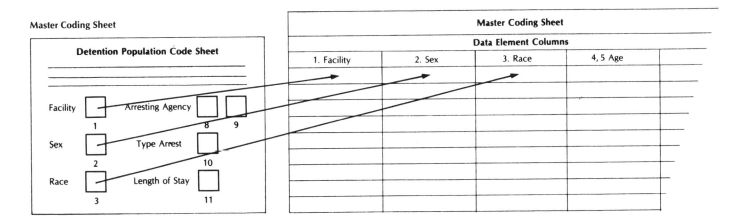

Task 2. Once data forms are all posted on the coding sheet, each line entry (one line per inmate) is analyzed, and all unsentenced male prisoners are identified.

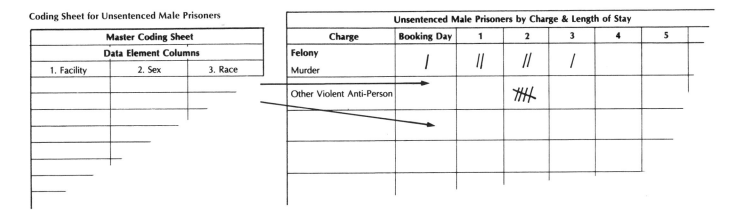

Task 3. Booking charge and length of stay data for each of the unsentenced male prisoners are transferred to a second tally sheet as shown in the example of a coding sheet for unsentenced male prisoners.

Task 4. Results are totalled in each data cell and then for each column and row, and percentages are calculated.

Manual tabulation and computation to construct a single chart like this would take **three to four hours** for a relatively small sample. Given the various ways that planners will want to consider the data, manual tabulation requires a major commitment of staff time and/or severely limits the county's ability to analyze its data. If your jail population exceeds fifty to seventy-five, you should very seriously consider computerized tabulation, which is described in the next section.

Computerized Tabulation

There are a variety of computerized statistical packages that your county can use to speed analysis of profile results and expand the planning team's capability to examine issues raised by the profile data. Standard packages like SPSS (Statistical

Package for the Social Sciences) can be employed to produce tables from data comparable to the jail profile.

These statistical packages can be used for both the **preliminary level** of portraying the entire population by two variables (such as primary booking charge versus length of stay), and for the **refined level** of portraying a specific subcomponent of the population by two variables (such as unsentenced male inmates by primary booking charge versus length of stay).

Statistical packages are available at many data processing centers and can be used by a county for a modest charge. For example, in-depth analysis of a profile sample of 500 to 1,000 inmates can be accomplished for approximately 750 to 1,500 dollars in data processing charges. You will also need some assistance in coordinating your data and writing the special instructions that SPSS (or another system) needs in order to construct the tables you will want. A programmer/analyst experienced in using the package can prepare the instructions required for in-depth analysis of profile results in forty to sixty person hours.

If county staff are not familiar with SPSS or other systems, data processing centers generally maintain lists of individuals you could contract for assistance. Most colleges and universities have SPSS and may be able to help you.

No matter which analysis technique you decide to use, once data collection activities are complete you will need to construct several tables to portray the basic characteristics of jail inmates. If more than one facility was included in the study, prepare tables both for the combined sample of inmates as a whole and separately for each facility. Once completed, the results should be reviewed with the advisory committee to provide a basic understanding of the composition of the jail population and some indication of the county's current performance in the use of pretrial release programs.

Preliminary Analysis of the Jail Population Profile

The following material outlines suggested preliminary analyses. These analyses develop information useful in examining policy concerning three critical issues:

- Sentence status of the jail population
- Length of stay for unsentenced inmates
- Proportion of inmates accorded pretrial release

For each of these issues, the table content is specified and its format illustrated. In addition, "primary analytical questions" you should ask (and answer) as you review each table are provided. Also provided are "triggers for additional analysis" that the data may suggest.

Analytical Issue 1: Sentence Status of the Jail Population

Table Content

Jail population is divided by **sentence status** (sentenced or unsentenced) and **primary charge** (felony and misdemeanor, with subcategories as listed on profile data form. Note that offense categories are listed in Appendix G by common penal code categories. Your state's categories may be different). Prepare a separate table for each county facility and for the population as a whole.

Primary Analytical Questions

What proportion of the population of each facility is comprised of unsentenced misdemeanants? What charges are levied against unsentenced misdemeanants?

If multiple facilities are operated by the county, how do the populations of these facilities compare in terms of sentence status and charge characteristics? Considering the level of charges associated with components of the population, is there a pattern of housing allocation, taking into account the security offered at each facility, sentence status, and charge characteristics of the population at each one? Are appropriate housing decisions being made?

Table 14-4. Sentence Status

Primary Charge	Facility: Main Jail					
	Sentenced		Unsentenced		Total	
	No.	% of Total Population	No.	% of Total Population	No.	% of Total Population
Felony						
Murder/related violent crime						
Other violent anti-person crime						
Sub-total Felony						
Misdemeanor						
Violent Offense—Civilian						
Violent Offense—Police Officer involved						
Burglary related						
Sub-total Misdemeanor						
Total						

Triggers for Additional Analysis

Do unsentenced misdemeanants comprise a significant proportion of the population of any facility? (More than 5 to 10 percent should raise questions about misdemeanor citation and other pretrial release practices.)

Are there substantial portions of the sentenced population who have been convicted of nonviolent felonies and/or misdemeanors housed in high-cost maximum- or medium-security facilities?

Analytical Issue 2: Length of Stay of Unsentenced Inmates

Table Content

The population analyzed in this table is limited to those who are **unsentenced.** Construct the table to divide the population by **primary charge** (felony or misdemeanor, with subcategories as listed on profile data form) and **length of stay** since booking. Prepare a separate table for each county facility and one for the population as a whole.

Table 14-5. Charge & Length of Stay for Unsentenced Inmates

Facility: Main Jail														
		Length of Stay for Unsentenced Inmates in Days												
Felony	Booking Day	1	2	3	4	5	6	7	8–14	15–28	29–56	57–84	85–112	113+
Murder/related violent crime														
Other violent anti-person crime														
Violent crime involving police officer														
Family violence														
Sub-total felonies														
Misdemeanor														
Violent offense—civilian														
Violent offense—police officer involved														
Burglary related														
Family violence														
Sub-total Misdemeanors														
Total														

Primary Analytical Questions

How many (or what proportion) of the population are unsentenced misdemeanants who have been in custody beyond the booking day?

What is the length of stay distribution of the unsentenced felony population? Are most under fifty-six days or is there a substantial portion whose length of stay exceeds sixty days? (Sixty days is used as a guideline because of the statutory limitation—in the absence of a time waiver—on taking a criminal case to trial.)

What proportion of the population in custody beyond municipal court arraignment and/or preliminary hearings are individuals charged with nonviolent felonies?

Triggers for Additional Analysis

Presence of misdemeanants with stays in excess of one day should trigger questions about misdemeanor citation and own-recognizance release practices. Why are these people in custody? Why were these people not cited rather than booked? Why have they failed to qualify for release on own recognizance if unable to post bail? What are the barriers (or characteristics) of either the inmates or existing programs that have kept these people in custody?

If a high proportion of the population is comprised of unsentenced felons whose stays exceed sixty days, this may indicate that court processing is backed up and this is influencing the jail population.

If a substantial portion of the population consists of unsentenced inmates charged with nonviolent felonies and who have been in custody beyond municipal court arraignment (generally one to three days), this may suggest that pretrial release practices ought to be further analyzed.

Analytical Issue 3: Proportion of Inmates Accorded Pretrial Release

Table Content

Means of release of pretrial inmates by **length of stay** before being released. This table presents data documented through the analysis of releases, to portray the use of various release options according to the average length of stay of inmates being released.

Table 14-6. Means of Release by Length of Stay

Means of Release Release Option	Booking Day	Length of Stay From Booking Until Release in Days														15–21	22–28	29–36	37–44	etc.	Total
		1	2	3	4	5	6	7	8	9	10	11	12	13	14						
Bail/Bail Bond	2	8	10	5	20	1	–	6	3	9	5	–	2	1	–	7	–	3	2		
10% Bail																					
OR																					
SOR																					
Misdemeanor Citation																					
Transfer to Other Agency																					
Diverted—Released																					
Trial Complete and/or Case Disposed																					
849(a)/849(b)(1)																					
849(b)(2)																					
849(b)(3)																					
Total																					

Primary Analytical Questions

What proportion of inmates is accorded pretrial release? To develop this indicator, use the totals for each pretrial release option listed in the table and compute the percent of inmates released under each option in relation to the total sample. Compute the percent of inmates who are held in custody until disposition of their cases.

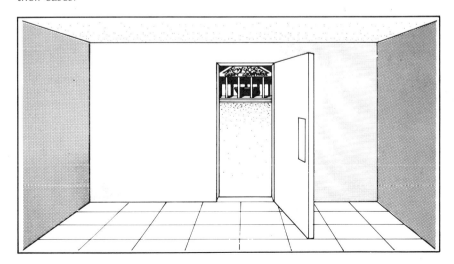

What is the average length of pretrial stay? What is the average length of stay for each release option and for those who are held in custody until court disposition? Compute average length of stay using the weighted-average technique shown below. For illustrative purposes, the bail bond option is used to show how to develop a weighted average.

Multiply the number of hours or days in custody by the number of inmates released, as recorded in the appropriate cell in your completed version of the table shown in Table 14-7. The table lists the possible days in custody in the first column. The number of inmates released on each of those days is then entered in the second column. The last column, weighted inmate days, is equal to the first column times the second column. Note that hours are coded as fractions of a day as follows:

$$\text{Less than 4 hours} = 0.2 \text{ days}$$
$$\text{4--7 hours} = 0.3 \text{ days}$$
$$\text{8--12 hours} = 0.5 \text{ days}$$
$$\text{13--23 hours} = 0.7 \text{ days}$$

Table 14-7. Inmate Days

Days from Booking to Release	×	Number of Inmates	=	Weighted Inmate Days
0.2		3		0.6
0.3		4		1.2
0.5		6		3
0.7		8		5.6
1		9		9
2		8		16
3		12		36
4		7		28
5		3		15
6		5		30
7		0		0
8		3		24
9		0		0
10		2		20
11		2		22
12		0		0
13		2		26
14		0		0
15		4		60
16		1		16
17		0		0
18		2		36
21		1		21
23		2		46
27		1		27
35		1		35
42		1		42
TOTAL:		87		519.4

Then, divide the total weighted inmate days (519.4 in the above example) by the number of inmates released this way (87 in the example) to compute the average length of stay associated with this option. In the example, the average length of stay for inmates released by bail or bail bond is 5.97 days.

Once average length of stay for each release option is calculated, combine these data to compute the average length of pretrial stay associated with each booking, given the county's existing mix of pretrial release policies and performance. Follow the procedures described above, applied to the "total" entries at the bottom of the table you have created (Table 14-7), to compute overall average length of pretrial stay.

Triggers for Additional Analysis

If the average length of stay for own-recognizance releases exceeds four or five days, it may suggest opportunities to accelerate pretrial release decision-making and reduce the jail population.

If the average length of stay of inmates held in custody until disposition exceeds twenty or thirty days, further explore in-custody average length of stay by type of charge in order to isolate average length of stay of felony defendants. If it exceeds sixty days, you may need to explore court processing activities (or delays) and their impact on jail population.

Further Analysis of Release Options

More information will be needed about release options. For example, you should analyze each **release option** by **type of charge.** This analysis will put in perspective existing pretrial release programs and strategies employed by your county.

Additional analyses of the profile data are suggested in Steps 3 and 4 of Part 3 (Chapters 16 and 17), which evaluate existing pretrial release programs, court processing performance, and the use of sentencing alternatives as they affect current and future jail population levels.

Present Results of the Preliminary Analysis to the Advisory Committee

The results of the preliminary analysis should be presented to the advisory committee. Include a selection of tables that demonstrate major findings.

- Provide a table showing the composition of the population in each facility by charge and sentence status (refer to Table 14-4).
- A second table should show the length of stay of the pretrial population by charge (refer to Table 14-5).
- Present this in conjunction with a third table showing the use of various pretrial release mechanisms for inmates facing various charges (refer to Table 14-6).

Accompany these tables with a narrative highlighting the existing use of pretrial release mechanisms and the resulting composition of the jail population.

Cautions in Analyzing Profile Data

The profile will provide extensive information on the characteristics of the jail population. However, as you construct tables from the data and analyze components of the population, you will find that some cells in the tables have only a small number of entries. Be careful not to lend too much weight or draw significant conclusions from cells with less than 10 or 12 percent of the total sample. They are subject to considerable potential error since such small numbers may not be representative of your jail's continuing population. In these instances, you will have to combine cells and draw conclusions about the population at a lower level of detail. In addition, averages for many of the kinds of data included in the profile can hide significant variations within the population. For example, an average length of stay of 6.8 days could be comprised of many people who stay about seven days or—more likely—a number of people who spend less than two days, some people who stay from two to seven days, and a small percentage who stay up to a year. Thus the distribution of results must be studied, not only the average.

Need for Supplementary Studies

It is important to realize that information from the population profile will not resolve **all** issues that you may encounter in the course of the needs assessment. When you find issues that need further clarification, your most effective course of action will be to conduct supplementary "ministudies" to develop information that will help resolve these issues. The following example illustrates the use of a supplementary study.

Example of a Supplementary Study

Your review of jail profile data indicates that felony defendants who are not released before trial have an average length of stay until sentencing of 98.7 days. This finding raises questions about the impact of court performance on jail population levels. It does not, however, provide sufficient information to support a conclusion about opportunities to improve court processing.

To resolve the issue, you would conduct a supplementary study of court operations that could consist of the following steps.

- Identify in-custody cases on one week's worth of sentencing calendars.
- Pull and analyze case files for each of those cases.
- Evaluate such performance indicators as time for continuances granted and time for psychiatric evaluations.
- Based on the supplementary study, determine if there are specific elements of court performance that could be improved that contribute to the average length of stay data identified through the profile.

Summary and Conclusion

The preceding material has described Step 1, techniques for documenting and analyzing a variety of characteristics of the sentenced and unsentenced people who pass through your jail.

Data developed from profiling provides the basis for analysis of inmate services, as well as pretrial and postsentence programs—all of which need to be evaluated before capacity projections can be made and facility needs evaluated. The next chapter discusses Step 2, an analysis of the need for inmate programs and services.

References

Lakner, Edward. 1976. **A Manual of Statistical Sampling Methods for Corrections Planners.** National Clearinghouse for Criminal Justice Planning and Architecture. Urbana, IL: University of Illinois. A valuable guide to sampling issues and methods.

Nie, Norman H., et al. 1975. **SPSS: Statistical Package for the Social Sciences.** 2d ed. New York: McGraw-Hill. This manual explains the use and capabilities of SPSS and also introduces its many available statistical techniques. SPSS has now been adapted to run on personal computers such as the IBM PC.

15. Step 2: Analyze Existing Inmate Programs

Introduction

An important aspect of corrections planning is to identify issues concerning the provision of programs and services to inmates. This analysis focuses on two areas:

- How decisions are made about housing inmates within existing facilities. Inmate classification systems are intended to fulfill these functions.
- Meeting the service needs of the incarcerated population by responding to inmate needs that arise in the jail as well as those related to the inmate's life outside (family, employment, and so forth).

Your jail may or may not now have the staff it needs to carry out proper classification or other programs, and it may lack the proper space to segregate various classifications or to offer programs that you want—or that standards require. This chapter presents a method to help you examine current programs and classification procedures and shows you how to gather information on inmate needs. This information will provide a basis for planning to improve current practices and projecting future needs. As you enter into this analysis, be sure to involve representatives of the agencies that play key roles in providing services to the jail.

Inmate Classification and Housing

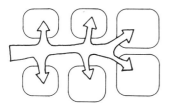

Classification is the process by which jail staff reviews various inmate characteristics and determines where in the jail inmates will be housed and which programs they should (or may) take part in. These decisions should include consideration of security requirements, service needs, and inmate and staff safety.

Procedures employed to classify inmates can have major impact on how current facilities are used and on the type of facilities and staff required to meet future needs. Therefore attention should be paid to existing classification procedures and housing decisions. Issues you need to explore are listed below; a more detailed analysis is contained in subsequent sections.

- Who has responsibility for making the classification decision?
- When is the classification decision made? Are inmates classified immediately after booking, or after spending several days in the facility?
- What criteria are employed to make the classification decision? Has a formal classification scheme been developed? If not, how are housing decisions made?
- What data sources are employed to make the classification decision?
- Are the specific service needs and problems of individual inmates incorporated into the classification decision? This would include consideration of such problems as medical needs, mental health problems, segregation, previous escape history, and behavior that poses security problems for inmates or staff.
- To what extent are medical staff and mental health staff who work with jail inmates involved in the classification decision?

Analysis of Classification Procedures

Analysis of the classification process involves examining not only how classification decisions are made but also the procedures currently used to collect information about inmates at intake and during previous stays in the facility. To document and understand the classification system in light of these issues, you need to answer the following questions:

- What information is currently collected about the inmates at intake? Are medical problems identified? What about other problems that might help in anticipating the inmate's behavior while in the facility?

- Are permanent jail files maintained for each individual who passes through the jail? If not, why not? If so, are these files available to staff during classification decision making? Do these files record experience with the inmate's problems and service needs during previous stays in the facility? Is this historical information incorporated into the classification decision?

- Are inmates kept separate from the general population prior to the classification and housing decision? Is sufficient time allowed to observe individuals in segregated circumstances to identify potential behavior problems before making the classification and housing decision?

- Is there consistency in the classification evaluation and decisions? For example, are inmates typically held in maximum security during the pretrial period, only to be sentenced to the local detention system and transferred to lower security upon sentence? If so, does this make sense or are there less costly approaches?

Developing answers to these questions will help you evaluate the effectiveness of existing classification procedures. As you evaluate those practices, ask other counties about advantages and disadvantages of the classification schemes they use. Also refer to the studies listed at the end of this chapter that synthesize a broader range of experience.

How to Evaluate the Effectiveness of Classification Procedures

It is important to develop quantitative indicators which demonstrate the effectiveness with which classification decisions are made. The jail population profile developed in Step 1 provides a data base that can be used to analyze existing classification practices. To conduct this analysis, you will need to accomplish the tasks that follow.

Task 1: Select Inmate Security Criteria. In conjunction with classification and custody staff, select criteria that could be or are employed to determine the security level in which an inmate should be housed. For example, criteria such as current violent behavior, escape risk, prison gang member, enemies in the general population, or current violent mental health problem could indicate individuals who need to be housed in a maximum security setting. By contract, inmates accused or convicted of nonviolent offenses with no behavioral problems, no escape history, and no serious mental health or medical problems could be considered for housing in less secure settings.

Task 2: Compare Current Housing Choices to Preferred Scheme. Once the criteria have been established, use them to analyze the population as it is currently housed compared to the way it would be housed using the preferred criteria. This can be accomplished through use of the analysis techniques described in Chapter 14. As noted there, you may have to develop indicators of inmate characteristics through interviews with jail personnel if a formal classification system is not in use.

The analysis involves developing a table that profiles the population in each of your county's facilities by individual inmate characteristics (especially custody problems) compared to actual housing assignment. Table 15-1 was produced using these variables.

Task 3: Interpret Results. Based on the analysis, identify the proportion of the population that appears to be inappropriately housed and determine **why** that is the case. Ask questions such as the following:

- How many people are inappropriately housed given the behavior characteristics documented in the profile?

- Why have these people been housed this way?

- To what extent does the existing facility contribute to housing problems?

- Does the existing classification system result in inappropriate housing decisions?

Table 15-1. Current Housing by Custody Problem

First Custody Problem	Current Housing Assignment					
	Admin. Seg.	General Pop.	Medical Unit	Mental Health Unit	Single Cell	Multiple Cell
Suicidal						
Violent						
Prison Gang						
Homo-sexual/ Trans-sexual						
(Etc.)						

Answers to these questions can be used two ways:

- To identify improvements that could be made in the existing classification system.
- To provide indicators of the type of housing required to deal with current and projected jail populations.

If possible, explore ways to correct this, given your current facility. Longer-range solutions are developed in later chapters.

Cautions in Interpreting Existing Classification Procedures

Caution

Consider certain limitations of the above analysis as you proceed with its interpretation and as you project facility and service needs responsive to classification issues.

If you are using existing classification documents, bear in mind that classification systems often reflect the characteristics of the available **facility** as much as characteristics of the **inmates.** Once data have been tallied and displayed, review results with custody personnel and temper interpretations based on their reactions. Determine the extent to which classification decisions would be different if the available detention space were configured to provide classification flexibility.

In addition, it is generally accepted that inmates' behavior often reflects the environment of the jail. Often, inmates who are pegged as behavior problems in an overcrowded and outdated facility would behave quite acceptably under better, less crowded, more modern, conditions—as many jails have found when they constructed and began to operate according to current standards.

Because of these factors, classification indicators recorded in the profile should be viewed as general indicators of current conditions, not as definitive indicators of how inmates can be expected to behave if positive changes are made in conditions and treatment.

Analysis of Inmate Service Needs

The planning team, the advisory committee, and policy makers should learn about the needs of the inmate population. This information is important in shaping service programs to provide rehabilitative opportunities to inmates, to minimize the problems they face while incarcerated, and to limit the potential for disruptive behavior.

Requirements for the provision of inmate programs and services need to be analyzed to meet two planning functions. First, as part of the overall correctional planning effort, it is important for the county to provide services that meet standards and are consistent with its correctional philosophy and mission statement.

To this end, inmate needs for both correctional and re-entry services should be documented and considered in the formulation of any plan.

Second, the entire range of services, from medical and mental health services to recreation or job counseling, must be considered when planning facility changes, since they require specific kinds of spaces in specific locations.

The paragraphs that follow introduce the analytical steps both to document service needs and to evaluate the scope and effectiveness of available service programs.

Inmate Needs Survey

Analysis of data contained in the jail profile (Step 1, Chapter 14) will partially satisfy the requirement to document and analyze inmate service needs. This analysis shows the proportion of inmates suffering from medical, mental health, or substance-abuse problems.

Limitations of the Step 1 Jail Profile. While the jail profile provides the information mentioned above, it does not identify other service needs. This is because most available jail records provide little information about the individual characteristics and situations of inmates. The kinds of needed information that may be lacking include:

- Educational achievement level
- Family problems
- Job skills or employment opportunities upon release
- Financial resources available after release
- Housing opportunities after release

Conducting an Inmate Needs Survey

To add to your understanding of service needs, you may wish to conduct interviews with a sample of inmates. The results can be used both to evaluate existing programs and to identify unmet program and service needs. Appendix G, "Inmate Needs Survey Form," provides a sample questionnaire that can be used to conduct inmate interviews. Feel free to adjust it to reflect the situation in your county. When conducting the survey, follow the following five guidelines.

First, if possible, conduct personal interviews with inmates. Face-to-face interviews allow clarification of questions and responses. Unless very carefully conducted, written-response questionnaires may be less reliable and more difficult to interpret.

Second, unless the jail is very small, it is unnecessary to interview the entire inmate population to develop representative findings and conclusions. A sample of 15 to 20 percent of the inmate population is usually sufficient to draw valid conclusions. Follow the sampling guidelines in Appendix C to determine the proportion of the inmate population that you should interview.

Third, to the extent possible, keep the interviewing team small—no more than three to five persons. This will provide greater consistency in recording inmate responses to questions.

Fourth, interviewing should be conducted after thoroughly documenting programs and services. A knowledge of existing programs and services will enhance interviewers' ability to interpret inmate responses. (See section below.)

List of Programs and Services

Classification	Mental Health Services
Counseling	Recreation
Drug/Alcohol Abuse Programs	Re-entry
Education	Religion
Food Service	Social Services
Legal Services	Visiting/Mail/Telephone
Library	Vocational Training
Medical Services	Work Furlough

Fifth, the interviewers should be trained, and the questionnaire should be "pretested" to ensure that it can be easily used and will produce valid responses. Pretest the questionnaire by conducting several pilot interviews with inmates to identify any problems with the wording of questions or the recording of responses.

Analyzing the Results of the Inmate Survey

If you tabulate the survey results manually, you will probably be limited to looking at the frequencies of responses to various questions together with the construction of a few tables. If you analyze the results by computer, you will have more options in developing tables to refine your interpretation. In either case, refer to the analysis section of Chapter 14 for guidance. At a minimum, you should look into the following issues.

- What are inmate prospects at release? Are existing services and correctional approaches meeting re-entry needs?
- What do inmates perceive as their major problems during incarceration? Are these problems consistent with the existing set of services?
- How do inmates view the day-to-day operations of the facility? Where do they see opportunities for improvement? While this may be surprising to some, inmates are often a valuable resource to identify opportunities for improving the efficiency and effectiveness of detention facility operations.

Evaluate Existing Inmate Programs and Services

As noted above, you need to document and understand thoroughly the programs currently provided in the jail. The "Checklist for Evaluating Inmate Programs and Services" is provided; see boxed text. Use the checklist to document how existing programs work and to identify program efficiency and effectiveness, consistency with the needs of the inmate population, and physical "fit" within the existing facility.

When reviewing the program needs and operations, be sure to involve both jail staff and representatives of service agencies who are or could be directly involved in providing jail programs. This may be done by interviewing key individuals or by including them on a special task force that would also take responsibility for implementing recommended program changes.

Checklist for Evaluating Inmate Programs and Services

This list of elements and questions about potential issues is intended to provide examples that you may apply directly or modify in evaluating inmate programs and services in your jail.

Program:
Medical Services

Analytical Element 1: Screening

Are inmates routinely screened for medical problems at or shortly after booking? If medical personnel are unavailable to conduct screening, have specific procedures been developed (and booking personnel trained in their use) to ensure that nonmedically trained personnel are sensitive to potential medical problems at booking? Are inmates required at booking to complete a medical questionnaire listing current medications and medical problems? Is this sheet routinely reviewed by medical personnel?

Potential Issues:

Are medical problems adequately screened at intake? Is the jail operation adequately structured to identify potential life-threatening situations at intake? Are there adequate qualified medical personnel available to identify quickly and deal with medical problems at intake?

Analytical Element 2: Facilities

What type of in-jail medical facilities are available to support the delivery of medical services to inmates? Are adequate facilities available to:

1. Support sick-call requirements, enabling private examination of inmates by medical personnel?
2. Provide adequate, controlled storage of medications and other required medical supplies?
3. Enable segregation of sick or disabled inmates who do not require hospitalization?
4. Provide resources for recuperative patients/inmates to minimize time spent in hospitals?

Potential Issues:

To what extent are significant numbers of injured/sick inmates housed in local hospitals for recuperative purposes? If recuperative facilities were available in the jail, what proportion of hospital costs could be eliminated?

Checklist for Evaluating Inmate Programs and Services, continued

Mental Health Services	**Analytical Element 1: Need for Services and Facilities**

What proportion of sentenced and unsentenced inmates are characterized by mental health problems? Use the jail population profile to isolate the proportion of the population with mental problems (using analytical steps outlined in Step 1, Chapter 14). Use the profile's mental health problem indicators: (1) suicidal, mental problem, violent entries in the classification field; and/or (2) problem entries in the alcohol or mental field. Employing these selection criteria, construct separate tables for sentenced and unsentenced prisoners, arraying the population according to housing in the facility and length of stay.

Once the tables are constructed, ask the following questions:

1. Are inmates with mental problems and potentially violent behavior housed differently and apart from the general population?

2. Based on profile results, how many inmates with mental health problems are there in the general facility population?

3. Are inmates with mental health problems concentrated among the sentenced or unsentenced population?

What psychiatric services are provided to inmates with mental health problems? What methods are employed to deal with inmate behavior problems? What proportion of the incarcerated population is receiving behavior-controlling medications?

Have services been established to review the unsentenced population and identify inmates with nonviolent mental health problems and to attempt to place selected inmates in mental health treatment programs as an alternative to pretrial incarceration? If not, what proportion of the population sample could be considered as service targets for such a program?

Potential Issues:

Are psychiatric services available to inmates? If not, why not?

To what extent are behavior-control drugs used to alleviate housing and service deficiencies in dealing with mental health problems?

Are adequate housing facilities available to deal with inmates with mental health problems?

Analytical Element 2: Screening

What procedures (if any) are used to screen inmates at booking to identify mental health problems? To what extent are mental health screening activities coordinated with classification and housing decisions in day-to-day operations?

Potential Issues:

Without some level of mental health screening, how are existing or potential mental health problems identified and accounted for in housing decisions?

Analytical Element 3: Housing and Security Level

Are there opportunities to deal with inmates with mental health problems in lower security settings with increased in-facility mental health services?

Potential Issues:

Would establishment of a mental health program allow transfer of selected inmates to lower/different security level facilities? Considering the impact on facility needs, would such a program be cost-effective?

Program: **Drug/Alcohol** **Abuse Services**	**Analytical Element 1: Detoxification**

Detoxification services provided to both sentenced and unsentenced inmates.

Potential Issues:

Are booking/intake procedures structured to identify real or potential detoxification problems?

Are medical and/or mental health services staffed and structured to provide detoxification services to inmates at and after booking?

Are classification procedures and housing configurations sufficient to enable medical and/or custodial personnel to deal with detoxification problems?

Analytical Element 2: Services

Drug/alcohol abuse education and training services provided in the facility(ies). Re-entry services provided to inmates with alcohol/drug abuse problems.

Potential Issues:

Are public and private agencies encouraged to come into detention facilities to conduct orientation/recruitment programs?

Is any attempt made to provide substance abuse education and treatment services to inmates?

Prior to release, are inmates with alcohol/drug abuse problems oriented to placement and treatment opportunities available in the community? Are resources made available to link inmates about to be released with available community-based services?

Checklist for Evaluating Inmate Programs and Services, continued

Program: **Basic Education/GED Training**	**Analytical Elements:** What in-facility services are provided to inmates designed to upgrade basic educational skills? Educational upgrading needs of the inmate population. Regular procedures to identify inmate educational achievement levels and needs. If programs/services are currently available in the facility, to what extent are they used by inmates: 1. Over the last six to twelve months, how have class enrollment levels compared to class capacities? 2. How do dropouts compare to total enrollment? 3. For GED classes, how many certificates have been earned as a proportion of total enrollments? 4. What grade level achievement improvements have been realized? **Potential Issues:** Are educational upgrading opportunities made available to inmates on a continuing basis? What steps have been taken to mobilize community based resources to provide in-facility educational services? Have local school districts been tapped to provide in-facility educational training? Have procedures been established to assess the educational needs of sentenced inmates?
Program: Recreational Services	**Analytical Elements:** Presence of scheduled recreation for inmates in the various types of facilities operated by the county. Includes minimum hours per week scheduled recreation for inmates. **Potential Issues:** Are recreation areas within the facilities sufficient to serve existing and future inmate population?
Program: Correctional and **Re-entry Services**	**Analytical Elements:** What programs are provided within correction and detention facilities to plan for smooth inmate re-entry to the community upon release? These can involve a wide variety of approaches and activities, including the correctional philosophy employed (with special emphasis on how sentenced inmates are dealt with while they are incarcerated), and re-entry programming designed to reintegrate inmates into the community in order to alleviate chances that repeat offenses will be committed shortly after release. **Potential Issues:** To what extent are the key actors in the criminal justice system involved in defining and monitoring the implementation of a correctional philosophy? Or are operations solely at the discretion of the sheriff? Are there procedures to identify inmates with motivation to change, and to provide privileges to inmates who participate and succeed in rehabilitative oriented programs? Are programs like work furlough used for re-entry purposes? Are inmates who meet in-facility behavior requirements (and who are serving longer sentences) assigned to work furlough in order to have access to the community to find work, job training, or educational placement opportunities upon release? What proportion of inmates have few or no financial opportunities, places to live, or employment opportunities upon release? What services and resources are available to deal with these problems? Have community resources been mobilized to the maximum extent possible to meet these needs? Have links been established with other county programs to solve re-entry problems?
Program: Use of Volunteers and **Community Resources**	**Analytical Elements:** Community service organizations that currently provide services in detention facilities. Identify service type, frequency, number and type of inmates dealt with on a weekly or monthly basis. Document steps taken by custodial staff to encourage community organizations to provide service in detention facilities. Develop an inventory of community organizations (volunteer and paid) to include service content, service capability, and interest in providing services to inmates. **Potential Issues:** Compare results of inmate needs survey with existing mix of services provided by volunteer organizations. Analyze inmate reaction to services provided. Determine whether or not custodial managers and staff are supportive of volunteer service organizations or create barriers to them. Compare services with results of inmate needs survey. Determine if there are opportunities to fill service gaps by mobilizing available community resources. Determine the extent to which custodial and rehabilitation staff have established links with community programs to ease inmate re-entry.

Your analysis of programs and services coupled with results of the inmate survey should help highlight the critical program and service issues your jail faces and establish priorities for dealing with them.

Present Results to the Advisory Committee

Once you have documented and evaluated inmate programs and reviewed the results of the inmate needs survey, present your findings to the advisory committee. Provide a briefing paper to the committee about the programs and the issues you have identified. Your paper should present the following:

- Brief narrative summaries of each of the inmate programs documented and analyzed. Summaries should include types of services delivered, when services are delivered to inmates (between booking and release), as well as staffing and program cost.
- Display of inmate responses to questionnaires. Use a blank questionnaire form to record your tabulation of the inmate responses.
- Summary of key issues and unmet needs identified in the study.

As the presentation, discussed should focus on the policy issues identified in the study. Implications for planning should be pointed out, and the committee should be encouraged—after adequate discussion—to recommend policy directions to the board of commissioners.

The next step in the process involves analyzing key components of the criminal justice system which impact jail population levels.

References

American Justice Institute with the National Council on Crime and Delinquency. 1979. **Classification Instruments for Criminal Justice Decisions.** Four volumes: Pretrial Release; Probation/Parole Supervision; Institutional Custody; Sentencing and Parole Release. Washington, DC: National Institute of Corrections.

California Board of Corrections. 1980. **Survey of Programs In California Jails.** Sacramento, CA. Contains useful descriptions of programs now operating in California jails, including samples of various forms used by them.

Hippchen, Leonard, ed. 1978. **Handbook on Correctional Classification: Programming for Treatment and Reintegration.** Rockville, MD: American Correctional Association.

National Council on Crime and Delinquency Research Center. 1979. **Improving Classification: a Guide to Evaluation.** San Francisco: NCCD Research Center.

In addition, refer to standards listed at the end of Chapter 3, most of which include specific requirements for program and service operations.

16. Step 3: Document Current Criminal Justice System Operations

Introduction

The third step in analyzing your jail's space and program needs involves studying how the county criminal justice system currently functions. County practices affecting **pretrial release, timeliness in court processing,** and **use of alternative sentencing** programs can have a major effect on jail population levels. Indeed, many counties across the United States have found that by adjusting justice system decision-making and programs, they can moderate both current and future detention facility needs.

It is important that the planning process include intensive analysis of how these and other aspects of the criminal justice system currently function. Because the county has considerable discretion for making adjustments in each of the above areas, they offer means for exerting a degree of control over who is incarcerated and for how long. Thus it becomes necessary to test the effects of varying philosophies and performance levels on jail requirements now and in future years.

The sections that follow provide a step-by-step process for documenting and evaluating existing country pretrial release programs, timeliness in court processing, and sentencing alternatives. The goals of this phase of the analysis are to make the county aware of possible programs and philosophies in these areas so it can consider their use. Later, Chapter 17 examines the impact of alternative programs.

Relationship of Pretrial Process and Programs

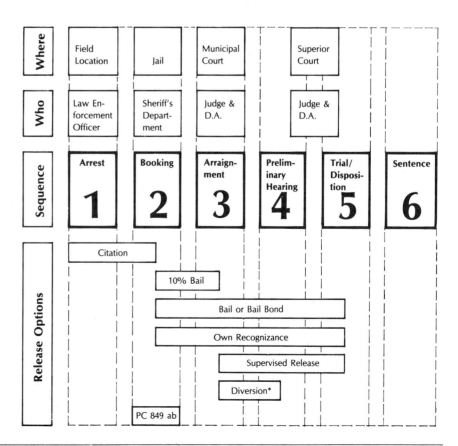

*PC 1000 Drug/Substance Abuse
PC 1000.6 Domestic Violence
PC 1001 General Diversion

An Overview of Pretrial Programs

The main purpose for incarcerating people before they have been found guilty of a crime is to assure their appearance in court. Another reason is to protect the public. In recent years, major steps have been taken across the United States to study and expand pretrial release for accused individuals. Special projects have been designed, implemented, and evaluated. Research findings repeatedly document the fact that many people can be released during the pretrial period with very little risk to public safety and little likelihood of their failure to appear in court.

The accompanying illustration shows pretrial release options open to counties. It relates each option to the flow of a defendant through the system, beginning with arrest and culminating in disposition of the case in court. As can be seen from the figure, release options tend to overlap, come into play at varying points during the pretrial process, and involve a variety of decision makers.

Discretion in Pretrial Release Programs

In recent years, legislation has been enacted in most states to provide opportunities for pretrial release of individuals who are unable to post bail. While the legal authority for these options is clearly established, their implementation leaves significant discretion to the county and to specific actors within the justice system. That discretion begins with the arresting officer, continues with the jail officer, and culminates with the judge. Pretrial programs and services that are open to counties are described below.

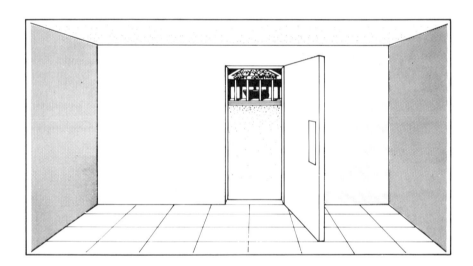

Citation Release

The decision to release a person on a citation is up to the arresting officer in the field or booking personnel at the jail. Penal code sometimes requires the arresting officer to indicate why the detainee was **not** given a citation release.

Potential Impacts of Citation Release

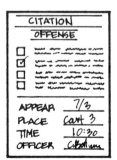

The citation release option can be one of the most effective methods of limiting jail population. If most of the people arrested for misdemeanor and minor felony offenses are cited and released in the field, relatively few low-risk offenders will occupy jail beds or consume the time of booking and intake staff. Studies have repeatedly shown that, as a general rule, persons arrested for misdemeanor offenses who have ties to the community (permanent residence, family ties, employment) are excellent risks for field citation and release.

When citation releases are used to the maximum by county law enforcement agencies, they reduce the burden on other agencies as well. They increase the available effective time of field officers who would otherwise be required to transport arrestees to jail. Citation release programs enable courts to distribute daily workload more evenly by reducing the number of individuals involved in in-custody arraignments. Finally, they reduce judges' involvement in bail adjustment and own-recognizance motions.

Steps to Enhance Citation Release Programs

Citation release activities appear to be most effective in those counties where the following conditions are fulfilled.

- With the county taking the lead, uniform citation release policies are formally adopted by all law enforcement agencies in the county.

- Given the adoption of uniform citation release policies, individual law enforcement agencies train and encourage field officers in the use of this method.

- Law enforcement agencies delegate substantial decision-making responsibility to individual officers in granting citation releases.

Citation Release Standards

Several different national organizations suggest standards for use of citation release by local agencies. The relevant standards offered by two major organizations follow.

The American Bar Association's standards for pretrial release, enunciated in 1968, suggest the following policy:

> Legislative or court rules should be adopted which enumerate the minor offenses for which citations must be issued. A police officer who has grounds to charge a person with such a listed offense should be required to issue a citation in lieu of arrest or, if an arrest has been made, to issue a citation in lieu of taking the accused to the police station or to court.

When assessing existing citation release programs, a county should consider two main issues. First, how many relatively minor misdemeanants are booked at the jail even though there is no reason to deny them field citations? Second, how many relatively minor misdemeanants are held in pretrial custody beyond the one to two hours required for booking and consideration for citation release?

The National Advisory Commission on Criminal Justice Standards and Goals set the following citation release standard in 1973:

> Every police agency should adopt policies and procedures that provide guidelines for the exercise of individual officers' discretion in the implementation of state statutes that permit issuance of citations and summonses, in lieu of physical arrest or prearraignment confinement.

Bail

Bail is an integral part of a county's pretrial release system. Formal bail is mandated by the Eighth Amendment to the United States Constitution and by most states' constitutions or by statutes that prohibit excessive bail.

Unlike other pretrial release options, bail directly relates an individual's pretrial custody status to his or her financial resources. Pretrial release can be gained only if an individual has enough money or property to post the required bail or to obtain a bail bond.

In conjunction with other pretrial release options, bail strongly affects the jail population. When relatively high bail amounts are established, jail populations increase—unless alternative pretrial release options are used for individuals who cannot meet bail.

The bail device partially shifts authority for the pretrial release decision from the criminal justice system to the private bail bondsman, allowing them to "share" that decision with the court.

In California, 10 percent bail has recently been authorized for misdemeanants. This allows an individual to post 10 percent of the bail established for the offense in lieu of posting the full amount or making arrangements with a bail bondsman. A relatively new enactment, little data is available on the impact of the procedure on counties. Principal questions include the extent to which the 10 percent bail option acts as a substitute for other pretrial release options; the extent to which counties have increased misdemeanor bail schedules to counteract the impact of 10 percent bail; and its impact on failure-to-appear rates.

Release on Own Recognizance and Supervised Release

Since the mid-1960s, release on own recognizance (OR) has been formally established in many jurisdictions across the United States. In the intervening years, considerable research has been conducted to determine the impact of OR programs on jail population levels, failure-to-appear rates, and public safety.

The authority for own recognizance release is often found in the state's penal code. A variety of own recognizance is "supervised own recognizance release."

Discretion over Release Criteria

Implementation of an own recognizance or supervised release program is entirely at the discretion of the local courts. The types of offenses considered as well as the required characteristics of candidates vary substantially from county to county. In some areas of the country OR release is limited to relatively minor misdemeanants. In that situation it acts primarily as a replacement for misdemeanor citation releases. In other areas a wide variety of defendants is considered, including individuals accused of various felonies. Similarly, the organization of the pretrial release program and the timing of the release decision vary substantially across the state.

Where jail booking volume is insufficient to justify a full-time pretrial release officer, jail booking personnel screen pretrial release candidates. In counties with somewhat greater booking volumes, individuals with specific responsibility for pretrial release screening come to the jail in the early morning and in the evening to interview individuals booked during the intervening periods.

In counties with a high volume of bookings, separately staffed pretrial release programs may be available to provide in-jail interviews and screening, deliver formal recommendations to the bench for pretrial release consideration, and provide supervision for defendants released on conditional or supervised own recognizance.

Four Models for Pretrial Release Programs

Just as there are different ways to staff and deliver pretrial release services, there are four organizational models for assigning responsibility for their operation.

The **first model** assigns responsibility for day-to-day interviewing and screening to an existing criminal justice agency such as the district attorney, the probation department, sheriff's staff, public defender's office, or marshal's office. A number of the release programs currently operating follow this model. Its advantage is that day-to-day delivery of services can easily be integrated into the overall functioning of the justice system. Especially in those areas where work volume is low, responsibilities can be assigned on a part-time basis to available staff. A disadvantage of this model is the danger that pretrial release services and recommendations will be unduly influenced by the philosophical orientation of the agency that is responsible for its operation.

The **second model** gives responsibility to an existing county agency, but requires a policy board of county criminal justice agency heads, police chiefs, bar association members, judges, and interested community members to provide direction to the program. The role of the policy committee is to establish criteria and to offset the potential philosophical influence of the agency responsible for day-to-day operations. The extent to which this balancing occurs depends, of course, on the composition of the board.

The **third model** involves the delivery of pretrial release services by associations or community groups interested in the criminal justice system. In San Mateo

County, California, one of the older contracted programs is operated by the County Bar Association. Similarly, in Alameda County, California, OR release services have been provided under contract with a private community-based agency.

In the **fourth model,** the court directly controls the day-to-day operations of the release program. Some state penal codes allow courts to employ an investigative staff for the purpose of recommending whether or not defendants should be released on own recognizance. This method minimizes potential conflicts since the court directly sets policy and makes release decisions.

Whichever organizational model is instituted in a county, the ultimate responsibility for both pretrial release policy and decision making lies with the courts. Through these decisions, judges directly control the population level of unsentenced detainees. Their flexibility in defining pretrial release criteria has major impact on a county's immediate and long-range detention system needs.

Impact of Release Criteria on Bed Space Needs

Pretrial release criteria substantially influence bed space needed in the jail. Thus there are several issues counties should consider when deciding what type of release on own recognizance and supervised release programs to implement.

One factor is the types of offenses that will be considered for pretrial release. Are pretrial release programs to be limited to relatively minor misdemeanants, or will they be expanded to consider individuals accused of felony offenses?

A second consideration is how information is gathered and provided to the bench to support pretrial release decisions. Research indicates that when judges have more and better information about release candidates, they tend to make much more use of this option.

A third issue is **when** the release decision is made. If interviewing staff and a duty judge are available, pretrial release decisions for many defendants can be made immediately or shortly after booking. Otherwise the decision is delayed until formal arraignment in court. The timing of the decision, because of its impact on length of stay, significantly influences the size of the pretrial population detained in the jail.

The final factor is how recommendations for pretrial release are formulated and presented to the court. Some programs rely on subjective interviews and informal submission of information for consideration of pretrial release. In other jurisdictions, the pretrial release recommendation is based on a point score that has been validated by monitoring the results of its weightings over a period of time. The latter arrangement is preferred since it can be better controlled.

In each of the above issues, the county has wide latitude in formulating and implementing its own policy and programs. The programs can have major impact on jail population and as a result affect long-term facility needs. The hypothetical example that follows is intended to demonstrate this impact.

A Comparative Example of the Use of Pretrial Programs

Consider two counties with identical booking volumes involving similar types of offenses. County A is prepared to implement a relatively expansive release on own recognizance and supervised release policy that includes consideration of felony defendants. County B has decided to pursue a far more restrictive policy that limits consideration for pretrial release to misdemeanants.

As a result of the more expansive policy, County A will be able to release approximately thirty felony defendants per month, while County B will hold comparable individuals in pretrial custody until disposition. The average length of stay in pretrial custody in County B is sixty days until disposition. Therefore County B will be required to dedicate sixty beds to hold individuals comparable to those who will be released by County A.

Both County A and County B face jail overcrowding problems and need to increase capacity. While arrest and booking volumes are identical in both counties, because of County A's more generous pretrial release policies it needs to build 60 fewer pretrial beds than does County B. To County A, this represents a savings of approximately $3 million in construction and perhaps $400,000 to $500,000 per year in operating costs.

While it is important to recognize that a county pretrial release program needs to reflect the circumstances, goals, and philosophy of that county, it is equally important to understand the financial ramifications of varying levels of pretrial release. The illustration above vividly points to the financial impact of different approaches.

Pretrial Release Programs Work

Jurisdictions across the United States have up to twenty years' experience in conducting pretrial release programs. Research on the performance of these programs has produced a number of findings about the risk factors associated with varying levels of pretrial release. The greatest concerns apparently are whether released individuals will appear in court and whether they will commit further crimes while waiting for trial.

Most research suggests that appearance rates for individuals released on their own recognizance and individuals who have posted bail are similar. Many studies show that appearance rates for individuals released on OR are actually better than for those who post bail.

Higher proportions of release on own recognizance and supervised release are generally found in those jurisdictions where effective, formalized pretrial release recommendation procedures have been developed and are provided to judges for decision making.

Some failures to appear by those accorded OR release have shown to be neither willful nor flights to avoid prosecution. Instead, they often involve simple forgetfulness. Many jurisdictions have found that court appearance notification programs have significantly reduced failure to appear rates.

Research involving felony defendants afforded pretrial release indicates that there is little relationship between the seriousness of the original charge and the likelihood that an individual will fail to appear or will commit an additional offense during the pretrial release period (Pryor and Allen 1980).

The financial impact of pretrial release programs suggests that most counties need to take a close look at existing and potential approaches to pretrial release. You should review the research and evaluate both existing programs and the population held in pretrial custody as outlined in a later section of this chapter. The references at the end of the chapter list some recent relevant research on pretrial release.

Diversion Programs

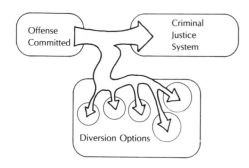

Some states' penal codes provide authority to "divert" certain types of alleged offenders without formal processing through the criminal justice system. Substance abuse and domestic violence cases, for example, may normally be diverted to community-based treatment programs.

One representative state law provides the authority to divert selected individuals who are charged with narcotics and substance-abuse offenses. Under its provisions, the district attorney has the option of referring cases that meet certain criteria. These criteria limit diversion candidates to individuals who have no previous convictions for narcotics or controlled-substance offenses; who are not charged with an offense involving violence; who have not had parole or probation revoked; and whose criminal history does not include diversion or a felony conviction within the last five years.

The potential impact of drug diversion on the jail population depends both on the type of pretrial release program operated by the county and on the number of potential candidates in the jail. In counties where pretrial release programs are rather expansive, most diversion candidates are released from pretrial custody before diversion is formally considered.

Another representative law authorizes diversion of selected domestic violence cases under comparable conditions to those outlined for drug diversion. Again, diversion recommendations are made by the district attorney and generally involve individuals with limited previous offense histories.

Yet another representative diversion law expands potential diversion to include **any** defendant. This legislation provides counties the opportunity to experiment with broad-based diversion programs. The district attorney is not required to make the diversion referral. Instead, judges may make diversion referrals, which the district attorney may support or oppose. Although such diversions are dependent on the criteria established by the local bench, the potential impact on the jail's unsentenced population can be significant.

Arrest and Charging Practices

Arrest and charging practices can also have a major impact on the jail population. One factor is the extent to which law enforcement agencies arrest and book individuals on whom formal charges are not filed. This can involve instances in which officers make an arrest and book an individual into custody, but the law enforcement agency opts not to file a case with the district attorney for review and possible prosecution. Inmates in this category can be held for a specified time period, often forty-eight hours, before release. Because people released in this manner have been held in custody, jail space is occupied by individuals on whom formal complaints will not be filed (and who therefore should not be in jail).

Apart from law enforcement agencies, the district attorney may opt not to file a formal complaint against an individual who has been arrested and held in pretrial custody. Some jurisdictions have experimented with stationing deputy district attorneys at the jail booking area to review arrests immediately at booking, thus attempting to control the amount of jail space and court time occupied by individuals who will ultimately be released.

The level of charges filed can also increase the jail population. In some jurisdictions, prosecutors choose to invoke the highest possible charge because they anticipate that plea bargaining will ultimately reduce it. In fact, there is often a substantial deterioration in charges from arrest and arraignment to ultimate disposition. When "high charging" occurs, jail population increases, since the existence of relatively serious charges may make it impossible for a person to be considered for pretrial release under reasonable bail or OR options.

Nonprosecution Alternative to Arrest

Often law enforcement officers must arrest and book an individual because of the absence of any alternatives for dealing with the immediate situation. To handle these problems, some jurisdictions have experimented with a variety of programs, such as neighborhood mediation for resolving family or neighborhood disputes and domestic violence counseling. Programs like these also may reduce jail populations.

The material presented in the preceding paragraphs indicates that counties have a wide degree of discretion in dealing with the pretrial period. Philosophy and policies regarding pretrial treatment will have major impact on a county's current and projected jail population. For this reason, closely analyze the entire pretrial area as part of the planning process. The following sections provide guidelines for conducting this evaluation.

Evaluating Pretrial Release Practices

Evaluation of pretrial release programs and practices should focus on quantifying existing activities and identifying opportunities to adjust and expand operations. The accompanying boxed text outlines approaches you may employ to evaluate existing or potential pretrial release programs in your county. The evaluation methods presented therein have the following features.

• Performance indicators have been established for each pretrial release option, quantifying the impact of existing operations.

• Rather extensive information is required to develop the performance indicators and to answer questions about existing program effectiveness. Sources are suggested for required information.

• Evaluative questions are presented for each pretrial release option. By following the sequential analysis given in the boxed text, you will develop a comprehensive portrait of both the scope of existing pretrial release programs and their implications for facility requirements.

• Like the questions presented in Step 1, suggested analyses have been classified as basic or secondary to assist you in establishing priorities for your analysis.

Each option should be quantified in terms of the proportion of the total population involved in the program, the proportion that fails to qualify for existing pretrial programs, the length of time required to make pretrial release decisions, and the length of time spent in custody for individuals who failed to qualify for pretrial release.

Through use of the jail profile data developed in Step 1 (Chapter 14), it is possible to analyze the implications of shifting pretrial qualification criteria on population levels and, ultimately, facility requirements. As explained in more detail in Chapter 17, these data can then be employed to project the impact on jail populations.

The evaluation of pretrial release options is the first step in analyzing the impact of the criminal justice system on jail operations and requirements. The next section analyzes the court system and its effect on the jail.

Method for Assessing Pretrial Release Programs

The following figure provides sample performance indicators for assessing pretrial release programs and mechanisms. The priority of each indicator is classified either as "basic" (B) or "secondary" (S), indicating its relative importance in the analysis. For each performance indicator, the type of information needed and its source are indicated. Finally, evaluative questions which may be raised are suggested for consideration.

Program: Citation Release

Performance Indicator:

Percent of misdemeanor arrests cited and released by each law enforcement agency in the county. (B)

Information Needed (Source):

Misdemeanor arrests by offense group for the last 12 months or the most recent calendar year reported for each law enforcement agency in the county.

Misdemeanor citations by offense group for the past 12 months or the most recent calendar year. (Source: Agency responsible for collecting and analyzing criminal statistics. Also, request each law enforcement agency to supply the data.)

Evaluative Questions:

To what extent do misdemeanor citations as a percent of arrests vary among law enforcement agencies? Are some agencies making only limited use of this release device?

Have all law enforcement agencies established formal policies regarding use of misdemeanor citations? Are these policies uniform?

Performance Indicator:

Percent of misdemeanor bookings cited and released by jail personnel, broken down by arresting agency. (B)

Information Needed (Source):

Misdemeanor bookings for last 12 months. (Source: Jail booking records.)

Percent of misdemeanor bookings cited and released by jail personnel. (Source: Inmate Profile.)

Average length of stay of individuals cited and released. (Source: Inmate Profile.)

Evaluative Questions:

If a substantial portion of misdemeanor bookings are cited and released by jail personnel, why were these people not cited and released in the field by law enforcement officers?

Could law enforcement agency policies/procedures be improved? Would a uniform countywide policy improve individual law enforcement agency performance?

Performance Indicator:

Percent of in-custody population that meets citation release criteria and average length of stay associated with that population. (S)

Information Needed (Source):

Establish selection criteria for potential misdemeanor citation candidates and produce table from profile data showing selected population by offense class and length of stay. Suggested selection criteria: misdemeanor charge; on-view arrest; no warrants or holds; unsentenced; no custody problems involving suicidal or violent behavior, or mental problems; no escape history; local residence; no drug/alcohol/medical problems; no previous failures to appear (FTA). (Source: Inmate Profile.)

Evaluative Questions:

Are there people in custody who could be cited and released? Why have they not been released?

If police misdemeanor citations expanded, what could be the impact on jail population and average length of stay of unsentenced population?

Method for Assessing Pretrial Release Programs, continued.

If eligible candidates in the jail population were cited and released, what could be the impact on average length of stay for the unsentenced population? What impact on unsentenced population levels?

Program: **Bail Bond**	**Performance Indicators:** Proportion of bookings who make bail; proportion of bookings who post 100% bail; existence of formal, court approved bail schedule available to jail booking personnel. (B) **Information Needed** (Source): Copy of current bail schedule and copies of bail schedules collected from other counties. (Source: Jail personnel/court administrative personnel. Also, contact other counties, same size and larger; collect their bail schedules.) **Evaluative Questions:** Compare bail established for various county offenses. Determine if high or low compared to other counties. Would judges consider modification of bail schedule? What basic reasons underlie current bail levels established in the existing bail schedule? Are these reasons sound?
	Performance Indicator: Description of county actions taken to implement a reduced-percentage bail program, if available in your state. (B) **Information Needed** (Source): By offense class, compute proportion of bookings released on bail/bail bond and reduced bail. Determine average length of stay associated with each release option. (Source: Booking/release data from release analysis or longitudinal profile.) **Evaluative Questions:** How do misdemeanor bail schedules compare before and after implementation of the reduced-percentage bail schedule. To what extent were bail schedules increased to offset impact of reduced-bail program? Why?
Program: **Release without Complaint**	**Performance Indicators:** Extent to which jail space is occupied by people who have been arrested but will not have a complaint filed against them and will subsequently be released. Proportion of arrests/bookings resulting in releases, broken down by arresting agency. Average length of stay. (B) **Information Needed** (Source): By offense class and arresting agency, compute proportion of bookings resulting in releases without complaint filings. Estimate number of jail beds occupied by inmates who are subsequently released. Calculate as follows: (1) use proportion of releases computed above; (2) multiply total annual bookings by that percentage; (3) multiply the results by the average length of stay associated with these releases; (4) divide the product of (3) by 365 to estimate the average jail beds occupied by individuals who will be released without complaint filings. (Source: Release analysis.) Collect data on statewide and other comparable county release rates for felony offenses. (Source: Your state's criminal statistics agency.) **Evaluative Questions:** Do some law enforcement agencies have a higher proportion of releases than others? What arrest types are predominantly associated with these releases? Do the arrest types (by offense class) indicate anything about law enforcement agency arrest practices? For example, are public inebriation arrests associated with a high release rate? If so, is the jail serving as housing for detoxification? If public inebriates were dealt with in alternative fashion, what would be the impact on jail population? In addition, for arrests involving violent offenses, is the action of the arresting officer a major contributor to the release? Are some law enforcement agencies more likely to be involved than others? For felony offenses, how does your county compare to other comparable counties and statewide averages in regard to released-without-complaint rates?
Program: **Own Recognizance Release (OR)**	**Performance Indicators:** Percent of individuals booked who are granted an OR release. Display and analyze by offense class. (B) Percent of individuals booked who are interviewed and considered for an OR release. Display and analyze by offense class. (S) Percent of individuals interviewed who are granted an OR release. Display and analyze by offense class. (S)

Method for Assessing Pretrial Release Programs, continued.

Average length of in-custody stay for individuals who are granted OR releases. (B)

Percent of OR releases who have failed to appear (FTA rate). (S)

Information Needed (Source):

For sample period (past three to six months), review jail records and document number of bookings, OR interviews, and OR releases—by arresting charge. (Source: Release analysis; jail/interview program record.)

Evaluative Questions:

What types of offenders are granted OR interviews and releases? Is OR limited to misdemeanants or does it include felons?

Are all people who are booked subsequently interviewed and considered for OR? If not, why (by specific group)?

Information Needed (Source):

Develop narrative description of how the county's existing OR program operates. Include the following: (1) who is responsible for interviewing; (2) if a separate program/staff from jail booking personnel, staffing and cost of the OR program; (3) around-the-clock assignments/staffing to conduct interviews; (4)specific OR policies formulated by judges in the county; (5) specific criteria employed to determine whether or not an individual qualifies for an OR release; (6) timing and schedule for when OR decisions are made—key questions include types of inmates who will be considered for OR release at booking and those who are held until arraignment before consideration for OR release; (7) how responsibility for OR decision is exercised (to include decision making flexibility delegated by judges to jail level interview staff). (Source: Meet with OR personnel; interview staff and review records. Interview judges.)

Evaluative Questions:

How long after booking are OR decisions made? Are substantial portions of releases granted directly after booking or do most arrestees have to wait until arraignment (or after) for the OR decision? Have jail-level OR personnel been delegated release-decision-making authority for certain types of defendants by judges (e.g., misdemeanants and selected types of felons)? During nonbusiness hours, is a "duty" judge available to review release recommendations by pretrial release/jail staff for those defendants who cannot be released without the approval of a judge?

Information Needed (Source):

Observe interviewing activities at jail during peak periods; estimate elapsed time between booking, interview, and release during these periods. Assess staffing and "backup" adequacy. (Source: Meet with OR personnel; interview staff and review records. Interview judges.)

Evaluative Questions:

Does periodic overcrowding occur because staff are unavailable to interview and process OR releases in a timely fashion?

Information Needed (Source):

Contact other counties and find out how they provide OR services. Document: (1) type of offenders considered for OR release; (2) specific criteria employed to determine if arrestees qualify; (3) how/when OR decisions are made to include any delegation of decision making authority by judges to jail staff; and (4) quantitative performance indicators to include: % of bookings interviewed for OR release; % of those interviewed who are released; % of those booked who are given OR releases. Collect comparative release data where possible, differentiating between felons and misdemeanants. Also, collect FTA data. (Source: Contact with other counties. Also, release analysis.)

Evaluative Questions:

Are quantitative (e.g., a point score) criteria used to assess whether or not an individual qualifies for pretrial release? If not, why not? What criteria are employed? Are they overly subjective?

Information Needed (Source):

Based on above research, explore impact of adjustments in existing OR programs on current and future detention population levels. Using jail profile information as a base, construct tables (as explained in Step 1, Chapter 14) to construct tables with selection criteria based on adjusted pretrial release parameters. In structuring tables, portray the selected population by charge versus length of stay. Repeat the analysis several times, employing alternative criteria for selection portion of the incarcerated population which might qualify if released under adjusted pretrial release policies and approaches. (Sources: Inmate Profile; release criteria documented through contact with other county pretrial release programs.)

Method for Assessing Pretrial Release Programs, continued.

Evaluative Questions:

Are there opportunities to accelerate the pretrial release decision making process by delegating release decisions now made at arraignment to jail interview staff for decision shortly after booking? Would establishment of quantitative release criteria accelerate decision making? To what extent would accelerated decision making reduce average length of stay of pretrial prisoners? What impact would reduction in length of stay have on existing jail population?

When alternative pretrial release criteria are applied, what is the impact on pretrial/unsentenced population incarcerated in local detention facilities?

Given the experience of other counties that use these criteria, what FTA rates can be expected if these criteria are employed? How do these compare with current FTA rates in the county?

Program:
Supervised Release

Performance Indicator:

Proportion of bookings provided supervised release. (B)

Information Needed (Source):

Statistics maintained at the jail and by the agency responsible for operation of the supervised release program. Data needed include (by offense): bookings, referrals for supervised release considered/evaluation, and grants of pretrial releases. (Source: Pretrial release program records; jail records.)

Performance Indicator:

Proportion of unsentenced inmates considered/referred for supervised release who are granted pretrial release. (S)

Information Needed (Source):

Contact other counties to document how they provide supervised release, pretrial release. Collect the following information: (1) how the supervised release program is organized and staffed; (2) scope and intensity of supervision services; (3) types of pretrial defendants dealt with on the program; (4) criteria employed to qualify defendants for supervised release; (5) procedures used to evaluate defendants for supervised release; and (6) types of defendants placed on supervised release. (Source: Contacts and interviews with other counties.)

Evaluative Questions:

If the county has a supervised release program, are there opportunities to accelerate decision making and reduce time in custody for those individuals who receive pretrial release? What impact would reduction in length of stay have on overall unsentenced population levels in county detention facilities?

Performance Indicator:

Average length of stay in custody for individuals who are granted supervised release. (S)

Information Needed (Source):

Review jail population profile data and analyze characteristics of the in-custody population. Compare to the types of inmates dealt with by supervised release programs in other counties— structure criteria and table formats that isolate potential release population components by charge and length of stay. (Source: Release analysis.)

Evaluative Questions:

If the county does not have a supervised release program, what impact would establishment of one have on the unsentenced population levels in county detention facilities considering proportion of population impacted? Would a supervised release program significantly increase pretrial releases and reduce length of stays associated with unsentenced inmates? Or would supervised release simply "replace" OR and have little incremental impact on the pretrial release rate?)

Program:
Charge Progression and
Charging Practices

Performance Indicator:

Extent to which "fall-out" occurs when initial arrest and booking charges are compared to disposition charges. (B)

Information Needed (Source):

Review proportional progression of charges from arrest to disposition; note "fall out" in terms of charge reduction, dismissals, etc. Compare performance in your county with other counties and statewide averages.

(Sources: Available local and state criminal statistics; special study as required.)

Evaluative Questions:

Do "fall out" rates in your county exceed statewide averages/other comparable counties? Does this suggest overcharging at arrest and/or initial arraignment? To what extent does this affect qualification for OR release or lesser bail? Could DA charging practices and case decision making be accelerated?

Assessing Adjudication Processes

Impact of Court Processing Time on the Jail Population

Court processing affects inmates' lengths of stay and therefore the jail population. Courts exert influence at every step in the adjudication process—from initial arraignment through trial and disposition. Principal areas where courts can influence jail populations include the following:

The elapsed time from booking to ultimate disposition for in-custody individuals is largely a function of **court scheduling** and the **availability of judicial, prosecution, and defense** resources. When courts are unable to handle criminal trials on a timely basis and when prosecutors and public defenders must continue cases because of excessive workloads, the stay of in-custody inmates is lengthened. As average lengths of stay are extended, jail populations rise.

The **scheduling of arraignments** for in-custody inmates can have significant impact on the length of stay for both misdemeanants and felons. Since many criminal cases are disposed of at arraignment, scheduling of the arraignment calendar determines the elapsed time to disposition and affects the granting of pretrial releases.

When courts are lenient in **granting continuances,** trial times are often extended. Extended trial time for in-custody individuals expands the jail population.

If **presentence investigations** are not conducted promptly, the adjudication process is lengthened. The availability of probation officers to conduct presentence investigations, as well as clerical staffing and paper flow, influence the time it takes to complete a presentence investigation. As this process is extended, convicted but unsentenced individuals are required to stay in local custody longer, contributing to an expansion of the jail population.

These factors clearly indicate that the analysis of jail population issues requires a close look at court processes.

Questions Raised by Extended Lengths of Stay

The boxed text illustrating the method for assessing court processing provides a series of evaluative questions that can help you determine the extent to which court processing affects the jail population. Again, the jail profile serves as the basis for the analysis.

The first step is to review the lengths of stay of unsentenced inmates. If a substantial portion of that population stays in excess of sixty days, court processing problems may be contributing to length of stay, although this conclusion cannot be drawn for certain at this point. The lengths of stay may reflect features of the adjudication system over which little control can be exercised, such as the complexity of serious criminal cases.

Method for Assessing Court Processing

The following figure presents a guide to the kinds of questions to ask—and the data needed to answer the questions—in evaluating court processing and its impact on the jail population. The relative importance of each question is indicated by their priority: "basic" (B) or "secondary" (S).

Evaluative Question:

What proportion of in-custody, unsentenced inmates have lengths of stay in excess of 60 days? (B)

Data Needed:

Profile unsentenced population by charge and length of stay (see Step 1, Chapter 1), noting proportion of unsentenced population with lengths of stay in excess of 60 days. Use these data to assess whether or not court processes are having an impact on detention population or overcrowding problems.

Evaluative Question:

Do extended periods of pretrial custody result from trial backlogs in county courts? (B)

Data Needed:

Document current court system performance in terms of elapsed time between readiness dates and commencement of trial for criminal cases which are held in-custody. Collect required data by following these steps:

Meet with judges having criminal case responsibility. Document current calendaring practices and case backlog problems. Determine if criminal case backlog problems exist and are related to court availability. Through discussions with judicial personnel, estimate court expansion (courtrooms, judges, support personnel) necessary to reduce criminal case trial backlog problems.

Analyze existing calendaring and case scheduling documents available within the county court system(s). Then:

1. Compute elapsed time between date cases ready for trial and trial date set.

2. Estimate trial frequency for felony cases as a percent of felony arrests by reviewing available criminal statistics.

3. Multiply result times felony bookings last 12 months.

4. Multiply that result times the average elapsed readiness to trial setting computed above.

5. Divide the result by 365 to develop an estimate of the number of unsentenced inmates, given existing practices, who are awaiting trial. Use these data to estimate the impact of reducing court backlog on detention facility unsentenced populations.

Evaluative Question:

Are prosecution and/or defense practices and operations contributing to extended adjudication processing? (B)

Data Needed:

Review length of stay data analyzed above. If data suggest a high proportion of long-stay, unsentenced inmates, this may indicate extended trial and disposition times resulting from workload problems and staffing shortages in the district attorney's and/or public defender's office(s). Case overload for trial attorneys can result in extension of trial disposition time for in-custody, unsentenced individuals. Analyze and identify the problem as follows:

Review length of stay data related to the in-custody population developed above.

Interview the public defender, district attorney, and judges and document their perspectives on whether or not caseloads contribute to extension of disposition times for unsentenced, in-custody defendants.

If staffing is considered to be a problem, attempt to quantify the impact in terms of continuances and related trial time or disposition time extension. Conduct the following analysis:

1. Pick several trial attorneys in both the public defender's and district attorney's offices who handle trials at the superior court level.

2. Review their current case load and identify in-custody cases that have been delayed because of lack of readiness. Review continuances noted in case files and estimate number of days case disposition extended because of workload problem.

3. In conjunction with public defender and/or district attorney, reach consensus about attorney staffing adjustments and their impact on the acceleration of disposition/trial.

4. Employing the number of days reduction in the trial and/or disposition time of in-custody defendants, convert to estimated impact on jail population as follows. Employing jail profile and arrest and booking data, document proportion of total felony arrests held in-custody until disposition. Review statistical data to approximate what proportion of those adult felony arrests are ultimately disposed of at the superior court level. Multiply the result by the estimated reduction in trial time which could be achieved with staffing adjustments to quantify the estimated impact on jail population. Divide the result by 365 to approximate reduction in average daily jail population that could be achieved.

Evaluative Question:

Are backlogs in the preparation of presentence investigation (PSI) reports extending lengths of stay for unsentenced prisoners and increasing overcrowding? (S)

Data Needed:

Review length of stay data from the jail profile compared to the sentence/adjudication status of inmates. Document proportion of in-custody inmates who are convicted and awaiting sentencing. If the data indicate lengths of stay that exceed 14 days postconviction and presentence, this may suggest that lengths of stay are extended as courts await completion of presentencing reports. Conduct the following steps to determine if this is an issue which impacts the jail population:

1. Sample probation department files to document turnaround time for presentence investigation reports; select a two- to four-week period to record date the referral is received from court; date officer completes investigation and report writing; and date report(s) are completed by clerical production units and forwarded to the court.

2. Compute average elapsed time for the sequences noted above.

3. Determine which of the sequences contributes to extension of the process.

4. Meet with probation managers and reach agreement on adjustments (staffing, procedural adjustments, etc.) required to reduce PSI turnaround time.

5. Set estimated target in number of days turnaround time would be reduced if adjustments were made.

6. Convert these estimated reductions into impact on jail population. Follow the procedures noted above to quantify impact on jail population.

However, extended lengths of stay may suggest that not enough courtrooms or judges are available, prosecutors and public defenders are overloaded, or court administrative practices lengthen trial and disposition time.

To resolve how much these problems are increasing demand for jail beds, follow the analysis sequence outlined in Method of Assessing Court Processing. In addition:

- **Develop** a thorough understanding of how the criminal courts currently function in terms of the various elements specified in the chart.

- **Interview** prosecutors, public defenders, and judges about what they consider to be problems in the court system.

- **Document** current performance of the court system in terms of elapsed times, calendaring and scheduling processes, caseload assignments for both prosecution and defense attorneys, in-court tactics of prosecutors and public defenders, and the functioning of various support agencies that are critical to efficient and effective court operations.

Collecting the data and answering the questions will help you identify whether or not problems exist in your local court system. Once issues are pinpointed, you can quantify their impact on jail population levels. Subsequent chapters will explain how you can develop solutions to these issues and resolve jail space needs or overcrowding problems.

Sentencing Alternatives

Somewhat less direct control can be exercised by the county over sentenced population levels, since the sentencing decision is at the discretion of the court. However, facility needs can be affected—and costs moderated—by how the sentenced population is dealt with. For example, if additional sentenced beds are needed, a less costly work furlough facility might be constructed in lieu of more costly higher security facilities. Further, participation in such programs can be more productive for some offenders than simply spending time in jail. To make this type of decision, sentencing options need to be considered.

Because of the authority of the courts over the use of most of these programs, it is essential that judges be involved in consideration of sentencing options. Major sentencing options include those that are largely under the control of corrections as well as those that are within the purview of the courts or other justice agencies. These two are discussed separately below.

Sentencing Options: Judicial and Justice System Programs

Community Service Programs. These allow individuals to provide a service of value to the community in lieu of a fine, probation, or incarceration. Many counties have developed and implemented such programs. While they vary substantially in size, organization, and funding, most have the common thread of serving as clearinghouses for individuals to find community service opportunities. It is important to consider which inmates would qualify for community service programs: more serious offenders, or only those who would otherwise receive modest sentences such as fines or probation.

If there are individuals currently serving sentenced time because they are unable to pay fines, a sentencing alternatives program may be appropriate and useful for a component of the sentenced population. Judicial use of alternatives such as **restitution programs** in lieu of incarceration can prove a more positive option for many convicted offenders while costing the county much less to operate.

Probation Services. These can include both presentence investigations and supervision services. In evaluating probation services, examine whether probation officers consider sentencing alternatives when developing presentence reports. Have guidelines been developed to establish consistency in sentencing recommendations?

What are probation officer's supervision caseloads? Do high caseload levels influence judges in favor of incarceration over probation? Are intensive supervision services an option for individuals who might otherwise be incarcerated?

Diversion of Substance Abusers. Frequently jails house offenders with severe alcohol or drug-abuse problems. As a result it is important to be aware of and to use the resources available to deal with such offenders. The size and scope of programs available through both institutional and community resources, criteria for admission, costs of operation, and awareness by judges of their availability all affect how much they are used in lieu of jail.

Job Programs. Job training, education, and placement programs can also affect sentenced population levels. Frequently judges will consider participation in such programs as alternatives to serving time. It is important to document resources that are available as well as their costs and performance levels. Then you can assess whether judges are aware of and use them, and whether additional programs might be needed.

Sentencing Options: Corrections Programs

The second set of sentencing programs is more directly under the control of local corrections. These programs include work furlough, county parole, and weekend jail.

Work Furlough. This option involves daily release from the jail to work in the community while spending all other time at the jail. When analyzing work furlough, consider whether or not the work furlough program is maximized as an alternative to traditional incarceration. In addition, quantify the proportion of available beds that are or would be occupied by individuals in a work furlough program. If a substantial number of these beds are located in secure facilities, look for another less expensive setting to house work furlough inmates and relieve pressure on the more costly secure facilities.

County Parole. County parole is a program through which the county can have direct impact on facility population levels. Analysis should focus on how the parole program is currently administered, the proportion of inmates who are granted county parole, assessment of the adequacy of supervision for parolees after release, and judicial attitudes toward county parole practices. To the extent county parole can be expanded without compromising judicial sentencing, jail population pressures can be relieved.

Weekend Jail. Weekend jail is a device that enables individuals to continue employment and maintain family responsibilities while suffering some level of incarceration. Identify whether weekend sentencing practices contribute to jail overcrowding, jail staffing, or management problems; whether other sentencing alternatives such as community service could substitute for weekend jail; whether "weekenders" could be required to report to the jail during daylight hours but sleep at home to eliminate overcrowding problems; and how weekenders spend their time while incarcerated.

In recent years some counties have experimented with variations on the weekender theme. These include, as mentioned above, requiring individuals with weekend sentences to report to jail facilities for work during the day and to return home during weekend evenings. This converts a weekend incarceration program into a weekend work program. Participants can accomplish tasks that reduce county operating costs in such areas as part or road maintenance, trash collection, or weed clearing.

Another "crisis"-oriented mechanism for temporarily reducing jail overcrowding when the jail count exceeds its capacity is accelerated release. The sheriff can request permission from the court to release a limited number of inmates before their sentences would otherwise end. Obviously this is not a program that should be built into a county's long-term planning.

Analysis of Sentencing Options

Determine the proportion of the current jail population that could be considered for alternative sentence programs. The Method for Assessing Postsentence Programs in the accompanying boxed text provides a procedure for analyzing your county's performance in using sentencing options. As in previous examples, suggested performance indicators are provided; information required to evaluate both existing and potential programs is outlined in some detail; data sources are identified; and a series of evaluative questions are presented. By going through the steps, you can identify the factors affecting facility and program needs of the sentenced population in your county.

Method for Assessing Postsentence Programs.

This figure presents a framework for evaluating the use of postsentence options. For each potential program, performance indicators are listed, with their relative priority: "basic" (B) or "secondary" (S). For each performance indicator, the type of information needed (and its source) is listed and evaluative questions are suggested.

Program:
Rapid Transfer to State

Performance Indicator:

Proportion of the jail population that has been sentenced and is awaiting transfer to the state penal system. (B)

Information Needed (Source):

Using jail profile data as the base, segregate that component of the population that has been sentenced to a state correctional facility and is awaiting transfer. For the group in question, document average elapsed time between sentencing and transfer. (Source: Jail profile.)

Evaluative Questions:

Are more than one or two beds occupied by people who are awaiting transfer to state prison? How long have they spent between sentence and current date/actual transfer? Why?

Information Needed (Source):

Document current procedures and decision time frames to process state prison transfers. Identify barriers. (Source: Interview custodial personnel.)

Evaluative Questions:

To what extent could transfer be accelerated? If transfer were accelerated, what impact on jail population levels could be expected?

Program:
Community Service
(for counties with these programs)

Performance Indicators:

Proportion of convicted felons and misdemeanants who are referred to sentencing alternative/community service programs, probation, restitution, etc. (B)

Proportion of current sentenced population that could be dealt with in alternative programs involving community service if such programs were available. (B)

Information Needed (Source):

If county has sentencing alternative/community service programs, collect data to indicate the extent to which these programs are used and whether or not there are opportunities to expand usage and affect the sentenced jail population. To conduct this evaluation, collect the following information:

1. Document type of current program operated to include cost to the county, type of inmate accepted in terms of charge (by offense class), referral source, and available criminal history and demographic data;

Method for Assessing Postsentence Programs, continued.

2. Collect information describing total felony and misdemeanor convictions in the county for the most recent calendar year;

3. By meeting with judges, document criteria they employ to refer or sentence people to alternative programs.

(Sources: Interviews with operators of current community service programs. Annual report of your state's judicial council providing conviction data for courts. Also, your state's criminal statistics agency.)

Evaluative Questions:

To what extent are available sentencing alternative and community service programs employed to deal with sentenced offenders?

Through analysis of program content and participant characteristics, determine the extent to which the program operates as an alternative to a fine rather than to incarceration. Base your conclusions on the results of interviews with judges and analysis of program participant characteristics.

Information Needed (Source):

Develop a profile of the sentenced incarcerated population. Use selection criteria to identify people who could qualify for alternative sentencing. Criteria could include: no previous felony convictions, no behavior problems such as violent or suicidal behavior, no serious mental problems, no current drug or major alcohol problems, fewer than three previous misdemeanor convictions, and other selection criteria determined appropriate for your county given judicial sentencing philosophy. Structure a table arraying the selected population by convicted charge versus length of sentence. Review results and discussions with judges and program personnel. Isolate population components that could qualify for an alternative sentence and compute as percent of jail population when profile was taken. (Source: Jail profile.)

Evaluative Questions:

Are there components of the existing sentenced population that could be considered candidates for a community service program as an alternative to sentenced incarceration? Why are they incarcerated? Are there opportunities to increase use of alternatives by familiarizing judges with program content and capabilities? To what extent could sentencing alternative options be expanded?

What impact would expansion have on jail and detention facility populations? Which facilities would be affected? What steps need to be taken to increase judicial use of available sentencing alternative resources?

Program:
Community Service
(for counties without these programs)

Performance Indicator:

Proportion of existing sentenced populations that could be considered candidates for alternative programs if resources were available. (B)

Information Needed (Source):

If the county does not have sentencing alternatives or community srvice programs, contact counties that do operate such programs and document program services and characteristics in terms of the elements noted above. (Source: Contacts with other counties.)

Meet with superior and municipal court judges. Discuss their potential use of an alternative program if one were available. Review results of contacts with other counties and develop tentative criteria they would employ to sentence convicted defendants to such a program. Based on these criteria, determine if the program would reduce sentenced jail population. (Source: Interview judges.)

Develop several profiles of the sentenced population using selection criteria noted above with the following modifications: vary criteria related to previous conviction history to select population components and construct tables based on no previous felony or misdemeanor convictions; no previous felony convictions and only one previous misdemeanor conviction; no previous felony convictions and two previous misdemeanor convictions. Analyze population components selected according to the recommended criteria by convicted charge versus sentence length. Identify what proportion of sentenced population could be considered as candidates for such a program and estimate bed space impact. (Source: Jail profile.)

Evaluative Questions:

If a sentencing alternative were available, how many of the inmates who are currently incarcerated would be sentenced to such a program, considering experience of other counties and attitudes of the local judiciary?

Would a sentencing alternative serve as an alternative to probation or fine or would it impact incarceration rates?

What would such a program cost to establish?

To what extent would it alleviate bed space requirements for sentenced people?

What type of detention facilities would be affected?

Method for Assessing Postsentence Programs, continued

Program: **Drug/Alcohol Treatment**	**Performance Indicator:** The proportion of the sentenced population has documented drug and/or alcohol abuse problems and could be considered candidates for participation in alternative treatment programs. (B)

Program:
Drug/Alcohol Treatment

Performance Indicator:

The proportion of the sentenced population has documented drug and/or alcohol abuse problems and could be considered candidates for participation in alternative treatment programs. (B)

Information Needed (Source):

Document resources available to judges and probation officers as sentencing alternatives for individuals with drug and/or alcohol problems. Document criteria employed by judges for sentencing (condition of sentence) to these programs. Determine adequacy/availability of placements. Document costs of maintaining sentenced individuals in alternative residential or outpatient treatment settings. (Sources: Interview judges and representatives of the probation department. Contact operators of programs currently used as referral sources.)

Employing the jail profile data as a basis, identify population components that could be considered as candidates for participation in alcohol or drug treatment programs as an alternative to incarceration. Develop selection criteria such as the following: no behavior problems, nonviolent, no mental problems (violent), no current or documented alcohol and/or drug problem(s), criminal history limited to no previous felony convictions. Then establish and test the effects of more relaxed criteria related to criminal history, including no or one previous felony conviction(s) and relevant misdemeanor conviction history. Once selection criteria are identified, conduct the following analysis:

Alcohol Program Suitability Analysis:

Current charge versus previous conviction history (by type of conviction). Focus on identifying population components with current and previous convictions involving alcohol related offenses. If this population reflects a relatively significant number (more than five to ten), isolate by length of stay.

Drug Program Suitability Analysis:

Current charge versus previous conviction history (by type of conviction). Focus on identifying population components with current and previous conviction histories involving drug related offenses. As above, if this population subcomponent reflects a relatively significant number (more than five to ten), isolate this population subcomponent by length of sentence.

Evaluative Questions:

Are there significant proportions of the sentenced, in-custody population that appear to be primarily alcohol or substance abuse related offenders? Is the detention system being used as a "warehouse" for alcohol offenders? Why? Are other housing and treatment resources available? If so, could they be used for people being dealt with in county detention facilities? Would it be more cost-effective to deal with these people in an alternative setting? If available, would judges use a sentencing alternative? Considering population component size and length of sentence, what impact would alternative programs have on existing facility populations?

Program: County Parole

Performance Indicators:

Number of county paroles granted over the last 12 months. (B)
County parolees as a percentage of sentenced prisoners released from jail and detention facilities over the last 12 months. (B)

Information Needed (Source):

Rules, administrative procedures, and current operating practices related to conduct of the county parole program. At a minimum, collect the following information: (1) criteria employed to qualify inmates for county parole; (2) application, review and approval procedures; approaches employed to monitor parolee performance once release granted; including responsibility assignments, supervision practices, and parolee reporting requirements. (Source: Interview appropriate members of the sheriff's department and other members of the county parole board.)

Performance Indicator:

Reduction in average daily population resulting from paroles granted (number of paroles times average reduction in sentenced time actually served divided by 365). (S)

Information Needed (Source):

Review recent county paroles. Analyze the following characteristics of the parolee population: (1) types of convicted offenses paroled; (2) personal characteristics of parolees to include community ties, marital status, family ties, previous conviction history, and behavior characteristics. (Source: Interview appropriate members of the sheriff's department and other members of the county parole board.)

Performance Indicator:

Over the last two years, proportion of county paroles granted where parolee failed and was returned to incarceration. (S)

Method for Assessing Postsentence Programs, continued.

Information Needed (Source):

Apply current (and/or relaxed) parole qualifications criteria to the jail population profile and determine what proportion of the sentenced population could be expected to qualify for parole. Estimate impact on current facility population levels. (Source: Jail profile.)

Evaluative Questions:

Is use of the existing parole program being maximized? What steps could be taken to expand parole? Are the current criteria employed to review and act on parole application overly restrictive? What are the barriers to expanding the current parole program (parole board philosophy, lack of resources available to supervise parolees once released, other)? If these barriers were overcome, how could the parole program be expanded and what impact might expansion have on facility population levels?

Program:
Work Furlough

Performance Indicators:

Proportion of total sentenced population involved in work furlough. (B)

Proportion of Type II and Type III beds occupied by individuals involved in the work furlough program. (S)

Information Needed (Source):

Rules, administrative procedures, and current operating practices related to conduct of the work furlough program. At a minimum, collect the following information:

1. Criteria employed to screen and qualify inmates for work furlough (e.g., pre-employment required? specific conviction types prohibited? work furlough available to those who are job seeking? work furlough used to provide "re-entry" opportunities for longer-stay, sentenced inmates?).

2. Where work furlough participants are currently housed and average daily number of beds generally occupied by work furlough participants.

3. For the last three to six months, number of work furlough applications made, number approved, average daily work furlough population, and number of work furlough failures/withdrawals.

4. Fees charged to work furlough participants.

5. Direct program costs.

Profile the current work furlough population (convicted offense, employment status at time of application, conviction history, current employment status, school enrollment, enrollment in job training program, length of sentence).

Contact other counties and document their approach to work furlough, to include:

1. Convicted offenses, if any, prohibited from work furlough participation.

2. Use of work furlough for re-entry purposes.

3. Provision of job finding services to help people qualify for work furlough.

4. Allowing people on work furlough who are enrolled in school or in job training programs.

5. Where/in what security level facilities work furlough people are housed.

Based on findings noted above, review contents of existing work furlough program compared to other counties. Determine if there is potential to adjust existing work furlough program to expand participation or increase the rehabilitation orientation of program. If so, apply relevant selection criteria to sentenced component of the detention profile and identify scope of existing nonwork furlough sentenced population which could be considered for participation.

(Sources: Jail records/custody files; work furlough case files; work furlough policies and procedures.)

Evaluative Questions:

Where are work furlough inmates housed? Are they integrated with the rest of the sentenced population? What custodial problems does integration pose?

Are work furlough inmates occupying beds that presentenced and sentenced inmates could occupy? How many? Would it be more cost-effective to house work furlough inmates in a residential facility separated from secure detention facilities? How many beds would be needed? What impact would provision of these beds have on existing secure facility utilization patterns and current/future overcrowding problems?

Is work furlough being used as a component of overall correctional facility rehabilitative activities, or solely as a device to enable selected unsentenced inmates who had jobs at time of sentencing to maintain employment during their sentence? Potential uses that could be considered include:

1. Using work furlough as a re-entry device for longer term sentenced inmates—this could involve employing work furlough for last 30 to 60 days of longer-term sentences by allowing inmates work furlough privileges to find employment/job training upon release.

2. Allowing qualified inmates access to work furlough to enable them to participate in job training or educational programs outside facilities during the period of their sentence.

Method for Assessing Postsentence Programs, continued.

Program: Weekend Jail

Performance Indicators:

Percent of average weekend jail population comprised of people serving weekend sentences. (B)

Percent of weekend days jail population exceeds rated housing capacity. (S)

Information Needed (Source):

For last six to twelve months, develop Saturday night population figures for each detention facility operated by the county.

For a comparable period, document proportion of the Saturday night population comprised of weekenders. Document specific housing practices related to weekenders to include specific facilities to which they are assigned and the type of beds occupied.

Determine rated capacity for each county operated facility. (Your state may provide this.)

(Source: Jail records. If unavailable from normal data sources, take a Saturday night "snapshot" documenting: (1) number of "weekenders" housed; (2) by facility and security type, where weekenders are housed.)

Evaluative Questions:

Do current practices include housing people overnight in detention facilities as they serve weekend sentences?

What potential exists to operate a weekender program under which people report to facilities during days for work assignments but sleep at home? If this approach were implemented, what impact would it have on weekend population levels and related overcrowding problems.

Present Findings to the Advisory Committee

The analysis of criminal justice programs conducted in this step should be presented to the advisory committee so that the members can understand the use and performance of existing programs as well as the kinds of programs that are possible.

When documenting results for the advisory committee, prepare brief profiles for each of the aspects of the criminal justice system. Structure these profiles to provide a brief narrative description of the program area and include the following:

- A listing of existing policies covering the type of inmates involved in the program
- When the decision is made to use the program
- A quantitative description of program performance
- A summary description of the planning issues you have identified

On completion of Step 3, you will have developed a picture of the major criminal justice program issues that have direct and measurable impact on jail population levels and facility requirements. The results of Step 3 will be used in Step 4 to evaluate the impact of program adjustments on facility needs.

References

American Bar Association Section of Criminal Justice. 1974. **Comparative Analysis of Standards and Goals of the National Advisory Commission on Criminal Justice Standards and Goals with Standards for Criminal Justice of the American Bar Association.** Washington, DC: American Bar Association.

Board of Directors, National Association of Pre-Trial Services Agencies. 1978. **Release: Performance Standards and Goals for Pre-Trial Release and Diversion.** Washington, DC: National Association of Pre-Trial Services Agencies.

Galvin, John. 1977. **Instead of Jail: Pre- and Post-Trial Alternatives to Jail Incarceration.** Washington, DC: Pre-Trial Services Resource Center.

Goldkamp, John. 1979. **Two Classes of Accused: A Study of Bail and Detention in American Justice.** Cambridge, MA: Ballinger.

Kirby, Michael. 1977. **"Findings 1," Recent Research Findings in Pre-Trial Release.** Washington, DC: Pre-Trial Services Resource Center.

Miller, Herbert, William McDonald, Joseph Romero, and Henry Roseman. 1975. **Second Year Report on the Evaluation of the Conditional Release Program.** Washington, DC: Institute of Criminal Law and Procedure of Georgetown University Law Center.

Pryor, Donald, and D. Allen Henry. 1980. "Pre-Trial Practices: A Preliminary Look at the Data." **Pre-Trial Issues.**

Roth, Jeffrey and Paul Wice. 1978. **Pre-Trial Release and Misconduct in the District of Columbia.** Washington, DC: Institute for Law and Social Research.

Silver, Nathan, Martin Sorin, and Mary Toborg. 1979. "The Outcomes of Pre-Trial Release: Preliminary Findings of the Phase II National Evaluation." **Pre-Trial Services Annual Journal,** Vol. II.

Thomas, Wayne. 1976. **Bail Reform in America.** Berkeley: University of California Press.

Venezia, Peter. 1973. **Pre-Trial Release with Supportive Services for "High Risk" Defendants: The Three Year Evaluation of the Polk County (Iowa) Department of Court Services County Corrections Project.** Davis, CA: National Council on Crime and Delinquency.

17. Step 4: Evaluate Alternative Programs

Introduction

Thus far, Part 3 has attempted to provide a step-by-step process for collecting and interpreting data. The first three steps of the data-gathering process involved documenting major characteristics of jail populations and programs as well as criminal justice system operations. In Step 4, you will draw on the results of each of these analyses to identify and evaluate actions that could be taken to moderate detention facility population levels (and therefore future construction and operating costs).

From this point forward, it will not be possible to illustrate and evaluate all the potential alternatives that you may consider in your county. Because of that, this chapter provides a **framework** rather than a specific methodology for evaluating the data that you have collected and for considering the impact of alternative programs on future capacity needs and operations. Illustrative examples are presented to provide the framework for establishing hypotheses, for testing the impact of these hypotheses on the existing system, and for assessing their cost-effectiveness.

Three major analytical issues are explored. These involve changes in pretrial release programs, court processing improvements, and the expanded use of sentencing options. Before embarking on the analysis, the next sections introduce a range of alternative programs that may provide a potential for reducing jail space needs.

Examples of Alternative Programs

The list given here presents some of the steps taken in one or more of seven counties across the United States that have participated in projects designed to reduce jail overcrowding. (Based upon a telephone survey conducted by Fred Campbell.)

Pretrial Improvement Projects

Selected projects undertaken to expand (or accelerate decision making for) pretrial release programs include:

- Expanding release on own recognizance to include low-risk felonies.
- Liberalizing bail schedules.
- Eliminating cumulative bail on multiple charges.
- Expediting decisions on whether to press charges (including accelerating both law enforcement agency preparation and case forwarding, as well as the district attorney's charging decision).
- Accelerating arraignment on weekends and/or evenings.
- Providing duty judges at booking facilities on weekends and during evenings to facilitate pretrial release decision making.
- Expanding use of citation release by establishing uniform policies among all law enforcement agencies in the county.
- Revising intake procedures to include review of all bookings for possibility of own recognizance release.
- Establishing around-the-clock central intake and pretrial release services at booking facilities.
- Notifying OR releasees of court appearance dates shortly before the required appearance to reduce failures to appear due to forgetfulness.
- Eliminating public inebriation arrests.

- Broadening the use of diversion.
- Installing a supervised own recognizance release program.
- Treating most mental cases outside of the jail setting.
- Releasing individuals arrested for driving under the influence to a responsible party within four hours or less.
- Establishing a broad-based advisory committee to oversee pretrial release decisions and policies.
- Assigning deputy district attorneys to the jail to review charges at intake to expedite release decisions, on persons arrested without having complaints filed against them.

Programs to Expedite Court Processing

Changes in court practices, procedures, or staffing that might be considered include these possibilities:

- Provide superior court arraignment immediately after preliminary hearings in municipal court.
- Shorten the time required to develop and provide presentence investigation reports (improve procedures or add staff).
- Adopt and enforce limitations on continuances granted in criminal cases.
- Establish and maintain an accelerated trial calendar for in-custody defendants.

Sentencing Alternatives

Programs that offer options other than straight jail time for sentenced offenders include these possibilities:

- Expand the use of county parole for sentenced inmates.
- Use more intensive probation supervision for individuals as an alternative to jail time or to expanded county parole. Expand probation officer staffing and assign special supervision caseloads.
- Expand the use of restitution and/or community service.
- Expand the use of weekend work projects and work furlough for sentenced individuals.
- Expand alcohol and drug programs available to individuals now sentenced to jail.
- Expand the capacity of local alcohol rehabilitation centers and shift individuals convicted of alcohol-related offenses to treatment centers rather than detention facilities.

By permission of Tom K. Ryan and Field Enterprises, Inc.

Upgrading Jail Operations

Changes that could be considered for implementation within the jail include the following:

- Provide special training for jail-classification staff to ensure that inmates are classified and housed in a way consistent with realistic security requirements.
- Transfer all individuals sentenced to state prison to state authorities within forty-eight hours of sentencing.

All changes listed above present a partial menu of steps that could be taken either in lieu of expanding detention facilities or in order to moderate future expansion requirements. When proceeding with Step 4, develop and test the potential of some or all of these programs in your county.

Analysis of Alternative Programs: The Basic Approach

The same basic approach applies to the analysis of each potential project or operating adjustment, no matter which phase it affects. The accompanying illustration, Analyzing the Impact of Program and Processing Adjustments, provides an overview of the sequence used to evaluate alternative programs. The sequence includes six tasks.

Analyzing the Impact of Program and Processing Adjustments

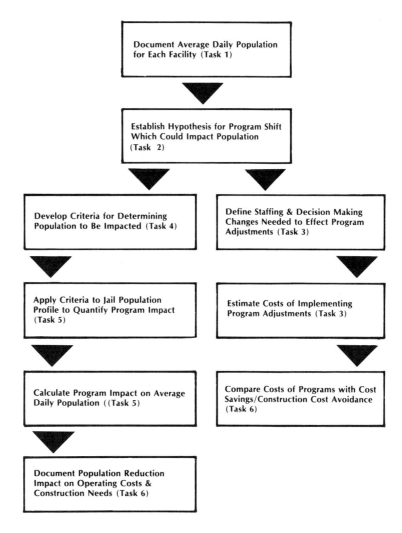

Task 1: Gather Base Data

The first task is to establish a base on which to calculate the impact of processing adjustments. For this purpose, **average daily population** (ADP) for each detention facility is used. To establish ADP, review detention facility records and compute average daily population for each facility for the most recent twelve-month period available. To the extent possible, document the following:

- Average daily population by facility and systemwide.
- The proportion of average daily population in terms of unsentenced and sentenced inmates in each facility.
- In multiuser facilities, specific identification of male, female, and juvenile inmates.

Once average daily population is documented, it is possible to assess the impact of alternative programs on reducing that population.

Task 2: Establish Hypotheses to Test

The next task is to establish a set of potential program changes, each of which might reduce jail population. Drawing on the results of your analysis of the criminal justice system (accomplished in Step 3, Chapter 16), identify specific processing or program adjustments that you think could have an impact on the jail population. Each of these program adjustments represents an hypothesis to test in terms of cost-effectiveness.

Once a set of hypotheses is developed, Tasks 3 and 4 should be completed for each one to determine its cost-effectiveness.

Task 3: Document Program Changes and Costs Required to Implement Each Hypothesis

Document the specific changes and costs required to implement the program or processing adjustment that you are testing. Implementation costs that need to be estimated include staffing costs, operating expenses, facility costs, and the like.

Task 4: Establish Criteria for Assessing Population Impact

Similarly, you need to develop specific criteria for determining which inmates would be affected if this program or processing adjustment were made. For example, if your hypothesis is the expansion of pretrial release activities, you need to specify the particular inmate characteristics which would qualify them for the expanded release program.

Task 5: Apply Criteria to Population Profile

Apply these criteria to the jail population profile developed in Step 1 (Chapter 14). Using the techniques in Step 1, isolate that portion of the existing jail population that fits the criteria. To quantify the number of inmates who could be involved in this alternative program, compare this population component to the total population at the time the jail profile was taken. Multiply the resulting percentage times the average daily population to yield the impact of the program if it were implemented today.

Task 6: Compare Costs and Benefits of Program Implementation

The final step in the analysis is the comparison of the cost of program implementation (to include both quantifiable and subjective costs) with its attendant cost savings or cost avoidance. ("Subjective" costs involve factors such as community acceptance or resistance.) Start by carefully estimating the cost of implementing the program. Be conservative when estimating existing staff's ability to absorb more workload.

In the estimation of cost reduction or avoidance, consider the impact on bed space requirements in light of the county's likely need for additional beds in the future. If the county faces capital construction for detention facilities, each bed reduced will save the cost of building that bed in the future. This impact can be quantified as follows:

- Estimate the cost of replacing that detention facility bed (see Chapter 26 for current estimated costs of constructing jail facilities).
- If you are comparing cost avoidance with the cost of implementing a program on an annual operating basis, compare the annual costs of program operation with the annual cost of jail beds saved. This can be done by dividing the construction cost of those beds by their useful life. The three examples in the boxed text given later in this chapter show procedures for amortizing jail bed costs.
- If the county needs to borrow money to build additional beds, evaluate the finance charges that will be incurred. Estimate their costs on an annual basis and include those in the comparison.

Impact on Operating Costs. You will also need to calculate what effect reduced bed space or non-construction of facilities will have on lowering facility operating costs or avoiding future increases in them. A common error is to treat the cost of each bed as if it were simply an equal part of the total cost—for instance, dividing the annual operating budget by the average daily population and assigning the resulting value as the unit cost associated with each bed.

Such an approach fails to recognize that facility operating costs are not necessarily responsive to small fluctuations in the population. If one bed is removed or one less inmate housed, total operating costs are not likely to be changed at all. The bulk of facility operating costs involve custody staff; and that is influenced significantly only by large shifts in inmate population.

The impact on operating costs is more accurately estimated by per-inmate support costs and the population reduction thresholds at which staff might be saved. First calculate the actual or estimated cost of supporting each prisoner in the jail for each day. These costs involve food, medical service, laundry, and the like. They generally run from three to six dollars per day in California facilities (1980 dollars). Then estimate the scope of population reduction necessary to eliminate one post in the detention facility. (Refer to the discussion of staffing estimates in Chapter 31.) Remember that it takes approximately five to six employees to staff one fixed post on a 24-hours-per-day, seven-day-per-week basis. Use this level of population reduction to estimate the impact of a reduction in bed space requirements on operating costs.

Compare Costs/Benefits. When you have completed each of these tasks, you can compare program implementation costs and savings in detention bed construction and operations, including subjective factors. In some instances you will find that program implementation costs will exceed savings. However, the program may have subjective benefits in terms of more timely adjudication or potential rehabilitative impact on inmates.

Conversely, a potential program adjustment may be very effective in avoiding measurable costs, while running counter to prevailing community philosophy. These factors need to be balanced in evaluating each program alternative.

Policy Review

These, then, are the analytical steps you need to follow to calculate and evaluate each potential program's cost implications. Once developed, these potential adjustments should be reviewed in detail by the advisory committee and policy makers to determine which are appropriate for implementation in your county. (See the final section of this chapter for suggestions on this presentation.)

In examining the impact of alternative programs, it is important to remember that **each individual can be released only once.** That is, someone who is released under a 10 percent bail program would not be affected by a new own recognizance program. Thus if you are considering more than one program, be careful not to "double count" people who might be eligible under both programs.

The sections that follow present examples of the application of the analytical steps to program alternatives related to pretrial release, court processing, and sentencing options. Each example includes two components: use of jail profile data to assess impact on capacity requirements, and an evaluation of the cost impacts of the changes. You need to understand that in both instances, these analyses have been designed to illustrate the techniques and not to suggest the actual issues that must be analyzed in your county.

How to Use Snapshot Profile Data to Evaluate Pretrial Release Options

The analysis that follows shows how to use data from the snapshot profile to evaluate a change in pretrial release policy. The tables referred to here have the same format as those constructed in Step 1 (Chapter 14), though in each case they require focusing on separate segments of the population. The analytical questions are also different.

Analytical Issue 1: Changes in Pretrial Release Programs

The following example of the analysis of the impact of pretrial release programs demonstrates how to assess the cost and impact of policy and program changes in pretrial services. The example features a county with an overcrowded jail and a pretrial release program limited to misdemeanants. The example evaluates an expansion of own recognizance release to include felony defendants, which entails rethinking release policies and criteria. The purpose of the analysis is to identify how many inmates might be affected by the revised criteria.

Example of the Analysis of the Impact of Pretrial Release Programs

Task 1. Establish a Hypothesis	Expansion of pretrial release opportunities to selected felony defendants would substantially reduce in-custody unsentenced populations in county detention facilities.
Task 2. Define Changes Required to Implement the Program Adjustment	**Required Change:** Development of criteria for own-recognizance (OR) release. What criteria would be employed to qualify selected felony defendants for OR release? **Implementation Process:** Review results of visits/contacts with other counties having OR programs that release felony defendants. Identify specific selection and qualification criteria that could be employed (e.g., type of offense, residence requirements, previous conviction history, etc.). **Required Change:** What expansion in OR interviewing at booking would accompany program adjustments? What would be the impact on booking or interview staff workload? Would additional staff be required? How many? What would expansion cost? **Implementation Process:** Analyze booking data for the last six to twelve months. Document daily felony booking volumes. Identify peak, average, and low volume periods by day of the week. Review jail records. Identify distribution of bookings by time of day. Estimate time required to conduct interviews and verify information related to considering felony defendants for OR. Multiply time requirements per booking by number of felony bookings to estimate staff time commitments required to support program expansion. Review current staff workload and determine if additional staff would be required. Estimate how many. Determine salary and fringe benefit costs necessary to support program expansion.
Task 3. Estimate Impact of Program Adjustment on Population	Using qualification criteria established in Task 2 above, select the component of existing detention facility populations which could be considered to be candidates for expanded OR releases.

Selected Unsentenced Felons Potentially Eligible for OR

Current Charge	Length of Stay Since Booking in Days								
Felony	Booking Day	1	2	3	4	5	6	7	8+	Total
Murder	0	1	0	0	1	0	0	1	4	7
Other Violent Crimes	1	2	0	4	0	1	0	0	7	15
Violent Crime, Police involved	0	1	0	0	1	0	1	0	3	6
Family Violence	0	0	1	0	0	0	0	0	1	2
Sex Offense	1	0	0	1	0	0	0	0	2	4
Commercial Sex Offense	0	0	0	0	0	1	0	0	0	1
Burglary	2	2	4	0	3	0	1	0	15	27
Weapons	0	1	0	2	0	0	1	1	4	9
Other Nonviolent Property Crime	2	5	2	1	1	2	3	2	18	36
Drug Use/Possession	0	1	1	0	2	0	0	1	3	8
Drug Sale	1	0	1	2	0	1	0	4	7	16
Automobile Violation	0	0	0	3	0	0	0	1	4	8
Property Violation	1	0	2	0	0	0	1	0	5	9
Miscellaneous	0	0	0	1	0	1	0	0	2	4
Total	8	13	11	14	8	6	7	10	75	152

Example of the Analysis of the Impact of Pretrial Release Programs, continued

Select specific criteria to determine which portion of the unsentenced facility population would be affected. Review the data elements in the Snapshot Profile Data Form (Appendix A) and specify those most consistent with the criteria documented in Task 2. For illustrative purposes, assume these criteria to be: (1) unsentenced; (2) current felony charge; no wants or holds from other jurisdictions; (3) no previous failures to appear; (4) local residence; (5) some community ties.

In addition, consider other factors judges might consider reflecting public safety and/or appearance risks. For illustrative purposes, assume these to be: no violent behavior, escape history, no mental, violent, or suicidal problem (in the "Custody Problem" section of the profile form); no drug addiction at time of booking (in the "Alcohol/Drug Abuse/Mental Health Problem" section of the profile form).

Once these criteria have been established, select specific inmates from the jail/detention facility population profile and display that population in a table showing length of stay by current charge.

The table on the previous page shows that, on the day the jail population profile was constructed, 152 unsentenced inmates out of the total population met the selection criteria. The next step in the analysis involves translating the data displayed in the table into a realistic assessment of the impact of the program adjustment of detention population levels. However, not all of the individuals—or jail days—represented in the table could be affected by a release program.

For example, even if the program were implemented, population components shown as being in the facility on the booking day would continue to occupy some space while awaiting interview and the release decision. In addition, not all offenses can be considered as automatic candidates for release. While this decision is clearly up to the local judiciary, for illustrative purposes assume that nonviolent felony offenders who meet the selection criteria can be considered as OR release candidates. From the table above, this would include individuals charged with burglary, other nonviolent property crimes, drug-use/possession, automobile violations, miscellaneous, and commercial sex offenses. Using this approach, the table which follows isolates the selected population by offense class.

Felony Offense	Booking Day	1 Day	2 Days	3+ Days	Total
Commercial Sex Offense	0	0	0	1	1
Burglary	2	2	4	19	27
Other Nonviolent Property Crime	2	5	2	27	36
Drug Use/Possession	0	1	1	6	8
Automobile Violation	0	0	0	8	8
Probation Violation					
Miscellaneous	0	0	0	4	4
Total	4	8	7	65	84

To assess impact on jail population, a further assumption needs to be made about when release would be granted. If the program was designed to identify candidates at booking and to release them after telephone confirmation or in-person check with a duty judge, population reduction would include all those inmates with a stay of one day or more—80 inmates in the example above. On the other hand, if the program was designed to consider candidates at arraignment, population reduction would be somewhat less. To estimate impact, you need to review the results of the court system analysis (Chapter 16) to estimate average elapsed time from booking to arraignment. For illustrative purposes, assume booking to arraignment requires two days. As a result, population reduction would be 65 inmates.

The last step involves comparing the effect of program expansion on the total jail population. This indicator is shown in the table below:

Population Component	Total Population on Profile Day	Population Reduction From Program Adjustments	Percent Population Reduction
Sentenced	128	0	0
Unsentenced	467	−65	−11.8%
Total	695	−65	− 9.4%

These percentages will be employed to analyze and project detention bed space needs later in this example.

Example of the Analysis of the Impact of Pretrial Release Programs, continued

Task 4. Analyze the Cost Impact of Program Implementation

The final task in the analysis involves assessment of the costs to implement each program modification compared to potential cost savings resulting from implementation. For the example given, assume the following cost impact.

Cost Increases: Your analysis indicates that OR program expansion will require more interviewing personnel. Based on workload estimates, your data suggest three jail interviewers will be required. Compute the cost.

Position	No.	Salary	Total
Jail Interviewer	3	17,500	$52,500
		Fringe Benefits @ 25%	$13,125
		Total Annual Cost Increase	$65,625

Cost Reduction/Cost Avoidance Impact: This program reduces population by 9.4%. The equivalent of 58 beds (in a jail where the average daily population equals about 624). The cost impact is computed as follows.

If it prevents expanding the facility or building a new facility, assume cost avoidance equivalent to population reduction times the cost per bed of new facilities. For illustrative purposes, assume population reduction avoids cost of building 58 new beds at a per bed cost of $60,000. Construction cost avoidance would total $3,480,000. To evaluate construction cost avoidance fully, you should also incorporate the cost of financing additional beds. In our example, assume 10% per year for 30 years. Estimated annual debt service is $348,000.

The program also reduces direct inmate support costs (meals, laundry, medication). For illustrative purposes, assume $5.75 per day per inmate (1980 costs). Annual cost avoidance with 58 bed reduction (5.75 X 58 beds X 365 days): $125,028. (Note: In estimating direct cost savings associated with bed and/or population reductions, be careful to avoid the mistake of taking total facility operating costs and dividing by average daily population, then multiplying the number of beds reduced by the result to estimate cost savings. This approach fails to recognize that the bulk of any facility's operating costs involve custodial staff, and that incremental reductions in single beds could not be accompanied by comparable staffing reductions.)

To estimate staffing impact, analyze the facility's staffing pattern and estimate the impact of reducing population on the fixed post pattern in the facility. To the extent that fewer fixed posts are required, reduce staffing costs. In the example, we will assume that a reduction of 58 in average daily population would eliminate (or avoid) the need for one fixed post. This will save about 5 deputies (to staff the post 24 hours per day, 7 days per week). Cost savings would be:

Position	No.	Salary	Total
Deputy	5	$20,000	$100,000
		Salary Cost Total	$100,000
		Fringe Benefits @ 25%	$25,000
		Total Annual Cost Reduction	$125,000

Total cost impact of implementing the program could then be displayed as follows:

Annual Operating Costs Only:

Item	Amount
Cost Increase: Add interview staff	$65,625
Cost Decrease: Custodial staff	($125,000)
Prisoner support costs	($125,028)
Annual Cost Increase (savings)	($184,403)

Annual Operating Costs Plus Construction Costs: If analysis indicates that construction will be averted, this saving should also be taken into account.

Construction cost: 58 beds X $60,000/bed = $3,480,000. To develop an equivalent annual cost of constructing the additional beds, an assumption needs to be made about how long new beds

Example of the Analysis of the Impact of Pretrial Release Programs, continued

will last. In this case, assume the new construction would have a 30-year life. Thus the annualized cost of construction would be $3,480,000 divided by 30 years, or $116,000 annually. The cost impact then would be displayed as follows:

Item	Amount
Cost Increase: Add interview staff	$65,625
Cost Decrease: Custodial staff	($125,000)
Prisoner support costs	($125,025)
Amortized construction	($116,000)
Construction financing	($348,000)
Annual cost increase (savings)	($714,025)

Task 5. Consider Quantitative Impact of Program Implementation

Based on contacts with other jurisdictions, estimate the impact on the failure to appear (FTA) rate which might be associated with program expansion. Concurrently, estimate the potential impact on the rearrest rate (people who commit additional offenses and are rearrested while on OR release).

As can be seen from the boxed chart, a variety of data sources needs to be used to conduct the analysis. Much of the information will be drawn from the Step 3 documentation of current program operations. Some additional data will need to be developed through special "ministudies." In addition, data collected for the inmate profile will quantify the impact of program adjustments on the inmate population. The analysis is demonstrated in the sections below.

Examine Length of Stay for Misdemeanants and Felons

Table Content. Document the county's existing formalized criteria for consideration for pretrial release. Select the data elements on the tally sheet most consistent with these criteria and use these criteria to structure a table that portrays the misdemeanant and felon unsentenced population by charge and length of stay. For illustrative purposes, the table below displays the population selected from the total profile by employing the following selection criteria: no murder-related violent crime charge, no holds or felony warrants from other jurisdictions, no previous failure to appear, no current drug addiction, a local residence.

Table 17-1. Length of Stay by Primary Charge

Length of Stay Since Booking Unsentenced Inmates																
Primary Charge	Booking Day	1	2	3	4	5	6	7	8	9	10	11	12	13	14	15+
Felony																
·																
·																
·																
Misdemeanor																
·																
·																
·																

Primary Analytical Questions

What proportion of the unsentenced population is composed of people whose characteristics fit the criteria you have established as "pretrial release qualifiers"?

Are there substantial numbers of these people in custody whose length of stay exceeds the typical time frame required to make pretrial release decisions (one to five days)?

Why are these people still in custody?

Are there significant numbers of qualified misdemeanants and "less serious" felons whose length of stay exceeds one day?

Triggers for Additional Analysis

A "yes" answer to one or all of the suggested analytical questions might suggest two possibilities:

First, existing pretrial release criteria may not be uniformly applied.

Second, there may be opportunities to accelerate pretrial release decision making by establishing procedures for that purpose at booking. This may require formalizing judicial policies, using a "duty" judge to review release candidates based on data collected at booking by jail or pretrial release interview staff and the like, to accelerate the application of **existing** pretrial release criteria. Elapsed time in custody would provide an estimate of the potential impact of accelerating releases or reducing length of stay, thus lowering the jail population.

To validate these tentative conclusions, some additional analyses would be required.

Examine Custody Problems of Inmates with Substance Abuse or Mental Health Histories

If the results of the above analysis indicate that substantial portions of the population might be affected, further segment the population to identify behavior characteristics that judges might take into account when considering inmates for OR release.

Table Content. Construct a table that profiles the population (selected according to existing pretrial release criteria as above) to show which inmates with substance abuse or mental health problems displayed various custody problems.

Table 17-2. Substance Abuse/Mental Health History by Custody Problem

First Custody Problem	Alcohol/Drug Abuse/Mental Health Problems				
	Active Drug Addiction	Past Drug Addiction	Alcoholic	......	No Problem
Violent Behavior					
Suicidal					
Escape History					
.					
.					
No Problem					

Primary Analytical Questions

If a significant number of the already selected inmates are classified as "no problem" from both perspectives, there may well be problems with existing pretrial release criteria. Conversely, if most of these inmates have other behavior or substance abuse problems, this may explain why judges have not granted pretrial releases. Even so, this could suggest a potential to expand pretrial release by providing service placement options to people who have no apparent barriers except drug or alcohol problems.

The next step in the population analysis involves conducting a more in-depth review of the unsentenced population. This review will identify potential barriers to pretrial release for lower risk misdemeanants and felons as well as provide data on opportunities to relax existing release criteria or accelerate release processes. To do this, the planning team should select a level of "relaxation" of pretrial release criteria and apply them to the population profile to determine what portion of the unsentenced population fits. Several examples of this type of analysis follow.

Examine the Warrant/Hold Status of Misdemeanants and Felons

Determine the impact of holds and minor warrants from local as well as other jurisdictions on providing pretrial release given **existing** pretrial release criteria.

Table Content. For illustrative purposes, it is assumed that release criteria are the same as those employed earlier in this section (no murder-related violent crime charge, no previous failures to appear, no current drug addiction, a local residence). Add the additional selection criteria of no indicators of violent behavior based on entries of violent behavior, mental problem-violent, or suicidal in terms of custody problems. Then, for the population selected based on these criteria, structure a table that portrays warrant/hold status ("wanted by other jurisdictions") on one axis of the table and the nature of the hold or warrant on the other (See Table 17-3).

Table 17-3. Warrant/Hold Status of Unsentenced Misdemeanants and Felons

Warrant/Hold Status of Unsentenced Inmates							
Nature of Charges in Other Jurisdictions	No Warrant or Hold	Parole Hold	Arrest Warrant Other County	Arrest Warrant State Agency	Arrest Warrant Federal Agency	Arrest Warrant Local Agency	Probation Hold
Felony							
.							
.							
.							
Misdemeanor							
.							
.							
.							

Primary Analytical Questions

Are there people who fit the pretrial release criteria and have no warrants and holds but who are still in custody? Why? (Refer to Table 17-1 to pursue this issue in terms of length of stay and charge characteristics of these people.)

Are there people charged with misdemeanors or traffic offenses in other jurisdictions who are still in custody?

Do parole holds account for the people who otherwise meet the county's pretrial release criteria yet remain in custody?

Do local traffic warrants appear to be a significant reason that people who meet pretrial release criteria are still in custody?

Do probation holds appear to be a major reason people are held in pretrial custody?

Triggers for Additional Analysis

If holds by parole agencies comprise a significant proportion of the population under analysis, a program to "clear" holds could expand the pretrial release program without adjusting existing criteria, thus reducing jail population.

Do minor warrants from other or local jurisdictions comprise a significant proportion of the population? If so, could a program to clear warrants earlier expand pretrial release activities within existing criteria?

If positive answers result from any of the above questions, the planning team will wish to profile the population further by length of stay to accomplish two things. First, to assess whether lengths of stay for the population groups noted above exceed one day. If so, this may suggest that a hold and/or minor warrant clearing program can have some impact. Second, to quantify the impact of potential population reduction on future facility requirements.

Additional analyses of pretrial release issues would look further at the unsentenced population, portraying characteristics that suggest the risk of failure to appear and potential threats to public safety, factors that formally or informally have an impact on pretrial release decision making. Several illustrative tables follow below.

Examine Criminal History of Misdemeanants and Felons

Determine whether the criminal history of pretrial inmates suggests that some might be considered for release.

Table Content. Use as selection criteria no previous failures to appear, no holds or felony warrants, current local residence, some family ties, no current drug addiction, no violent behavior problem, and no escape history. Portray the population that meets these criteria by current charge versus previous conviction history as shown in Table 17-4.

Table 17-4. Criminal History by Current Charge

	Criminal History						
Current Primary Charge	More than 2 felony convictions	One felony conviction	No previous felony conviction	No misdemeanor conviction	One misdemeanor conviction	More than two misdemeanor convictions	Population Total
Felony							
.							
.							
.							
Misdemeanor							
.							
.							

Primary Analytical Questions

Is a significant proportion of the people in the table those with limited criminal histories as measured by previous felony convictions?

What proportion of these people are charged with misdemeanor or nonassaultive felonies?

What proportion of these people have no previous convictions?

Triggers for Additional Analysis

What length of stay is associated with the population noted above? If lengths of stay exceed three to five days for individuals without a serious prior conviction, relatively low risk people may have failed to qualify for pretrial release because of existing criteria or practices. The next step is to analyze this population further by length of stay, adding the additional selection criteria of conviction history.

However, remember that current charge and conviction histories apparently do not affect whether people will make court appearances. Nonetheless they are factors that many judges informally take into account when setting bail and considering people for pretrial release. As a "real world" analyst, you need to consider these issues and present them to the advisory committee for practical consideration of pretrial release adjustments.

Re-examine Length of Stay for Misdemeanants and Felons

This step takes you back to the format of table 17-1, this time to look at length of stay for people meeting a larger set of criteria.

Table Content. Select that portion of the jail population that fits these criteria: no previous failure to appear, no holds or felony warrants, current local residence, no current drug addiction, no violent behavior problem, no escape history, and no more than two previous felony convictions for nonviolent felony offenses.

Primary Analytical Questions

Given the selection criteria, what proportions of the population have a length of stay beyond the thresholds of one day, two days, and three days? These generally represent people who did not qualify for pretrial release or could have been released earlier.

What proportion of the unsentenced population do these people represent? What proportion of the total detention population?

Triggers for Additional Analysis

Considering the cost of pretrial detention facility beds in terms of new construction (over $60,000 per bed), is it cost-effective to hold these people in pretrial custody?

Can the county's pretrial release program be expanded without compromising the adjudication process or endangering public safety?

Analytical Issue 2: Court Processing Improvements

The second major issue for analysis concerns how effectively the court system (and related services) can process the individuals held in custody in the jail. Obviously the length of time each court proceeding takes will have a direct effect on how long a pretrial or presentenced individual spends in jail, and therefore on the jail's required capacity.

The boxed text displays an analytical sequence for evaluating how court processing improvements might affect jail population levels. To conduct the analysis of potential court processing improvements, you will want to use a variety of resources, including the following:

- The jail population profile developed in Step 1 (Chapter 14).
- The results of the analysis of criminal justice system operations carried out in Step 3 (Chapter 16).
- Special studies done to resolve issues identified during the criminal justice system analysis in Step 3 (Chapter 16).

When using these data to evaluate the impact of court system processing improvements, investigate issues such as the following.

• Profile the unsentenced population by length of stay versus adjudication status and determine the proportion of disposed cases at the various key points in the adjudication process. Analyze results to assess how much court processing backlogs contribute to the jail's unsentenced population. Identify convicted population groups that are awaiting sentence. If the elapsed time is significant, conduct further analysis to determine if probation department presentence report services are backlogged and if this backlog is influencing in-custody population levels.

• Similarly, profile the unsentenced population by length of stay versus adjudication status. Identify sentenced population groups that are awaiting transfer to the state correctional system. Conduct further analysis to determine ways to accelerate transfer to reduce local facility populations and moderate future facility expansion needs.

Example of the Analysis of the Impact of Court Processing Improvements

Task 1. Establish a Hypothesis	By increasing staff resources available to the district attorney and public defender, disposition time for in-custody defendants could be accelerated and jail population reduced.
Task 2. Define Changes Required to Implement the Court System Processing Improvement	**Required Change:** How many additional deputy district attorneys and deputy public defenders would be required to accelerate disposition time?
	Implementation Process: Document current workload of district attorney and public defender staff assigned responsibility for superior court cases.
	Meet with managers from the district attorney's and public defender's offices. Review workload data and reach a consensus on number of additional staff required to speed disposition. Ensure staffing requirements are documented in terms of both attorney and clerical positions.
	Required Change: If staffing were increased, how much would dispositions be accelerated?

Example of the Analysis of the Impact of Court Processing Improvements, continued.

Implementation Process:

Review elapsed processing time in the criminal justice system. Analyze impact of staffing increases on caseload distribution and potential readiness of trial staff in both offices. Based on the analysis, develop (and review with managers from both offices) potential disposition acceleration as an estimated number of days.

Task 3. Estimate the Impact of Processing Improvements on Population Levels

Display the felony unsentenced population (documented in the jail profile) in a table that arrays the population by length of stay versus charge. If you have previously determined that the felony unsentenced population can be reduced through expansion of pretrial release activities, make sure that you do not include in the table those who will be released. For example, if analysis resulted in plans to expand pretrial release, the portion of the unsentenced population analyzed in this table would exclude all of population component which could qualify for expanded pretrial release. To structure a table, reverse the selection criteria used to select pretrial release candidates.

	Unsentenced Felons									
	Length of Stay Since Booking									
Primary Charge	0–20	21–28	29–35	36–42	43–49	50–56	57–63	64–70	71–77	Total
Felony										
Murder	2	1	2	0	1	1	2	1	3	3
Other violent	6	0	1	2	3	1	1	0	1	15
Violent—police officer involved	3	0	2	0	0	1	0	0	0	6
Sex Offense	1	0	0	1	1	0	1	0	0	4
Commercial Sex Offense	0	0	0	0	1	0	0	1	0	2
Weapons	4	1	0	2	1	0	3	1	4	16
Burglary	2	3	5	4	4	5	7	9	10	49
Other Property	7	1	0	2	1	0	3	1	4	19
Total	25	6	10	11	12	8	17	13	22	124

Review the data displayed in the table and attempt to assess the impact of disposition time acceleration on the unsentenced jail population. Follow these three steps:

First, determine what proportion of the population would be affected by accelerated court processing. In the example above, assume that only those inmates who have been in custody more than 21 days would be affected. In this example, it is assumed that people in this category would have their cases in process at the superior court level, and that disposition acceleration would affect that group. From the table above, the inmates affected would total 99 (the 124 total less the 25 whose length of stay is less than three weeks).

Second, calculate the average length of stay of the population using the weighted average technique. Use the midpoint of each length of stay range for computational purposes (e.g., 29 to 35 days would be treated as 32 days: 29 + 35 = 64 divided by 2 = 32 days). Then divide the

Total Inmates in the Category		Midpoint Length of Stay		Jail Days
6	×	24.5	=	147
10	×	32	=	320
11	×	39	=	429
12	×	46	=	552
8	×	53	=	424
1	×	60	=	1,020
13	×	67	=	871
22	×	74	=	1,628
Total 99				5,391

Example of the Analysis of the Impact of Court Processing Improvements, continued.

weighted days by the total inmates to estimate average length of stay (5,391 divided by 99 = 54.5 days).

Third, calculate the impact on the in-custody sentenced population. For illustrative purposes, assume that staffing increases for the public defender and district attorney would reduce disposition time by ten calendar days. To convert that reduction to impact on in-custody population, perform the following calculations:

Subtract the reduction from the documented average length of stay (54.5 days − 10 days = 44.5 days).

Multiply 44.5 days by the number of inmates above (99 × 44.5 = 4,405.5).

Divide that result by the total jail days represented by the population (5,391). The calculation would be:

4,405.5 divided by 5,391 = .817

Multiply the number of inmates by that result.

99 inmates × .817 = 81

Subtract the result from the current number of inmates to document the expected population reduction:

99 − 81 = 17 beds

Divide the result by the facility population on the day the profile was taken:

Population Component	Total Facility Population on Profile Day	Population Reduction From Program Adjustment	Percent Population Reduction
Sentenced	68	0	0
Unsentenced	314	−17	−5.4
Total	382	−17	−4.4%

These percentages would subsequently be employed to analyze and project detention facility bed space needs later in this process.

Task 4. Analyze Cost Impact of Program Implementation

First, estimate the cost of implementing the adjustment. In this example, assume that achieving disposition time reduction would require the addition of two staff attorneys to both the public defender's and district attorney's office. In addition, the increase in attorney staff would require one additional clerical support position in each office.

Position	Number	Salary	Total
Deputy District Attorney	2	$30,000	$60,000
Deputy Public Defender	2	30,000	60,000
Clerical	2	14,000	28,000
		Salary Cost Total	$148,000
		Fringe Benefits @ 25%	37,000
		Total Annual Cost Increase	$185,000

Then, following procedures comparable to those shown in Table 17-4, compute capital cost and operating cost avoidance impact. For illustrative purposes, assume that average daily population is 415; and recall that this adjustment has the potential to reduce facility population by 4.4%. Thus it reduces bed space requirements by (415 × 4.4%) 18 beds.

If this reduction avoids expanding the facility or building a new facility, estimate the construction cost of the facilities that would not need to be built. For illustrative purposes assume the acceleration of disposition eliminates the need to build 18 pretrial beds at a per bed cost of $60,000. Construction cost avoidance would total $1,080,000. To evaluate fully construction cost avoidance, you should also incorporate the cost of financing additional beds. In the example, assume 10% per year for 30 years. Estimated annual debt service would then be $108,000.

Example of the Analysis of the Impact of Court Processing Improvements, continued.

In the illustration, assume that the bed space reduction is insufficient to lead to either a reduction in current custodial staffing levels or to avoid the addition of new custodial staff positions in future years.

Compute the reduction in direct inmate support costs (food, laundry, medicine, etc.). Estimate per day, per inmate support costs at $5.75; total yearly savings are ($5.75 × 18 × 365 =) $37,777.50 per year. The total impact of program implementation is as follows.

Annual Operating Costs:

	Item	Amount
Cost Increase:	Increase District Attorney and Public Defender staff	$185,000
Cost Decrease:	Inmate support costs	(37,777)
Annual Cost Increase (Savings):		$147,223

Annual Operating Costs Plus Construction Costs:

If analysis indicates that construction will be averted, include these savings in the analysis.

	Item	Amount
Cost Increase:	Increase District Attorney and Public Defender staff	$185,000
Cost Decrease:	Inmate support costs	(37,777)
	Amortized Construction	(36,000)
	Construction financing	(108,000)
	Annual Cost Increase (Savings):	(3,223)

Task 5. Consider the Quantitative Impacts of Program Implementation

Are there sufficient courts and judges available to accelerate processing if prosecution and defense resources are expanded? Would staffing resource increases really achieve disposition acceleration estimated, or would selected defense tactics (e.g., delay to influence deterioration of prosecution's case) offset all or a portion of the expected impact?

Analytical Issue 3: Use of Sentencing and Housing Options

The final issue for analysis is the potential impact of sentencing alternatives on the jail population. A closely related issue is the potential of adjusting housing patterns to alter the security level used for sentenced inmates (and therefore to reduce the cost of facilities needed by your county, now and in the future).

The example of the analysis of custody and security requirements supplied in the boxed text presents a case study of the potential impact of adjusting classification criteria to improve the cost-effectiveness of in-facility housing practices.

Jail profile data may also help determine other potential opportunities to control facility populations by providing sentencing alternatives, using programs such as court parole, or using alternative facilities like work-furlough facilities, community-based re-entry residences, or other approaches.

Example of the Analysis of Custody and Security Requirements

Task 1. Establish a Hypothesis	There are inmates who can be held in less than a high cost, maximum security bed without adversely affecting their safety, or the safety of other inmates or custodial staff. Many pretrial inmates are held in maximum security during the pretrial period but if convicted, will be housed in lower security sentenced facilities. Is this cost effective?
Task 2. Define Changes Required to Improve the Cost-Effectiveness of Housing Practices	**Required Change:** Are there pretrial inmates likely to be sentenced to time in county facilities? **Implementation Process:** Analyze the previous conviction history of sentenced inmates. Identify common threads. **Required Change:** How would existing classification practices have to be changed to incorporate "predicting" sentences for inmates if convicted. **Implementation Process:** Contact probation department and document criteria employed to make sentencing recommendations in pre-sentence investigation reports. Identify ways to incorporate these criteria into existing classification practices.
Task 3. Estimate the Impact of Housing Program Adjustments on Bed Type Requirements	As the first step, structure a table which shows the criminal history of sentenced inmates using the jail population profile data as a base.

Previous Conviction History of Sentenced Inmates							
Charge	No Prev. Conv.	More than 3 Fel. Conv.	Two Fel. Conv.	One Fel. Conv.	More than 3 Misd. Conv.	Two Misd. Conv.	One Misd. Conv.
Felony							

Analyze results and identify criminal history/conviction records that appear to be closely associated with a local rather than a state prison sentence. Then, construct a second set of tables to determine where sentenced inmates and unsentenced inmates are currently housed.

Sentenced Inmates			
Charge	Housing Assignment		
Felony	Main Jail Cell	Main Jail Dorm	Jail Farm

Unsentenced Inmates			
Charge	Housing Assignment		
Felony	Main Jail Cell	Main Jail Dorm	Jail Farm

Example of the Analysis of Custody and Security Requirements, continued.

Compare the tables and see if the hypothesis that sentenced prisoners are generally held at lower security levels holds true. If so; construct a third table to determine what proportion of the unsentenced population could be considered as candidates for housing in a lower security facility.

Apply the following criteria to select the potential population component: no custody problems which would influence housing; currently housed in maximum security setting; length of stay over seven days (need to allow sufficient time to enable custodial staff to monitor behavior to ensure there are no custody problems associated with individual inmates); and other selection criteria as you deem appropriate.

	Selected Unsentenced Inmates		
Charge	**Housing Assignment**		
Felony	Main Jail—Cell	Main Jail—Dorm	Jail Farm
Murder	7	0	0
Other Violent	4	8	0
Burglary	6	15	2
Other Property	0	8	3
Misc.	0	9	1

(circled totals: 6, 15, 8, 9 → 38)

Analyze the results and identify rehousing candidates. For this example, assume all non-violent felons who meet the selection criteria can be transferred to a lower security housing situation.

The next step would involve comparing the results of program expansion or modification to total jail population (at the time the sample was taken) to develop an impact indicator. In developing this indicator, analyze the impact only on the facility where population will be reduced. Assume the maximum security main jail in this instance.

Population	Total Main Jail Population on Profile Day	Population Reduction	Percent Population Reduction
Sentenced	38	0	0
Unsentenced	291	−38	−13.1%
Total	329	−38	−11.5%

In this example, it must be remembered that this step does not involve a population reduction but rather a transfer within the detention system. As a result, the increase in the population of lower-security facilities caused by population transfer must be quantified. For illustrative purposes, assume that inmates when reclassified would be transferred to the jail farm.

Compute the average daily population of both the main jail and jail farm. Then multiply main jail average daily population by the percentage reduction noted above and add the result to the jail farm population.

Facility	Average Daily Population	× %	=	Number
Main Jail	316	11.5		36
Jail Farm	214 + 36 = 250 Revised ADP.			

Example of the Analysis of Custody and Security Requirements, continued.

Task 4. Analyze the Cost Impact of Housing Program Changes

The cost impact of reclassification and intrasystem transfer depends on the status of existing facility overcrowding. If existing facilities are not overcrowded, the transfer is unlikely to have either major operating capital cost avoidance impact.

On the other hand, if both the main jail and jail farm have populations that exceed capacities, the transfer would have the impact of reducing the additional higher security beds needing to be built and increasing the number of lower security beds. Analysis of the cost impact would be the differential between construction and financing costs as follows (assume 30-year financing at 10%).

Cost Component	Amount
Main Jail Expansion	
Construct 36 beds @ $60,000	$2,160,000
Financing costs (10% for 30 years)	6,480,000
Subtotal	$8,640,000
Jail Farm Expansion	
Construct 36 beds @ $25,000	900,000
Financing costs (10% for 30 years)	2,700,000
Subtotal	$3,600,000
Cost Avoidance Differential	$5,040,000

If the main jail is overcrowded but the jail farm has excess capacity and could absorb the population without constructing additional beds, then the cost differential would be the total amount required to build the higher security main jail beds.

Present Results to the Advisory Committee

Summarize the results of the analysis of alternatives for the advisory committee and decision makers so that issues of policy and cost can be resolved. Prepare narrative and statistical profiles that describe each alternative to use when presenting the results.

Open the discussion of each alternative with a section describing the program adjustment and how it could affect the jail population.

Provide a second section showing the requirements to implement the program, including organizational changes, staffing increases, policy, and procedural changes. Show the costs of implementing these changes. Where other pros and cons are identifiable, list them.

Show the impact of the program on the jail population, including a detailed description of the assumptions underlying your assessment of the impact. Support your analysis of each alternative with enough data to justify your findings, but be careful not to overwhelm the committee.

Finally, prepare a summary table comparing the cost, risk, and benefit of each alternative.

Summary and Conclusion

By following the techniques outlined in this section, you can quantify the impact of specific alternative programs and processing improvements on both current jail overcrowding and likely future capital requirements. Remember, however, that you can release each individual only once and that cumulative programs or policies may show diminishing returns.

Once you have evaluated all the potential alternative programs, project future detention facility population and capacity requirements in the next steps.

18. Step 5: Document Trends and Project Future Volumes

Introduction

The purpose of Step 5 is to develop projections of the jail population **given current incarceration strategies** (including existing pretrial release programs and services, court processing procedures, sentencing alternatives, and jail management techniques).

While it is recognized that this is only a temporary step, the projection that results assumes that **no adjustments** are made in policies or programs. Once this projection has been developed, you must examine and test the impact of alternative courses of action on adjusting the projection. This will be done by varying pretrial release policies, improving court operations, adjusting sentencing practices and the like. These adjustments produce the **final projection** and are covered in Step 6, Chapter 19.

Accuracy of Projections

When projecting future population and facility needs, it is well to bear in mind that there is no "magic" approach to making projections. No one can predict the future. At best you can make intelligent use of available information on past practices, look at recent developments, make reasonable assumptions, and decide how in the future you will treat the factors over which you can exert some control. These principles form the basis for the methods presented here and in Step 6. But how accurate can you expect a projection to be?

It is possible to use either complex methods of projection that involve mathematical models, or relatively simple methods. Perhaps surprisingly, jurisdictions using either method have experienced about the same range of accuracy. Some developed projections that closely paralleled actual needs, while others missed by substantial factors; the method used to arrive at the projection did not affect the outcome. Since so many issues can influence future jail populations, the projection method may be less important than other aspects of planning, coordination among agencies, and the regular updating of data and projections.

Obviously it is more difficult to project farther into the future than to project short term. This book uses a twenty-year projection because that period of time allows a perspective that relates to the useful life of the construction under discussion. Greater emphasis is placed on the first ten years than on the second ten, and more detailed projections are developed for the earlier period. In fact, once projections are developed they should be updated annually (or even more frequently), considering and quantifying changes in the assumptions upon which the initial projections were based.

Overview of the Projection Process

No matter how complex the projection method, the same basic steps are required. The figure provides a graphic illustration of the main steps in the projection sequence. The paragraphs that follow introduce you to the overall projections sequence and provide two alternative methods that you can use to project likely detention population levels in your county.

Projecting Detention System Needs

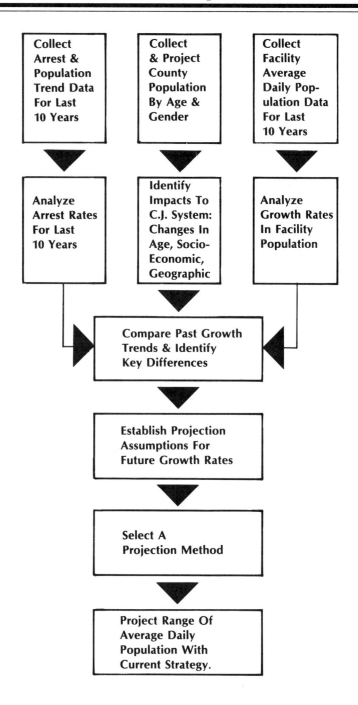

Obtain and Analyze Background Data

Any projection approach requires you to review and analyze key trends in your county over the last five (or preferably ten) years in both the general county population and the criminal justice system. Among important types of available historical and future projection information are the following four:

- **Historical arrest data** for your county for at least the last ten years.
- **Average daily population data** and bookings (by facility) for the last ten years.
- **Historical county population data** for the past ten to twenty years.
- **County population projections** that cover the twenty-year planning period.

Historical Arrest Data

Obtain the most recent available copy of your county's criminal justice statistics. Extract adult felony and adult misdemeanor arrest data for the last ten years. Array these data on a chart (or set of charts) depicting volume of arrests by offense class for each year over the ten-year period. (Use caution in interpreting these data, however, if the reporting base has changed within the last ten years.)

Compute the average annual percentage changes for total adult misdemeanor arrests and total felony arrests, and then by specific offenses within those categories. Do this separately for males and females.

Average Daily Population Data

Review jail records and extract average daily population data for the last ten years. Compute average daily population for each year over the ten-year period and, to the extent possible, determine what proportion was comprised of sentenced and unsentenced individuals. If your county has more than one detention facility, collect and display these data for the whole system and for each facility. Where appropriate, break down average daily population data into males and females. At the same time, collect annual booking data for the same period.

Example of Historical Population Data

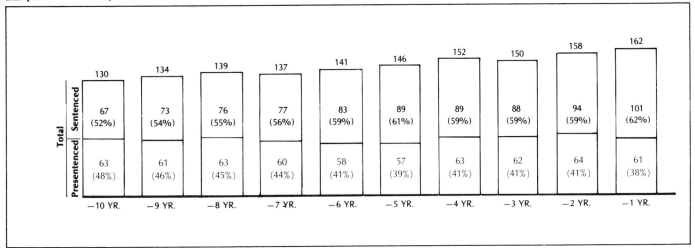

Historical County Population Data

Obtain county population data for the same period. Your county planning department should be able to provide you with relatively detailed population data based on the 1960, 1970, and 1980 United States Censuses. Array these data on a second chart and show annual percentage increases in total county population and for males and females.

County Population Projections

Collect and evaluate all available projections of future county population. Sources to investigate may include your state's finance or economic development departments; your county's general plan; and multijurisdictional agencies including school districts, metropolitan transportation commissions, associations of government, and the like. Many of these institutions develop and maintain up-to-date population projections as part of their planning services. Local sources can also identify key planning assumptions that need to be incorporated in your projections.

Select a Population Projection. Once you have collected available population projections, review them in detail and select the one that will be most useful in corrections planning. In other words, select the forecast that appears to be most consistent with existing and likely future political trends in the county—including assumptions about land use, migration, and the like.

Rely on the projection that takes into account the most recently documented and validated trends in county historical population. The 1980 U.S. Census invalidated many earlier population projections.

Identify High Impact Population Groups. Once you have selected a population projection, analyze it thoroughly to identify county population components that are likely to have special impact on the nature and scope of criminal justice system growth. Consider such questions as locations of the growth and probable composition by age and socioeconomic characteristics.

• Where in the county is growth expected to occur? What implications does this have for future facility location?

• What do projections say about the expected age composition of the overall county population? Is the age group generally associated with high levels of criminal activity (eighteen to thirty years old) expected to grow at rates faster, slower, or the same as general county population? If this age group grows at a rate different than overall county population, criminal justice system trends could be expected to grow at differing rates as well.

• What do projections say about the general socioeconomic composition of the population? Are unemployment rates projected to increase or decrease? What implications do shifts in socioeconomic trends have for the criminal justice system?

Once you have completed an analysis of expected trends, the next step is to review information about the past to determine relationships among trends in general population, detention population, and general justice system volume.

Compare Various Growth Trends and Identify Key Differences

Conduct a comparative analysis of past trends in felony and misdemeanor arrests, general county population, and average detention facility population for the last ten years. As you review these data, compare general population growth and increases in arrest volume. Have arrests grown at a faster rate, at the same rate, or more slowly than general county population?

In conducting this analysis, you will find it useful to convert total arrests into the arrest rate or number of arrests per hundred thousand population for each year under analysis. Using annual changes in arrest rates for each of the offense categories, you can compare change in criminal justice system activity to change in overall county population.

In analyzing arrests, you will need to look beyond changes in overall arrests or arrest rates. Analyze changes for each class of offense and note differences between patterns of change in total arrests and changes in specific types of arrest. If you observe different rates of change by offense class, ask the following questions:

• Which offenses seem to be growing at a faster rate? Are these high growth rates uniform over the entire ten-year period? Have they been growing at a faster rate in more recent years? Or was higher growth registered at the beginning of the ten-year period?

• What specific factors can you relate to observed changes in rates of growth or decline for the various offense classes? For example, if the data indicate that felony drug arrests have generally declined or grown slowly over the ten-year period, consider the following issue. In many areas, decriminalization of certain substance abuse offenses in the early and mid-1970s resulted in significant declines in arrest rates for these offenses. To a great extent, this decline has leveled out in recent years. Given this pattern, can a future decline be expected?

Compare trends in general county population (and its composition) with trends in arrest rates over the past ten years. Attempt to identify relationships between shifts in county population composition and trends in arrests and arrest rates.

Review trends in average daily population in county detention facilities (both for total and for unsentenced and sentenced components) and compare them to trends in both general county population and overall arrests and arrest rates. Again, attempt to identify relationships. Ask such questions as:

• Have detention populations grown at approximately the same rate that arrests have grown during the ten-year period?

• Is there consistency between general population growth, arrest growth, and growth in average daily detention population? If not, are there proportional differences between these factors?

Once you have completed these comparative analyses, identify past growth trends that appear to relate directly to growth and detention facility population. In addition, identify key factors in recent trends in overall growth in adult arrests. Specifically, draw conclusions about the following issues:

- Is there a direct relationship between detention system population and criminal justice system volume? Has that relationship generally held over the last ten years?
- What relationship can be found between arrest volume, average daily population, length of stay, and growth in general county population? Have these relationships held constant over the past ten years?
- Are there recent changes that are likely to affect these relationships? Are local political decisions or law enforcement emphases likely to adjust these trends in coming years? How?
- Therefore, what recent trends can be observed that you can use in projecting future detention populations?

Once you have answered these questions, you are ready to define some specific assumptions which will form a basis for projecting future growth rates.

Formulate Projection Assumptions

The analysis of trends in general population and criminal justice system indicators culminates in defining specific projection assumptions that should incorporate the following:

- Whether you expect criminal justice system activity in the county to grow at a rate faster than, equal to, or less than general county population.
- Whether you expect arrests for all types of offenses to grow at comparable rates. Are rates of growth for arrests that generally result in detention likely to grow faster or more slowly than more minor offenses?
- Whether projected shifts in the age composition of the population are likely to have major impact on the growth of criminal justice system volume and future detention populations? If so, how?

Once your projection assumptions have been formulated, write them down, review them with the advisory committee, revise them as appropriate, and proceed with the selection of a specific projection technique.

Select the Projection Methodology, and Project Average Daily Population Given Current Incarceration Strategies

As noted earlier in this section, you can use a variety of accepted techniques to project facility population. All involve studying changes in average daily detention population, general county population, and arrest volume to determine future detention facility needs. Two methods are provided in Part Three.

Method 1 is preferred if adequate data and staff time are available. It is preferred because it involves thorough analysis of the trends and performance factors that affect jail population. In addition, it requires you to develop planning assumptions that incorporate local law enforcement policies, political developments, external influences such as state legislative trends, and shifts in population composition. Method 2, which is described in Appendix H, is a simpler approach that relies primarily on available historical data. Principal components of the two methods are described below.

Method 1: Projection Based on Arrests and Pretrial Release Practices

Method 1 is a more involved approach than the second method. It is based on arrest data and specific assumptions about growth rates that reflect analysis of a variety of community and population characteristics that are likely to influence future changes.

Future projected arrest volumes are converted into inmate populations by studying the average length of stay in terms of current pretrial release and disposition practices. These include the current proportion of booked inmates who are released on bail, released on OR, held in custody until disposition, and the like.

Method 2: Projection Based on Average Daily Population

Method 2 involves projecting detention populations based on observed trends in average daily population and length of stay. It primarily involves reviewing historical trends, identifying relationships among these factors, and projecting the relationships into future years. Differing projection assumptions can be employed to forecast ranges of populations. While Method 2 may be somewhat less reliable than Method 1, it is worthwhile using it as a crosscheck.

Making the Projections

Both methods include suggested procedures to break down gross inmate population projections into sentenced and unsentenced components. The two methods also project both male and female population components. This means that, if possible, arrest, average daily population, and preferably county population data all need to be recorded separately for males and females.

With each method, the techniques that can be used to project the trend include either simpler "straight line" techniques or more sophisticated mathematical techniques such as linear regression analysis.

Thoroughly document each step in the projection exercise. It will be important in subsequent steps to be able to defend and explain potentially controversial points. Likewise, as you formulate projection assumptions, review them with the advisory committee to insure that these critical foundations to your work reflect a consensus.

With either method, the next chapter (Chapter 19) will show how to adjust the projections for future changes in incarceration strategy—a crucial step in preventing the error of the simple projection of current practices into the future.

The section that follows presents illustrative examples of Method 1's application along with blank forms to use in developing your county's projections. Appendix H describes Method 2 and provides similar illustrative examples and blank forms.

Method 1: Projection Based on Assumed Shifts in Criminal Justice System Activity and Trends in Average Length of Stay

Method 1 involves several basic steps, divided into fifteen specific tasks. The accompanying illustration, Tasks in Projecting Future Capacity Requirements, shows the relationship between the basic steps and the specific tasks.

Tasks in Projecting Future Capacity Requirements

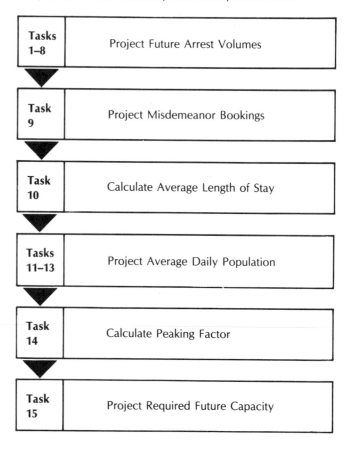

Tasks 1–8	Project Future Arrest Volumes
Task 9	Project Misdemeanor Bookings
Task 10	Calculate Average Length of Stay
Tasks 11–13	Project Average Daily Population
Task 14	Calculate Peaking Factor
Task 15	Project Required Future Capacity

Task 1: Document Historical Arrest Trends

Document historical trends in the volume of annual felony and misdemeanor arrests for males and females over the past ten years. Review trend data by specific offense class and compute average annual increases for both felony and misdemeanor arrests. Use criminal justice statistics as your source for the data. Then calculate the trends in arrest data as displayed in the following example.

Table 18-1. Example of Historical Trends in Arrest Volumes

Offense Category	Annual Rate of Change Last 10 Years	Annual Rate of Change Last 5 Years
Felony Arrests		
Crimes Against Persons	2.4%	3.1%
Crimes Against Property	1.8%	2.9%
Drug Violations	2.8%	1.3%
All Other	1.5%	1.6%
TOTAL FELONIES	2.6%	1.5%
Misdemeanor Arrests		
Assault and Battery	1.2%	2.6%
Property	1.4%	1.3%
Drug Law Violations	1.9%	3.4%
Sex Offenses	.8%	.9%
Prostitution	.6%	1.8%
Public Drunk	1.9%	.7%
Drunk Driving	2.8%	3.9%
Other Auto	1.6%	2.8%
All Other	3.6%	2.1%
TOTAL MISDEMEANORS	2.9%	3.6%

Table 18-2. Your Computation of Historical Arrest Trends

Offense Category	Annual Rate of Change Last 10 Years	Annual Rate of Change Last 5 Years
Felony Arrests		
Crimes Against Persons		
Crimes Against Property		
Drug Violations		
All Other		
TOTAL FELONIES		
Misdemeanor Arrests		
Assault and Battery		
Property		
Drug Law Violations		
Sex Offenses		
Prostitution		
Public Drunk		
Drunk Driving		
Other Auto		
All Other		
TOTAL MISDEMEANORS		

Once you have computed rates of change by offense class and displayed them in the format shown above, compare growth rates for the entire ten-year period and for the last five years for each offense class. Identify which offenses appear to be growing at faster rates and slower rates over the last five years than over the entire decade. Then identify factors contributing to recent trends and determine whether or not these are likely to continue in future years.

Given the data you have developed, consider the following questions:

- To what extent do local enforcement strategies (anti-drunk-driving campaigns; clearing the streets of public drunks; antiprostitution campaigns; and others) contribute to acceleration of arrests in certain categories? Are they likely to be maintained in future years?

- Can changes in legislative mandates that affect arrests and sentences (such as decriminalization of drug offenses) be identified with shifting trends? Are they likely to be maintained in future years?

Task 2: Compute Arrest Rates

Document population growth trends over the same period. Compute felony and misdemeanor arrest rates per 100,000 population of the period. Convert arrests to arrest rates by offense class by arraying arrest and population data for each year over the last ten years.

- Divide population by 100,000 to get the percentage factor. In the example (for 1976), the population of 250,748 divided by 100,000 results in a factor of 2.51.

- Divide total arrests in each category by the factor to obtain the rate per 100,000 population. For example, in 1976, the 751 felony crimes against rates yields a rate per 100,000 population of 299.2.

The illustration below shows the calculation for a two-year period. You will need to make this calculation for each year included in your analysis.

Table 18-3. Example of Computation of Arrest Rates

1976

Offense Category	Number of Arrests	÷	County Population (000,000)	=	Arrest Rate Per 100,000
Felony					
Crimes Against Persons	751	÷	2.51	=	299.2
Crimes Against Property	1,268	÷	2.51	=	505.2
Drug Violations	598	÷	2.51	=	238.2
All Other	486	÷	2.51	=	193.6
TOTAL FELONIES	3,103	÷	2.51	=	1,236.2
Misdemeanor					
Assault and Battery	1,380	÷	2.51	=	549.8
Property	1,428	÷	2.51	=	568.9
Drug Law Violation	1,850	÷	2.51	=	737.1
Sex Offense	628	÷	2.51	=	251.2
Prostitution	751	÷	2.51	=	299.2
Public Drunk	4,821	÷	2.51	=	1,920.7
Drunk Driving	3,968	÷	2.51	=	1,580.9
Other Auto	2,175	÷	2.51	=	866.5
All Other	1,182	÷	2.51	=	470.9
TOTAL MISDEMEANORS	18,183	÷	2.51	=	7,244.2

1977

Offense Category	Number of Arrests	÷	County Population (000,000)	=	Arrest Rate Per 100,000
Felony					
Crimes Against Persons	805	÷	2.53	=	318.2
Crimes Against Property	1,398	÷	2.53	=	552.6
Drug Violations	478	÷	2.53	=	188.9
All Other	504	÷	2.53	=	199.2
TOTAL FELONIES	3,185	÷	2.53	=	1,258.9
Misdemeanor					
Assault and Battery	1,396	÷	2.53	=	551.8
Property	1,301	÷	2.53	=	593.3
Drug Law Violation	1,728	÷	2.53	=	683.0
Sex Offense	711	÷	2.53	=	281.0
Prostitution	1,186	÷	2.53	=	468.8
Public Drunk	4,810	÷	2.53	=	1,901.2
Drunk Driving	4,264	÷	2.53	=	1,685.4
Other Auto	1,813	÷	2.53	=	716.6
All Other	1,204	÷	2.53	=	475.9
TOTAL MISDEMEANORS	18,613	÷	2.53	=	7,356.9

Table 18-4. Example of Computation of Arrest Rates

Year _____

Offense Category	Number of Arrests	÷	County Population (000,000)	=	Arrest Rate Per 100,000
Felony					
Crimes Against Persons		÷		=	
Crimes Against Property		÷		=	
Drug Violations		÷		=	
All Other		÷		=	
TOTAL FELONIES		÷		=	
Misdemeanor					
Assault and Battery		÷		=	
Property		÷		=	
Drug Violation		÷		=	
Sex Offense		÷		=	
Prostitution		÷		=	
Public Drunk		÷		=	
Drunk Driving		÷		=	
Other Auto		÷		=	
All Other		÷		=	
TOTAL MISDEMEANORS		÷		=	
Repeat for each year.					

Task 3: Compute Rate of Change in Arrest Rates

Compute the annual percent change in arrest rates per 100,000 population by the same offense classes used above.

Table 18-5. Example of Rate of Change in Arrest Rates

Offense Category	Arrest Rate		Change	
	1976	1977	Number	%
Felony				
Crimes Against Persons	299.2	318.2	19.0	6.3%
Crimes Against Property	505.2	552.6	47.4	9.4%
Drug Violations	238.2	188.9	−49.3	−20.7%
All Other	193.6	199.2	5.6	2.9%
TOTAL FELONIES	1,226.2	1,258.9	22.7	1.8%
Misdemeanor				
Assault and Battery	549.8	551.8	2.0	.4%
Property	568.9	593.3	24.4	4.3%
Drug Law Violation	737.1	683.0	−54.1	−7.3%
Sex Offense	251.2	281.0	29.8	11.9%
Prostitution	299.2	468.8	169.6	56.7%
Public Drunk	1,920.7	1,901.2	−19.5	−1.0%
Drunk Driving	1,580.9	1,685.4	104.5	6.6%
Other Auto	866.5	716.6	−149.9	−17.3%
Other Misdemeanors	470.9	475.9	5.0	1.1%
TOTAL MISDEMEANORS	7,244.2	7,356.9	112.7	1.6%

Table 18-6. Your Computation of Rate of Change in Arrest Rates

Offense Category	Arrest Rate		Change	
	—	10—	Number	%
Felony				
Crimes Against Persons				
Crimes Against Property				
Drug Violations				
All Other				
TOTAL FELONIES				
Misdemeanor				
Assault and Battery				
Property				
Drug Law Violation				
Sex Offenses				
Prostitution				
Public Drunk				
Drunk Driving				
Other Auto				
Other Misdemeanors				
TOTAL MISDEMEANORS				

Repeat the calculation for each year over the last ten years.

Task 4: Calculate Average Annual Changes in Arrest Rates and Analyze Results

Once you have calculated annual percent changes in rates for each offense category, calculate averages for the last ten years and the last five years. The example shows one offense category, felony crimes against persons.

Table 18-7. Example of Average Annual Change in Arrest Rates

Offense Category: Felony Crimes Against Persons

Period	Percent Change	Cumulative Total % Change
1973–74	1.2	1.2
1974–75	(1.5)	(0.3)
1975–76	3.8	3.5
1976–77	4.2	7.7
1977–78	(0.5)	7.2
1978–79	6.3	13.5
1979–80	(1.7)	11.8
1980–81	(1.3)	10.5
1981–82	0.3	10.8

Average annual change last 10 years (1973-82): 10.8 divided by 9 = 1.2%
Average annual change last 5 years (1976-82): 3.6 divided by 4 = 0.9%

Repeat the calculation shown above for each offense category. If your county's results are erratic or exhibit sudden changes over the past few years, try to determine the cause of these changes.

Table 18-8. Your Calculation of Average Annual Change in Arrest Rates

Offense Category

Period	Percent Change	Cumulative Total % Change
19___ to 19___		
19___ to 19___		
19___ to 19___		
19___ to 19___		
19___ to 19___		
19___ to 19___		
19___ to 19___		
19___ to 19___		
19___ to 19___		

Average annual change last 10 years ____ divided by 9 = ____%
Average annual change last 5 years ____ divided by 4 = ____%

Array the results of your calculation in a table like the following:

Table 18-9. Summary Table of Average Changes in Arrest Rates

Offense Category	Average Annual % Change Last 10 Years	Average Annual % Change Last 5 Years
Felonies		
Crimes Against Persons		
Crimes Against Property		
Drug Violations		
All Other		
TOTAL FELONIES		
Misdemeanors		
Assault and Battery		
Property		
Drug Law Violation		
Sex Offenses		
Prostitution		
Public Drunk		
Drunk Driving		
Other Auto		
All Other		
TOTAL MISDEMEANORS		

Analyze the contents of the table and identify differing growth rates among and within offense categories for both the total ten-year period and the most recent five years.

Task 5: Make Projection Assumptions

Review population forecasts and identify projected growth rates for the twenty-year planning period. Analyze trends in terms of absolute growth, age distribution of the population, and economic composition. Isolate those factors that are likely to affect criminal justice system volume.

Example of Assumptions

Population Growth. Data indicate that annual population growth in the county is projected to be about one percent for the next ten years, slowing to 0.5 percent for the remaining ten years of the planning period. In part, this reflects the political assumption that land use policies limiting growth to current urban areas will be maintained.

Age Distribution. Moderate aging in population, with limited growth in the crime-prone eighteen-to-thirty-year-old age group. Projections indicate that this group should grow at half the rate of the overall population.

Economic Composition. Projections suggest an increase in the lower income population resulting from immigration.

Summary Conclusion. Growth in lower income groups may cancel out the benefits of the age shift. Assume that recent trends (last five years) in arrest rate increases may be experienced over the planning period in some offense categories.

Your Assumptions

Population Growth.

Age Distribution.

Economic Composition.

Summary Conclusion.

Task 6: Convert Assumptions to Estimated Annual Arrest Rate Changes for Each Offense Category

Combine your analysis of future population trends with your analysis of arrest rate trends completed in Task 5. Make specific estimates of the impact of your assumptions in terms of their magnitude. Project changes in arrest rates by offense category over the planning period. Analyze potential changes on an offense-by-offense basis and select rates of change for arrest rates that could be expected to be maintained over the planning period. Use statistical techniques or intuition to make growth assumptions.

Table 18-10. Example of Assumed Changes in Arrest Rates

Offense Class	Annual Change in Rate Per 100,000		Planning Assumption	Projected Change in Arrest Rate
	5 Years	10 Years		
Felony Crimes Against Persons	1.2%	.9%	Shift in age distribution of population indicates accelerating growth unlikely to be maintained. Assume will still increase at faster rate than population but only at half the recent rate.	+0.6%
Drug Violations	−0.7	1.1	Recent decrease over last five years reflects decriminalization of some drug offenses. Impact largely felt, and decrease in rate unlikely to be maintained. Will grow with population.	no change
Misdemeanor Drunk Driving	1.9	.8	Enforcement emphasis last five years has accelerated growth rate. Public pressure suggests increase faster than population will be maintained.	+1.9%
(etc.)			(Complete assumptions for each offense on the list.)	

Table 18-11. Example of Overall List of Assumed Changes in Arrest Rates

Offense Category	Assumed Annual Change
Felony	
Crimes Against Persons	0.6%
Crimes Against Property	0.5%
Drug Violations	NC
All Other	NC
TOTAL FELONIES	
Misdemeanor	
Assault and Battery	0.6%
Property	1.0%
Drug Law Violation	NC
Sex Offense	NC
Prostitution	NC
Drunk Driving	0.8%
Other Auto	NC
Other Misdemeanors	0.5%
TOTAL MISDEMEANORS	

Table 18-12. Your Listing of Overall Assumed Changes in Arrest Rates

Offense Category	Assumed Annual Change
Felony	
Crimes Against Persons	
Crimes Against Property	
Drug Violations	
All Other	
TOTAL FELONIES	
Misdemeanor	
Assault and Battery	
Property	
Drug Law Violation	
Sex Offenses	
Prostitution	
Drunk Driving	
Other Auto	
All Other	
TOTAL MISDEMEANORS	

Task 7: Project Future Arrest Rates

Use your county's most recent twelve months of data to convert arrest rate growth into anticipated future arrest rates (Task 7.1) and annual rates of increase in arrest rates (Task 7.2). These factors will be used in Task 8 to project the arrest rates and volumes expected for the twenty-year planning period.

Task 7.1: Convert Arrest-Rate Change Assumptions into Projection Factors for Future Arrest Rates

Convert arrest-rate change assumptions to revised arrest rates for felonies and misdemeanors by using the last twelve months' arrest rate data calculated from available criminal justice profile reports in Step 2 to develop weighted average factors.

Table 18-13. Example of Revised Arrest Rates

Offense Category	Projected* Growth Rate From Task 6	×	Arrest Rate Last 12 Months	=	Revised Arrest Rate
Felony					
Crimes Against Persons	1.006	×	319.1	=	321.0
Crimes Against Property	1.005	×	560.6	=	563.4
Drug Violations	1.000	×	182.5	=	182.5
All Other	1.000	×	204.3	=	204.3
TOTAL FELONIES			1,266.5		1,271.2
Misdemeanor					
Assault and Battery	1.006	×	563.9	=	567.3
Property	1.010	×	590.1	=	596.0
Drug Law Violation	1.000	×	685.0	=	685.0
Sex Offense	1.000	×	283.4	=	283.4
Prostitution	1.000	×	470.1	=	470.1
Public Drunk	1.000	×	1,904.5	=	1,904.5
Drunk Driving	1.008	×	1,686.3	=	1,699.8
Other Auto	1.000	×	720.4	=	720.4
All Other	1.005	×	478.6	=	481.0
TOTAL MISDEMEANORS			7,382.3		7,407.5

*Add 1.0 to percent growth estimates for calculation purposes. Note that rates can also **decline,** in which case the factor would be less than 1.0.

Table 18-14. Your Computation of Revised Arrest Rates

Offense Category	Projected* Growth Rate From Task 6	×	Arrest Rate Last 12 Months	=	Revised Arrest Rate
Felony					
Crimes Against Persons		×		=	
Crimes Against Property		×		=	
Drug Violations		×		=	
All Other		×		=	
TOTAL FELONIES					
Misdemeanor					
Assault and Battery		×		=	
Property		×		=	
Drug Law Violation		×		=	
Sex Offense		×		=	
Prostitution		×		=	
Public Drunk		×		=	
Drunk Driving		×		=	
Other Auto		×		=	
All Other		×		=	
TOTAL MISDEMEANORS					

Task 7.2: Compute Annual Arrest-Rate Increase

Then compute the composite arrest-rate increase factors to use for projection purposes by subtracting the total rate for felonies and misdemeanors for the last twelve months from the revised arrest rate for felonies and misdemeanors. Divide the results by the felony arrest rate and the misdemeanor arrest rate for the last twelve months to calculate the annual arrest rate increases you will use to project future arrests.

Table 18-15. Example of Arrest-Rate Increase

Felony Arrest Annual Growth Rate:

Revised Arrest Rate	−	Arrest Rate Last 12 Months	=	Remainder	÷	Annual Arrest Rate Last 12 Months	=	Annual Change in Arrest Rate
1,271.2	−	1,266.5	=	4.7	÷	1,266.5	=	.37%

Misdemeanor Arrest Annual Growth Rate:

Revised Arrest Rate	−	Arrest Rate Last 12 Months	=	Remainder	÷	Annual Arrest Rate Last 12 Months	=	Annual Change in Arrest Rate
7,407.5	−	7,382.3	=	25.2	÷	7,382.3	=	.34%

Table 18-16. Your Computation of Arrest-Rate Increase

Felony Arrest Annual Growth Rate:

Revised Arrest Rate	−	Arrest Rate Last 12 Months	=	Remainder	÷	Annual Arrest Rate Last 12 Months	=	Annual Change in Arrest Rate

Misdemeanor Arrest Annual Growth Rate:

Revised Arrest Rate	−	Arrest Rate Last 12 Months	=	Remainder	÷	Annual Arrest Rate Last 12 Months	=	Annual Change in Arrest Rate

Task 8: Project Arrest Rates and Volumes

Project arrest volume for the twenty-year planning period by using the annual weighted average arrest rate increase to project felony and misdemeanor arrest rates. Use the felony and misdemeanor arrest rates for the last twelve months as the projection base and expand by year for ten years and then at five-year intervals for the twenty-year planning period.

Table 18-17. Example of Arrest Rate Projections

Factor and Operation	Felony Arrest Rate	Misdemeanor Arrest Rate
Last 12 Months' Base Rate	1,266.5	7,382.3
×	×	×
Annual Projected Change	1.004	1.002
=	=	=
1st Projection Year Arrest Rate	1,272	7,397
×	×	×
Annual Projected Change	1.004	1.002
=	=	=
2nd Projection Year Arrest Rate	1,277	7,411

(Continue calculation process for 20-year planning period.)

Table 18-18. Your Projection of Arrest Rates

Factor and Operation	Felony Arrest Rate	Misdemeanor Arrest Rate
Last 12 Months' Base Rate		
×	×	×
Annual Projected Change		
=	=	=
1st Projection Year Arrest Rate		
×	×	×
Annual Projected Change		
=	=	=
2nd Projection Year Arrest Rate		

(Continue for 20-year planning period.)

Convert the arrest rate projections into estimated arrest volume by multiplying the arrest rate calculated above by total county population projections (converted by dividing each year's population projection by 100,000 and multiplying the result times the projected felony and misdemeanor arrest rate for the year) to project total annual arrest volume. The examples that follow show calculations for projecting felony arrests. Use the same techniques to project felony **and** misdemeanor arrests.

Table 18-19. Example of Projected Felony Arrests

Year	Projected Population	÷	100,000	=	Factor	×	Arrest Rate	=	Projected Arrests
1st Year	256,182	÷	100,000	=	2.56	×	1,272	=	3,256
2nd Year	258,744	÷	100,000	=	2.59	×	1,277	=	3,307
3rd Year	261,331	÷	100,000	=	2.61	×	1,282	=	3,346
(etc.)									

Table 18-20. Your Projection of Felony Arrests

Year	Projected Population	÷	100,000	=	Factor	×	Arrest Rate	=	Projected Arrests
1st Year		÷	100,000	=		×		=	
2nd Year		÷	100,000	=		×		=	
3rd Year		÷	100,000	=		×		=	
4th Year		÷	100,000	=		×		=	
5th Year		÷	100,000	=		×		=	
6th Year		÷	100,000	=		×		=	
7th Year		÷	100,000	=		×		=	
8th Year		÷	100,000	=		×		=	
9th Year		÷	100,000	=		×		=	
10th Year		÷	100,000	=		×		=	
15th Year		÷	100,000	=		×		=	
20th Year		÷	100,000	=		×		=	

Task 9: Convert Projected Misdemeanor Arrest Volumes to Projected Misdemeanor Bookings

Convert projected misdemeanor arrest volumes into projected misdemeanor bookings for the twenty-year planning period. A two-stage analysis is required to accomplish this task. The first is to develop an indicator of the proportion of misdemeanor arrests that actually result in bookings at the jail. Second, projected misdemeanor arrests are adjusted by this factor to estimate future bookings. Once misdemeanor bookings are projected, they will be used in combination with projected lengths of stay to estimate the average daily presentenced population.

To accomplish Task 9, review the results of Step 3 (Chapter 16) and document the proportion of misdemeanor arrests cited and field-released by law enforcement agencies. If these data are unavailable from your local law enforcement agencies, an alternative way to develop estimates of field citation volume includes the following:

- Extract misdemeanor arrest data from available criminal justice statistics.
- For each year over the last five years, compare pretrial misdemeanor bookings at the jail to total reported misdemeanor arrests and calculate the difference (bookings should be lower than arrests).

- Then, for each year divide the result by total misdemeanor arrests. The calculated percentage will approximate misdemeanor prebooking releases.
- Finally, add up the results and develop an average for the period analyzed. Deduct these arrests from the total arrest volume projected in Task 8.

If the alternative method is used, considerable caution should be maintained because the criminal justice profiles may underreport arrests. This would lead to an erroneously high estimate of bookings. Therefore it is important to attempt to verify the data with local law enforcement agencies. The data should not be accepted unless they seem reasonable and consistent.

Results of Step 3 (Chapter 16) indicate that 14.8 percent of misdemeanor arrests are cited in the field. Subtract this factor from 1.00 (1.00 - .148 = .852) to calculate the percentage of misdemeanor arrests that are booked. Then multiply projected misdemeanor arrests by this factor to calculate misdemeanor bookings.

Table 18-21. Converting Misdemeanor Arrests to Bookings

Year	Total Projected Misdemeanor Arrests	×	Cite Release Adjustment Factor	=	Misdemeanor Bookings
1st Year	18,936	×	.852	=	16,133
2nd Year	19,194	×	.852	=	16,354
(etc.)					

Table 18-22. Your Projection of Misdemeanor Bookings

Year	Total Projected Misdemeanor Arrests	×	Cite Release Adjustment Factor	=	Misdemeanor Bookings
1st Year		×		=	
2nd Year		×		=	
3rd Year		×		=	
4th Year		×		=	
5th Year		×		=	
6th Year		×		=	
7th Year		×		=	
8th Year		×		=	
9th Year		×		=	
10th Year		×		=	
15th Year		×		=	
20th Year		×		=	

Task 10.1: Compute Current Average Length of Presentenced Stay by Offense

Compute current average length of presentenced stay for arrestees in each offense category. Use data from the snapshot jail profile (from Chapter 14) for this computation.

Table 18-23. Example of Average Length of Presentenced Stay by Offense

Offense Category	Average Length of Stay (days)
Felony	
Crimes Against Persons	18.1
Crimes Against Property	7.6
Drug Violations	9.4
All Other	8.3
TOTAL FELONIES	
Misdemeanor	
Assault and Battery	1.7
Property	1.8
Drug Law Violation	1.3
Sex Offense	4.8
Prostitution	1.2
Public Drunk	2.8
Drunk Driving	.5
Other Auto	.2
All Other	.8
TOTAL MISDEMEANORS	

Table 18-24. Your Computation of Average Length of Presentenced Stay by Offense

Offense Category	Average Length of Stay (days)
Felony	
Crimes Against Persons	
Crimes Against Property	
Drug Violations	
All Other	
TOTAL FELONIES	
Misdemeanor	
Assault and Battery	
Property	
Drug Law Violation	
Sex Offenses	
Prostitution	
Public Drunk	
Drunk Driving	
Other Auto	
All Other	
TOTAL MISDEMEANORS	

Task 10.2: Calculate "Weighted" Length of Presentenced Stay by Offense

Calculate the "weighted" length of presentenced stay (ALS) factor for each category of misdemeanor and felony offense. This is done by multiplying the average length of stay related to a given offense (from Task 10.1) by the past twelve months' volume of arrests for that offense.

Table 18-25. Example of Weighted Length of Presentenced Stay by Offense

Offense Category	Average Length of Stay	×	Last 12 Months Volume	=	Total Weighted Factor
Felony					
Crimes Against Persons	18.1	×	807	=	14,607
Crimes Against Property	7.6	×	1,418	=	10,777
Drug Violations	9.4	×	462	=	4,343
All Other	8.3	×	517	=	4,291
TOTAL FELONIES			3,204	=	34,018
Misdemeanor					
Assault and Battery	1.7	×	1,427	=	2,426
Property	1.8	×	1,493	=	2,687
Drug Law Violation	1.3	×	1,733	=	2,253
Sex Offense	4.8	×	717	=	3,442
Prostitution	1.2	×	1,189	=	1,427
Public Drunk	2.8	×	4,818	=	13,490
Drunk Driving	.5	×	4,266	=	2,133
Other Auto	.2	×	1,823	=	365
Other Misdemeanor	.8	×	1,211	=	969
TOTAL MISDEMEANORS			18,677		29,192

Table 18-26. Your Calculation of Weighted Length of Presentenced Stay by Offense

Offense Category	Average Length of Stay	×	Last 12 Months Volume	=	Total Weighted Factor
Felony					
Crimes Against Persons		×		=	
Crimes Against Property		×		=	
Drug Violations		×		=	
All Other		×		=	
TOTAL FELONIES				=	
Misdemeanor					
Assault and Battery		×		=	
Property		×		=	
Drug Law Violation		×		=	
Sex Offense		×		=	
Prostitution		×		=	
Public Drunk		×		=	
Drunk Driving		×		=	
Other Auto		×		=	
Other Misdemeanor		×		=	
TOTAL MISDEMEANORS		×		=	

Task 10.3: Calculate Consolidated Average Length of Presentenced Stay for Misdemeanants and Felons

For both misdemeanants and felons, divide the total weighted factor by the sum of the last twelve months' arrests to develop the consolidated average length of stay for these two major offense categories.

Table 18-27. Example of Consolidated Average Length of Stay

Felony Arrest Average Length of Stay

Total Weighting Factor	÷	Total Last 12 Months' Arrests	=	Weighted Average Length of Stay
34,018	÷	3,204	=	10.6 days

Misdemeanor Arrest Average Length of Stay

Total Weighting Factor	÷	Total Last 12 Months' Arrests	=	Weighted Average Length of Stay
29,192	÷	18,677	=	1.6 days

Table 18-28. Your Computation of Consolidated Average Length of Stay

Felony Arrest Average Length of Stay

Total Weighting Factor	÷	Total Last 12 Months' Arrests	=	Weighted Average Length of Stay
	÷		=	days

Misdemeanor Arrest Average Length of Stay

Total Weighting Factor	÷	Total Last 12 Months' Arrests	=	Weighted Average Length of Stay
	÷		=	days

Note that adjustments to average length of stay due to program or processing improvements (which can have considerable impact on the jail population) are taken into account in Step 6.
Projection Method Two (in Appendix H) builds part of this adjustment into its calculation of length of stay (Method Two, Task 8) and, if desired, a similar adjustment could be incorporated here.

Task 11: Project Average Daily Presentenced Population

Convert projected arrest volumes into average daily unsentenced population by multiplying the consolidated average length of stay calculated in Task 10.2 by projected and adjusted arrest volumes, and dividing the results for each year by 365.

Table 18-29.
Example of Average Daily Presentenced Population

Year		Projected Arrests	×	Avg. LOS	÷	365	=	ADP
1st Year	Misdemeanors	16,133	×	1.6	÷	365	=	71
	Felonies	1,272	×	10.6	÷	365	=	95
				1st Year Total Presentenced ADP			=	166
2nd Year	Misdemeanors	16,354	×	1.6	÷	365	=	72
	Felonies	3,307	×	10.6	÷	365	=	96
				2nd Year Total Presentenced ADP			=	168

(Continue for each year of the 20-year planning period.)

Table 18-30. Your Computation of Average Daily Presentenced Population

Year		Projected Arrests	×	Avg. LOS	÷	365	=	ADP
1st Year	Misdemeanors		×		÷	365	=	
	Felonies		×		÷	365	=	___
				1st Year Total ADP			=	
				1st Year Total Presentenced ADP			=	
2nd Year	Misdemeanors		×		÷	365	=	
	Felonies		×		÷	365	=	___
				2nd Year Total Presentenced ADP			=	

(Continue for each year of the 20-year planning period.)

Task 12: Project Sentenced Population

There are two approaches to estimating sentenced population for the planning period. Each is described and illustrated below.

Method 12.1: Base Sentenced Population Projection on Proportionate Relationship with Unsentenced Population. Review historical population data and document the percentages of sentenced and unsentenced inmates in the average daily population. If proportions are relatively constant, use them to extrapolate the projected unsentenced population to the total average daily population.

Method 12.2: Base Sentenced Population Projections on Average Length of Stay of Sentenced Inmates. This information comes from the jail profile and processing performance data (Chapter 14). Tasks required to complete this method follow.

Document the number of individuals sentenced for the last several years to county jail time (see 12.2a below).

Calculate the number of sentenced individuals as a percentage of felony and misdemeanor arrests (adjusted with citation releases removed) for the period analyzed (see 12.2a below).

Analyze the sentenced component of the jail population profile to calculate average sentence, using weighted average techniques described earlier (see 12.2b below).

Multiply the average sentence length by the number of sentences each year and divide by 365 to estimate average daily population for each year over the planning period (see 12.2c below).

Method 12.1: Base Sentenced Population Projection on Proportionate Relationship with Unsentenced Population

Table 18-31. Calculation of Percent of Population Unsentenced

Year	Average Daily Population Unsentenced	÷	Total ADP	=	Percent Unsentenced
1978	136	÷	211	=	64.4
1979	142	÷	214	=	66.3
1980	145	÷	220	=	65.9
1981	139	÷	221	=	62.9
1982	148	÷	215	=	68.8
TOTAL:					328.3

Then, divide the total percentage by 5 to develop 5-year average:

328.3 ÷ 5 = 65.7% Unsentenced.

Table 18-32. Your Computation of Percent of Population Unsentenced

Year	Average Daily Population Unsentenced	÷	Total ADP	=	Percent Unsentenced
5 Yrs. Ago		÷		=	
4 Yrs. Ago		÷		=	
3 Yrs. Ago		÷		=	
2 Yrs. Ago		÷		=	
1 Yr. Ago		÷		=	
TOTAL:					

Total _____ ÷ 5 = _____ % Unsentenced.

For each year of the projection period, divide projected unsentenced population by the percentage computed above to calculate total, projected average daily population.

$$\text{Total Projected Average Daily Population} = \frac{\text{Projected Unsentenced Population}}{\text{Percent Unsentenced Population}}$$

Table 18-33. Example of Projected Average Daily Population

Year	Projected Unsentenced ÷ % Unsentenced	=	Projected ADP
1st Year	166 ÷ 0.657	=	253
2nd Year	168 ÷ 0.657	=	256
(etc.)			

This example uses 67.5% unsentenced.

Table 18-34.
Your Projection of Average Daily Population

Year	Projected Unsentenced ÷ % Unsentenced	=	Projected ADP
1st Year	÷	=	
2nd Year	÷	=	
3rd Year	÷	=	
4th Year	÷	=	
5th Year	÷	=	
6th Year	÷	=	
7th Year	÷	=	
8th Year	÷	=	
9th Year	÷	=	
10th Year	÷	=	
15th Year	÷	=	
20th Year	÷	=	

Method 12.2: Base Sentenced Population Projections on Average Length of Stay of Sentenced Inmates

Use the jail profile completed in Step 1 (Chapter 14) to calculate average length of sentence **actually** served. Then, review criminal justice system data collected in Step 3 (Chapter 16) to document how many people were sentenced to local time over the last full calendar year. Calculate this number as a percent of total felony and misdemeanor arrests reported in your county and apply this percentage to projected arrests to calculate total sentenced population by year. Then, for each year, multiply by the average length of stay data and divide by 365 to calculate average sentenced daily population.

Subtask 12.2a: Estimate Proportion of Arrests Resulting in Local Sentences

$$\frac{\text{Last 12 Months' Felony and Misdemeanor Arrests}}{\text{Number Sentenced to Local Time, Last 12 Months}} = \text{Sentenced Population Factor}$$

Computation of Sentenced Population Factor

$$\frac{1,045}{19,458} = .054$$

Your Computation of Sentenced Population Factor

$$\frac{\quad}{\quad} =$$

Subtask 12.2b: Project Sentenced Population

Multiply the projected felony and misdemeanor arrests calculated in Task 9 to calculate projected sentenced people per year.

$$\text{Total Projected Felony and Misdemeanor Arrests} \times \text{Factor} = \text{Total Sentenced People}$$

Table 18-35. Example of Total Sentenced People

Projection Year	Total Projected Felony & Misdemeanor Arrests	×	Factor	=	Total Sentenced People
1st Year	18,936	×	.054	=	1,022
2nd Year	19,194	×	.054	=	1,036

(Continue calculation through the 20-year planning period.)

Table 18-36. Your Computation of Total Sentenced People

Projection Year	Total Projected Felony & Misdemeanor Arrests	×	Factor	=	Total Sentenced People
1st Year		×		=	
2nd Year		×		=	
3rd Year		×		=	
4th Year		×		=	
5th Year		×		=	
6th Year		×		=	
7th Year		×		=	
8th Year		×		=	
9th Year		×		=	
10th Year		×		=	
15th Year		×		=	
20th Year		×		=	

Subtask 12.2c: Calculate Projected Average Daily Sentenced Population

Multiply the total sentenced population calculated above by average length of sentenced stay and divide by 365 for each year over the planning period to calculate projected average daily sentenced population.

$$\text{Total Sentenced Population} \times \text{Average Length of Stay} \div 365 = \text{Average Daily Sentenced Population}$$

Table 18-37. Computation of Average Daily Sentenced Population

Projection Year	Total Sentenced Population	×	Average Length of Stay	÷	365	=	Avg. Daily Sentenced Population
1st Year	1,022	×	30.4	÷	365	=	85
2nd Year	1,036	×	30.4	÷	365	=	86

(Continue calculation through the 20-year planning period.)

Table 18-38. Your Computation of Average Daily Sentenced Population

Projection Year	Total Sentenced Population	×	Average Length of Stay	÷	365	=	Avg. Daily Sentenced Population
1st Year		×		÷	365	=	
2nd Year		×		÷	365	=	
3rd Year		×		÷	365	=	
4th Year		×		÷	365	=	
5th Year		×		÷	365	=	
6th Year		×		÷	365	=	
7th Year		×		÷	365	=	
8th Year		×		÷	365	=	
9th Year		×		÷	365	=	
10th Year		×		÷	365	=	
15th Year		×		÷	365	=	
20th Year		×		÷	365	=	

Task 13: Combine Unsentenced and Sentenced Projections

This step involves combining unsentenced and sentenced population projections.

Table 18-39. Projecting Total Average Daily Population

Projection Year	Projected Unsentenced Population (From Task 11)	+	Projected Sentenced Population (From Task 12.2c)	=	Total Projected Avg. Daily Population
1st Year	166	+	85	=	251
2nd Year	168	+	86	=	254

(Continue calculations through the 20-year planning period.)

Table 18-40. Your Projection of Total Average Daily Population

Projection Year	Projected Unsentenced Population (From Task 11)	+	Projected Sentenced Population (From Task 12.2c)	=	Total Projected Avg. Daily Population
1st Year		+		=	
2nd Year		+		=	
3rd Year		+		=	
4th Year		+		=	
5th Year		+		=	
6th Year		+		=	
7th Year		+		=	
8th Year		+		=	
9th Year		+		=	
10th Year		+		=	
15th Year		+		=	
20th Year		+		=	

Task 14: Calculate Factor for Adjusting Projections to Accommodate Periodic Peaks

This step involves adjusting the projections to reflect periodic peaks above average daily population.

Review daily population data for the last six to twelve months. Compute average high or peak population by noting high or peak population each month and dividing by 12. To calculate the adjustment factor, compare to the average daily population for the same period and divide by the number of months analyzed.

Table 18-41.
Example of Peak Population Factor

Table 18-42.
Your Computation of Peak Population Factor

Month	ADP	Monthly High
Dec.	243	258
Jan.	241	260
Feb.	240	258
Mar.	236	249
Apr.	242	258
May	240	253
TOTAL:	1,442	1,536
AVERAGE:	240	256

Then, compute the peak adjustment factor as follows:

Six-month average high population	256
Less average daily population	−240
Difference	16

$$\frac{\text{Difference (16)}}{\text{Average Daily Population (240)}} = \text{Peak Adjustment Factor (.067)}$$

Month	ADP	Monthly High
One		
Two		
Three		
Four		
Five		
Six		
TOTAL:		
AVERAGE:		

Compute the peak adjustment factor:

Six-month average high population	( )
Less average daily population	−( )
Difference =	( )

$$\frac{\text{Difference ( )}}{\text{Average Daily Population ( )}} = \text{Peak Adjustment Factor (.)}$$

Task 15: Adjust Population Projections to Account for Peak Periods

Use the adjustment factor calculated in Task 14 to increase the population projections developed in Task 13. The resulting figure represents future capacity needs including population fluctuations.

Table 18-43. Computation of Capacity Needs

Projection Year		Unsentenced				Sentenced			
	ADP	×	Peak Factor	=	Total Unsent.	ADP	×	Peak Factor	=	Total Sent.	Total Peak Pop.
1st Yr.	166	×	1.067	=	177	85	×	1.067	=	91	268
2nd Yr.	168	×	1.067	=	179	86	×	1.067	=	92	271

(Continue calculations through the 20-year planning period.)

Table 18-44. Your Computation of Capacity Needs

Projection Year	Unsentenced				Sentenced				Total Peak Pop.
	ADP	×	Peak Factor	=	Total Unsent.	ADP	×	Peak Factor	=	Total Sent.	
1st Year		×		=			×		=		
2nd Year		×		=			×		=		
3rd Year		×		=			×		=		
4th Year		×		=			×		=		
5th Year		×		=			×		=		
6th Year		×		=			×		=		
7th Year		×		=			×		=		
8th Year		×		=			×		=		
9th Year		×		=			×		=		
10th Year		×		=			×		=		
15th Year		×		=			×		=		
20th Year		×		=			×		=		

Update Projections Periodically

Regardless of the projection method you used, the validity of your projections rests upon the validity of the data and assumptions developed in making the projections. As time passes, conditions will change and new data will be available to test your projections against. Therefore it is critical to the continued success of your planning effort that you periodically (at least annually) review projections and assess the extent to which changing local conditions require adjustment of your assumptions. If your projections need to be modified to reflect changing conditions, adjust your assumptions and make the related changes in your projections.

Summary and Conclusion

Completion of Step 5 provides projections of capacity requirements for the next twenty years. However, remember that these projections reflect **existing release, court processing, and sentencing practices.** They do not yet take into account the potential reduction in bed space needs that can be realized through the use of alternative programs or processing improvements.

The next step in the analysis will be to convert these general projections into specific facility requirements and to examine the potential moderating influence of alternative programs and processing improvements. Step 6 carries the projection exercise to its conclusion.

19. Step 6: Forecast Capacity and Program Needs

Introduction

Three major tasks are necessary to complete the projections of needed capacity and programs.

- Convert the general population projections completed at the end of Step 5 (Chapter 18) into **bed space needs by security level.**
- Calculate the potential impact of alternative programs and court processing improvements on the **reduction of projected jail capacity needs.**
- Assess the impact of alternative programs and processing improvements on **costs of future jail construction and operations.**

The sections that follow demonstrate the tasks required to develop information in each of these areas.

Convert Population Projections to Bed Space Needs by Security Level

Completion of Step 5 provides a forecast of the general detention population for the twenty-year planning period. Before costs can be calculated or facilities planned, these general projections need to be broken down by security levels so that facility types as well as total bed space needs can be specified. This section provides a task-by-task procedure for the conversion. The population will be divided into the following components:

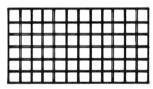
High Security Facility

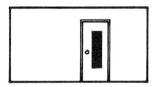
Lower Security Facility

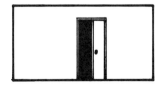
Work Furlough Facility

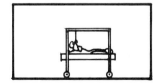
Medical Facility

- The proportion of the sentenced and unsentenced population requiring housing in a high security facility.
- The proportion of the sentenced population that can be housed in a lower security facility.

- The proportion of the sentenced population that can be housed in a work furlough facility.
- The proportion of the population with special service needs that can be housed in a correctional medical facility, mental health facility, or the like if such were available.

While this breakdown of the population will allow more accurate cost and facility projections, it will be necessary to study this further as detailed facility planning progresses. At that point, questions of living unit size and staffing will be considered and flexibility for classification taken into account.

Refining general facility population forecasts into more detailed projections of likely bed space needs by security level will require you to accomplish three main tasks. Each task, including an illustrative example and forms you may use to accomplish your analysis, is described in the sections that follow. Complete the task sequence separately for male and female inmates.

Task 1: Document Requirements for Various Security Levels

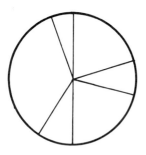

Analyze the results of the jail profile to develop estimates of the numbers of each type of bed required to meet current and projected needs. Use the same techniques as those in Step 1 (Chapter 14) to define the criteria to determine which sentenced and unsentenced inmates will require varying levels of security. These security levels are generalized here as high security, lower security, work furlough, and special service facilities. Selection criteria for the levels could include:

- **Unsentenced, high security:** Violent felony offense, behavior problems, escape history, gang member, enemies.
- **Unsentenced, lower security:** Nonviolent felony or misdemeanor, no behavior problems, no escape history, no characteristics requiring segregation (not a gang member, no enemies, and so forth).
- **Sentenced, high security:** Any behavior problems or problems requiring segregation.
- **Sentenced, lower security:** No behavior problems or problems requiring segregation.
- **Work furlough:** People on work furlough, or people who could qualify for housing in a work furlough facility if one were available.
- **Special service needs:** Mental health problems—inmates requiring individual housing, and/or those who could function in group housing with service/ treatment. Medical problems—inmates requiring housing in a medical unit within a detention facility.

A further refinement that your county may wish to consider is the separate classification of short-stay inmates. For individuals who are released in less than twenty-four hours, a waiting room may be more appropriate (and less expensive) than a cell. Some jurisdictions also provide a separate intake unit for initial screening and classification. These approaches can be built into the following calculations.

Use your county's selection criteria and the table-producing techniques described in Step 1 (Chapter 14) to analyze the jail population profile. Produce a table comparable to Table 19-1.

Table 19-1. Security Level by Sentence Status

Security Level	Unsentenced	Sentenced	Total
High	312	87	399
Lower	149	291	440
Work Furlough	0	86	86
Medical	8	9	17
Mental Health	7	7	14
TOTAL	476	480	956

Table 19-2. Your List of Security Level by Sentence Status

Security Level	Unsentenced	Sentenced	Total
High			
Lower			
Work Furlough			
Medical			
Mental Health			
TOTAL			

Use the data contained in the table to calculate the percent of the total population that each component represents. Transfer your calculations to a table like Table 19-3.

Table 19-3. Percent of Population by Housing Need

Component	Number	% of Jail Profile
Meet Unsentenced High Security Criteria	312	32.6%
Meet Unsentenced Lower Security Criteria	149	15.6
Meet Sentenced High Security Criteria	87	9.1
Meet Sentenced Lower Security Criteria	291	30.4
Meet Sentenced Work Furlough Criteria	86	9.0
Mental Health Problem—Segregation Required	17	1.8
Medical Problem—Medical Housing Required	14	1.5
JAIL PROFILE TOTAL	956	100.0

Table 19-4. Your Listing of Percent of Population by Housing Need

Component	Number	% of Jail Profile
Meet Unsentenced High Security Criteria		
Meet Unsentenced Lower Security Criteria		
Meet Sentenced High Security Criteria		
Meet Sentenced Lower Security Criteria		
Meet Sentenced Work Furlough Criteria		
Mental Health Problem—Segregation Required		
Medical Problem—Medical Housing Required		
JAIL PROFILE TOTAL		

Task 2: Calculate Type of Beds Required over the Planning Period

Apply the percentages developed above to projections of the peak inmate population found in Step 5 (Chapter 18, Task 14) to refine estimates of bed needs by facility type over the planning period. For illustrative purposes, only two years are shown in the example.

Table 19-5. Number of Beds Needed by Bed Type

| Bed Type | | 1984 | | 1985 | |
Description	% of Jail Profile	Projected Average Peak Population	Bed Space Needs	Projected Average Peak Population	Bed Space Needs
High Security, Unsentenced	32.6	1,039	339	1,119	365
High Security, Sentenced	9.1	1,039	94	1,119	102
Lower Security, Unsentenced	15.6	1,039	162	1,119	175
Lower Security, Sentenced	30.4	1,039	316	1,119	339
Work Furlough	9.0	1,039	93	1,119	101
Medical	1.8	1,039	19	1,119	20
Mental Health	1.5	1,039	16	1,119	17
TOTAL			1,039		1,119

Table 19-6. Your Computation of Number of Beds Needed by Bed Type

| Bed Type | | 1st Year | | 2nd Year | |
Description	% of Jail Profile	Projected Average Peak Population	Bed Space Needs	Projected Average Peak Population	Bed Space Needs
High Security, Unsentenced					
High Security, Sentenced					
Lower Security, Unsentenced					
Lower Security, Sentenced					
Work Furlough					
Medical					
Mental Health					
TOTAL					

Calculate bed space needs for each year of the planning period.

Task 3: Identify Bed Space Deficiencies over the Planning Period

Develop a chart that compares projected facility needs with available resources. When displaying the capacity of existing facilities, use rated capacities adjusted to reflect any potential reduction in capacity that might result from remodeling or changes in use.

Table 19-7. Example of Bed Space Deficiency Computation

Facility Type	1984	1985	1986	1987	1988	(etc.)
High Security						
Available	450	450	450	450	450	
Required	433	467	504	543	584	
Excess (Deficiency)	17	(17)	(54)	(93)	(134)	
Lower Security						
Available	575	575	575	575	575	
Required	478	514	553	596	643	
Excess (Deficiency)	97	61	22	(21)	(68)	
Work Furlough						
Available	100	100	100	100	100	
Required	93	101	110	121	132	
Excess (Deficiency)	7	(1)	(10)	(21)	(32)	
Mental Health Beds						
Available	5	5	5	5	5	
Required	16	17	19	20	21	
Excess (Deficiency)	(11)	(12)	(14)	(15)	(16)	
Medical Beds						
Available	15	15	15	15	15	
Required	19	20	22	23	24	
Excess (Deficiency)	(4)	(5)	(7)	(8)	(9)	

Table 19-8. Your Computation of Bed Space Deficiencies

Facility Type	1st Yr.	2nd Yr.	3rd Yr.	4th Yr.	5th Yr.	(etc.)
High Security						
Available						
Required						
Excess (Deficiency)						
Lower Security						
Available						
Required						
Excess (Deficiency)						
Work Furlough						
Available						
Required						
Excess (Deficiency)						
Mental Health Beds						
Available						
Required						
Excess (Deficiency)						
Medical Beds						
Available						
Required						
Excess (Deficiency)						

Upon completion of Task 3, you will have detailed information indicating facility deficiencies by year and by type of facility for the twenty-year period. The results will indicate the county's facility expansion requirements if existing incarceration and system processing strategies are followed.

Assess the Impact of Alternative Programs and Processing Improvements on Projected Capacity Requirements

Projections developed to this point are still based on the assumption that no changes will be made in existing county pretrial release policies, court processing performance, or use of sentencing alternatives. These projections display facility requirements if your county continues "business as usual." For policy makers and the advisory committee to make informed planning decisions, the potential impacts of alternative programs and processes need to be clearly displayed.

The following sections demonstrate how to assess the potential impact of program adjustments on moderating future facility requirements. For illustrative purposes, two potential program adjustments are shown: expansion of pretrial release, and acceleration of court processing of in-custody cases. The discussion includes general instructions on how to complete each task and an example of its application. While these examples result in shorter lengths of stay—and therefore reductions in required capacity—other changes which could result in **longer** stays for sentenced or unsentenced inmates should also be taken into account.

Task 1: Estimate the Impact of Program Alternatives on Forecasted Space Needs

General Instructions

As the first step, array population projections and facility requirements for the twenty-year planning period. Display population projections and facility requirements by type of facility.

Review the results of your analysis in Chapter 17, and select those program alternatives and processing improvements that analysis has indicated may have major impacts on detention population levels and future facility requirements. Apply the percentage reductions in population computed in Step 4 to the detention system population projections developed in Step 5. Follow the analytical sequence outlined in the following pages.

When applying the potential population reduction impact of various alternative programs, certain cautions need to be observed. First, be sure that population reductions are applied to the proper type of detention population. For example, if previous analysis has suggested that expansion of pretrial release programs could substantially reduce the inmate populations, reduce **unsentenced** populations only.

Second, if you are estimating the impact of more than one alternative program, do not double count potential impacts of each one. For example, if your initial program involves extending own recognizance releases to low-risk felons held in pretrial custody, compute this population reduction impact first. Then, if you are considering the potential impact of other programs that affect pretrial population, apply these percentage reductions to the **reduced population** computed after the potential impact of the expanded pretrial service program has been considered.

No matter what mix of programs you are considering, examine them in priority order and isolate specific components of the jail population that are likely to be affected by each one. Eliminate overlaps as you compute potential population reductions.

Task 1.1: Array Population Projections

Record the population projections from Task 1 as divided into facility types noted earlier in this chapter.

Table 19-9. Example of Projected Unsentenced Population

Projected Unsentenced Population	1981	1982	1983	(etc.)
High Security	339	365	393	
Lower Security	162	175	187	
TOTAL PROJECTED UNSENTENCED POPULATION	501	540	580	

Table 19-10. Your Projection of Unsentenced Population

Projected Unsentenced Population	1984	1985	1986	(etc.)
High Security				
Lower Security				
TOTAL PROJECTED UNSENTENCED POPULATION				

Task 1.2: Develop Factors for Assessing Impact of Program and Processing Adjustments on Population Projections Statement of Program Improvement Changes

From the Step 4 analysis (Chapter 17), you have determined that expansion of the pretrial release program to include unsentenced low-risk felony defendants could reduce the unsentenced population by 15.2 percent. The impact factor for calculation purposes will be 0.152.

In addition, increasing prosecution and defense services could accelerate disposition of in-custody defendants whose cases are dealt with in superior court. Accelerated disposition was estimated to have the potential of reducing unsentenced population by 5.4 percent. The impact factor for calculation purposes will be 0.054.

Table 19-11. Impact of Program Adjustments

Program Adjustment	Population Reduction Impact		
	Component Affected	Reduction Impact	Calculation Factor
1. Modify pretrial release program	Unsentenced	5.2%	0.152
2. Accelerate disposition of in-custody defendants	Unsentenced	5.4%	0.054

Table 19-12. Your Computation of Impact of Program Adjustments

Program Adjustment	Population Reduction Impact		
	Component Affected	Reduction Impact	Calculation Factor
1.			
2.			
(etc.)			

Task 1.3: Apply Impact Factors to Population and Space Projections

Apply the estimates developed in Task 1.2 to the population and space projections to determine their impact on capacity needs. Do not double count reductions when more than one program is being considered.

For example, if pretrial release program activities are expanded, some of the inmates whose lengths of stays might be reduced if court processing were accelerated would be released on their own recognizance. To apply both programs' population reduction potential to the total unsentenced population would overstate their impact. As a result, consider the impact of alternatives you are considering and apply them sequentially.

Table 19-13. Reduction of Population Projections

	1984	1985	1986	(etc.)
Projected Unsentenced Population	501	540	580	
(times)	×	×	×	
Population Reduction Factor for Expanding Pretrial Release	.152	.152	.152	_____
(equals)				
Resulting Reduction	76	82	88	
Revised Population Projection	425	458	492	
(times)	×	×	×	
Population Reduction Factor for Accelerated Disposition	.054	.054	.054	_____
(equals)				
Resulting Reduction	23	25	27	
Net Population	402	433	465	

Table 19-14. Your Reduction of Population Projections

	1st Yr.	2nd Yr.	3rd Yr.	(etc.)
Projected Unsentenced Population				
(times)	×	×	×	
Population Reduction Factor for Expanding Pretrial Release	_____	_____	_____	_____
(equals)				
Resulting Reduction				
Revised Population Projection				
(times)	×	×	×	
Population Reduction Factor for Accelerated Disposition	_____	_____	_____	_____
(equals)				
Resulting Reduction				
Net Population				

Task 1.4: Divide Total Adjusted Unsentenced Population Among Facility Types

After program impact has been calculated, convert the total adjusted population to population by security type. Two steps will be required:

• Review projections developed in Step 5 (Chapter 18) and calculate the proportion of the relevant population component by security level before program impact has been considered.

• Use the resulting percentages to divide your adjusted population by security level. In dividing the adjusted population, be aware that certain reductions may affect one security level more or less than the other. While the division is shown as proportional here, you may wish to weight the reductions toward higher or lower security beds.

Table 19-15. Example of Division of Unsentenced Population

Population Component	1st Year Projection from Step 5	Percentage
High Security, Unsentenced	339	67.7
Lower Security, Unsentenced	162	32.3
TOTAL	501	100.0

Table 19-16. Your Division of Unsentenced Population

Population Component	1st Year Projection from Step 5	Percentage
High Security, Unsentenced		
Lower Security, Unsentenced		
TOTAL		

Then, apply these percentages to the adjusted population calculated in Table 19-14 above for each year over the planning period.

Table 19.17. Example of Projection Considering Program Impact

Population Component	Allocation %	1984 Projected Total	Division by Security Level	1985 Projected Total	Division by Security Level	etc.
High Security, Unsentenced	.677	402	272	433	293	
Lower Security, Unsentenced	.323	402	130	433	140	

Table 19.18. Your Computation of Projection Considering Program Impact

Population Component	Allocation %	1984 Projected Total	Division by Security Level	1985 Projected Total	Division by Security Level	etc.

Task 2: Compare Projected Bed Space Needs Under Current Incarceration Strategies to Requirements When Program Adjustments Are Considered

General Instructions

Array future facility needs in terms of total beds required by facility type compared to total beds available by facility type **without consideration of the impact of potential programs.** Show bed space deficiencies by year over the planning period under this option. Then, develop a similar projection of bed space requirements by facility type **incorporating the bed space reduction potential of alternative programs** and processing improvements.

Once you have arrayed both options, compare bed space requirements.

Clearly identify bed space differentials by year and by facility type.

Table 19-19. Comparison of Facility Needs with and without Adjustments

Projected Needs **without** Program Adjustments

Facility Type	1984	1985	1986	1987	1988	(etc.)
High Security Beds						
Available	450	450	450	450	450	
Required	433	467	504	543	584	
Excess (Deficiency)	17	(17)	(54)	(93)	(134)	
Lower Security Beds						
Available	575	575	575	575	575	
Required	478	514	553	596	643	
Excess (Deficiency)	97	61	22	(21)	(68)	
Work Furlough Beds						
Available	100	100	100	100	100	
Required	93	101	110	121	133	
Excess (Deficiency)	7	(1)	(10)	(21)	(33)	

Projected Needs **with** Program Adjustments

Facility Type	1984	1985	1986	1987	1988	(etc.)
High Security Beds						
Available	450	450	450	450	450	
Required	366	395	425	457	492	
Excess (Deficiency)	84	55	25	(7)	(42)	
Lower Security Beds						
Available	575	575	575	575	575	
Required	446	477	511	546	585	
Excess (Deficiency)	129	98	64	29	(10)	
Work Furlough Beds						
Available	100	100	100	100	100	
Required	93	101	110	121	133	
Excess (Deficiency)	7	(1)	(10)	(21)	(33)	

Table 19-20. Your Comparison of Facility Needs with and without Adjustments

Projected Needs **without** Program Adjustments

Facility Type	1st Year	2nd Year	3rd Year	4th Year	5th Year	(etc.)
High Security Beds						
Available						
Required						
Excess (Deficiency)						
Lower Security Beds						
Available						
Required						
Excess (Deficiency)						
Work Furlough Beds						
Available						
Required						
Excess (Deficiency)						

Projected Needs **with** Program Adjustments

Facility Type	1st Year	2nd Year	3rd Year	4th Year	5th Year	(etc.)
High Security Beds						
Available						
Required						
Excess (Deficiency)						
Lower Security Beds						
Available						
Required						
Excess (Deficiency)						
Work Furlough Beds						
Available						
Required						
Excess (Deficiency)						

Task 3: Analyze the Cost Impact of Alternative Strategies

Once bed space differentials have been identified, develop cost estimates for both potential courses of action. Assess the incremental cost to your county of pursuing existing incarceration strategies. This involves developing estimates for construction to expand facilities for projected population requirements, incremental prisoner support costs related to increased populations, and costs related to expansion of custodial staff to deal with more inmates. A number of relevant factors need to be considered in your cost analysis.

Staffing. Since staffing is critical to the operation and cost of a jail, it is important to estimate the impact of changes in programs, capacity, and operations on staff requirements. For a new or renovated facility, all three of these factors can be expected to change in relation to current staffing levels—often dramatically. Chapter 32 and Appendix J provide methods for estimating future staffing requirements under various facility population assumptions.

In using the staffing estimation techniques, you will have to make a number of assumptions. An important one concerns estimating the number of continuously staffed posts for custody and control functions. The number needed depends on philosophy (desired level of staff-inmate contact), operations, design and economics. The most direct reflection of this complex decision is the number of beds per staff station. This may range from a low of twelve or eighteen to a high of around one hundred. Clearly, the cost and level of services provided at these extremes are very different. Your county must begin to determine how it will approach staffing in order to make an initial estimate that has some degree of validity.

Construction Costs. Estimate construction costs for facility expansion. You may use the present day costs shown in this chapter's examples, or develop more detail using the techniques explained in Chapter 26. In any case, figures shown in this book must be adjusted for inflation and conditions in your area.

Operating Costs. Similarly, estimate direct inmate support costs including staffing costs associated with population growth in detention facilities.

Program Cost Comparison. Portray the costs to the county of implementing program adjustments and processing improvements over the same twenty-year planning period.

Total the twenty-year costs under both alternatives and compare them. In addition, discuss other potential subjective advantages or disadvantages related to implementing alternative programs and operating adjustments.

The following example compares construction of 235 beds with construction of 185 beds along with implementation of certain programs. The beds that are saved include both high and lower security facilities and result in savings of about a million dollars per year. Certain assumptions are made here, but you will have to make your own assumptions or calculations concerning staffing and costs (using the chapters cited above). In this example, average staff costs are taken at $25,000 per year. It is assumed that one staff post will be required for each thirty inmates (or fraction thereof) and that each post will need five persons to staff it.

For illustrative purposes, the analysis shown covers only a five-year period. As you prepare your plan, expand comparative cost analysis to the full twenty-year planning period.

Table 19-21. Example of Cost Differential Calculations

Costs Associated with Existing Strategies (235 beds)

Cost Element	Average Per Year	Total for Five-Year Period
Construct 134 High Security Beds @ $60,000/bed	—	$ 8,040,000
Construct 68 Lower Security Beds @ $40,000/bed	—	2,720,000
Construct 33 Work Furlough Beds @ $25,000/bed	—	825,000
Inmate Care Costs @ $5.75/day (x 365 days/yr)	$477,000	2,385,000
Plant Maintenance and Utility Costs @ $9.50/day (x 365 days)	$815,000	4,075,000
Security staff costs (for 8 posts or 40 staff)	$1,000,000	5,000,000
TOTAL		$23,045,000

Costs if Alternative Strategies Are Implemented (180 beds)

Cost Element	Average Per Year	Total for Five-Year Period
Construct 97 High Security Beds @ $60,000/bed	—	$ 5,820,000
Construct 50 Lower Security Beds @ $40,000/bed	—	2,000,000
Construct 33 Work Furlough Beds @ $25,000/bed	—	825,000
Inmate Care Costs @ $5.75/day (x 365 days/yr)	$377,775	1,888,875
Plant Maintenance and Utility Costs @ $9.50/day (x 365 days)	$624,150	3,120,750
Security staff costs (for 6 posts or 30 staff)	$750,000	3,750,000
Expand pretrial interview staff	$38,300	191,500
Expand District Attorney and Public Defender Staff	$88,500	442,500
TOTAL		$18,038,625

Table 19-22. Your Computation of Cost Differentials

Costs Associated with Existing Strategies (____ beds)

Cost Element	Average Per Year	Total for Five-Year Period
Construct (____) High Security Beds @ $(____)/bed	—	
Construct (____) Lower Security Beds @ $(____)/bed	—	
Construct (____) Work Furlough Beds @ $(____)/bed	—	
Inmate Care Costs @ $(____)/day (x 365 days/yr)		
Plant Maintenance and Utility Costs @ $(____)/day (x 365 days)		
Security staff costs (for (____) posts or (____) staff)		
TOTAL		

Costs if Alternative Strategies Are Implemented (____ beds)

Cost Element	Average Per Year	Total for Five-Year Period
Construct (____) High Security Beds @ $(____)/bed	—	
Construct (____) Lower Security Beds @ $(____)/bed	—	
Construct (____) Work Furlough Beds @ $(____)/bed	—	
Inmate Care Costs @ $(____)/day (x 365 days/yr)		
Plant Maintenance and Utility Costs @ $(____)/day (x 365 days)		
Security staff costs (for (____) posts or (____) staff)		
Expand program staff		
Expand District Attorney and Public Defender Staff		
TOTAL		

Summary and Conclusion

By following the techniques outlined in this chapter, you will have quantified the cost impact of following existing incarceration strategies in future years, and will as well have quantified the potential of reducing future capital and operations costs by implementing alternative programs and/or system operating improvements.

Once these differentials have been quantified, you should review them in detail with the advisory committee in order to develop recommendations covering program and facility strategies for your county's decision makers.

The next, and final, chapter in Part 3 outlines the content, organization, and presentation of the results of your entire analysis of corrections needs.

20. Step 7: Document Needs in a Final Report

Introduction

The product of Part 3 is a report to the advisory committee and policy makers regarding the choices that must be made before county detention facility plans can be finalized. The report identifies directions for the corrections system for years to come. Thus it needs the review and approval of the corrections system, the advisory committee, and the board of commissioners.

In organizing this report, lead readers through the six major steps that you took to determine facility needs and the impact of alternative programs. To make your report easier to understand, include graphic or tabular representations of major trends, needs, and options. You may wish to organize the chapters to answer a series of questions as suggested in the following topical outline.

Contents of the Report

Executive Summary

Start the report with an executive summary focusing on major findings and policy decisions. Include the "mission statement" developed by the advisory committee (see chapter 10) and one or two paragraphs on each of the six main steps.

County Corrections Needs Assessment Final Report

Chapter 1: How Have County Population and the Corrections System Been Changing?

In the first chapter of the report, describe the results of your analysis of county and corrections system trends and characteristics that have influenced planning assumptions about future change. Trace these trends over the preceding ten years. Include the following information:

- General county population growth over the past ten years.
- Observed changes in population composition and trends that could relate to increases or decreases in criminal activity.
- Major trends in felony and misdemeanor arrests over the past ten years. Show changes in the pattern of offenses that might affect projections of either criminal activity or detention facility requirements.
- Trends in average daily population in each county detention facility and overall.
- Indicators of shifts in the composition of the inmate population. These could include comparisons of sentenced to unsentenced inmates as propor-

tions of the total inmate population, comparative increases in male or female inmates, changes in length of stay, and the like.

Chapter 2: Who Is Incarcerated?

Provide a detailed description of individuals who are currently incarcerated in the county. Draw on the results of the jail profile to portray these characteristics. Include the following:

- Offense characteristics, sentence status, length of stay, use of release mechanisms, and the like.
- A perspective on inmates' criminal sophistication in terms of current charges as well as previous conviction and incarceration history.
- Special service needs of the inmates, as drawn from both the jail profile and the inmate survey.

In describing the inmate population, focus on those elements that are directly related to the potential alternative programs and processing improvements that you are going to ask policy makers and the advisory committee to consider.

Chapter 3: How Extensively Are Programs Used to Limit Jail Population?

Review county performance in using programs that can reduce detention facility requirements. At a minimum, discuss the extent to which misdemeanor citation policies have been implemented on a uniform basis in the county and the specific steps taken to implement pretrial release programs including bail, reduced percentage bail, release on own recognizance, supervised release, and diversion.

Trace the performance of pretrial release programs in the recent past. Show the extent to which county policies have expanded or restricted in response to changes in number of arrests or types of offense.

Provide indicators of current performance in court processing and sentencing alternatives in light of the analysis completed in Step 4 (Chapter 17).

Conclude this chapter with a review of findings about overall county response to growth in both population and criminal activity. Answer such questions as these:

- Have pretrial release programs expanded at a pace consistent with, greater than, or less than changes in arrests and bookings?
- As volume has increased, have court processes kept pace with demand for timely adjudication of individuals in custody?
- As criminal justice system volume has grown, have sentencing alternatives been available to provide adequate alternatives to incarceration for selected convicted offenders?

Chapter 4: If the County Continues Current Policies, How Can We Expect the Inmate Population to Grow?

Present the inmate population projections that were based on the assumption that existing incarceration strategies would continue. Provide information on the following:

- Major assumptions underlying the projections
- Methodology employed in the projections
- Projected inmate populations during the planning period

Convert those population projections into specific requirements by type of facility, compare them to available facility resources, and note deficiencies over the planning period.

Chapter 5: How Will the Inmate Population Grow if the County Changes Certain Practices?

Portray in some detail the potential impact of alternative programs and processing improvements on the inmate population expansion faced by the county. Include the following:

- The potential impact of each alternative program on facility requirements, operating costs, and capital improvement cost-saving opportunities.
- The costs, both quantitative and subjective, related to instituting each potential program or operating improvement.

In presenting your analysis, follow the same steps you covered in Chapter 19 and point out the potential benefits and drawbacks of implementing various programs.

Chapter 6: What Are the Planning Issues that Need to Be Resolved?

In the final section of your report, list the key planning issues that policy makers and the advisory committee need to consider. In general, the following issues should be included:

- Resolving trade-offs between facilities and programs.
- Settling on a specific set of facility projections for the planning period— either accepting or rejecting the program adjustments and operating improvements that you have evaluated.
- Setting up a continuing mechanism to insure implementation and monitoring of chosen program changes (such as a permanent advisory committee).

Appendices

Include a selection of the backup data that support the conclusions you have drawn. To keep the reader from bogging down, put most of this material in appendices after the main body of the text.

Summary and Conclusion

This major portion of the needs assessment process concludes with reporting on the results of—and making decisions about—your analysis, projections, and consideration of alternatives.

The next steps, presented in Part 4, involve assessing the feasibility of facility development and finding the best facility option for your county to pursue.

Part 4.
Determining the Feasibility of Developing a Correctional Facility

21. Introduction

Who Will Use Part 4

Primary Users
Project manager
Planning team
Task forces

Secondary Users
Advisory committee
Board of commissioners

Part 4 will help determine if it is feasible for your county to build the facilities it needs. Now that you have examined the operation of your county's corrections system, studied the impacts of justice system programs, and projected needed capacity in light of possible alternatives, it is time to figure out how and where to accommodate identified needs.

Part 4 will help:

- **Establish how much space is required** in a new or renovated facility (Chapter 22).
- **Evaluate existing facilities** to determine whether they are adequate for continued use or capable of being remodeled or expanded (Chapter 23).
- **Consider the options** that may be available for correctional facilities (Chapter 24).
- **Determine if a consolidated (or regional) correctional facility** would make sense (Chapter 25).
- **Calculate the costs** of building and operating a correctional facility (Chapter 26).
- **Explore the sources of funding** that may be available and develop a strategy for obtaining both money and community support for the project (Chapter 27).
- **Select the most feasible option** for accommodating corrections needs, whether that entails a new, expanded, or renovated facility (Chapter 28).

Part 4 will help you to structure your analysis of the options available for accommodating corrections needs in effective and affordable facilities. These options include:

- No major changes required
- Renovation of an existing facility
- Addition to an existing facility
- Construction on a new site
- Construction of a consolidated or regional facility

An early step in the feasibility study will be to develop an estimate of how much space will be needed in detention facilities both in the near and in the farther future. This will be a preliminary estimate for the purpose of exploring various options and will be refined greatly during the facility programming phase (see Chapter 32).

Once space needs are established, the next step will be to evaluate existing county jail facilities in terms of their physical condition and capabilities. This effort will benefit from some expertise in construction, engineering, and/or architecture. Help may be obtained from the county's public works or building department, a building inspector, the fire marshal, and/or a consultant.

Another aspect involved in the evaluation of your jail is its ability to satisfy state and national standards as well as the county's goals. Here it is important to be familiar with standards and trends in correctional practices and designs (refer to Chapters 3 and 4). Help in determining how your jail does—or could, if renovated—perform in terms of standards and goals can be obtained from the state jail inspectors (or the National Sheriffs' Association audit system or ACA Commission on Accreditation's evaluation process; see Chapter 3).

Arrange to visit other jails that have been built recently or renovated if you have not already done so as part of your exploration of current practices. These may stimulate ideas about what can be done. (See Chapter 4 for recommendations of jails to visit, or ask your state's agency responsible for local corrections.)

If your early assessment of the possibility of consolidated (regional) operations and facilities between your county and another city or county was positive or promising, a special task force should study this option. Help with legal and organizational issues will come from the county legal counsel and administrator, with advice on intergovernmental relations available from intergovernmental bodies such as a regional council of governments.

To evaluate options properly, it is necessary to assess their immediate and long-term costs. For construction costs, seek help from the public works department and a construction contractor or architect who is familiar with current correctional facility costs as well as local conditions. For operating costs, assistance will be available from the county administrative office or budget analyst, working in coordination with the jail administrator.

A finance task force may be required to explore avenues of funding. Again, county administrators, budget analysts, and legal counsel can be of help. Since the acceptability of certain options may depend on official and public support, the board of commissioners as well as members of the advisory committee should be involved. You may wish to form a community relations task force, as mentioned in Chapter 8, to handle media relations and develop community support.

The final result of the work done in Part 4 will be an evaluation of the feasibility of your project. This will be done by the planning team and presented to the advisory committee for deliberation. Their recommendation will be passed to the board of commissioners for a final determination.

22. Step 1: Establish the Need for Facilities: The Preliminary Program

Who Will Use This Chapter

Primary Users
Project manager
Planning team
Task force (?)
Corrections staff
Planning consultant (?)

Introduction

To select an effective and feasible option for facility development, the county must have a clear, if preliminary, picture of its needs and the demands they will place on the facility. This entails the development of a **preliminary program statement**, which is a "first pass" at the programming process detailed in Chapter 32.

The preliminary program should briefly cover the following topics:

- Review of goals and objectives
- Capacity projections (by facility type) over the planning period
- List of programs and services the jail runs or wishes to run
- Preliminary estimate of space needs for each function (based on the rules of thumb presented in this chapter)

If the county is considering including related justice or administrative facilities, such as courts, law enforcement, district attorney's offices, of the like, their needs must be accounted for as well.

Review of Goals and Objectives

This is one of the times when the **mission statement**, as developed in Chapter 10, should be reviewed. From the mission statement and list of correctional goals, review those that relate to operations and conditions in the jail. If little was said about these factors, use the techniques presented in that chapter (along with a review of standards and legal requirements from Chapter 3) to develop a concise statement of the major goals and objectives for the jail. These will form a basis for evaluating the existing facility and for planning any needed new facilities.

List the goals and objectives in the following spaces in order of priority with the most important first.

By permission of Johnny Hart and Field Enterprises, Inc.

Table 22-1. List of Major Goals and Objectives

1. _____

2. _____

3. _____

4. _____

5. _____

6. _____

7. _____

8. _____

9. _____

10. _____

(etc.) _____

_____

Review Capacity
Projections

Capacity projections for the planning period (as modified by the use of alternative programs) were one of the products of Chapter 19. Those projections, broken down by facility type, should be recorded here.

Table 22.2. Jail Capacity Projections

	Bed Space Needs by Year				
Facility Type	1st	2nd	3rd	4th	(etc.)
High Security					
Lower Security					
Work Furlough					
Medical Service					
Mental Health					
TOTAL					

List Jail Programs and Services

Programs and services to be offered in the jail will have considerable impact on the space that must be provided. Refer to Chapter 15, which discussed programs and services; review state standards, if any, and other national standards for programs to consider. In addition, consider the list of possible programs presented in Chapter 31.

List on the following chart those programs that will probably be offered in the jail during the period covered by this planning project.

Table 22-3. List of Jail Programs and Services

1. _____

2. _____

3. _____

4. _____

5. _____

6. _____

7. _____

8. _____

9. _____

10. _____

(etc.) _____

Estimate Space Needs

This section offers rules of thumb for preparing preliminary space needs estimates. The rules are based on state and national standards together with information derived from studies of a number of recently constructed facilities. Ranges of space provision are presented and guidance is provided to help you choose where in the range your future facility may fit. This will allow you to develop a reasonable picture of space needs for functions to be accommodated in the jail.

Your estimate of jail-space needs will provide you with a means to test how usable existing facilities and sites are, and also help to establish budgets or identify potential areas for cost savings.

If you are considering renovating your jail, some spaces may have to be compromised to smaller areas than standards require or than are really workable. While variances may be requested in relation to standards, loss of operational efficiency or effectiveness can be one of the drawbacks of jail renovation. However, do not start by compromising. Develop a picture of needed space and compare the possibilities offered by renovation (see Chapter 23 for facility evaluation methods).

Before presenting the space needs calculations, concepts of **net** and **gross area** and space **efficiency** are explained.

Net and Gross Area

Area calculations start in **net**—or usable—square feet. Net area includes that space inside of the walls actually available for use by people. People who use various spaces in a building perceive their **usable** area—not necessarily their **total** area. A calculation of net area, however, makes no allowance for general circulation space, wall thicknesses, or mechanical equipment rooms, all of which need to be included when estimating the actual area required. That total is called **gross** square footage and represents the actual area to be constructed.

Efficiency Factors

The ratio (or percentage) of net area divided by gross area is called the **efficiency** of the building. The higher the number, the more efficient the building. If the building were 100 percent usable, which is of course impossible, the net and gross areas would be equal and the efficiency factor would be 1.0. Even well-designed jails are not efficient compared to other buildings because of jails' generous corridors, special surveillance spaces, thick walls, special mechanical equipment areas and so forth.

While your jail building's actual proportion of usable and gross area depends on its design (and cannot be determined until that stage), a reasonable goal to aim for is efficiency in the range of 60 percent (or a factor of .60). Actual efficiency may vary from 55 to 65 percent, with the higher number the more efficient. To obtain the gross area that represents 60 percent efficiency, the net area is divided by .60 (or multiplied by 1.67, the figure used in the space needs calculations that follow).

As you will see in the calculations, the range of net areas runs from a minimum of 148 to a maximum of 333 net square feet, depending on what is included. When these figures are translated into gross area, the range runs from 247 to 555 square feet. (This range is broader than occurs in real life, since no jails have either the minimum or the maximum provision of all types of space. More realistic is a range from 350 to 450 gross square feet per bed.)

Preliminary Estimates

The figures provided here are for preliminary estimates only. Final space needs cannot be determined until a detailed program is completed (see "Facility Programming," Chapter 31).

The rules of thumb are based upon **square feet per bed** (SF/bed) in the facility. The footnotes provided for each of the types of space explain the basis of the ranges of square feet per bed and allow you to choose a figure or range responding to conditions faced at your facility. You may not need to provide certain types of space if those functions are already housed or can be accommodated elsewhere. For example, if administrative offices are in the sheriff's office, little space need be planned here.

Note that there are economies of scale for some types of spaces but not for others. That is to say, some areas are not directly dependent on capacity while

Relationship Between Capacity and Space per Bed*

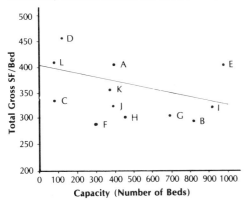

Each Letter Represents a Surveyed Facility Program
*From Surveyed Facility Programs

others are proportional to capacity. For instance, while each inmate will require the same space for sleeping and dayroom activities, laundry or food service may need to grow by only one-third or one-half for a jail capacity of 200 compared to one with 100. In general, there appears to be a moderately clear relationship between a jail's capacity and its total area per bed, as illustrated in the accompanying diagram.

Use Table 22-4 to obtain a rough idea of how much area will be needed in the jail. For each type of space, there is a range of "area per bed"; this is the number of net square feet (SF) for each inmate that your facility will be designed to accommodate. Before you fill in the part of the chart for each type of space, read the corresponding footnotes. These explain what the ranges are based on. In cases where the footnote indicates that the space per bed is more or less for certain types or sizes of facilities, you should use a narrower range than the one in the columns. In determining ranges of space provision, be certain to involve representatives of the various operations accommodated within the jail.

Table 22-4. Space Needs: Preliminary Calculations

TYPE OF SPACE	NET SF/BED	NO. OF BEDS	RANGE OF SF From–To
Sleeping Rooms: Single Occupancy Cells:	60–80[a]		–
Beds In Multioccup. Rooms:	35–60[b,c]		–
Day Rooms:	35–70[d]		–
Intake/Release/Processing:	8–30[e]		–
Central Control:	0.8–3[f]		–
Administration:	3–10[g]		–
Staff Stations:	0.7–2[h]		–
Visiting/Lobby:	6–12[i]		–
Program Space:	16–50[j]		–
Indoor Recreation:	3–15[k]		–
Medical Services:	5–12[l]		–
Kitchen/Food Service:	6–22[m]		–
Laundry:	1.5–8[n]		–
Receiving/Storage/Maintenance:	8–19[o]		–

TOTAL NET SQUARE FEET:			
For facility with all single cells:	153–333[p]		
For facility with 50% single cells, 50% multiple rooms	148–333[p]		

Multiply total net square feet times "efficiency factor":

All Single Cells

Low Range: _____ × $\frac{1.67}{\text{efficiency factor}}$ = _____
net square feet   gross square feet

High Range: _____ × $\frac{1.67}{\text{efficiency factor}}$ = _____
net square feet   gross square feet

50% Single Cells

Low Range: _____ × $\frac{1.67}{\text{efficiency factor}}$ = _____
net square feet   gross square feet

High Range: _____ × $\frac{1.67}{\text{efficiency factor}}$ = _____
net square feet   gross square feet

RANGE OF TOTAL GROSS SQUARE FEET: From _____
To _____

Note that the "number of beds" for each kind of residential sleeping room will, when added together, equal the total number of beds in the facility. The total will then apply to all types of spaces other than sleeping rooms.

Table 22-4. Space Needs: Preliminary Calculations continued

a. Most standards mandate between 60 SF and 80 SF. Often there is an inverse relationship between SF and the amount of time per day inmates are out of their cells. The Commission on Accreditation for Corrections (CAC) recommends a minimum of 70 SF in new facilities, 60 SF in existing detention facilities, and 50 SF in existing holding facilities.

b. California standards mandate a minimum of 35 SF per person and no more than 8 people per cell. CAC recommends 50 SF per person but allows multiple occupancy only in existing facilities.

c. California standards allow rooms to accommodate up to 16 **presentenced** inmates with at least 50 SF each in existing facilities, and up to 50 in an existing dormitory.

d. American Public Health Association (APHA) calls for at least 39 SF per person for dining and dayroom activities. Many recent facilities have more generous dayrooms (some of which accommodate other activities), which may have as much as 100 SF per person. CAC recommends a minimum of 35 SF.

e. SF standards do not exist. Most facilities surveyed have between 13 and 30 SF per jail bed, with no clear relationship between total capacity and amount of intake area per bed. The variation may be due to the number of holding cells, related services or amount of storage provided at that location.

f. Based on surveyed facilities, there is no apparent correlation with capacity. Variation can be due to number of functions handled at central control versus unit or floor control rooms.

g. Surveyed facilities and Washington State Jail Commission (WSJC) standards suggest that more administrative space per bed is needed for small jails (10 SF/bed for capacity of 25) than large jails (2.9 SF/bed for capacity of 1,200). This can also vary depending on whether the jail shares administrative space with the rest of the sheriff's department.

h. Most surveyed facilities have 48 to 96 beds per staff station.

i. Surveyed facilities and WSJC standards suggest more visiting space per bed for smaller jails (10 SF/bed for capacity of 25) than larger jails (6.1 SF/bed for capacity of 25). Variation can be due to provision of contact visiting space or scheduling of visiting hours (more hours of operation, fewer spaces needed to provide same number of visits).

j. Most surveyed facilities have 16 to 25 SF/bed; one has 54 SF/bed. These are rather highly programmed facilities. The list of programs created earlier in this chapter should be reviewed to determine how much space is needed to accommodate them.

k. This range is for indoor recreation and is based on only a few facilities. How much indoor recreation space is needed for your county depends upon climatic conditions, outdoor provisions, and the number of postarraignment inmates. CAC recommends at least 1,500 SF for **indoor and outdoor recreation** areas for jails with a capacity greater than 100 inmates. CAC suggests at least 15 SF per inmate for smaller facilities.

l. Surveyed facilities and WSJC standards recommend more space for smaller facilities (10 SF/bed for capacity of 25) than larger facilities (6.43 SF/bed for 1,200 capacity). California mandates an infirmary and a medical exam room with at least 100 net SF.

m. Most surveyed facilities are at the lower end of the range, less than 13 SF/bed. Smaller jails tend to have more foods service space per bed. The American Public Health Association recommends 7 to 9 SF/bed. The National Sheriffs' Association recommends 10 SF/bed for small jails, less for large jails. This will vary considerably depending on local conditions, with possibilities for the jail either to be serviced from another 24-hour, 7-day-per-week kitchen (which would eliminate much of the space requirement) or to serve other institutions (which would require more space). CAC recommends at least 200 SF, or 10 SF per person in smaller facilities.

n. Surveyed facilities range from 1.4 to 7.6, with most in the middle of the range. WSJC standards recommend a range from 7 SF/bed for capacity of 25 to 1.66 SF/bed for capacity of 1,200. As for food service, this depends on the possibility of shared services.

o. California mandates 80 cubic feet of storage space per inmate (excluding receiving and maintenance). Actual provision depends on supply logistics and reserve stocks to be held.

p. These ranges are very wide since no facility has the minimum or maximum area/bed for all or even most types of space. A more realistic net SF range is from 210 to 270, with gross SF ranging from 350 to 450 SF per bed.

Preliminary Estimate of Parking Needs

Numerous factors will determine how many parking spaces your facility will need. These are detailed in Chapter 31. While there are no formulas for deriving a preliminary estimate of the required number of spaces, the following should be anticipated:

- Number of staff on the two largest consecutive shifts
- Number of visitors anticipated at one time (depends on number of inmates and extent of visiting hours)
- Access to and adequacy of public transportation
- Other departments housed on the site
- Provision for service vehicles (law enforcement, trash, delivery, court transport)

Summary and Conclusion

Having completed the tasks in this chapter, you have developed a preliminary description of county needs for jail facilities. The next chapter allows you to assess the ability of existing facilities to meet these needs, with or without renovation.

References

See the references in Chapter 3 for sources on standards and those in Chapter 31 for sources on facility programming.

Kaplan/McLaughlin, Architects. n.d. "Area Comparisons of Seven Detention Facilities." Mimeographed report. A survey of seven recently constructed jails.

Naramore, Bain, Brady, and Johanson, Architects. 1979. **Architectural Programming Study for Local Correction and Detention Facilities.** A report to the Washington State Jail Commission.

————.1979. **Final Report: King County Jail/Correctional Facilities.** Reviews space provisions in a number of recent facilities.

23. Step 2: Evaluate Existing Facilities for Continued Use, Remodeling, or Expansion

Who Will Use This Chapter

Primary Users
Project manager
Planning team and/or
Evaluation task force

Introduction

There are several options your county can consider to make use of its existing jail:

- Use the facility as is.
- Make minor or major renovations.
- Build minor or major additions.
- Use it along with another existing or new building.

Although your county may believe it cannot continue to use its detention and correctional facility, an evaluation of the facility may prove otherwise, particularly if justice system changes developed in Part 3 limit or change the detention population.

This chapter takes your county through the building evaluation process. First, it spells out the purpose of an evaluation and describes which people should do the evaluating and what general and focal issues they should address. Then it spells out evaluation methods: taking charge, reviewing other evaluations, determining criteria, reaching agreement and prioritizing needs, estimating costs, and reporting back to the project manager. The Facility Problem and Solution Checklist is provided to use in the evaluation.

Purpose of the Evaluation

The primary purpose of evaluating your existing detention and correctional facility is to determine whether it has potential for some level of continued use. This potential depends on whether it can satisfy correctional standards and legal requirements (Chapter 3), your county's goals (Chapter 10), and your county's program objectives and needs (Chapter 22).

Although your county may have a good idea of what it will learn from the evaluation, there can be surprises that may help you decide whether to renovate, construct additions, or replace the facility. Therefore the evaluation must be objective and comprehensive.

The Evaluators

To evaluate your facility, your county has three choices. You can charge the **planning team** with this task, commission **consultants** with expertise in engineering, architecture, and corrections, or form an **evaluation task force.** Factors to consider in deciding who should conduct the evaluation include how thorough an evaluation you want, the availability of appropriate personnel, financial resources, and time.

Regardless of which group conducts the evaluation, select its members carefully. Choose people with expertise in different areas, including day-to-day operation of the jail, construction, architecture, engineering, life safety, and cost analysis. The group should be small enough to function as a working team but large enough to include at least one person who is well informed about each prime area.

The evaluators might be chosen from among the following: correctional officer and administrator (who work in the facility), budget analyst, planner, public works official, county health or sanitation official, local fire marshal, engineer, architect, an interested citizen or community leader, and, if possible, an inmate or former inmate. In addition, your county may request assistance from your state's local corrections agency's field representatives.

If the planning team will conduct the evaluation, it may choose to invite some of the people mentioned above to help. Or you may choose to hire a consultant to perform either all or part of the evaluation (such as investigating the structural and mechanical systems). Alternatively, the consultant could develop the evaluation instruments, the county could collect the data, and then the consultant could analyze and interpret the data.

General Issues for Evaluation

While some evaluation issues will be of special concern to your county, others should be addressed by every county. Every evaluation should address compliance with state laws and respond to capacity projections, goals, objectives, and future needs. Each of these topics is discussed below.

Standards and Legal Requirements

Your county must comply with state standards and laws that prescribe practices, conditions, types, and amounts of space. For instance, although there may be enough beds for all projected inmates, the renovated facility may have too little space per person to meet minimum legal requirements. Or, while your county may not view extremely low light levels in residential areas as a problem, the law prescribes minimum light levels. (See Chapter 3.)

Capacity Projections

Can the existing facility house the projected number of inmates of each type (for example, presentenced adult females)? If the answer is no, the task force should attempt to determine what combination of renovation and new construction would meet projections.

Goals and Objectives

Goals and objectives, including those identified in the mission statement, should be reviewed to determine which ones the facility currently achieves and which ones could be satisfied by renovations or additions.

For instance, one goal may be to provide surveillance from a single control point. To assess the facility's current performance, determine whether all the cells in the existing facility are visible from a guard post. If not, would surveillance be possible with renovations to an existing post or by relocating a post within the existing structure?

Or, while total square feet and number of beds indicate enough space per person, sleeping areas for sentenced offenders may house more than one person. If the county wishes to follow the recommendations of many criminologists, it will look to see whether or not the existing facility could be made to provide single cells for all inmates.

Future Needs

Future needs and flexibility must be considered, since a renovation or addition can add many years to the life of the facility. Correctional programs and populations, laws, and judicial practices are likely to change considerably. Hence the facility should accommodate desired programs and projected populations for a defined period after present changes are made. If the investment is to be large, the facility should serve as more than an interim solution.

In considering future needs, many variables must be examined. Can the existing facility grow or change? Although multiperson cells are permissible now, they may not be in the future. Could the facility adapt to such a change? Are site, orientation, and building configuration compatible with conversion to passive or active solar energy systems? Could air conditioning be added by using the existing duct system or would major construction work and expense be necessary? Could you add to intake, visiting, or residential spaces?

Focus of the Evaluation

In addition to the general issues described above, the evaluation should concentrate on nine focal areas. These are derived from state laws and national standards together with functional and design issues that are likely to reflect your county's concerns. You may wish to add other focal areas that respond to the local situation.

Building Soundness and Adaptability

Consider how adequate, safe, and sound are the facility's structural, mechanical, electrical, and plumbing (sewage and water supply) systems. Which walls are load bearing and which are partitions that could be more easily moved? Can appropriately sized spaces be created within existing physical constraints (for example, load-bearing walls)? Is the facility adequately braced to withstand earthquakes and wind storms? Is there easy access to critical parts of the plumbing system? Can the electrical system be added to so that it can support future equipment requirements? Engineers and architects should have chief responsibility for answering these questions.

Fire and Life Safety

Are all building materials and furnishings in inmate areas fire resistant? Does the facility meet codes concerning the number and locations of points of egress, fire extinguishers, alarms, and smoke removal systems? If not, what is necessary to meet the codes? For example, are there at least two means of egress from all occupied areas? Could secure exits be added? The local fire marshal should help explore these fire and safety questions.

Security and Safety

Access for the Handicapped

To what extent does the building facilitate order and control; prevent escapes, break-ins (to break inmates out), and mass riots; and minimize attacks on inmates and staff? Is there now or is the building amenable to incorporating an adequate communications system, an electronic surveillance system, and a mechanical locking system for residential areas? Can problem inmates, such as those prone to violence, suicide, or escape be kept in separate, more secure areas? Are all intake, residential, activity, and circulation areas secure and easily observable? Is there a secure perimeter around all inmate areas? Are there provisions for physically handicapped inmates and visitors? What changes would have to be made to satisfy these concerns? Architects, security staff, electrical engineers, and criminologists can make these safety and security determinations.

Separation

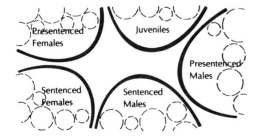

Does or can the facility enable a classification plan to be carried out? Can different population types—males, females, juveniles, adults, presentenced, and sentenced inmates—be kept separated? Can special classes of inmates, such as those being disciplined or the mentally disturbed, be separated? Is the facility flexible enough to accommodate increases and decreases of each of these population types?

How many inmates share each sleeping, dining, living, and bathing area? How many residential units are there? Can "small" units (of eight to twenty-four) be accommodated within the existing facility? Are physical and acoustical separations between areas adequate to facilitate management and control as well as to limit interaction between residential units in case of a disturbance? Jail staff, administrators, and classification officers, along with architects, should study these separation issues.

Comfort and Humane Conditions

How adequate is the heating, air conditioning, and ventilation (air flow, fresh air, air quality)? How is the artificial lighting—is there a minimum of glare and are light levels appropriate for work, sleep, or surveillance? Is there natural lighting in all residential areas? Is there too much noise in staff work areas, residential areas, and program areas? How much space is there per inmate for sleeping and living (dining, TV) in each type of cell, room, or dorm? Is there enough space to accommodate activities, programs, and recreation? What are the conditions of the materials and furnishings of the spaces used by the inmates? Is there adequate separation between eating and toilet areas? These issues should be evaluated by engineers, architects, and jail staff, with input from other staff and inmates?

Appropriate Spaces for Programs and Services

Is there adequate space for jail functions (intake, booking, holding, administration, food service, laundry, storage, sleeping, activities, and programs)? If the facility must increase the residential area to accommodate more inmates, will other areas be adequate in size? Are the spaces appropriate, or can they be remodeled so that they are suitable for and supportive of their functions? (For instance, there may be adequate square footage in dayrooms, but if they are very long and narrow, they will not be conducive to socializing and shared activities.) Can acoustical privacy be obtained in spaces used for interview or counseling? Do the residential areas allow for a degree of privacy? Jail staff and architects should respond to these questions.

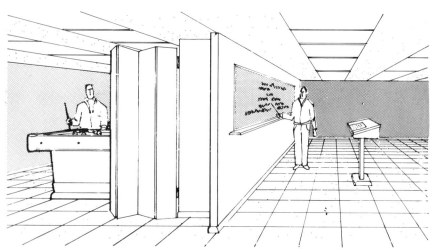

From National Clearinghouse for Criminal Justice and Architecture, **Harris County Corrections Plan.**

Sanitation

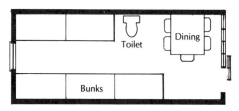

Configuration Not Conducive to Sanitation

Are there adequate provisions for staff and inmate toilets in residential, intake, program, activity, and recreation areas? What provisions are there for bathing in intake and residential areas? Can inmates obtain privacy for hygiene? Can residential, intake, dining, food service and preparation areas be thoroughly cleaned? Can vermin be prevented from infiltrating residential, intake, food preparation, food storage, and dining areas? The evaluators should consult inmates and appropriate jail staff about these sanitation concerns.

Efficiency

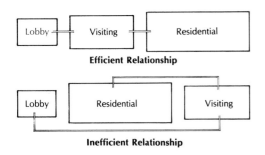

Efficient Relationship

Inefficient Relationship

Are the relationships and circulation paths between areas logical and efficient (for example, lobby near visiting, dayrooms near cells)? Are the most frequently traveled routes relatively short? Could the facility make do with fewer staff if the layout were more efficient? Jail staff, administrators, and architects should help answer these questions.

Scale

Is the scale of the residential areas oppressive and institutional? If so, could large areas be subdivided to better accommodate individuals and small groups? Can different areas reflect different security levels by using a variety of building materials or configurations? (See the section "Normalized Environment" in Chapter 4.) An architect can help with these questions of scale.

Other Issues

If there are other issues and concerns that have been identified during the planning process that are not covered above, you may wish to ask questions about them in your facility evaluation.

Method

Choose a Leader

To begin, the evaluators should select a leader—perhaps the project manager—who will ensure that an evaluation plan and timetable are established and followed.

Review Previous Evaluations

Before conducting your county's evaluation, the evaluators should review previous audits and evaluations to learn of problems that have already been identified. These records may consist of jail inspection reports, grand jury reports, and those from the state or county fire marshal and county building inspector. If your county has gone through an evaluation using the National Sheriff's Association (NSA) audit system or if the Commission on Accreditation for Corrections has conducted an accreditation visit, study these as well. Audit system materials may be ordered from NSA for your use (see Chapter 6).

Evaluate Your Facility

Your facility should be examined to determine how well it responds to relevant laws, capacity projections, goals, objectives, standards, and future needs, as described above. While you are compelled to deal only with issues and concerns mandated by law, you will undoubtedly identify additional functional objectives and concerns to evaluate.

Questions should be developed for evaluating each area of the facility. The questions can be of two types.

One, does the area presently support desired functions? For example, does the recreation area facilitate exercise and serve as an outlet for tension? Is it secure and easy to supervise?

Two, if not, could the area be effective if modified? Table 23-1, the "Facility Problem and Solution Checklist," may be used as the basis for your evaluation. You may use it as is or modify it to correspond better to the issues at your facility, or you may develop your own form. In any case, all evaluators should use the same form so that all will be clear about what to look for. However, since some evaluators will not be able to answer some questions, the leader should assign sections of the form to evaluators (including consultants, if necessary) who can answer them. For example, engineers should be assigned questions about structure but not necessarily about convenience. Advice from appropriate resources should also be obtained. For example, in evaluating the kitchen, the cook should be questioned.

Each area should be independently evaluated by more than one person and, when possible, by people with different perspectives, in order to ensure that questions are answered fairly. For example, the adequacy of dayrooms for specific activities could be studied by a correctional officer, an architect, and an ex-offender.

Going from one part of the facility to another with the checklist, the evaluators should independently consider each problem, identifying its presence, describing it, noting potential solutions and ranking its priority on a scale from 1 to 5 as follows:

1 = lowest priority: not necessary to alleviate
2 = low priority: would like to solve, after others
3 = medium priority: try to solve
4 = high priority: make considerable effort to solve
5 = highest priority: vital to solve this problem

Reach Agreement, Establish Priorities, and Summarize Needs

After the individual evaluations are done, the entire task force should discuss and agree upon the presence and relative importance of the problems. To accomplish this for each area and concern, add together all rankings, then divide by the number of raters. List the problems in descending order, with the most important first. Then the evaluators should discuss possible solutions to these most important problems, reach a consensus, and develop a statement of the identified problems and needs, dividing them into priority groupings. Depending on the nature of the solutions, some may be implemented immediately. More extensive remedies should have their costs assessed and be held for consideration along with other potential solutions that go beyond the existing facility (these are discussed in Chapter 24).

Estimate Costs

If, after the evaluation, continued use of the facility appears at least somewhat feasible, roughly estimate costs. If several different approaches are possible, such as a major renovation or a minor renovation plus additions, the costs of each approach should be figured and compared with other options. More thorough and accurate cost estimates can be conducted later (see Chapter 26).

Prepare and Submit Report

The major problems with the existing facility, their possible solutions, and the rough estimate of their construction costs should be briefly discussed. Submit the report to the advisory committee and the board of commissioners.

If your county has more than one type of any area (such as two differently configured inmate sleeping areas), make extra copies of the following form so that each area can be evaluated.

Table 23-1. Facility Problem and Solution Checklist

AREA & ISSUE	EXISTING PROBLEMS			POTENTIAL SOLUTIONS
	Yes?	Rank	Description	Description
INMATE SLEEPING AREAS				
Enough beds	[ ]	[ ]	_____	_____
Size, potential for relocating walls	[ ]	[ ]	_____	_____
Access to plumbing chases	[ ]	[ ]	_____	_____
Fire-resistant materials	[ ]	[ ]	_____	_____
Fire-resistant furnishings	[ ]	[ ]	_____	_____
Fire escapes	[ ]	[ ]	_____	_____
Smoke alarms	[ ]	[ ]	_____	_____
Smoke removal	[ ]	[ ]	_____	_____

Table 23-1. Facility Problem and Solution Checklist, continued

AREA & ISSUE	EXISTING PROBLEMS			POTENTIAL SOLUTIONS
	Yes?	Rank	Description	Description
Control over entry	[ ]	[ ]	————————	————————
Secure from other inmates	[ ]	[ ]	————————	————————
Provisions for handicapped	[ ]	[ ]	————————	————————
Heating, ventilation	[ ]	[ ]	————————	————————
Lighting	[ ]	[ ]	————————	————————
quantity	[ ]	[ ]	————————	————————
quality (glare, etc.)	[ ]	[ ]	————————	————————
Natural light (sun)	[ ]	[ ]	————————	————————
Noise	[ ]	[ ]	————————	————————
Toilets	[ ]	[ ]	————————	————————
enough	[ ]	[ ]	————————	————————
condition	[ ]	[ ]	————————	————————
privacy	[ ]	[ ]	————————	————————
furniture	[ ]	[ ]	————————	————————
equipment	[ ]	[ ]	————————	————————
SHARED INMATE AREAS				
Dayrooms				
existence	[ ]	[ ]	————————	————————
number shared by each	[ ]	[ ]	————————	————————
size (per person)	[ ]	[ ]	————————	————————
fire safety	[ ]	[ ]	————————	————————
adequate for dining	[ ]	[ ]	————————	————————
adequate for activities	[ ]	[ ]	————————	————————
light	[ ]	[ ]	————————	————————
noise	[ ]	[ ]	————————	————————
heating, ventilation	[ ]	[ ]	————————	————————
proximity to cells	[ ]	[ ]	————————	————————
furniture	[ ]	[ ]	————————	————————
Sallyport				
ample size	[ ]	[ ]	————————	————————
secure	[ ]	[ ]	————————	————————
surveillance	[ ]	[ ]	————————	————————
STAFF AREAS				
Surveillance of:				
cells	[ ]	[ ]	————————	————————
dayrooms	[ ]	[ ]	————————	————————
corridors	[ ]	[ ]	————————	————————
program areas	[ ]	[ ]	————————	————————
Control of:				
cells	[ ]	[ ]	————————	————————
dayrooms	[ ]	[ ]	————————	————————
corridors	[ ]	[ ]	————————	————————
fire escapes	[ ]	[ ]	————————	————————
outside spaces	[ ]	[ ]	————————	————————
Secure control areas	[ ]	[ ]	————————	————————
Provisions for:				
breaks	[ ]	[ ]	————————	————————
meals	[ ]	[ ]	————————	————————
training	[ ]	[ ]	————————	————————

Table 23-1. Facility Problem and Solution Checklist, continued

AREA & ISSUE	EXISTING PROBLEMS			POTENTIAL SOLUTIONS
	Yes?	Rank	Description	Description
Restroom	[ ]	[ ]	_____	_____
Lockers	[ ]	[ ]	_____	_____
ADMINISTRATIVE AREAS				
Sufficient office space	[ ]	[ ]	_____	_____
Appropriate spaces	[ ]	[ ]	_____	_____
Security	[ ]	[ ]	_____	_____
Staff training	[ ]	[ ]	_____	_____
Access (public lobby, etc.)	[ ]	[ ]	_____	_____
SUPPORT AREAS				
Food service				
fire-safety provisions	[ ]	[ ]	_____	_____
surveillance of inmate workers	[ ]	[ ]	_____	_____
ventilation	[ ]	[ ]	_____	_____
cold and dry storage	[ ]	[ ]	_____	_____
cleanliness	[ ]	[ ]	_____	_____
vermin control	[ ]	[ ]	_____	_____
convenience to dining	[ ]	[ ]	_____	_____
Showers				
quantity	[ ]	[ ]	_____	_____
privacy	[ ]	[ ]	_____	_____
condition	[ ]	[ ]	_____	_____
location	[ ]	[ ]	_____	_____
Residential units				
number inmates in each	[ ]	[ ]	_____	_____
number of units	[ ]	[ ]	_____	_____
provisions for separating population types	[ ]	[ ]	_____	_____
PROGRAM AREAS				
Recreation				
indoor provisions, for what activities	[ ]	[ ]	_____	_____
outdoor provisions, for what activities	[ ]	[ ]	_____	_____
Activity areas for:				
counseling	[ ]	[ ]	_____	_____
group programs	[ ]	[ ]	_____	_____
classes	[ ]	[ ]	_____	_____
library	[ ]	[ ]	_____	_____
vocational/crafts	[ ]	[ ]	_____	_____
VISITING AREAS				
Noncontact visits	[ ]	[ ]	_____	_____
Contact visits	[ ]	[ ]	_____	_____
Lawyer visits	[ ]	[ ]	_____	_____
Public parking	[ ]	[ ]	_____	_____
Public reception	[ ]	[ ]	_____	_____
Public waiting	[ ]	[ ]	_____	_____
INTAKE AREA				
Adequacy for:				
search	[ ]	[ ]	_____	_____
booking	[ ]	[ ]	_____	_____
holding	[ ]	[ ]	_____	_____

Table 23-1. Facility Problem and Solution Checklist, continued

AREA & ISSUE	EXISTING PROBLEMS Yes?	Rank	Description	POTENTIAL SOLUTIONS Description
processing (fingerprint, photo, shower, clothing issue)	[ ]	[ ]	———————	———————
storing	[ ]	[ ]	———————	———————
surveillance	[ ]	[ ]	———————	———————
alcohol recovery	[ ]	[ ]	———————	———————
OR program	[ ]	[ ]	———————	———————
interviewing	[ ]	[ ]	———————	———————
court assembly	[ ]	[ ]	———————	———————
Medical Service				
outpatient provisions	[ ]	[ ]	———————	———————
inpatient provisions	[ ]	[ ]	———————	———————
Laundry				
adequate space	[ ]	[ ]	———————	———————
ventilation	[ ]	[ ]	———————	———————
Trash Disposal	[ ]	[ ]	———————	———————
FACILITYWIDE CONCERNS				
Circulation				
efficiency	[ ]	[ ]	———————	———————
security of routes	[ ]	[ ]	———————	———————
convenience	[ ]	[ ]	———————	———————
adjacencies among areas	[ ]	[ ]	———————	———————
Structural soundness	[ ]	[ ]	———————	———————
Adequacy of plumbing	[ ]	[ ]	———————	———————
Electrical system				
safety	[ ]	[ ]	———————	———————
adequacy	[ ]	[ ]	———————	———————
Fire safety				
materials	[ ]	[ ]	———————	———————
exits, egress	[ ]	[ ]	———————	———————
alarms	[ ]	[ ]	———————	———————
smoke removal	[ ]	[ ]	———————	———————
Security				
from within	[ ]	[ ]	———————	———————
from outside	[ ]	[ ]	———————	———————
communications	[ ]	[ ]	———————	———————
provisions for violent inmates	[ ]	[ ]	———————	———————
Provisions for handicapped	[ ]	[ ]	———————	———————
Scale	[ ]	[ ]	———————	———————
On-site storage	[ ]	[ ]	———————	———————
Housekeeping provisions	[ ]	[ ]	———————	———————
OTHER AREAS AND CONCERNS				
———————	[ ]	[ ]	———————	———————
———————	[ ]	[ ]	———————	———————
———————	[ ]	[ ]	———————	———————
———————	[ ]	[ ]	———————	———————
———————	[ ]	[ ]	———————	———————
———————	[ ]	[ ]	———————	———————
———————	[ ]	[ ]	———————	———————

References

American Institute of Architects, Committee on Architecture for Justice. 1978. **Design Resource File: Planning Justice Facilities, 1978.** Washington, DC: AIA. Includes an evaluation checklist for law enforcement facilities.

Farbstein, Jay, Richard Wener, and Patricia Gomez. 1980. **Evaluation of Correctional Environments: Instrument Development Report.** San Luis Obispo, CA: Farbstein/ Williams & Associates. Describes the development of a set of instruments that measure the impact of the jail environment on inmates and staff.

Miceli, Charles, and Alton Golden, Jr. 1979. **Fire Behind Bars: An Administrator's Guide for Prevention and Control.** Durham, NH: The New England Coordinating Council, Inc. Provides a yardstick for measuring the fire safety status of a correctional facility.

National Clearinghouse for Criminal Justice Planning and Architecture. 1976. **Cellhouse Renovation Potentials.** Clearinghouse Transfer No. 8. Urbana, IL: University of Illinois. Describes and illustrates several possible jail renovations.

————. 1975. **El Paso County Corrections Plan.** Urbana, IL: University of Illinois. This plan and the two that follow include analyses of the corrections systems, inmate characteristics, future needs, and recommendations.

————. n.d. **Harris County Corrections Plan.** Urbana, IL: University of Illinois.

————. 1977. **Hennepin County Corrections Plan.** Urbana, IL: University of Illinois.

24. Step 3: Develop and Consider Facility Options

Who Will Use This Chapter

Primary Users
Project manager
Planning team and/or
Evaluation task force

Secondary Users
Advisory committee
Board of commissioners

Introduction

Once the evaluation task force has studied your existing facilities, your county will want to look at many building-related options. Some of these involve continued use of the existing facility (as is, with renovations and/or additions, or with another facility), while others involve replacing the existing facility with a new one.

Criteria for Evaluating Options

The criteria for evaluating the options are the same as those used for the existing facility (refer to "General Issues for Evaluation" in Chapter 23). These criteria include compliance with laws and standards, ability to accommodate your county's capacity projections, goals and objectives, and flexibility for possible future change.

In addition to the criteria previously discussed, consider the initial and life-cycle costs of each alternative (see Chapter 26 on costs). The team will use cost comparisons to help choose among options. To make these estimates, they may seek help from people with expertise in cost estimation, construction, and design of correctional facilities.

The Options

There are a number of building-related options to consider at least briefly before concentrating on the ones that appear promising. The options include:

- No construction
- Minor renovation
- Major renovation
- Minor addition
- Major addition
- Using another existing building
- Constructing a satellite facility
- Constructing a new (replacement) facility

Of course, there are many combinations and permutations of these options that may deserve consideration. Some may provide interim solutions while longer range plans are being developed. Each option is discussed below.

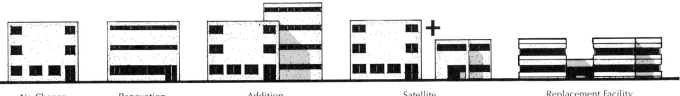

| No Change | Renovation | Addition | Satellite | Replacement Facility |

No Construction

It is assumed that if you are reading this chapter, your county has some need for construction or renovation.

Minor Renovation

If your facility evaluation indicates a close but not perfect fit between the existing building and county needs, consider minor renovation. This entails relatively inexpensive changes that can be implemented with a minimum of disruption. Included are such alterations as covering "hard" surfaces (metal, concrete) in minimum security residential areas with "soft" materials (carpet, acoustical tile, treated wood), adding fire exits, and subdividing a large space into several small spaces.

Major Renovation

If the findings from your evaluation disclose that many parts of your facility are adequate but rather considerable changes are needed to meet present criteria, then your county should consider a major renovation. This involves substantial (and often expensive) alterations, such as inserting windows in load bearing walls, constructing firestairs within an existing space, tearing out steel "cage" cells, or installing a new plumbing system.

If there is a need for more space and the correctional facility is within a building that houses other functions, your county could consider moving the other departments and expanding the jail into that space. Existing attics and basements may also be renovated to accommodate certain functions.

Minor Addition

If your correctional facility is adequate except for some relatively small areas that cannot fit within the existing building, your county may want to consider one or more minor additions. For example, these may involve adding firestairs next to existing residential areas and expanding the lobby.

Major Addition

If your building as a whole is adequate even though one or more of its areas needs more space to accommodate specific functions, your county should consider major additions. For instance, this may involve adding a wing of residential units or a program area.

Another criterion for additions must be considered: how much room is there for expansion where you need it on the site? When looking at the possibility of major additions, currently occupied land should be considered as well as open space. Demolition and reconstruction may be cost-effective.

Furthermore, many government buildings are constructed to support the future addition of more stories. Study the building's plans and structure to determine whether this is a possibility.

Using Another Existing Building

Explore the possibility of moving some functions that currently take place within the correctional facility to another existing building. Necessary adjacencies must be considered since it is not wise to separate such functions as residential, programs, recreation, and visiting. However, other functions can operate relatively independently; for instance, intake services (in a large system), long-term storage, or work furlough might be relocated to other buildings. This would free space for the remaining functions to expand. For example, the residential area may take over the work furlough area, or the kitchen may use the long-term storage area.

Sometimes there are other advantages to relocating a function. Moving work furlough to a separate facility, for example, can reduce the possibility of contraband being brought to the general population. Furthermore, living in a more "normal" environment can facilitate adjustment to living in society after release.

Constructing Satellite Facilities

Another option is to continue using the existing jail and add one or more additional buildings. Satellites generally work best if they are designed for inmate subgroups who should be housed separately, such as presentenced men, women, the mentally ill, or work releasees. Satellite buildings may be located on the same site, on an adjacent site, or in a more remote location.

For populous counties, a side benefit of using satellite buildings for residential purposes is that these smaller facilities help keep down institution size, thus reducing the possibility of the jail becoming unmanageable, impersonal, overwhelming, or dehumanizing. Furthermore, for minimum security and work furlough satellite units, construction costs can be considerably lower than for maximum security housing. On the other hand, operational costs for staffing, food service, and so on must be evaluated because some of these costs may be greater when operating more than one facility.

Transportation costs should be studied before deciding to construct satellite facilities, particularly on outlying sites, since moving inmates between facilities can be expensive. Because of transportation costs between detention and court, it may make more sense for outlying satellites to accommodate sentenced offenders.

Constructing New Facilities

The most obvious option may be to replace the existing facility completely. It may be the best choice if other options are unfeasible. For example, a new facility may be preferred if there is not enough space for necessary additions, or if renovation costs exceed new construction costs or would not be worth the relative savings in terms of quality.

When considering a new facility, your county should look at two options: building on the same site (with or without demolition of the existing facility), or building on a different site. The direct and indirect costs of building on a different site should be weighed, including transportation between the courts and the new facility as well as ease of access for visitors and staff.

If you may be building on the same site, study interim housing arrangements for the affected jail population. These include the use of portable buildings, temporarily housing inmates in other jurisdictions, or building in stages.

Combinations of Options

Besides considering each of the options on its own, your county should review combinations of options. Workable combinations include a minor renovation with a major addition, and a major renovation plus the construction of a satellite facility.

Interim Solutions

Your county may find that it needs to make some changes in its present facility before a new facility is completed. Or, that what is needed may be too costly or politically unfeasible at the present time. If this is the case, reconsider renovations, minor additions, and using existing facilities as interim temporary solutions. Then, when the necessary political and financial support is available, a new facility can be built.

Interim solutions should concentrate on remedying the worst physical problems of the most highly used areas, such as overcrowded living spaces. Obviously, since these solutions are intended to be temporary, they should be either as inexpensive as possible or include elements that can be used in the eventual new facility. An example of a relatively inexpensive remedy is removing beds that were added to single cells and making up for the diminished capacity by leasing an existing apartment house for work furlough or prerelease programs. An example of movable elements is buying dayroom furniture that can also be used in a new facility.

When exploring an interim solution, recognize that many planned "short-range" renovations last much longer than intended. Therefore find temporary solutions that the county can live with.

Examine the Implications of Renovations or Additions

If it appears that your current facility can meet basic criteria when renovated, consider the additional factors that follow.

Ramifications of Changes

Be careful that the solution to one problem does not create others. View prospective changes individually and as a whole to insure that they do not negatively affect other areas of the facility. For instance, surveillance may be compromised by creating smaller, shared activity spaces. Or, the ideal place to add a program area may be the same limited space in which you need to add a residential unit.

Expense of Changes

Besides the "usual" costs of construction, maintenance, and staffing, consider two other factors that affect costs.

First, construction may disrupt the operation of a facility. It may create noise, debris, and confusion, which can increase staff and inmate tension. Inmates must be shuffled around, possibly to other facilities. Costs incurred by paying another jurisdiction to keep inmates, extra staffing, and transportation between the courts and remote, temporary facilities can be extensive.

Second, permanence is a factor that should be considered. Your county should estimate how long the renovated facility will serve compared to a new facility. If the renovations and additions are relatively inexpensive, then a short new life for the facility may be acceptable. If a new facility costs more but its anticipated life is much longer, then a new facility may be the more cost-effective option in the long run.

Generate and Evaluate Options

To ascertain which of the previously discussed options is more feasible for your county, briefly review each one. For those that seem most practical, a more careful study should be conducted.

Table 24-1, the "Facility Options Checklist" at the end of this chapter, can be used to summarize the positive and negative attributes of each option. This should help screen out the options that are less appropriate. Then, a more thorough evaluation of the surviving options should be undertaken. This will include an analysis of costs (see Chapter 26) and the selection of the most feasible option (see Chapter 28).

Renovation and Addition Possibilities in Typical Jail Layouts

Here are some solutions to typical problems in jails. They may or may not be realistic given conditions in your facility, but they are offered to show some possibilities.

Single Cells Too Small

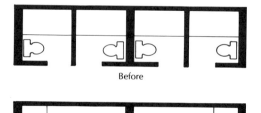

Before

After

If your facility has single cells that do not provide adequate space and do not meet minimum standards, you may wish to consider several possible solutions. If cells run along a corridor with an outside wall, build a new corridor beyond the wall and add space from the old corridor to each cell. Or, walls between each pair of cells can be removed, providing the walls are not structural. More extensively, the interior of the residential area can be gutted and fewer, larger cells constructed.

Housing in Large Dormitories

To meet national standards and to facilitate inmate control, eliminate large dormitories. You could construct walls and create units comprised of single cells and a shared dayroom. Alternatively, you could change dormitories into a medical unit, program space, or offices. Or, with minor renovation, a dormitory could support other functions that are suitable for large spaces, such as recreation or dining.

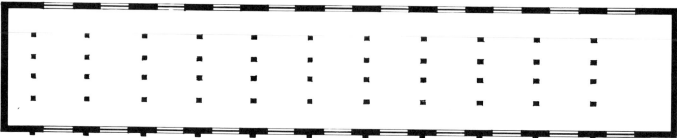

Before

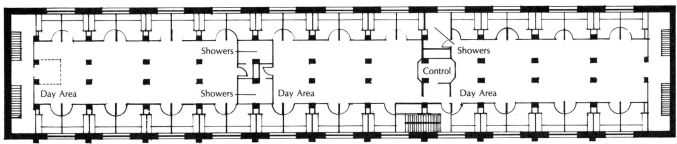

After   Adapted from National Clearinghouse for Criminal Justice Planning and Architecture, **Clearinghouse Transfer: Cellhouse Renovation Potentials.**

Residential Units without Dayrooms

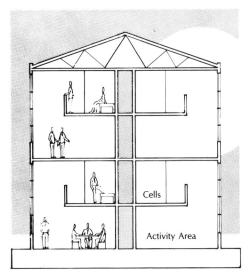

Adapted from National Clearinghouse for Criminal Justice Planning and Architecture, **Clearinghouse Transfer: Cellhouse Renovation Potentials.**

If cells are about the right size but there are no dayrooms, several cells could be combined to become a dayroom. Or, if ceilings are very high or the jail contains more than one residential floor, two-story units could be created by combining cells on one level to become a dayroom space for the inmates whose cells are above or below it. If cells are near an outside wall and if the site permits, dayrooms can be added.

Dayrooms Too Small

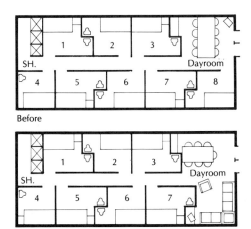

Before

After

If there is insufficient space in existing dayrooms to meet standards and accommodate desired activities, there are two approaches your county can take. The first might be to move some activities, such as dining (for minimum security inmates), to another part of the building. The second approach can be to add on to the dayrooms by combining one or more cells into the dayroom. Or, these cells could be kept as separate rooms to provide a variety of dayroom spaces. This will keep groups small and minimize noise transference from one area to another.

Inadequate Visiting Space

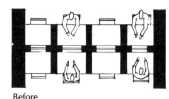

Before

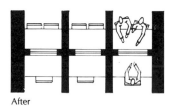

After

If visiting areas are deficient, consider these remedies. If there is no place for contact visiting, space adjacent to or near the lobby could be converted or could "moonlight" for this purpose. For example, your facility may contain an underutilized chapel. During specified hours it could become a contact visiting room. You could convert cells into attorney visiting rooms. If visiting booths are too small and do not provide adequate privacy, partitions can be upgraded and faced with sound-absorbent materials. If this results in too few booths (and additional booths cannot be added elsewhere), visiting hours can be increased.

Corridors Too Long

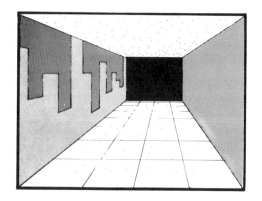

Long, straight corridors may be noisy, difficult to manage, or dehumanizing. A partial solution is to make corridors appear shorter by using graphics on walls, ceiling, or floor. For noise control, sound-absorbent materials can be added.

Program Space Inadequate

ROOM	SCHEDULE
TIME	MONDAY
7am	GYMNASTICS – GROUP 4
8	GYMNASTICS – GROUP 5
9	GYMNASTICS – GROUP 6
10	
11	READING – GROUP 2
12pm	MATH
1	DRAMA
2	ORIENTATION GROUP
3	PRE - RELEASE GROUP
4	
5	ART CLASS – 4
6	ART CLASS – 5
7	DRUG GROUP
8	READING – GROUP 3
9	ALCOHOLICS ANON.

If the space allocated for education, library, counseling, and similar activities is inadequate, consider adding space if the site allows. Or, if the site is too tight, convert program space in another area that is easily accessible to residential areas. As stated previously, dormitories can be converted to multipurpose rooms, libraries, and so forth. Another alternative calls for management rather than construction. Programs can be scheduled more efficiently, thus using an existing program area more intensively (for example, twelve hours per day instead of eight).

Examples of Renovations and Additions

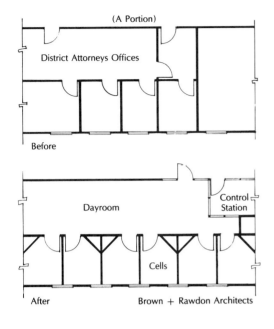

(A Portion)

District Attorneys Offices

Before

Dayroom

Control Station

Cells

After   Brown + Rawdon Architects

Riverside County Jail, California

Problem
Crowded cells; as little as 13 sq. ft. per person. Too many inmates per cell.

Solution
As an interim solution, public defenders vacated adjoining space within same building. Offices were gutted, women's unit built with single cells, dayrooms, control station, visiting rooms, medical exam room, showers.

Lack of detoxification unit.

Part of existing residential area became detoxification unit.

Too few fire exits.

Added fire exits.

El Paso County Jail, Texas

Problem
Most housing was in dorms, each with approximately 26 beds.

Proposed Solution
Created residential units with about 14 single rooms, dayroom/dining room, and visiting room.

Intake functions were isolated from each other and their spaces insufficient. Intake population consisted of large numbers of low security risk people for less than six hours.

Relocated booking, holding, and medical exam to one location. Planned informal intake lounges.

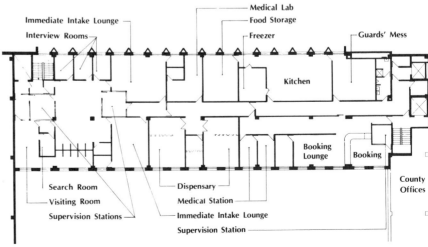

Immediate Intake Lounge
Interview Rooms
Medical Lab
Food Storage
Freezer
Guards' Mess
Kitchen
Booking Lounge
Booking
County Offices
Search Room
Visiting Room
Supervision Stations
Dispensary
Medical Station
Immediate Intake Lounge
Supervision Station

From: National Clearinghouse for Criminal Justice Planning and Architecture, **El Paso County Corrections Plan.**

San Luis Obispo County Jail, California

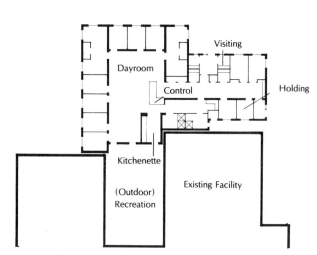

San Luis Obispo County Jail Addition
Farbstein/Williams and Associates, Architectural Programmers
MPW Associates, Architects

Problem
The jail, including the womens' and medical units, was overcrowded. During intake, women were verbally abused by male inmates.

Using the same recreation area for men and women caused scheduling and access problems.

Proposed Solution
Added a larger, self-contained female unit that has its own intake area. Converted former women's unit to medical unit.

New unit was placed so that a seldom-used partially enclosed courtyard became a recreation area. It is accessible from the womens' dayroom.

Hennepin County Jail, Minnesota

Problem
At 54 sq. ft., single cells were too small, but defined by service and concrete walls.

Lack of hot water in cells.

Distant and unsuitable dining space (in gym).

Proposed Solution
Too expensive to create larger cells; replacement facility planned for future.

Added hot water.

Moved dining to dayrooms; converted one cell per residential unit to food dispensing and receiving room.

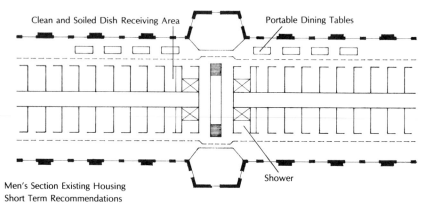

Men's Section Existing Housing
Short Term Recommendations

Adapted from National Clearinghouse For Criminal Justice Planning And Architecture, **Hennepin County Corrections Plan.**

Manhattan House of Detention for Men (The Tombs), New York

Problem

Very large and institutional facility. No spaces for small groups and few activity spaces.

Proposed Solution

Gutted interior, removed some floors. Designed split-level residential areas with single cells along perimeter and activity and dining areas for small groups, plus staff stations, in center.

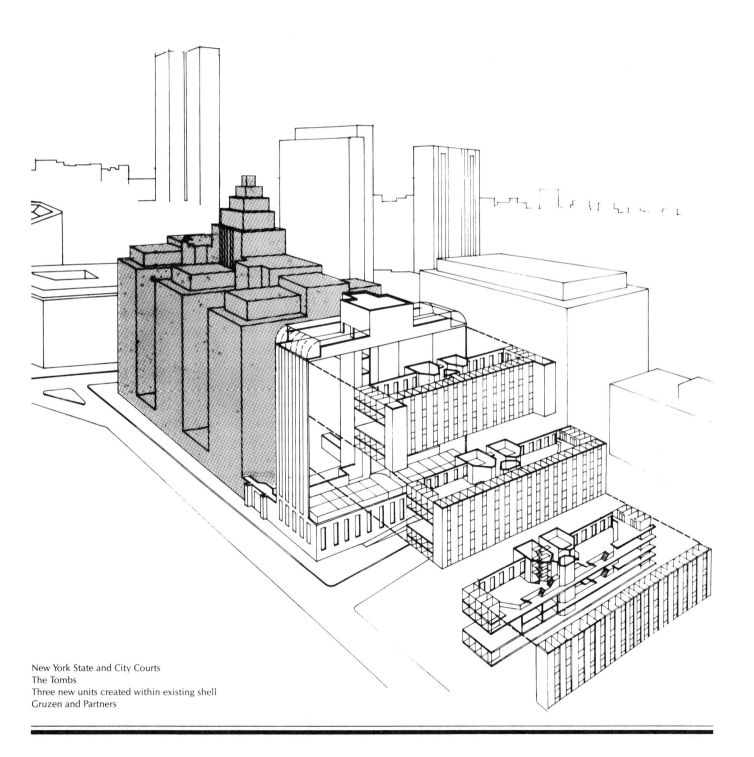

New York State and City Courts
The Tombs
Three new units created within existing shell
Gruzen and Partners

Table 24-1. Facility Options Checklist

Complete this form for each reasonable facility option.

Option: _____

Focal Concern	Positive Attributes of this Option	Negative Attributes of this Option
Building Soundness and Adaptability		
Fire and Life Safety		
Security and Safety		
Separation		
Scale		
Comfort and Humane Conditions		
Appropriate and Adequate Spaces for Programs, Services		
Sanitation		
Efficiency		
Other concerns— indicate _____		
Ramifications of the Change		
Summary		

Conclusion

There are many options for correctional facility development. In assessing potential solutions to your county's facility needs, consider the range of possibilities before deciding how to proceed. If new construction is anticipated, be sure that plans for existing facilities (including, perhaps, decommissioning or demolition) are formulated.

One option deserves special consideration. The next chapter covers the possibility of sharing or consolidating facilities with another jurisdiction.

References

American Institute of Architects. 1980. **1980 Architecture for Justice Exhibition Directory.** Washington, DC: AIA. Published annually, this illustrated directory briefly describes selected current designs.

National Clearinghouse for Criminal Justice Planning and Architecture. 1976. **Cellhouse Renovation Potentials.** Clearinghouse Transfer No. 8. Urbana, IL: University of Illinois. Describes and illustrates possible and actual jail renovations.

————. 1975. **El Paso County Corrections Plan.** Urbana, IL: University of Illinois. Includes an analysis of the corrections system, inmate characteristics, future population needs, and recommendations.

————. n.d. **Harris County Corrections Plan.** Urbana, IL: University of Illinois. Includes an analysis of the corrections system, inmate characteristics, future population needs, and recommendations.

————. 1977. **Hennepin County Corrections Plan.** Urbana, IL: University of Illinois. Includes an analysis of the corrections system, inmate characteristics, future population needs, and recommendations.

————. 1976. **Jackson County, Kansas City, Missouri: A Model Health Care Unit.** Clearinghouse Transfer No. 3. Urbana, IL: University of Illinois. Describes and illustrates renovations for health-care units.

————. n.d. **Ocean County Corrections Plan.** Urbana, IL: University of Illinois. Includes an analysis of the corrections system, inmate characteristics, future population needs, and recommendations.

————. 1976. **St. Louis County, Clayton, Missouri, Intake Service Center.** Clearinghouse Transfer No. 6. Urbana, IL: University of Illinois. Describes and illustrates renovations for an intake center.

25. Step 4: Consider Consolidated Correctional Facilities

Who Will Use This Chapter

Primary Users
Project manager
Planning team
Facility consolidation
    task force

Secondary Users
Advisory committee
Board of commissioners
Affected agencies and departments

Facility Consolidation Task Force

If consolidation appears to have some merit, a task force should be formed to study the question. It should include representatives of each jurisdiction that might be involved, such as county supervisors, city or town council members, and county and/or city attorneys. The sheriff or other law enforcement agency representatives may also be involved, but for obvious reasons representatives of corrections-related agencies that might be abolished because of a consolidation should not be involved at this stage.

If consolidation appears likely, care should be taken to coordinate data gathering and analysis as well as feasibility study efforts between the jurisdictions — you may even wish to combine efforts from the outset.

Introduction

More and more communities are seriously considering consolidating their correctional facilities. This emerging trend follows closely on the heels of increasing demands to upgrade or replace antiquated facilities, the growing difficulty of smaller communities to hire and retain qualified personnel, increasing constitutional requirements for more and better services and programs, and the significantly higher costs to build and maintain these facilities and services.

This chapter is designed to assist communities that are considering mergers in properly planning and implementing such systems. Key aspects of this chapter describe the subjects that should be examined when studying the feasibility of consolidation, the legal basis for joint operation of facilities, financing of consolidated systems, and administering the jail.

Before examining these subjects, however, let us first define what a consolidated correctional facility is and show why some communities use them. In understanding these two basic elements, you may be able to assess whether your community should consider consolidating with a neighbor for all or part of your correctional facility needs.

Consolidated Jails: Definition and Types

The regional, multijurisdictional, multicounty, or consolidated jail is "a facility with a joint agreement by two or more units of governments to organize, adminis-ter, and operate a jail facility[ies] to be used exclusively by participating govern-ments for all pretrial and sentenced inmates" (Price and Newman 1979).

Within this definition, several types of organizational arrangements are possible. Full consolidation would involve sharing one or more facilities that jointly accom-modate all detainees. Alternatively, jurisdictions may maintain separate pretrial (or sentenced) facilities. The lowest degree of sharing is where one jurisdiction con-trols all operations will accepting certain inmates from another jurisdiction on a fee-for-service basis.

The range of merger options is quite extensive. You may consider a merger to house a special inmate population group such as females, or to provide a special program such as work release. Or you may be looking to utilize more fully a facility that is underpopulated or better suited to a different security level than it currently houses. The consolidation may involve another community, a city, a county, or another jurisdiction in the same community, a city-county, or several city jurisdictions.

Possible Compositions of Consolidated Jails

	City or County A's Facility		Regional Facility	City or County B's Facility	
No consolidation	○	●		●	○
Complete Consolidation			○●●○		
Sentenced Only	○		● ●		○
Partial Consolidation	◖	◖	◗ ◗○	●	

Key: ○ = Pretrial Inmates

● = Sentenced Inmates

The Impetus to Consolidate

In many cases, communities consider consolidating their facilities either because funding is available from federal or state sources or because day-to-day use is so light that a single jurisdiction operating its own facility is uneconomical (Price and Newman). Yet other factors may contribute to a community's decision to consolidate.

Current demands from the courts, prisoners' rights groups, professional coalitions for jail reform, and others call for changes in the design and operation of correctional facilities (see Chapter 3 on legal issues). Most significant among these demands are the introduction of health care provisions, and the requirement to deliver separate services to those awaiting trial and to those serving sentences.

The provision of such specialized services is expensive, not only in terms of building costs but also in terms of equipment and staffing. To provide them for special populations, such as maximum security inmates, or to isolate male from female or sentenced from pretrial inmates in service, program, and residential areas further escalates the costs.

Small or Rural Communities

Consider, for example, the problems of a small or rural community whose resources are limited and whose inmate population is also small but varies considerably throughout the year. First, facilities built to comply with regulations are often underutilized (for instance, medical examination rooms). Second, staff for these special functions (medical, counseling, and others) may not be readily available in the area, but bringing in someone to fill such positions is not justified because of limited demand. Third, flexibility in the utilization of a particular type of space is limited because of requirements for housing certain special populations (such as maximum-security, female, or work-release prisoners).

Because of problems such as these, the National Advisory Commission on Criminal Justice Standards and Goals stated: "A regionalized service delivery system should be developed for service areas that are sparsely populated and include a number of cities, towns, or villages. Such a system may be city-county or multi-county in composition and scope . . . " (Standard 9.1.1). Some small jurisdictions have even found that by combining their requirements, a smaller total capacity could serve their needs. This is due mainly to reduced allowances for peak periods.

Other Conditions Indicating Consolidation

However, consolidation is not limited to small or rural communities, nor called for only because of increased mandates or fiscal belt-tightening. Other conditions may exist that would influence a community to consider consolidation regardless of its size or location. These include the following:

- Crises or problems (for example, financial or manpower shortages, union pressures, charges of racial discrimination or corruption) that raise questions regarding the desirability and/or ability of the current single-jurisdiction system to meet future community needs.
- The existence of and confidence in a nearby provider agency, be it a public agency or a community resource with services attainable through coordination rather than competition.
- A history of interjurisdictional cooperation that serves as a precedent for merger.
- Desired detachment from local administrative efforts, such as the maintenance of personnel and payroll or the recruiting, training, and retraining of personnel.

Reasons to Consolidate

In all, your community should consider the possibility of consolidating with other jurisdictions for one or more of the following reasons:

- If consolidation would mitigate conditions that limit or reduce the effectiveness of correctional services, such as jurisdictional overlap, disputes, jealousies, or competition for either public or private resources.
- If consolidation would permit a broader range and level of programs and services than is financially possible through small independent facilities and operations (for example, work release, psychiatric care, juvenile detention).
- If consolidation would result in higher quality personnel or services through better training, supervision, organization, and working conditions.
- If consolidation would tend to reduce per-inmate costs or would result in the provision of more or better-quality programs and facilities for the same dollar invested.
- If consolidation would mitigate conditions that do not comply with various court decisions and applicable statutes.

Formally Assess the Feasibility of Consolidation

Decisions to consolidate should be based on careful planning and study, not on a general review of needs by local correctional facility administrators. The latter route may too easily lead to system-financing problems, such as one jurisdiction going "bankrupt" from poor financial planning, or discrepancies in expected services and programs, such as misunderstandings as to what programs or what capacity the consolidated facility is either intended or able to provide.

At the minimum, the task force considering consolidation should:

- List the correctional services that are currently required by applicable statutes or court decisions in the area to be served.
- List additional services that are necessary to comply with your jurisdiction's goals and philosophy.
- List present deficiencies in the delivery of required correctional services.
- Analyze the contribution of consolidation to alleviating those deficiencies.
- Outline the possible formal relationships between the participating governmental bodies.
- Invite representatives of the candidate agencies to discuss consolidation plans (if they are not already involved).
- Develop and consider a formal plan before committing the jurisdiction to any long-range course of action.

In some cases a relatively quick, informal study is sufficient—especially if it is the intention to contract on a fee-for-services basis for minimal services. However, a more formal study can be beneficial for several other reasons.

- A formal study can thoroughly assess the benefits and costs of consolidation.

- If a merger is found to be feasible, the resulting information can be useful in promoting implementation, since the documentation offers an objective assessment of available alternatives.
- Such planning also produces baseline data necessary for subsequent monitoring and evaluation.

A formal study should not only include the full data collection and analysis process discussed in Part 3 but should also include additional information on issues of compatibility between jurisdictions and the specific impacts of consolidation on other components of the criminal justice system in each jurisdiction. Because the data should be collected and analyzed in all jurisdictions involved, it is best to coordinate all efforts as early in the process as possible, even if a single jurisdiction's independent survey first proposes the consolidation option.

The differences, therefore, between studying the feasibility of any option and that of consolidation involve coordination between jurisdictions and additional attention to a few critical issues. These issues include facility location, financing, jail administration, management and staffing standards and procedures, and the legality of consolidation. Each of these issues is briefly addressed in the following sections.

Location

Possible Locations For a Facility Shared By Two Counties and a City

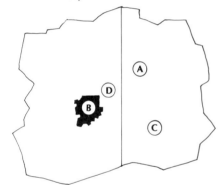

The location of consolidated facilities can be beneficial or costly to a jurisdiction. Benefits might include proximity to better community services (such as health-care or work-release jobs), qualified personnel (such as psychiatrists), or major components of the criminal justice system (such as courts).

On the other hand, a given location can add to transportation time and cost for a remotely located participating jurisdiction. These increases would result from transporting detainees the long distances required for court appearances and the consequent taking of personnel and equipment away from patrols and other police duties for extended periods of time.

A remote location can also create inconvenience and added costs to follow up investigations for the jurisdictions as well as for private attorneys, family, and friends, who must travel longer distances for visits. A faraway location may also affect community attitudes and inmate behavior if accessibility to the facility for visits and services is hampered.

Consolidation therefore functions best when central sites can be found that are relatively close to the population and administrative centers of participating jurisdictions.

Financing a Consolidated System

There are two choices for financing consolidated services: pro rata and fee-for-services.

The pro rata method allocates a predetermined percentage of the annual operating budget to each participating jurisdiction. The fee-for-services method entails payment of an established per diem charge to the receiving institution based on the number of inmates housed.

The pro rata arrangement tends to encourage a fuller regional commitment, while participating jurisdictions tend to operate more as consumers in the fee-for-services arrangement. However, in some areas the latter has proven easier to implement.

Administering a Consolidated Jail

Three basic models of jail administrations are used in consolidated correctional institutions:

- Administration by the sheriff or chief of police
- Administration by civilians
- Either or both of the above with a joint powers board

The first model is used by about 75 percent of all jails in the U.S.; however, a civilian jail administrator or director operating with the advice or consent of the joint powers board may be more common in a regional arrangement (Price and Newman).

Generally the joint powers board consists of elected officials who are responsible for policy formulation, budget development, fiscal control, and/or direct jail operation. Such boards, especially in pro rata arrangements, can help insure participating jurisdictions a means of control. In general they help maintain the necessary coordination and ongoing working relationship between jurisdictions. The director in most cases is responsible for day-to-day operations and, though advised or directed by the board, is ultimately responsible to a sheriff. It is possible, however, to operate the jail directly through the sheriff without a director.

Regardless of the administrative structure chosen, it will probably alter the organizational structure of all or some of the correctional agencies in each jurisdiction. This means changes in the power and authority of some individuals, perhaps even their jobs. Such "turf" issues must therefore be handled with sensitivity and prudence to avoid alienating participants and to insure fair allocation of control.

Management, Staffing, and Equipment Compatibility

The current compatibility, or the cost to make them compatible, of records, procedures, salaries, benefits, and equipment (from radios to word processors) is an important consideration when assessing the feasibility of consolidation. Varying management procedures may require retraining of staff. You may have to balance salary and benefit differences if staffs from several locations are merged. Equipment for basic operations, communications, personnel, and offices may need to be acquired, may need to be made interactive, or may need to be salvaged.

The Legal Basis for Joint Operation of Facilities

The consolidation of correctional facilities is aided in some states where legislation facilitates interlocal cooperation agreements. If this is the case in your state, consolidation must be sanctioned only at the local level by ordinance, resolution, or local referendum.

Ordinances or resolutions are the simplest and most common approach, requiring action only by legislative councils (board of commissioners or city council) of participating local governments. Usually such ordinances or resolutions articulate the need for consolidation and serve to approve officially a previously negotiated contract.

The time-consuming local referendum is bypassed by this approach, and generally the action can be revoked easily if the arrangement proves unsatisfactory. Public hearings are recommended before such action occurs to air and resolve conflict or opposition, particularly regarding location.

The use of a referendum to mandate consolidation is a much more involved process—similar to a political campaign. Passage of a referendum usually requires affirmation by either a majority of all voters or a majority of all voters in each participating locality.

Comparing the Advantages and Disadvantages of Consolidation

The advantages and disadvantages of consolidating correctional systems must be considered in order to make an informed decision. Essentially the test is to compare a proposed consolidated system to another system—consolidated or not.

One such method of comparison is the cost-benefit analysis. Compare the ratio of costs to benefits for one option to the ratios for other options. The objective is for benefits to outweigh costs as much as possible. A cost/benefit ratio greater than one indicates the feasibility of an option. Values less than one can also be used to compare the effectiveness of options.

A final decision should not be based solely on a cost-benefit analysis, however. While many costs and benefits are clear (construction, operations, and so forth), others are not so easily assessed. For example, how do you assess the costs of a family traveling a long distance to visit a detainee?

To the extent that such intangible costs and benefits are estimated, the analysis becomes more sophisticated, but it also becomes potentially less objective. Thus judgment is needed to interpret the value of intangibles.

Facility Consolidation Checklist

The following checklist summarizes the issues that should be considered in assessing the consolidation option.

Table 25-1. Consolidation Checklist

Impact on Jurisdictions and the Justice System?
- Time and transportation costs to the system, staff, and visitors
- Reuse of vacated facilities
- Access to community services and programs
- Availability of qualified personnel

How Will the Consolidation Be Financed?
- Availability of outside funds
- Type of financing (fee-for-services, pro rata)
- Type of service to be bought or sold
- Control over or through financing (by participating jurisdictions)

How Will the Consolidated Jail Be Administered?
- Type of administration
- Degree of participation/control by each jurisdiction
- Effects on power and authority—"turf"

Compatibility of Systems Being Merged?
- Job classifications and descriptions
- Salaries, benefits, etc.
- Recordkeeping
- Training, manuals, etc.

Compatibility of Equipment?
- Operations equipment (cameras, fingerprinting kits, medical)
- Vehicles
- Communications equipment (radios, teletype)
- Personal equipment (uniforms, leathers)
- Office equipment (furniture, typewriters, reproduction)

Public and Political Acceptability?
- Current relationships between jurisdictions
- Attitudes toward correctional services
- Attitudes toward consolidation
- Elected officials
- Sheriff, chief of police, corrections administrators
- Press and media
- Community groups
- Prisoners and families

Summary and Conclusion

Facility consolidation is not a cure-all for correctional problems. Consolidation, however, may represent a viable option that warrants your consideration if it can do the following:

- Improve the overall effectiveness of correctional services.
- Permit more or better quality programs.
- Provide better quality personnel.
- Reduce cost per inmate.

Regardless of the type of consolidation, formally plan and study the feasibility of such a move. The study must involve all the jurisdictions considering participation to assess properly the needs, commitments, and resources of each.

Once the study is completed and alternatives are explored, the contract or agreement should be negotiated and ratification sought in the local jurisdictions. Negotiations should cover administrative and budgeting arrangements for building, maintaining, and operating the facility. Funding may be on a pro rata or fee-for-services basis. Administration options include management by a sheriff or civilian director and/or a board. The agreement should insure the proper balance of control for each jurisdiction.

References

Advisory Commission on Intergovernmental Relations. 1967. **A Handbook for Interlocal Agreements And Contracts.** Washington, DC: Government Printing Office.

Gressman, Wendy. 1977. **Multi-County Correctional Facilities.** Washington, DC: National Association of Counties Research Foundation: Factsheet. Brief description of three multicounty correctional facilities.

National Advisory Commission on Criminal Justice Standards and Goals. 1973. **Corrections.** Washington, DC: Government Printing Office. Suggestions for improvements in the delivery of correctional services.

National Sheriffs' Association. 1975. **Jail Architecture.** Washington, DC: Government Printing Office. A summary of predesign considerations and architectural guidelines for the comprehensive planning of jails.

Price, Barbara R. and Charles L. Newman. 1979. "Multijurisdictional and State Jails: A Study in Organization and Management." An unpublished report to the National Institute of Corrections. University Park, PA. Results of a nationwide study comparing the organization and management structures of multijurisdictional (consolidated) and state jails.

26. Step 5: Calculate Construction and Operating Costs

Who Will Use This Chapter

Primary Users
Project manager
Planning team
Cost estimator
Administrative analyst

Secondary Users
Advisory committee
Board of commissioners

Introduction

The cost analysis will be one of the most crucial parts of the feasibility study since it will delineate the relative affordability of various alternative project options.

Several cost categories need to be understood and estimated during jail planning:

- **First costs** or **project costs,** including construction.
- **Operating costs:** recurrent costs associated with running the facility.
- **Life-cycle costs:** first costs plus operating costs, considered over the economic life of the building.

Relative Costs

First Costs   Operating Costs   Future

To compare first costs properly with the operating costs of a proposed correctional facility, it is necessary to consider life-cycle costs over approximately a thirty-year term.

These types of costs are discussed in detail in Chapter 5. This chapter tells how to estimate and limit the three types of costs for your project.

How to Estimate First Costs

First costs for corrections facilities vary considerably, depending on the required security level, the cost of building in different regions, the size or capacity of the facility, the kinds of building systems and finishes used, the type of construction (steel frame, prefabricated, concrete block, poured in place or precast concrete), and other variables. In addition, when the bidding and construction take place will determine the inflation-caused increase over the costs specified in this chapter.

Several regularly published construction cost estimates for various facility types are available from companies serving the construction industry (for example, the **Dodge Building Index**). These provide a valuable source of information about per square foot construction costs for comparable facilities and allow you to adapt the costs to your region and date of construction.

A five-step formula for estimating the first costs of a new facility follows.

Step 1: Determine Current per Square Foot Construction Costs. Determine the current construction cost per square foot for this type of correctional facility. This may be done by surveying other recent local projects and then adjusting for inflation to a current cost, or by consulting an estimating publication or service.

Current per square foot (SF) construction cost = $_____ per SF.

Step 2: Record the Total Gross Area of the Facility. Record the total gross area of the facility as described in Chapter 14. If a detailed estimate of space needs is not available, you may estimate from 350 to 450 square feet per inmate bed for a rough idea of space for a detention facility.

Total facility area (gross square feet) = _____ gross SF.

(Or number of beds (capacity _____) × about 400 SF/bed = _____ gross SF.)

Step 3: Calculate Current Total Construction Cost. Multiply the cost per square foot by the size in square feet to determine the current construction cost (CCC).

Current construction cost (CCC) = (cost per SF ($) _____) × (total area _____ (SF)) = $ _____.

Step 4: Adjust Construction Cost for Inflation. To gain a more realistic picture of the likely construction cost of your jail when it goes out to bid, the construction cost estimate must be adjusted to include inflation. This has run from .8 to 1.5 percent per month in recent years. Since the construction contractor will estimate costs over the period of construction, identify the number of months from the time of the estimate to the midpoint of construction.

Months to midpoint of construction = _____ months.

Assumed inflation rate = _____% per month.

Inflation factor = (_____ months) × (inflation rate_____ %/mo) × (1/100) = _____.

Inflated construction cost (ICC) = (inflation factor 1._____) × (current construction cost (CCC) $_____) = $_____.

Step 5: Calculate Total First Costs. In addition to construction, total first costs include the following (percentages adapted from Peña 1977):

- **Professional fees.** About 6 to 8.5 percent of construction.
- **Testing and expenses,** including printing documents and advertising bids. About one to 1.5 percent.
- **Furnishings and movable equipment.** Depending on how much and what quality, about 8 to 15 percent.
- **Administrative costs** (project representative, legal, accounting). About one percent. (These may be absorbed as general overhead rather than being assigned to the project.)
- **Site acquisition.** Depends on actual cost.
- **Site development,** including parking, landscaping, lights, fences, and signage. About 5 to 15 percent or more, depending on slopes, soils, and number of cars.
- **Contingency.** Allow 5 to 15 percent, depending on how far planning and design have progressed and how many unknowns can be identified (the further the progress, the lower the contingency allowance).

To develop the total first cost of the project, assumptions are made about the range of each of these line items and all except site acquisition are multiplied times the inflated construction cost (ICC). This process is illustrated in the example that follows.

Correctional Facility Construction Cost Estimation: An Example

This example of the use of the development of the construction cost formula is for a county that is about to start architectural design on a 300-bed jail. The site is county-owned land that is essentially flat and has all needed utilities.

Step 1. Look up cost per SF = **$125 per SF** (from Dodge Index for the county's region).

Step 2. Estimate facility size (from Chapter 22) = **120,000 gross SF** (about 400 square feet per bed).

Step 3. Calculate current construction cost. $125 per square foot (times) 120,000 square feet = **$15,000,000 current construction cost.**

Step 4. Adjust construction cost for inflation. Assume construction will start in 12 months and last 36 months (midpoint of construction is 24 months from now). Assume one percent per month inflation. Inflation factor = 24 months (times) one percent (times) 1/100 = 1.24. Multiply current construction cost (times) 1.24 to obtain inflated construction cost = **$18,600,000.**

Step 5. Add other first costs:

Professional fees (7%): **$1,302,000**

Testing and expenses (1%): **$186,000**

Furnishings and movable equipment (8%): **$1,488,000**

Administrative costs (0.2%): **$37,000**

Site acquisition (no cost): **$000**

Site development:

Parking (80 cars on grade at $1,000 each): **$80,000**

Other (2%): **$372,000**

Contingency (10%): **$1,860,000**

Total added costs: **$5,325,000**

TOTAL FIRST COSTS: **$23,925,000**

The result is a rather high total per bed cost of $79,750 at the assumed future date (if all the contingency is used).

This kind of estimate is of course very rough and must be refined when the precise facility size, site, and type of construction are known. It will, however, allow planners to develop an early cost figure to help determine feasibility and to compare alternatives. At a later stage, detailed "take-offs" will be done from the plans to develop a more accurate estimate. It is important to remember, however, that the actual cost will be known only when you receive a firm bid for construction and a contractor commits to that price. And even then, the final cost is subject to changes during construction.

Strategies for Limiting First Costs

If you wish to limit or reduce first costs, it makes sense to focus attention upon the components that contribute the most to those costs. These components will reflect the most significant differences when adjusted up or down.

Probably the most obvious potential way to cut costs is to reduce the capacity of the facility. We stated in Chapter 5 that per bed first costs are currently as high as $70,000. While each eliminated bed will not necessarily save this amount, the reduction can be substantial. This is because when subtracting a single cell, you achieve only a marginal reduction in cost—less than its full proportion of the total first cost—because taking out one cell will not allow proportionate reduction of shared systems and spaces. Thus, the first cost to build **one more** or less cell or room will be less than the overall per bed cost. If a number of cells are removed, reduction may indeed become proportional.

Another area for scrutiny is the overall provision of space and facilities. The figure of 350 to 450 square feet per bed is merely a rule of thumb. Some savings may be affected by reducing areas other than the residential space (such as administrative or program areas) or designing areas so that they serve dual purposes. Further reductions in first costs may be realized by any of the following strategies:

- Reduce security provisions for inmates who do not require them. (Special glazing, hardware, and fixtures are very expensive.)
- Reduce dependency on expensive mechanical and electrical systems.
- Utilize readily available building materials to avoid costs of transport and delays.
- Choose an easily buildable site requiring minimal site work.

- Reduce associated costs of interest and inflation during construction by using a "fast track" or phased construction process that may shorten time to completion.

With any of these strategies, most important is the ability to identify problems and solutions as early as possible. Possible costly delays may be avoided if a problem is identified before it takes its toll. The use of preliminary cost estimates, critical-path scheduling methods, testing of materials, and gauging of the project against established standards for size or costs may help identify problems before they delay the project.

How to Estimate Operating Costs

In the early planning stages, operating cost estimates are even rougher than those for first costs. More accurate estimates cannot be determined until numbers of staff, types of services, and many other factors are known. It is possible, however, to derive a "guesstimate" of the cost of operating the facility. To do this, you will need several kinds of information.

Average Annual Corrections Personnel Costs. A survey sponsored by the National Institute of Corrections (Center for Justice Planning 1980) found a national average of $17,492 salary and $2,045 fringe benefits (12 percent of salary), for a total of $19,537. Personnel costs accounted for about 70 percent of operating costs. Since these costs vary by region, calculate your county's current average personnel costs for jail staff.

Future Staffing and Bed Capacity Estimates. These may be taken from the estimates done in Chapter 19. National survey figures showed an overall average of one staff position per 1.98 inmates (or one security staff position per 3.11 inmates). On a per bed basis, the survey found an average staff cost of about $28.00 per day.

Annual Inmate Support Cost per Bed. This includes the cost of food, laundry, medical care, and so forth. Survey results showed an average cost of about $4.00 per day for each bed (times 365 days equals $1,460 annual cost per bed). Thus inmate support costs accounted for about 10 percent of operating costs.

Annual Plant Maintenance and Operations Costs per Bed. These averaged about $8.00 per day per inmate. Multiplying them times 365 derives an annual cost of $2,920 per bed. This accounts for about 20 percent of operating costs.

Total operating costs were found to be in the range of $40.00 per bed per day. The following sections show you how to make a more accurate projection of operating costs in either of two ways. Method One develops operating costs for a single year, while Method Two estimates the total operating cost of the facility over its life.

Method One: Estimate Single-Year Operating Costs

This method uses staffing and bed capacity estimates for the projected year ("n") of the analysis to determine estimated operating costs for that year. The formula involves determining the costs for future operations in current dollars (Task 1) and then adjusting that figure for inflation (Task 2).

Task 1: Project Operating Costs in Current Dollars

Current dollar operating costs for year "n"

=

Staff costs (number of staff projected for year "n" times current average personnel costs per staff)

+

Inmate support costs (bed capacity for year "n" times current average annual per bed inmate support costs)

+

Maintenance and utility costs (bed capacity for year "n" times current average annual per bed maintenance and utility costs).

Task 2: Adjust Operating Costs for Inflation

Select an estimated annual inflation rate from now until the projection year ("i" percent) and use the following formula to adjust estimated operating costs for inflation.

Operating costs for year "n"

=

Current dollar estimated operating costs

$\times$

$(1 + i\%)^n$.

Example: Assuming estimated current dollar operating costs at the twentieth year of $250,000 and an average 6 percent annual inflation rate, inflated operating costs at the twentieth year are calculated as follows:

Inflated twentieth-year operating costs

=

$250,000 \times (1.06)^{20} = \$801,783$.

Method Two: Estimate Total Period Operating Costs

This method uses average staffing and bed capacity estimates for the period of the analysis to determine total estimated operating costs over that period. The formula involves projecting the average number of staff and bed capacity (Task 1), determining the average annual cost of future operations in current dollars (Task 2), and projecting an inflated total operating cost for the period (Task 3).

Task 1: Develop Average Staffing and Bed Capacity Estimates

Example: Begin with 40 staff and 125 beds. Project that with steady growth in 30 years there will be 80 staff and 250 beds.

Average number of staff = $(40 + 80) \div 2 = 60$

Average bed capacity = $(125 + 250) \div 2 = 188$

Task 2: Calculate the Average Annual Operating Cost in Current Dollars

First, multiply average number of staff times average annual personnel cost. Then, multiply average bed capacity times annual prisoner support cost per bed. Finally, multiply average bed capacity times annual plant maintenance and utility cost per bed. The sum of these three figures is the average annual operating cost in current dollars.

Task 3: Compute Total Inflated Operating Costs

To compute the total inflated operating costs over the period under consideration, use the following formula, where "n" is the total number of years in the period and "i" is the assumed average annual inflation rate.

Total inflated operating costs

=

Average annual operating cost

$\times$

$$\frac{(1 + i\%)^n - 1}{i\%}$$

Example: Assume an average annual operating cost of $250,000 with an average of 6% annual inflation for a 30-year life cycle.

Total inflated operating costs =

$250,000 \times \dfrac{(1 + 6\%)^{30} - 1}{6\%}$

or

$250,000 \times \dfrac{1.06^{30} - 1}{.06}$

=

$250,000 \times 79.06 = \$19,760,000$.

This figure represents the total thirty-year operating cost at a compound annual inflation rate of 6 percent.

Strategies for Limiting Operating Costs

Suggestions for limiting operating costs include:

- Reduce overall space constructed, thus limiting the building area that must be staffed, heated, lit, and maintained.
- Design buildings that are efficient to staff.
- Design buildings that are energy efficient (perhaps exploring alternative energy sources or solar applications), thus reducing dependence on expensive fuel sources.
- Utilize mechanical systems that are low in maintenance and repair costs (for example, passive rather than active solar).
- Use quality building materials that will last longer.

To compare the savings in operating costs to costs or savings in first costs, both must be considered on an annual basis over the life of the building. This comparison is discussed in the next section.

How to Estimate Life-Cycle Costs

Life-cycle costing can provide information in two important areas. First, it can give an economic assessment of design and program alternatives. It provides a means for choosing among various program and facility options by measuring costs of operation and ownership. Second, it can give an overview of those costs on an annual basis. This may be used as a budgeting and operating tool by corrections and fiscal personnel.

Detailed life-cycle costing may be performed by your county or its consultants during facility design. You can, however, use a simplified life-cycle cost analysis to compare the effects of alternative building and program strategies.

To examine life-cycle costs for various options, you must first calculate total life-cycle operating costs for each option using Method Two above. To these will be added estimated first costs of construction for each building type included in the options. If funds are to be borrowed for first costs, financing charges must also be added (this is not shown here).

Example: Assuming per bed costs of $50,000 for detention space and per square foot costs of $50/SF for program and office space, examine the relative costs of a 250-bed jail versus a 150-bed jail supplemented by programs for 100 people.

Table 26-1. Example of Life-Cycle Cost Comparison

	250-Bed Jail	150-Bed Jail (J) 100-Person Programs (P)	
First Cost Estimates (build jail and/or program space)	$ 12,500,000	$ 7,500,000	(J)
		500,000	(P)
Total Operating Costs (30 years)	125,000,000	75,000,000	(J)
		25,000,000	(P)
Total Life-Cycle Cost (30 years)	137,500,000	108,000,000	
(divided by 30 =) Equivalent Uniform Annual Cost (30 Years)	4,583,333	3,600,000	

Summary and Conclusion

It is easy to see that the costs of building and operating jails are quite high. Your county should have a firm idea of what type of financial commitment it is making when it is deciding to build—and operate—a new facility. By using the estimating methods included here, you can develop your own estimate and decide if you need to reduce or can expand your plans. The methods for cost reduction will give you more tools to use in limiting the size of your fiscal commitment.

The next chapter will help you explore potential funding sources to finance your project.

References

Center for Justice Planning. 1980. **Costs of a New County Jail: Pay Now and Pay Later.** Champaign, IL: Center for Justice Planning.

McGraw-Hill Information Systems Company. 1981. **Dodge Digest of Building Costs and Specifications.** New York: McGraw-Hill.

National Council on Crime and Delinquency. 1977. **Prisons: The Price We Pay.** Hackensack, NJ.

National Moratorium on Prison Construction. 1975. **Jail and Prison Costs.** Washington, DC.: National Moratorium on Prison Construction.

Peña, William M., William Caudill, and John Focke. 1977. **Problem Seeking: An Architectural Programming Primer.** Boston, MA: Cahners Books.

For additional references, see Chapter 5.

27. Step 6: Pursue Funding Sources and Strategies

Who Will Use This Chapter

Primary Users
Project manager
Funding task force
Community relations
   task force

Secondary Users
Advisory committee
Board of commissioners

Task Forces

Since funding is such an important issue, the county should seriously consider forming a **funding task force** made up of individuals within county government who have backgrounds in finance or politics and community support. The county administrator, tax collector, treasurer, and county counsel as well as a member of the board of commissioners and advisory committee should be considered for inclusion. A **community relations task force** may also be formed if the advisory committee feels that your county will need one.

Introduction

Now that you are aware of the high costs that may be involved in building and operating a jail, this chapter looks at possible funding sources. Tight budgets and high costs are stimulating counties to search for innovative approaches, some of which are described here. Information about other approaches that may develop over time may be available through your state's local corrections agency.

Potential Funding Sources

There is a wide range of possible sources for funding the renovation or construction of county correctional facilities. Of course, sources may be used singly or in combination. This section reviews both traditional and innovative sources; a later section reviews state and federal government special programs for jail or justice facility construction.

General Fund

The county general fund capital improvement budget is one possible funding source. These monies traditionally have been derived from property taxes, fees, and other sources. Some counties may have funds set aside that are—or could be made—available for jail construction. However, in states where voter initiatives have limited county taxing abilities and pressures on county budgets have increased from inflation, few counties will find the capital improvement budget a practical alternative.

Revenue Sharing

Revenue sharing involves direct grants to the county from the federal government, in this case for capital construction. Amounts are based on county population. However, funds available from this source have been shrinking and may soon disappear totally. Furthermore, jail construction must compete with many other needs, such as schools, community-based organizations, and the daily operation of county government. Jail construction alone could require several years of the total revenue sharing funds available to the county.

Special Reserves

Two types of special reserves may be available to counties.

Accumulated Capital Outlay (ACO). Some counties have ACO funds approval accumulated through special tax rates. These might contribute a portion of the funds needed for jail construction.

Insurance Revenues. Many counties are presently self-insured for general liability and/or workers' compensation. As reserves grow, it may be possible for these insurance funds to lend money to the county building fund, much as private insurance companies invest premiums. Caution must be exercised to make certain that potential claims are covered and that sources for paying back the insurance fund are identified.

Bonds

Bonds may or may not provide a feasible funding option for jail construction. Although few counties have general fund monies available to retire long-term general obligation bonds, revenue bonds may be a useful approach. Interest rates on these bonds vary according to prevailing market forces and the county's credit rating (which in turn depends on its demonstrated ability to generate revenues to cover the bonds). Counties utilize underwriters to issue revenue bonds. Since the final market interest rate must be negotiated with the underwriter, it is best to contact several and choose one who has established success in this field.

Individual counties may wish to seek special legislation to help generate revenues with which to pay these bonds. This approach has been used by some counties to fund courthouse construction.

Tax Anticipation Notes

Tax anticipation notes are short term, and may be available to counties that anticipate an increased tax base in the near future (for example from population growth). While they generally have a higher interest rate than municipal bonds, counties may find tax anticipation notes useful to fund portions of the jail construction project, such as land acquisition or architectural and engineering fees.

Private Funds

Private lending institutions (or other nongovernment agencies) can finance county construction projects through loans or lease-purchase agreements. Generally higher interest rates, however, would make the total long-term cost of facilities financed in this manner more expensive. At least two major financial companies have entered the jail market and publish booklets on their sources (Hutton 1983; Shearson 1984).

Lease Purchase

In recent years private financing packagers have put together lease-purchase arrangements to build jails. The private jail developer finances construction through tax-exempt instruments such as revenue bonds or certificates of participation. The public agency designs and operates the jail, and leases it from the builder for a set number of years. At the end of the lease period, ownership passes from the builder to the public agency.

Possible Sources of Special Grants

Because of concern with the counties' ability to fund adequate correctional facilities, your state's legislature and/or the United States Congress may from time to time authorize grant funds for jail or justice facility construction. Should such programs be enacted, counties can expect to receive detailed information from the state's local corrections agency.

State Government

Check with your state's local corrections agency to see if state funds are available for county jails or if availability is anticipated. If so, ask about funding policies, procedures, and criteria.

Federal Government

At the time of writing, there are no federal grant programs to assist counties in financing jail construction. However, funds may be available for specific portions of the jail; you can find these by consulting the most recent amendments to the

Catalog of Federal Domestic Assistance published by the Office of Management and the Budget.

Funding: Conclusion

There are no easy answers to the question of how to fund jail construction. Some current and innovative possibilities are outlined here, but these programs may or may not be realistic approaches for your county. By the same token, new ideas or programs may surface at any time; you may even develop them in your county. When you start your research into funding options, check with your state's corrections agency for an update on current possibilities.

Most important, your county must plan for the continuing provision of adequate funds to staff and operate the jail during and after this construction project.

Community Relations: Selling the Project

While the professionals and citizens involved in the needs assessment and planning will understand and support the project, you may need to convince the rest of the community. This is particularly true when difficult funding or locational decisions are to be dealt with by the sheriff or the commissioners, especially during a bond issue election.

When the time has arrived to "sell" the project, the early involvement of community groups, special interest groups, and the media should pay off. Where any difficulties of acceptance and support are anticipated, a **community relations task force** and campaign should be organized. The following considerations may be of help.

- Refer to the chapters on participation, problem identification, and action planning (Chapters 8, 9, and 11) for general organizational information.
- Analyze the problem you are facing. Where is support? Where is resistance or opposition?
- What resources (people, organizations, media, events) can you mobilize for support? For example, would your cause be helped by articles in the newspaper or presentations on TV? What about visits to the jail by various groups or the general public?
- Are there recent examples of successful campaigns or bond issues in your county (or close by)? If so, learn how they were organized and see if their techniques or approaches can be adapted to your situation.

Many counties have found that technically sound planning in and of itself does not provide community support adequate to allow resolution of politically difficult site selection or of funding issues. Opening your county's planning process to community participation and mounting a concerted and well-organized community relations campaign can make the difference in obtaining your new facility.

References

Council of State-Community Affairs. **State Financial Management Resources Guide.** Washington, D.C. Published annually.

E. F. Hutton. 1983. **Innovative Alternatives to Traditional Jail Financing.** New York: Public Finance Group, E. F. Hutton.

Moody Investors Service. 1980. **Pitfalls in Issuing Municipal Bonds.** New York: Moody Investors Service.

Municipal Finance Officers' Association. **Resources in Review.** Washington, D.C. Published bimonthly.

Office of Management and the Budget. **Catalog of Federal Domestic Assistance.** Washington, DC: Government Printing Office. Published annually.

Shearson Lehman/American Express. 1984. **Financing Alternatives for State and Local Correctional Facilities.** New York: Public Finance Department, Shearson Lehman/American Express.

28. Step 7: Select the Most Feasible Option

Who Will Use This Chapter

Primary Users
Project manager
Planning team
Task forces (?)

Secondary Users
Advisory committee
Board of commissioners

Introduction

This chapter, the conclusion to Part 4, summarizes all the considerations that lead to the conclusion about the **need** for renovation or construction; and, if one or the other is needed, which is the **most feasible option** for your county to pursue.

The assessment of the feasibility of various building options will be organized by the project manager, who will focus the results of the work of a variety of planning team members or task forces. The results of this effort will be a feasibility study presented to the advisory committee for review and to the board of commissioners for a final determination about whether to proceed.

The following sections provide space in which to review and summarize the various factors that will contribute to the choice among options.

Capacity Needs

What is the total number of jail beds that the county will require now and over the planning period? Refer to "Step 1: Establish the Need For Facilities" (Chapter 22) or back to "Step 6: Convert Projections to Capacity and Program Needs" (Chapter 19). You may wish to complete separate charts for male and female inmates.

When considering planning targets, be aware that renovated or new facilities planned now will not be on line for two to five years.

Table 28-1. Total Required Capacity

	Now 19( )	In 1 Year 19( )	In 2 Years 19( )	In 3 Years 19( )	In 4 Years 19( )	In 5 Years 19( )	In 6 Years 19( )	In 7 Years 19( )	In 8 Years 19( )	In 9 Years 19( )	In 10 Years 19( )	In 15 Years 19( )	In 20 Years 20( )
High Security													
Unsentenced													
Sentenced													
Lower Security													
Unsentenced													
Sentenced													
Work Furlough													
Medical Service													
Mental Health													
TOTAL BEDS:													

How Much Additional Capacity Is Needed?

For each of the projected years, show how much current facility(ies)—either as is or renovated—can contribute toward meeting the capacity needs and determine how many more beds you need to meet projections. As for total capacity requirements, you may wish to complete this chart separately for males and females.

Table 28-2. Additional Capacity Needed

	Prov. Now 19( )	Needed Now 19( )	In 1 Year 19( )	In 2 Years 19( )	In 3 Years 19( )	In 4 Years 19( )	In 5 Years 19( )	In 6 Years 19( )	In 7 Years 19( )	In 8 Years 19( )	In 9 Years 19( )	In 10 Years 19( )	In 15 Years 19( )	In 20 Years 20( )
High Security														
Unsentenced														
Sentenced														
Lower Security														
Unsentenced														
Sentenced														
Work Furlough														
Medical Service														
Mental Health														
TOTAL BEDS:														

Options for Facility Development

Review the significant options you came up with for varied facility development approaches (see "Facility Options," Chapter 16) and list them below. Include the regional option if you consider it. List below four or more of the desirable options in order of preference, placing what you consider to be the best one first. Since options may meet both short- and long-term requirements, you may wish to explore these separately.

Table 28-3. Facility Development Options

Option	Description
OPTION 1:	
OPTION 2:	
OPTION 3:	

Table 28-3. Facility Development Options, continued

Option	Description
OPTION 4:	
etc.	

First and Operating Costs of Various Options

Use the techniques presented in Chapter 26 to calculate the first (project) and operating costs of the options under consideration. Enter the results below.

Table 28-4. Cost of Facility Options

Option	First Cost ($)	Operating Cost ($/yr)
OPTION 1:	$	$
OPTION 2:	$	$
OPTION 3:	$	$
OPTION 4:	$	$
etc.		

Note: Consider options for various time-projection periods.

Costs and Benefits of Options

Now that the costs of each option are established, what are the benefits? While the economic benefits will probably appear in the assessment of costs, what are the other, noneconomic costs and benefits? These may include such issues as the length of time required for implementation, the resulting quality of facilities, the effectiveness of the programs to be offered, the degree of operational disruption, of covenience or acceptability to the public, and so forth. List the major noneconomic costs and benefits in the chart below.

Table 28-5. Noneconomic Costs and Benefits

Option	Costs	Benefits
OPTION 1:		
OPTION 2:		
OPTION 3:		
OPTION 4:		
etc.		

Once you have listed these costs and benefits, review with the planning team the feasibility analysis as developed to this point. Discuss the needs and the merits of each option. Take the results of this discussion to the advisory committee and select the option that appears to provide the best solution for your county, subject to funding considerations.

Potential Funding Sources

Explore the funding sources listed in Chapter 27 to determine which, if any, of the desirable options your county can afford. If necessary, begin budgeting the planning and construction costs that will be involved. To determine if funds are available from certain sources, it may be necessary to prepare and submit grant applications. The availability of funds may have a considerable effect on which of the options is chosen.

Feasibility Determination

At the conclusion of the feasibility review, the planning team should have a clear idea of which approach will accommodate your county's projected capacity and needed programs. The final selection should be developed with the advisory committee and ratified by the board of commissioners.

If the most desired option is not achievable, consider scaled down or phased approaches. In addition, alternative programs that were rejected initially may well be more attractive in light of the cost analyses. If that is the case, it may be necessary to "recycle" the capacity projections done in Chapters 18 and 19, reconsidering the use of various alternatives to incarceration.

If the project proves to be viable, your county will move on to Part 5 as you become involved in the facility development process.

Part 5.
The Correctional Facility Development Process

29. Introduction

Part 5 presents material intended for counties who have determined that they need to—and can—renovate old jails or construct new jail facilities. Thus, this part covers the following topics:

- The **facility development process.** What steps you will go through, who will do what, and what the results will be as you work toward developing a building project (Chapter 30).
- The **impact of the jail environment** on inmates and staff (Chapter 31).
- **Facility programming.** The determination of detailed functional and architectural requirements for design (Chapter 32).
- **Staffing.** The ascertaining of the composition and number of staff needed to run the jail (Chapter 33).
- **The site analysis process.** The analysis and selection of a building site (if you do not already have one) and planning for its development (Chapter 34).
- **Ongoing project management.** The continuing corrections system and facility monitoring, planning, and management functions (Chapter 35).

Drawing by Eugene Mihaesco; reproduced with permission from **Psychology Today.**

The participatory planning structure that has been working from the beginning will continue to operate. The project manager will coordinate these steps and the planning team will consider information and formulate recommendations to the board of commissioners. The board will offer input and review of policy matters and approval of costs, funding, and contractual actions. The advisory committee will continue to review and offer input at each step.

As the project moves closer to reality, the continued involvement of the sheriff and corrections staff becomes ever more important in order to insure that the product is a facility they can live with for years to come. Specific task forces, drawn mainly from corrections staff, will carry out facility programming and conduct site and, perhaps, architect selection. One of the task forces to be formed during construction will be a transition team. It will be responsible for planning and coordinating the move into the new facility.

"Tumbleweeds" by Tom K. Ryan; reproduced with permission from Field Syndicate

30. The Correctional Facility Development Process

Who Will Use This Chapter

Primary Users
Project manager
Planning team
Advisory committee
Facility programming,
     site selection, and
     other active task forces
Board of commissioners

Secondary Users
County public works
     agency representatives
Planning and architectural
     consultants

Introduction

This chapter is intended to give you an overview of the entire facility development process, from needs assessment through construction and occupancy, up to the eventual obsolescence of the facility. For convenience, the process is shown as a step-by-step sequence from start to finish, even though in reality some steps can happen earlier or later and some may need to be repeated.

The steps in facility development are explained, in order to help each individual understand what lies in store as he or she enters into this long process. An even more important purpose is to encourage your county, especially the corrections department, to take **control** of the process rather than let it control you or bring you nasty surprises. The roles of the project manager, who sees the whole process through, and of the task forces, which provide input, are critical to the continued success of the project.

Your county should identify where it is in the process at the present time, then study with particular care the steps from that point on. (If you are at the beginning of the process, you might wish to refer to the final step below, "Obsolescence and Renovation," which may describe where you are now as well as a point to be reached again someday.)

Remember that for each stage of the process, there is a product (or conclusion) and a formal sign-off by responsible bodies.

Facility Development Process Chart

For each step, Table 30-1 shows four facets of the process: the name and **major activities** of the step, the people or **actors** involved, a list of typical **products,** and a roster of who must **sign off** on these products. Please note that "sign off" may mean either acceptance and endorsement of a product or, more formally, legal approval and contractual authorization to proceed.

The section on **actors** includes nine groups:

- The **board of commissioners.**
- The **sheriff,** and especially the **jail or corrections division.**
- Representatives of county **criminal justice agencies** such as courts and probation staff, some of whom may be on the advisory committee.
- The **county administrative officer** and staff from other **county departments** such as finance, planning, engineering, and assessing.
- The **project manager** of this facility development effort.
- The project's **planning team.**
- The **advisory committee.**

• **Task forces** with specific duties such as site selection, facility evaluation, consolidation, funding, or programming.
• **Consultants or contractors** employed to complete specified tasks, such as planning or architecture.
• **Agencies** that either have jurisdiction over particular products or offer advice, training, or other forms of support.

Phases in the Facility Development Process

The sixteen steps of the facility development process are divided into five main phases of work:
• Phase I: Prearchitectural planning
• Phase II: Site selection and planning
• Phase III: Architectural and engineering design
• Phase IV: Construction
• Phase V: Occupancy
The balance of this chapter elaborates on the tasks involved in each step.

Phase I: Prearchitectural Planning

Step 1. Corrections Needs Assessment Study and Master Plan. By now you are probably very familiar with the needs assessment process that helped your county identify the need to construct or renovate a facility (see Parts 1 through 3).

Step 2. Feasibility Study. The feasibility study is covered in Part 4. To continue with the development of your facility, the study must show your project to be economically viable. In fact, the economic feasibility analysis should continue as an issue throughout the design process—at least until construction bids are received. Only at that point is the true initial cost of the building established. Operating costs, especially staffing, should also be reviewed throughout the design phase since the layout of the building will have considerable effect on the number of staff required to operate it.

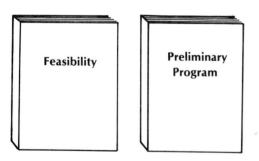

Step 3. Consultant/Architect Selection. Chapter 12 discusses the selection of architects and other consultants and contractors. To avoid needless delays or hurried work, consultants should be selected and hired sufficiently early to give them enough time to perform their tasks to your county's satisfaction. Before completion of the next step, it is wise to initiate the architect selection process so that the design team will be on board and ready to start work on site selection, architectural design, and perhaps programming.

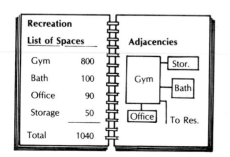

Step 4. Facility Programming. Facility programming includes both functional and architectural programming. While some architectural expertise is required for the latter, functional programming may be done largely by jail and other staff. At the conclusion of programming, set a realistic project budget.

If your county opts to use programming consultants, be sure to work very closely with them. You must explore and express clearly what you want from the facility, or the programmers and the architect will never know and the resulting building will not be responsive to your county's needs.

Chapter 32 deals with facility programming in some depth.

Phase II: Site Selection and Planning

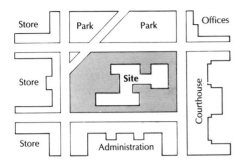

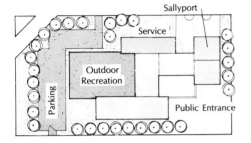

Phase III: Architectural and Engineering Design

Step 5. Site Analysis and Selection. Site selection is very important for functional, technical, economic, and political reasons. The site must support the amount and type of construction required. Its location will have major impact on the operations of law enforcement agencies and movement of prisoners to and from the courts. Political issues surrounding the acceptability of various locations are also of great significance. Unfortunately, politics sometimes result in a jail being placed other than where it would best be located.

Chapter 34 deals with site analysis, selection, and planning.

Step 6. Site Master Plan. Once the site has been selected, master planning activities center around examining and determining long-term site utilization. The master plan locates open space, parking, circulation routes, and security zones. It takes into account the long-term development of the site including required phasing over time. You may need to complete an environmental impact report at this stage of the project.

Step 7. Schematic Design. During schematic design, the most critical design phase, basic concepts emerge for how the facility will be organized. It is easy to make changes at this stage, but it gets more difficult as the design becomes more developed. Major changes after this stage can be costly too, since design work would have to be repeated or construction torn out and rebuilt. These cautions are not given as reasons against making changes later on if needed, but rather to stress the importance of making sure that you are getting what you need at this point.

The users and client must be actively involved in all phases of the design, directing the architect and not solely reacting to or approving his or her suggestions. At this stage, users are concerned with the design's performance on functional and organizational issues. Use the facility program to see where all the required spaces are and that they have all been accommodated. Review the required relationships between areas and imagine actually moving from one to another to carry out typical activity sequences. Where are security and control points? How many stories are proposed? Does the arrangement appear to satisfy your program and design goals? Have the architect explain **precisely** how the proposed design responds to your needs.

Be aware that there may be certain problems in how you will **understand** what the architect is showing you. It is difficult, for instance, to read and interpret plans. The nonarchitect can more easily understand scale models, especially larger-scale ones that show the interior of spaces or even full-scale mockups if warranted by the magnitude or innovation of the project.

Verify adherence to the budget at this point, before giving approval to proceed to design development.

Step 8. Design Development. During design development, review the same issues as during schematic design, particularly as related to any changes that have been made. As design progresses, information becomes more and more specific and refined, so you must continue to re-evaluate the building's performance as you learn more about what it will be like. As the outline specification evolves, it is important to be involved in and review the selection of systems and materials.

Your county and its architects may wish to employ specialists to conduct special studies during design development. These design studies may be necessary because of the complexity of the jail building and its sophisticated systems. It is probably better to rely on an expert (or even do considerable research and testing yourself) rather than depend upon the potentially biased advice of a vendor or manufacturer. By visiting jails at this point you can observe systems in practice and get valuable input from their operators.

Special design studies are not part of basic architectural services but may be contracted for in addition. They are normally coordinated by the architect, although the county can contract independently for them.

Step 9. Contract Documents. "Contract documents" are the plans (blueprints), specifications, and other bidding documents. Together, these form the basis for bids and for the contract, with the contractor specifying what will be built and at what cost. Since these documents establish what you will get for your money, they must reflect exactly the building you want. The final cost estimate is also done at this stage. Changes after this time, which will be by negotiation or by change order, can be highly disruptive and costly.

Contract documents are highly technical and, especially for larger projects, can be voluminous, sometimes running up to hundreds of pages of blueprints and text. The problem you face as a user or client is how to absorb and understand all this information. While you may trust your architect or public works representative, it is important to keep on asking questions about what is being provided in order to make sure that you get what you want.

Step 10. Agency Approvals. Your programmer and architect establish and maintain close liaison with review and approval agencies from the beginning of the project. While they should be familiar with many of the regulatory agencies and their requirements, the county stipulates required approvals, particularly from such local agencies as water or sewer districts. The architect normally takes care of submitting documents and obtaining required approvals. Even so, there may be times when user or client representatives wish to attend meetings or work directly with certain agencies to understand their concerns and participate more fully in solving potential problems.

Phase IV: Construction

Step 11. Bidding and Negotiation. There are a number of alternative bidding procedures. These include the standard design/bid/build sequence in which the architect prepares one set of bid documents that are bid on and constructed by one prime contractor and a number of subcontractors. Or the architect may divide the project into a number of separate "bidding packages," each of which covers certain parts of the project such as demolition plus site work, foundations, or structure. This is sometimes done to "fast track" the bidding and construction sequence so that one part of the construction can be started before design is completed on other parts.

Under certain circumstances, particularly when more than one construction contract is contemplated, counties use construction management services. Construction managers specialize in coordinating and scheduling the activities, professionals, and contractors involved in design, bidding, and construction. This expertise and accountability can be valuable. Note, however, that construction management services do not always deliver the time or money savings that their proponents may claim. Some counties have had problems with fast tracking, finding that decision-making time was cut down to the detriment of the design.

The use of one or the other of these methods must be determined very early on in the process, since which consultants are hired and **what** they are hired to do depends on the decision. Actually there are many variations and combinations of approaches. It is possible to have a relatively standard process where long lead items, such as security hardware, are bid and ordered in advance to save time—without the formality of a fast track process.

With any of these methods, once a set of construction documents is completed, the county advertises for bids, holds meetings with potential bidders to clarify the documents, and receives and opens the bids at an appointed time and place.

After the bids are examined and the qualifications of the bidders checked out, one bidder—usually the lowest one who is deemed qualified—is selected to be the construction contractor. Then the construction contract is negotiated and details are worked out. These involve questions about the inclusion of **bid alternates** (which may add or delete items or areas once the bottom line is known) and the substitution of materials.

Step 12. Construction. On-site construction begins, and then, after months or years of planning and design, a physical building finally emerges. During this phase, the architect is responsible for **administration of the construction contract.** He or she carries out site observations, coordinates **shop drawings** submitted by suppliers, and reviews materials tests and **change orders.**

Change orders indicate alterations or departures from the construction contract, such as additions, deletions, or substitutions. These can be minor, but sometimes involve major, important changes that affect the cost and function of the facility. The importance of careful review and monitoring of change orders for their cost and impact on operations or performance cannot be overstressed. Since in effect change orders modify the construction contract, their legal and fiscal impact must be evaluated and approved by the proper county authority (ultimately the board of commissioners).

In addition to on-site observations by the architect, the county may wish to have its own technically qualified representative or clerk of the works overseeing the work and representing county interests.

This is also the time to form the transition task force of jail operators and managers to prepare for the move into the new facility.

Step 13. Construction Completion. As the building and site development near completion, the county should be aware of and take part in a number of activities. The architect and contractor prepare a "punch list" of items remaining to be finished or repaired. As systems are completed, certain performance tests are conducted for all mechanical, electrical, plumbing, heating or air conditioning, security, and communications systems to insure that they work properly. Warranties and guarantees are delivered to the owner. A **users' manual** may be prepared to organize and synthesize these documents along with operating instructions and functional information.

A users' manual for a building is a rather new concept. As a single source of information about the systems, operations, and functions of the building, it can be a useful aid to the building's operation. It is remarkable that a car or appliance that costs up to a few thousand dollars comes with a detailed owner's manual while a building as complex as a jail often costing millions of dollars comes with the cutting of a ribbon and a handshake. Demand for a building users' manual may well grow.

The preparation of "as-builts" or record drawings that show how the building was actually constructed are a potential extra service. If carefully developed and kept up to date, they are an invaluable tool in the maintenance and alteration of the building and should be required in the architect's contract.

By this point, advance planning for the move to the new facility is well under way. Furniture or equipment not included in the construction contract have been ordered. Required personnel are hired and trained.

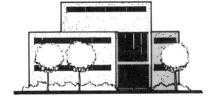

Phase V: Occupancy

Step 14. Movein and Startup. Several activities prepare jail staff for moving into the new facility. These include arranging of furnishings and movable equipment; planning the logistics of the move; shaking down all systems in operation; transferring prisoners and staff; and starting the actual operation of the jail. The more carefully and thoroughly you plan and execute the logistics of the transition, the smoother this difficult process will be.

Immediately upon movein, an ongoing preventive maintenance program should be initiated with an adequate budget for staff and materials. The jail is a 24-hour-per-day, seven-day-per-week facility, subject to intense use from its first day of operation. If maintenance or repair is deferred for long, it becomes much more difficult and expensive. Include in the construction contract extra replacement parts of special items such as windows, doors, and lights so they will be on hand when needed. Care for this expensive new facility should begin immediately with occupancy.

Step 15. Occupancy and Operation. The actual use of your new facility may not begin for three to five years or more after the initial planning. However, use will continue for the many years during which your county will occupy, operate, maintain, repair, and make minor alterations to the jail.

Once the new jail is on line it is extremely important to monitor its operations. As stated elsewhere in this book the jail is a **capacity-driven system** that can fill up or become overcrowded immediately if policies, programs, and population levels are not monitored continuously. Only with vigilance and early response to developing problems can your planning assumptions and forecasts be expected to work out.

Step 16. Obsolescence and Renovation. Eventually users begin to recognize certain bad fits between desired programs or goals and the actual performance of certain bad fits between desired programs or goals and the actual performance of the building. At that time, re-evaluate the jail building's potential to serve compared to alternatives. This evaluation may be informal, or it may involve a formal evaluation study that synthesizes the responses of jail administrators, staff, inmates, and maintenance personnel (see Chapter 23). It may be worthwhile to consider a number of building-related options at this time such as renovation, addition, or construction of satellite facilities (see Chapter 24). While obsolescence to some degree is inevitable, some flexibility may be built into the design to help alleviate future misfits.

It may seem a bit strange to end this description of the facility development process at precisely the point where most readers' facilities are now. However, recognition of this likely future state should help put the entire process into perspective as a continuing cycle of events.

Acknowledgment: The first draft of the material contained in this chapter was developed with support from the National Institute of Corrections Jail Center for use in its PONI program.

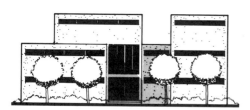

References

American Institute of Architects. 1971. **Statement of the Architect's Services.** Washington, DC: AIA. Describes the architect's responsibilities at each stage of design and construction.

American Institute of Architects. 1978. **You and Your Architect.** Washington, DC: AIA. Explains some of the client's responsibilities during the course of the project.

Table 30-1. Stages in the Correctional Facility Development Process

---

PHASE I: PREARCHITECTURAL PLANNING

Step 1.
Corrections Needs Assessment Study and Master Plan

Major Activities:

Organize planning team.
Set up advisory committee & task forces.
Review corrections issues: standards & legal; developments in operations & design; costs.
Develop mission statement.
Gather & analyze corrections system data.
Consider alternative programs.
Project corrections system & facility needs.

Actors' Roles:

Commissioners: help select & define roles & functions of planning team & advisory committee; evaluate, approve recommendations, needs assessment study, & master plan.

Sheriff and Corrections Staff: serve on planning team, advisory committee, & task forces.

Justice Agency Representatives: serve on planning team, advisory committee, & task forces.

Project Manager: coordinates; assigns tasks, manages work.

Planning Team: collects, analyzes information; prepares reports; makes recommendations; provides information for decisions; develops mission statement & functional program.

Advisory Committee: studies & evaluates planning team's recommendations/reports, & information; identifies criminal justice problems; considers policy issues.

Task Forces: receive assignments regarding topics of concern (e.g., site), conduct studies, make recommendations.

Consultant/Contractor: corrections planner may collect, analyze data, & provide information.

Table 30-1. Stages in the Correctional Facility Development Process, continued

Agencies: State, NIC, & regional planning agencies may provide input & assistance; state may have to approve needs assessment study (if application for state funds is made).

Products:

Mission statement
Needs assessment study
Corrections system master plan

Sign-off:

Citizens advisory committee
Sheriff/Corrections
Justice agencies (if their cooperation is required)
Board of commissioners

Step 2.
Feasibility Study

Major Activities:

Project facility needs.
Develop preliminary program statement.
Evaluate existing facilities.
Explore facility options.
Consider regional facility.
Analyze costs.
Explore funding sources/apply for grants.
Determine project feasibility.

Actors' Roles:

Commissioners: approve feasibility study report, determine whether or not to proceed.

Sheriff and Corrections Staff: provide & gather information.

Justice Agency Representatives: provide & gather information.

Project Manager: helps develop preliminary program; manages feasibility study.

Planning Team: develops preliminary program; conducts portions of feasibility study.

Advisory Committee: reviews & approves feasibility study report.

Task Forces: conduct portions of feasibility study: evaluate existing facility, consider building-related options, look at consolidation; explore funding possibilities.

Consultant/Contractor: may conduct facility evaluation.

Products:

Preliminary program
Feasibility study report
Grant application (?)

Signoff:

Advisory committee
Board of commissioners
Sheriff/corrections

Step 3.
Consultant/Architect Selection

Major Activities

Deciding if need consultants: for what, when.
Identifying, screening, hiring consultants & architects.
Managing & supervising consultants & architects.

Actors' Roles:

Commissioners (with their staff): define scope of services; solicit requests for proposals; screen, select consultants & architects; allocate funds for contracts; approve contracts.

Sheriff and Corrections Staff: help determine what types of consultants are needed; provide information to consultants.

Justice Agency Representatives: may help determine what types of consultants are needed; provide information to consultants.

Project Manager: identifies need for consultants; may help screen & recommend consultants; may help define scope of services; manages consultants.

County Departments: planning & building departments help determine what types of consultants are needed; facilities department may help select & manage architects & engineers.

Planning Team: works with, reviews, & critiques consultants' work.

Advisory Committee: provides input to and reviews consultants' work.

Table 30-1. Stages in the Correctional Facility Development Process, continued

Task Forces: monitor projects & plan meetings with consultants.

Consultant/Contractor: corrections planners, architects, & contractors; may also include master planners, facility programmers or evaluators, energy consultants, financial consultants, etc.

Products:

Contract(s)

Signoff:

Board of commissioners
Sheriff/corrections

Step 4.
Facility Programming

Major Activities:

Conduct functional programming.
Conduct architectural programming.
Estimate staffing.

Actors' Roles:

Commissioners: provide input to, review, & approve program.

Sheriff and Corrections Staff: may conduct functional programming; facility users provide input.

Justice Agency Representatives (if their spaces are affected): may conduct some functional programming; provide input.

Project Manager: supervise/manage programming effort.

Planning Team: contributes to program.

Advisory Committee: contributes to program.

Task Forces: may conduct programming.

Consultant/Contractor: may use facility programmers.

Agencies: input & technical assistance available from BOC.

Products:

Facility Program:
Functional program
Architectural program

Signoff:

Sheriff/corrections
Board of commissioners

PHASE II: SITE SELECTION AND PLANNING

Step 5.
Site Analysis and Selection

Major Activities:

Develop site requirements.
Identify available sites.
Evaluate available sites.
Consider technical & political issues.
Select & acquire site.

Actors' Roles:

Commissioners: review & approve site selection.

Sheriff and Corrections Staff: provide input.

Justice Agency Representatives: provide input.

Project Manager: helps review & select site.

Planning Team: provides input on site requirements & selection.

Advisory Committee: provides input on selection.

Task Forces: evaluate & recommend site.

Consultant/Contractor: traffic engineer, real estate assessor may advise.

Products:

Selection of site
Acquisition of site

Signoff:

Board of commissioners
Planning/zoning commission
Advisory committee
Sheriff/corrections

Table 30-1. Stages in the Correctional Facility Development Process, continued

Step 6.
Site Master Plan

Major Activities:

Plan the long-term utilization of the site once it has been selected.
Survey site characteristics (soils, utilities, vegetation, existing uses, circulation, etc.).
Conduct long-range planning & phasing.
Plan site utilization & organization (open space, parking, security, etc.).
Complete environmental impact report.
Complete site development guidelines & master plan.

Actors' Roles:

Commissioners: review & approve site development guidelines & site master plan.

Project Manager: manages master planning efforts.

Sheriff and Corrections Staff: contribute input to master plan.

Justice Agency Representatives (if affected): contribute input to master plan.

Planning Team: may compile/complete site development guidelines & site master plan.

Task Forces: may work on guidelines or master plan.

Consultant/Contractor: architect/planner/landscape architect may work on master plan, site development guidelines; geologist, surveyor, ecologist may contribute to environmental impact report.

Products:

Master plan document (plans & written report)
Site development guidelines
Environmental impact report (may be required)

Signoff:
Planning/zoning commissioners
Board of commissioners
Sheriff/corrections

PHASE III: ARCHITECTURAL DESIGN
Step 7.
Schematic Design

Major Activities:

Execute conceptual & schematic architectural design.
Develop preliminary engineering concepts.
Complete preliminary cost analysis.
Consult with applicable agencies.
Consider alternative bidding procedures (standard, construction manager, separate contracts, fast track).
Revise staffing analysis.

Actors' Roles:

Commissioners: review & approve schematics & budget; give notice to proceed.

Sheriff and Corrections Staff: provide input to designers.

Justice Agency Representatives: provide input to designers.

Project Manager: ensures schedules are met.

Planning Team: provides input to designers, uses program to test design.

Advisory Committee: provides input to designers, uses program to test design.

County Departments: fire marshal, building inspector review plans.

Consultant/Contractor: architects & engineers begin design; construction manager/cost estimator estimates costs.

Agencies: state local corrections agency reviews plans.

Products:

Schematic design drawings
Schematic cost estimate

Signoff:

Board of commissioners
Sheriff/corrections
State local corrections agency

Step 8.
Design Development

Major Activities:

Refine & develop architectural & engineering design.
Develop outline specification.
Conduct energy analysis.
Update/refine costs.

Table 30-1. Stages in the Correctional Facility Development Process, continued

May execute special design studies of security, equipment, communications, kitchen/food service, interior, graphics, furnishings, etc.

Actors' Roles:

Commissioners: review & approve design development, special studies, & budget; notice to proceed.

Sheriff and Corrections Staff: provide input to special design studies & design.

Justice Agency Representatives (if their spaces are affected): provide input to special design studies & design.

Project Manager: directs & supervises study teams; ensures schedule & budget are met.

Planning Team: provides input to study teams; reviews systems, selections, design.

Advisory Committee: provides input to study teams; reviews systems, selections, design.

County Departments: fire marshal, building inspector may review plans & specifications in progress

Consultant/Contractor: architects, engineers, construction manager/cost estimator; may have special study teams/consultants.

Agencies: state local corrections agency may review plans & specifications in progress.

Products:
Design development drawings
Outline specifications
Construction cost estimate

Signoff:
Board of commissioners
Sheriff/corrections

Step 9.
Contract Documents

Major Activities:
Complete plans (blueprints).
Complete specifications.
Develop bidding documents.
Execute final cost estimate.

Actors' Roles:

Commissioners: review & approve contract documents & final cost estimate (for bids).

Sheriff and Corrections Staff: provide input, review.

Justice Agency Representatives: (if affected) provide input & review.

Project Manager: ensures tasks are completed.

Planning Team: provides input & review.

County Departments: fire marshal, building inspector may review plans & specifications.

Consultant/Contractor: architects & engineers complete plans & specifications; construction manager/cost estimator determines cost estimate.

Agencies: state local corrections agency may review plans & specifications.

Products:
Plans (blueprints)
Specifications
Bidding documents
Final cost estimate

Signoff:
Board of commissioners
Sheriff/corrections

Step 10.
Agency Approvals

Major Activities:
Obtain building permit.
Procure regulatory agency approvals.
Seek/secure funding agency approvals.

Actors' Roles:

Project Manager: facilitates securing approvals, submits formally required documentation.

County Departments: fire marshal, building inspector approve contract documents.

Consultant/Contractor: architect aids in submission of documents & obtaining approvals.

Agencies: state local corrections agency approves contract documents.

Table 30-1. Stages in the Correctional Facility Development Process, continued

Product:
Written approvals

Signoff:
State local corrections agency
Fire marshal
County building department
County health department
Other regulatory agencies
Funding agencies

PHASE IV: CONSTRUCTION

Step 11.
Bidding and Negotiation

Major Activities:
Advertise for bids.
Open bids.
Select lowest qualified bidder.
Negotiate contract for construction.

Actors' Roles:

Supervisors: make decision on bids.

Project Manager: may manage bidding process, review bids, recommend bid to accept.

County Departments: facilities department may manage bidding process, review bids, recommend bid to accept; legal department reviews bids to ensure their legality.

Planning Team: reviews bids.

Consultant/Contractor: architect or construction manager receives & reviews bids & may manage process; building contractors (& subs) submit bids.

Product:
Contract for construction

Signoff:
Board of commissioners
Funding agency

Step 12.
Construction

Major Activities:
Work on site.
Administration of construction contract.
Conduct site observations.
Process payments (interim approvals).
Complete shop drawings.
Test materials.
Process change orders.
Set up transition team & start planning for move.
Begin hiring & training staff.

Actors' Roles:

Commissioners: appoint individual to review & approve change orders.

Project Manager: may manage interim approval process; may review & approve change orders; begins preparations for move.

County Departments: finance department processes payments; facilities department may manage interim approval process & may review and approve change orders; building department inspects.

Planning Team: monitors changes; begins preparations for move.

Task Forces: programming & design task force becomes and acts as transition task force.

Advisory Committee: helps with preparations for move.

Consultant/Contractor: architects approve change orders; architects & engineers monitor; construction manager supervises & coordinates; contractor & subcontractors build.

Product:
The building

Signoff:
Architect & representative of board of commissioners on change orders

Table 30-1. Stages in the Correctional Facility Development Process, continued

Step 13.
Construction Completion

Major Activities:

Compile "punch list."
Draft record or as-built drawings.
Secure warranties & guarantees.
Conduct performance testing.
Obtain waivers of liens.
Write users' manual.
Plan detailed logistics of move.
Secure occupancy permit.
Ensure furniture & equipment is enroute.
Hire & train personnel.

Actors' Roles:

Commissioners: accept building.

Sheriff and Corrections Staff: prepare for move; hire & train staff.

Justice Agencies (if directly affected): prepare for move.

Project Manager: coordinates preparations to move into building.

County Departments: building department issues occupancy permit.

Planning Team: may prepare users' manual, then phases out.

Advisory Committee: may help prepare users' manual.

Task Forces: Transition task force makes preparations for move, updates policy & procedures manual, carries out operational staffing analysis, coordinates hiring & training of new staff, conducts public relations efforts, may prepare users' manual.

Consultant/Contractor: architect & contractor prepare "punch list"; architect may prepare as-built drawings & approves certificate of completion; architect provides orientation to facility.

Product:

Completed building

Signoff:

Funding agency
Board of commissioners
Sheriff/corrections
Architect
Building department

PHASE V: OCCUPANCY
Step 14.
Movein and Startup

Major Activities:

Complete selection & training of personnel.
Install furnishings & movable equipment.
Transfer prisoners.
Begin operation.
Initiate data gathering & analysis of population, programs.
Initiate maintenance program.

Actors' Roles:

Sheriff and Corrections Staff: move into & begin using facility; start gathering and analyzing data; begin maintenance programs.

Justice Agencies (those affected): move into & begin use of facility.

Project Manager: facilitates move.

Task Forces: Transition task force manages move & orientation to facility, making use of users' manual; conducts public relations.

County Departments: building department (& sheriff, corrections staff) start maintenance program.

Advisory Committee: monitors correctional system performance & programs.

Product:

The building in use

Signoff:

None

Table 30-1. Stages in the Correctional Facility Development Process, continued

Step 15.
Occupancy and Operation

Major Activities:

Occupy facility.
Operate.
Maintain.
Repair.

Actors' Roles:

Commissioners: provide ongoing control & support.

Sheriff and Corrections Staff: occupy, operate, & maintain facility; continue collecting and analyzing data on populations & programs.

Justice Agencies (those affected): occupy & operate facility.

Advisory Committee: continues monitoring correctional system performance & programs.

Project Manager: phased out.

County Departments: building department makes minor repairs

Consultant/Contractor: may have facility planner/evaluator conduct post-occupancy evaluation; contractor makes repairs as needed.

Agencies: state & regional corrections agencies, provide technical assistance, training, support, & possible grants for programs, etc.

Product:

No physical product

Signoff:

None

Step 16.
Obsolescence & Renovation

Major Activities:

Review performance & maintenance of building.
Consider bad fits among facility, programs, & goals.
Evaluate building's potential (compared to building-related alternatives).
Fine-tune facility, consider renovations.

Actors' Roles:

Corrections: inspect facility, approve building-related changes (e.g. renovations, new facility).

Sheriff and Corrections Staff: operate, maintain facility; identify bad fits/problems of facility, recommend physical changes.

Justice Agencies (those affected): operate facility, recommend physical changes.

County Departments: grand jury inspects building; facilities department conducts inspections & coordinates/manages renovations.

Planning Team: may be reactivated if major changes are considered.

Advisory Committee: may be reactivated if major changes are considered.

Task Forces: may use evaluation task force for post-occupancy evaluation.

Consultant/Contractor: facility evaluator or architect may study building; architect & contractor make renovations/additions.

Agencies: inspections by state local corrections agency, state fire marshal.

Products:

Complaints (?)
Grand jury report (?)
Jail inspection reports (?)
Building evaluation study (?)
Renovations/additions/new facility (?)

Signoff:

If renovation/additions/new facility:

    Board of commissioners
    Sheriff/corrections
    State local corrections agency

31. Human Factors in Jail Design

Who Will Use This Chapter

Primary Users

Planning and design
  consultants
Project manager

Secondary Users

Planning team
Advisory committee

Introduction

The jail environment—its location, surroundings, layout and design—has very significant effects on the people who use this highly specialized facility. The purpose of this chapter is to discuss some of the many ways in which the physical environment of the jail may affect the behavior, attitudes, or feelings of its users.

A great deal has been written about the physical environment of the jail—how it is and how it should be. Much of this is opinion based on experience, common sense, or speculation. Where opinion has been codified, it becomes a guideline; where it has statutory power, a standard. Outside the realm of opinion, some of our knowledge is based on empirical research done in jails or other correctional environments. Although only perhaps thirty such studies have been done to date, this chapter reviews the results of this research in the hope that it may have some influence on decisions about jail design.

The concept that correctional design has effects on behavior is far from new. For example, the eighteenth-century "panoptican" plan of Jeremy Bentham manipulated the environment for behavioral ends, that is, to separate inmates while allowing supervision from a central point (Evans; Fairweather). What is new is that now scientists and designers are beginning to visit buildings and measure the relationships between environment and behavior—the impact of jail design on the users.

Jail Users

Everyone who visits the jail for any reason is a jail user. Jail users include inmates, staff, administrators, visitors, law enforcement officers, service and emergency personnel, and community members. The main factors that distinguish categories of users are: their situation, role, or amount of time involved in the facility; their degree of control over their situation; their attitudes, expectations, and objectives; and their socioeconomic status.

The inmates are the first and obvious but highly diverse grouping. To understand inmate needs and behavior, it is necessary to understand their situations—since this governs their relationship to the jail environment. One of the most stressful times for a detainee is usually intake, as this is his or her first contact with the jail system (especially for a first-time offender). At intake the main concerns are the uncertainty of one's status and what will happen in this environment. Information (written or posted), human contact, the appearance of the facility, and a view of the interior spaces can all be reassuring (Farbstein 1978). Access to a telephone, the possibility of immediate release, the ability to contact outsiders and arrange for obligations or property to be taken care of temporarily will be foremost in the detainee's concerns.

The concerns of the individual who remains in custody as a presentenced prisoner revolve around court appearances, conferences with attorneys, and access to legal information. Court appearances are of course stressful, as so much depends on their outcome. The environments experienced during movement to and from court may heighten or lessen tensions (for example, exterior views or distractions such as television).

An inmate who is sentenced to be detained at the jail has a different set of concerns. These revolve around "doing time" and the daily routines of jail life.

In general, inmates are far from typical of the population as a whole. They tend to be from lower socioeconomic groups and poorly educated. Minorities are consistently overrepresented. As a result, ethnic or racial polarization that exists in the outside world can be heightened in jail (see the section on territoriality for a discussion of how this relates to environment).

The second major group of jail users is the staff—including security, program, and support staff. Each has a different set of relationships with the inmates—and each makes different demands on the environment. The physical relationship between staff and inmate spaces, ease of visual surveillance, and the provision of program space will affect staff-inmate relations. In a security-oriented jail, "correctional" officers may not be able to perform a correctional function.

Depending on differences in their activities and locations in the jail, line and administrative staff may have very different needs and attitudes toward the jail environment. These do not always align as one might expect. For example, a study of the Federal Metropolitan Correctional Centers found that inmates and line staff had very similar attitudes concerning low levels of vandalism, while administrators held opposite views (Wener and Olsen 1978, 1980).

Visitors and community users are particularly sensitive to the jail's location and image. If the jail is to become a "community correctional center," as suggested by LEAA's National Clearinghouse for Criminal Justice Planning and Architecture (referred to henceforth as the National Clearinghouse), it must be accessible to the community and appear as a place that the public can tolerate to visit or have "next door."

Institutional and Residential Group Sizes

How large should a jail be? The answer depends, of course, on a detailed study of the needs of its community, including alternatives to incarceration. Consideration must also be given to evidence concerning the effect of jail and living unit size on the goals of the jail. A review of the literature on institution size concluded that "**size alone** creates organizational **pressures** toward custodial rather than treatment operations. The net effect of these pressures tends to alienate inmates from treatment involvement" (Knight 1971, p. 21; emphasis in the original).

For the jail itself, a maximum size of 300 (National Advisory Commission on Criminal Justice Standards and Goals 1973 to 400 (Moyer et al. 1971) is recommended. Above this size, regimentation and routinization seem inevitable, anonymity is fostered, and the institution's image tends toward rejection and security. Moyer quotes recommendations of a 100- to 125-bed capacity as allowing "for staff to recognize . . . every resident and to develop personal relationships with each individual (1977, p. 212).

Within the jail, "Small living-unit size is crucial to the implementation of effective and humanitarian treatment" (Knight 1971, p. 21). While there are no magic numbers, a living unit of from twelve to twenty encourages close, personal relationships to develop among inmates and with correctional staff. Moos found that unit population in and of itself has a significant effect on the unit's "social climate"—with smaller units achieving more "spontaneity, support and autonomy" and less submission. However, larger units may be designed, if they allow for some level of subdivision and smaller group identity. This was found to be successful at the New York Metropolitan Correctional Center (MCC), where six tiers of eight rooms each (with a shower, telephone and small conversation area) combine to form a 48-bed unit (Wener and Olsen 1978, 1980). The small size was felt by inmates to reduce vandalism and theft, because "strangers" were immediately recognizable.

Environmental Perception

The environment provides information that is received on sensory channels. Each sense has its unique ability to accept information. With light the eye sees, with sound the ear hears, the skin feels pressure, heat, and cold. When the senses lack adequate stimulation, boredom, frustration, and tension result. This can occur in jail, and so can its inverse effect: heightened sensory acuity, especially for smell and sound. Because of this, each of these sensory needs will be discussed relative to the conditions found in jail.

Light and View

Adequate light is required for the performance of visual tasks, especially reading and writing. Reading requires approximately 75 to 100 foot candles (a standard measure of illumination). Some jails do not provide these levels. A study in North Carolina, for instance, found only 30 foot candles at bunk levels, making reading difficult to impossible (Goldblatt 1972). Satisfactory lighting levels together with inmate control are required by the American Correctional Association (ACA) Committee of Accreditation and are recommended elsewhere.

Lighting can of course be made available naturally from windows, as well as from artificial sources. The debate concerning the psychological effects of windowless environments is considerable. Although (unbelievably) no research has been done in jails on this specific subject, results of studies in other settings would suggest that windows are more than just a luxury for the incarcerated. Studies of stressful situations find that a lack of contact with the outside world heightens the stress. For example, more than twice as many patients in a windowless intensive care unit developed postsurgical depression than those with windows. The author of the study theorized "that windows apparently provide some sort of necessary psychological escape from the grim realities of surgery" (Collins 1975, pp. 29-30).

A general review of the effects of windows—and the lack of them—concludes that "although a view out is generally regarded as desirable, in some restricted and monotonous situations, it becomes almost a necessity" (Collins, p. 76). There is little doubt that a jail cell fits this description. The proposed Nebraska **Jail Standards** state that:

> Transparent windows are not a mere luxury, but rather serve as a means by which inmates maintain vital links with the outside world . . . . at least five district courts have recognized the right of pretrial detainees to have transparent windows (Nebraska State Bar Association 1977, p. 61).

It may be somewhat ironic that the areas of highest stress in jails—isolation cells—are those that most commonly lack windows.

Color

Unlike other aspects of the sensory environment, color is not treated in jail standards or court cases. While its general psychological effects are significant and well studied, almost nothing has been done in the correctional field. The ACA **Standards** recommend that cells be painted a light color. Studies have found positive inmate response to bright colors (Wener and Clark 1977) and murals (especially ones they have designed and painted themselves; Goldblatt 1972). These are found to make the jail more attractive, brighter, more cheerful, and personalized—in general, less institutional. In concert with other factors, this positive physical appearance is thought by inmates and guards alike to improve morale and lessen tension somewhat. While great claims were made a few years ago about the calming effect of pink holding cells, there has been no conclusive evidence that it actually works.

Two rather similar articles on the use of color in correctional environments review its effects and recommend colors for various areas (Sweitzer 1977; Reeves 1985). Color can enhance light (brightening or subduing spaces), provide sensory stimulation, give directional and other information, and optically change the proportions of a room. Saturated colors are thought to be inviting and "reassuring," although only a "moderate level of stimulation" is recommended. According to Sweitzer, cells should be off-white, with a bright accent wall. Certain hues of blue, red, black, and yellow should be avoided because of their psychological or cultural connotations. Color can also be used to code doors or units, equipment, circulation spaces, and safety or emergency items. Reeves supplies a matrix of color recommendations to achieve desired behaviors in a variety of jail spaces. However, neither Sweitzer nor Reeves has conducted empirical studies to test their theories.

Noise

Noise is one of the jail environment's most persistent problems, even plaguing the new "soft" jails (Wener and Clark 1977). Noise is, simply, unwanted sound. In the presence of this unwanted sound, communication becomes difficult, conversations take place at a shout, sleep is often disturbed, and stress and discomfort are experienced (Gersten n.d.). A study of the prison environment (Moore 1985) found that noise, along with other invasions of privacy, resulted in increased use of health services by inmates.

Two major factors are at issue here. One is the **source** of noise. In many jails, the clang of metal on metal is common. Multiple conversations, radios, and televisions in the same space create an indeterminate, disorienting, and very high level of sound. Unexpected or unpredictable noise can be even more disturbing than a constant high level. The second factor is the hard, reflective quality of most jail **building materials**. Softer, more absorbent materials that could reduce sound levels are virtually unused.

Proposed standards distinguish between acceptable daytime sound levels of about 70 decibels or less, based on normal conversation (85 decibels requires shouting) and acceptable nighttime sound levels of about 45 decibels, based on sleep interference noise levels (Nebraska State Bar Association 1977, pp. 61-62).

Recommendations for reducing noise levels include: isolating or dispersing audio systems, utilizing sound-absorbing materials such as carpet or acoustic tiles, and limiting metal-on-metal contacts of structure, equipment, or furnishings.

Thermal Comfort

Thermal comfort—or discomfort—represents a complex of psychophysiological responses to conditions in the physical environment. These include temperature, humidity, and air movement, which in their turn result from a combination of outdoor climatic conditions, heat flow through the building structure, and the tempering effects of the building's mechanical systems. The outcome as experienced inside the jail depends on the individual's level of activity or exertion, quantity of clothing, and level of control over thermal conditions.

In general, thermal discomfort is very common, especially inside closed institutions. Inmates and staff frequently find conditions too hot, cold, drafty, or stuffy (Goldblatt 1972; Wener and Clark 1977). Though not documented for prisons, irritability undoubtedly increases with thermal discomfort, making aggressive behavior more likely—especially when it is too hot.

Even new correctional facilities often have difficulty achieving thermal comfort. Perhaps this is because jail buildings are frequently complex structures, with their spaces varying greatly in volume, exterior exposure, and occupant load. Such complexity increases the difficulty of mechanical system design.

Standards that apply to thermal comfort are normally based on building-code requirements; for example, the ACA Standards require 10 cubic feet per minute of fresh or purified air for a single room. Nebraska's standards propose that temperatures be kept between 60 and 85 degrees (a very wide range).

In addition, the desirability of some amount of inmate control should be recognized, given the considerable variety in individual responses.

Sensory Deprivation

Sensory deprivation implies a severe limitation on the stimulation available to one or more of the senses. A complete absence of stimulation is generally attempted in experimental studies (total darkness, complete sound absorption, and even emersion in body-temperature water). While this does not describe the jail environment, many jail isolation cells reduce stimulation to a very low level. A psychologist has pointed out that "very little is known about the effects of long-term confinement on sensory abilities" (Sommer 1971, pp. 18-19).

Generalizing from other settings, sensory deprivation can cause "difficulty in thinking, a shortening of time perception, distorted impressions of his own body, and hallucinations" (Leroy, p. 46). It has been suggested that monotony and boredom contribute to the vandalism common in jails; "with enforced idleness and sensory deprivation predominating...individual expression is suppressed, but not eliminated" (Moyer 1977, p. 56).

The lack of variety that results from limiting an individual's experience to a sixteen- or even fifty-person living unit for many months has also been questioned as possibly detrimental (Silver 1978). Thus the relatively open and noninstitutional MCCs are not always preferred by inmates over more traditional facilities that allow wider ranges of movement and more access to the outdoors (Wener and Clark 1977; Wener and Olsen 1978).

None of these sensory issues is simple. None acts singly on the individual—rather they act in concert as part of the total setting of the jail. Other aspects of this setting will be discussed in the next section, including some of the many ways that the jail building affects communications and social relationships: the jail's social environment.

The Social Environment

The ability to control one's sensory environment is closely linked with the ability to control one's social environment, that is, who one meets or communicates with and under what circumstances. In general, being in jail significantly reduces this control. However, specific physical arrangements of the jail environment have considerable effects on communications, privacy, territoriality, and crowding. All of these factors are treated in this section.

Communication and Social Interaction

Sensory information received from or transmitted to another individual forms the basis for communication or social interaction. The major types of interaction that are of concern in the jail involve staff and inmates (including staff interactions with other staff and inmates' interactions with other inmates). Depending on personal predilections or the goals of incarceration, specific interactions may be viewed as positive or negative. Helping, considerate exchanges are positive, while any unwanted or destructive exchange is negative. Staff-inmate interactions are desirable from correctional and security standpoints. The physical size, shape, and location of an area affects visual surveillance, since this depends on the ability of staff to see into certain inmate spaces.

Research in correctional settings has shown that physical design can affect the probability of positive or negative interactions taking place. A study of a Louisiana women's prison before and after a move into a new facility found that security became more formalized, surveillance became more obtrusive, and informal contacts decreased in the new facility because of problems with unobservable spaces. This was, of course, contrary to program goals (Prestholdt et al. 1976).

A study of various youth facilities found that the location of circulation routes and staff or control areas affected the frequency of staff-resident interactions. Informal outdoor spaces were also found to encourage informal personal interactions (McReynolds 1972; McReynolds and Palys 1975).

Locating staff in residential units—so-called direct supervision (Nelson 1983)—also increases contacts with residents. The planners of the MCCs consciously eliminated the staff station from residential units so that staff would circulate among inmates (Wener and Olsen 1978, 1980). One potentially negative outcome of this is that staff themselves may begin to feel isolated from one another (McReynolds 1972). This can increase their tensions, depending on the availability of other staff members. On the other hand, a study of the Contra Costa County jail found that direct supervision increases the ability of staff to control the jail through immediate interaction with the inmates (Frazier 1985). And, because it is more challenging than working in a remotely located control booth, it may also increase staff professionalism (Nelson 1983).

Territoriality

When a certain physical area is identified with or controlled by an individual or group, **territoriality** is in operation. On an individual level, inmates have been found to sense an intrusion into their personal territory when it is entered by others, especially strangers (Kinzel 1970). The size of this zone is much larger in violent inmates (about twenty-nine square feet) than for nonviolent ones (about seven square feet). For violent inmates, the rear of the zone may be larger than the front, although later research has questioned this result (Curran, Blatchley, and Hanlon

1978). In any case, the issue of personal territory has implications for sleeping and dayroom design, as size and layout affect distance and direction of approach.

On a group level, it is common in correctional settings for ethnic or other groups to habitually occupy—perhaps "take over"—certain areas. The reason for this may be that defined territorial boundaries clarify and control contact between groups, which in turn reduces tension, although it also increases ethnic polarization. In a study of territories in a youth training school, it was found that a change in furniture arrangement in a dayroom increased positive interracial contact. However, disruptive behavior also increased, perhaps as a result of the loss of clear territorial boundaries (Stokols and Marrero 1976).

Crowding, Privacy, and Stress

Stress in jail comes from many sources, including uncertainty about the future and exposure to danger, as well as from aspects of the housing environment such as crowding or lack of privacy. The effects of stress include elevated blood pressure, more frequent illness, an increase in sick call rates, as well as greater anger, assaultiveness, and violence.

Privacy is commonly defined as the ability to control one's immediate surroundings and to regulate one's interpersonal contacts. To do this one must be able to control physical, visual, and auditory separation. This does not imply isolation (which is less social stimulation than desired), but rather solitude, intimacy, anonymity, or reserve. At a given time, an individual may want more or less interaction, depending on situation and cultural background. Privacy in institutions is related to occupancy patterns (single versus multiple rooms) and to density (number of people per unit area). The manipulation of distance or barriers in the environment is only one mechanism for achieving privacy, but in jail it is a critical one. A barred cell provides physical separation but little visual or auditory isolation. In a dormitory, none of these separations is possible.

Lack of opportunities for privacy increases stress. Moore (1985) found that the cells in a Michigan prison that were more open and exposed generated higher utilization rates for health services, an indirect measure of stress. Similarly, a private room—when available—is often used by inmates as a retreat from stressful situations (Fleising 1973). As for bathroom use, the inability to achieve socially accepted norms of privacy for bodily functions contributes to dehumanization.

Privacy is closely related to crowding, which describes high levels of density. There is much evidence from research in correctional settings that increased spatial and social density cause numerous negative effects. Briefly, **social density** refers to the number of people who share a unit of the environment (lowest for single cells, highest for dormitories—especially large ones) and **spatial density** refers to the average amount of space that each person has.

There is no suggestion in the literature that increased density does not have negative effects. However, the research has not yet been so specific as to have identified thresholds either of square feet per inmate or number of inmates per living area. Much (if not most) of the research has been conducted in essentially substandard settings, where facilities offered little space per inmate, were overcrowded, old, and/or in poor condition. Rarely has it been possible for researchers to evaluate scientifically the differences in impact of settings that all met professional or legal standards. However, findings are highly suggestive.

Inmates themselves respond very differently to single rooms than they do to dormitories. Responses at the New York MCC showed that far more inmates in dormitories than in single rooms felt that privacy and space were insufficient and that conditions were crowded (Wener and Olsen 1978). In the same study, double-bunked conditions (before a court order forbidding it took effect) were compared to single-bunked conditions. Although the total population density was reduced only about 15 percent, perceived crowding and sick call rates were significantly reduced. (It should be noted that despite these ill effects—which, unfortunately, were not available to the court at the time of the ruling—the U.S. Supreme Court failed in **Bell v. Wolfish** to prohibit double bunking at that facility.)

In the most comprehensive study of the health and stress impacts of different housing densities, McCain, Cox, and Paulus (1980) were able to compare types of housing units. Their findings range from suggestive to rather conclusive and are summarized below.

Singles versus Doubles. Double cells or cubicles were found to have measurably greater negative effects than single-occupancy housing. Differences were observed in illness complaint rates, perceived crowding, and nonviolent disciplinary infractions, among other variables. The authors warn, however, that these findings are open to other interpretations since the doubles provided consistently less space than the singles.

Singles versus Small Multiple-Occupant Units (three to six persons). Illness complaints, perceived crowding, and other negative measures increased as the number of inmates increased. Here, it is primarily the social density that varied, with space per person actually greater for some of the multiple occupancy cells.

Singles versus Open Dorms. The authors assert that "if there is any one set of findings from this project or earlier work that seems beyond serious question, it is that dormitories have more negative consequences than one-man units" (p. 125). The dorms performed worse with illness complaints, perceived crowding, and other negative factors. Findings were consistent for all races, ethnic groups, security levels, program assignments, and lengths of time in the institution.

Doubles versus Dormitories. Dormitories were found to have more negative impacts than double cells or rooms.

Open versus Segmented Dorms. When dormitories were subdivided into bays with ten to twenty inmates, less negative effects were found compared to the open arrangement.

Cubicles versus Rooms. Generally, in terms of reducing stress, partitioning the inmate sleeping area within a dorm into cubicles can be almost as effective as providing a single cell. The more the cubicle resembles a single room (higher partitions, storage, desk space), the more it duplicates the positive effects of the room.

Cubicles versus Open Dorms. As expected, dorms with cubicles perform much better than those without them. The authors point out that "cubicles . . . represent an inexpensive means of affording privacy in otherwise open dormitories" (p. 127).

In another study, d'Atri (1981) found that inmates in dorms perceived guards more negatively than those in other housing units. He also found that as the number of people housed in the same living unit increases, so do their blood pressure and stress levels.

Ray, Huntington, and Wandersman (1979) found a direct relationship between density and anger. The threshold at which it occurs is not established, but it may be that inmates in multiple cells who have 35 to 50 square feet each may become more angry than if they are in single cells with 70 square feet each.

Thornberry et al. (1982), in a review of the literature, also reported more violence, sexual assaults, contraband, and medical emergencies in double-bunked cells than in single cells. It is unclear whether these differences are attributable to the amount of space, the number of people, or both.

All of this research suggests that more stress, anger, and assaultiveness are associated with multiple cells and dorms. Interestingly, the use of cubicles (or partitions) within dorms appears to mitigate some of their otherwise negative effects (McCain, Cox, and Paulus 1980).

Behavior and Activities

In addition to perception and to social relations, the jail environment affects several other aspects of human activity. Individuals perform a wide variety of observable behavior, much of which comes about as a result of programs or other goal-oriented activities and functions. The jail should be responsive to these activities both in providing spaces and facilities for them and in locating them so that they will be conveniently accessible to the people who carry them out. Activities and the objectives that jail users have for their environmental support— including safety and security—are discussed in this section.

Behavior in Jail

Behavior in jail—or what people do there—might seem to depend more on the people than on their environment. While this is partially true in that the experience of incarceration and the way people behave in jail are different than in the outside world, the physical setting also appears to have considerable impact.

One study of the jail environment divided observable behavior into simple categories: aggressive; isolated passive (sitting, sleeping); isolated active (exercising alone); social (playing games, talking); and traffic (movement). The results showed that sleeping accounted for a staggering 20 percent of all daytime activities (9 A.M. to 9 P.M.) and that, overall, inmates spent about 80 percent of their time engaged in isolated, low-energy behavior. Active game equipment was in constant use, but competition for this scarce resource limited the average inmate's involvement to about 2 percent of his time. Though this particular jail environment was "softer" and less monotonous than most, it still appears to have generated a withdrawn and "somnambulent" response (Wener and Olsen 1978).

A study of a new women's prison in Louisiana provides a further example of the facility's impact on behavior. It found that an easily accessible TV room replaced an outdoor yard as a natural congregation area. Consequently TV watching increased (Prestholdt et al. 1976). Other more casual observations of jail behavior would seem to bear out these studies.

These examples suggest that unless we are imprisoning people to sleep and watch TV, we must begin to ask how the jail building, together with its programs, can elicit more active, social, and involved responses.

Organized Activities

Jail programs and operations generate physical activities that are carried out by individuals and groups. These activities make demands upon the environment for space and facilities. If the space is not adequate, the activity may be hampered. If the space is not available or is too inconvenient, the activity may not take place at all.

The amount of area required for an activity depends on several behavioral factors. These include the number of people involved, the types of actions they carry out, the communication between them, and how frequently and for how long they perform the activity. Aspects of environmental support include the furnishings and equipment required, the provision of appropriate levels of light, heat, and ventilation, as well as the possible separation from other activities to achieve physical, visual, or acoustic privacy.

In order to judge the effectiveness of an environment in accommodating an activity, criteria such as comfort, convenience, or safety need to be established. Rather little research has been done in the correctional field concerning the effectiveness of jail spaces in accommodating activities. The lack of space for many kinds of activities documented in the **National Jail Census** was reported above. Other studies have found minor or major environmental faults that affected activity performance—either in design or in the inability of structures to adapt to changes over time (Wener and Clark 1977).

Change over Time

Change is a fact of life in corrections. While philosophies may change slowly, legislative and judicial mandates come overnight. Populations, crime, arrest and commitment rates, programs, and types of inmates have changed, are changing, and will change in the future. Yet jail buildings—because they have responded mainly to perceived security requirements—are perhaps the **least** flexible structures built.

Studies of obsolescence in other types of facilities (such as offices and housing) show a clear tendency for the effectiveness of accommodation to decrease over time. Even assuming it served its purpose well when constructed, changes in need eventually outpace the facility's ability to respond.

Guidelines have proposed designing significant flexibility into jails (National Sheriffs' Association 1975). Features such as added capacity beyond projections, planned expansion capability, modular units for program flexibility, and even movable partitions and mobile or prefabricated units are suggested. Flexibility, however, costs money—in redundancy, overprovision, or increased performance. Yet there have been no thorough studies of how flexibility has been used or how well it has been achieved in jails. Thus it would seem prudent to plan and design for the specific flexibilities that can be anticipated and afforded.

Accessibility and Security

The pattern of internal locations, distances, physical controls or barriers, and rules for use all act together to make parts of the jail more or less accessible to its users. In jail, of course, one group controls the access of another. Thus their concerns are quite different. Staff concerns focus around the distances they must walk to perform sequential activities, possible conflicts among the routes of groups or materials, and the control of secure boundaries. Inmate concerns focus around the limitations on their movement rather than time expenditure—since they have so much of it. Layout, space allocation, and operational rules define the areas for residential and program activities that are accessible to them.

Research has indeed verified that these issues are important to correctional settings. An evaluation of a structure that was held to be "probably one of the best jail or detention institutions in the country" in 1968 found that inmates had to pass through the hospital section to reach the visiting room, causing a conflict (American Foundation Institute of Corrections 1968). In the same facility, the X-ray room was in the hospital area, although its major use was as part of the intake procedure. A careful study of the activity sequence at intake could have avoided the inconvenience of wasted staff (and inmate) time.

In a high-rise jail, elevator control and response time are critical. At the Chicago MCC, a study estimated that each staff member spends eighty-seven hours per year waiting for elevators (Wener and Clark 1977). Even though walking distances to initiate and complete the trip are short, this is clearly excessive.

The discussion of accessibility is closely related to security issues, especially questions of the location of secure barriers. Three distinct options exist for a given level of security: local (at the cell), zone (at the tier or unit), and perimeter. Jails often include **all** of these, with additional intermediate levels as well. The debate on security acknowledges and agrees on the need to detain certain individuals, but then diverges on the level of constraint necessary after they are contained within the facility. Most writers (though writers are not necessarily representative of opinion in the corrections field) advocate a flexible approach to security with a choice of levels for inmates who exhibit varying behaviors. An advocate of high internal mobility points out that much internal constraint is necessary:

> It appeared in many of the places visited that the movement was unduly restricted and that the restrictions were a function of physical as much as programmatic considerations. The movement between cell block, corridor, and day room, for example, is frequently prevented by a locked door, which is locked largely because **the door is there and the lock is there.** We did see one such housing unit in which the doors were left unlocked (proving the rule by exception) and nothing seemed to happen except that the tension was clearly diminished [Gilbert 1971, p. 8; emphasis in the original].

Perimeter security arrangements appear to work, at least where research has examined them, as at the federal MCCs (Wener and Olsen 1978). However, a related problem has been raised by the designer of one of the MCCs, who is concerned that the relatively free movement in the residential unit is still not adequate. Findings bear out that, while the relative freedom is appreciated, the limited range and lack of access to the outdoors leads to boredom and an occasional preference for duller but larger facilities (Silver 1978). In context, however, the maximum acceptable mobility appears to be prized, beneficial, and workable.

Jail Safety

Aggressive behavior has already been discussed in relation to territoriality and crowding. More generally, aggression can be conceived of as being perpetrated against people (inmates against inmates, officers, or visitors; or officers against inmates) or against things (objects, surfaces, structures).

Safety in jail results from many complex factors, of which the housing environment is only one. First, **who are the inmates** in the jail? Obviously, threats to safety and security will come more from inmates with histories of violent behavior or, perhaps, charges for violent crime. Inmates who are more passive, weaker, or older are more likely to be victimized by the former group.

Perhaps the key factor in making a jail safe is its **staffing** (the number of officers, their location, competence, training, ability in "human relations," and so forth). Staff must be able to maintain control, provide security, ensure fire safety, and avoid or defuse potential major disturbances such as riots.

The physical **environment** of the jail also contributes to safety. Not only is the housing configuration (the focus of this study) to be considered, but also the visibility of inmate areas for staff surveillance, as well as access to stress-reducing activities and visitation.

Inmate Personal Safety: Suicides

While many inmates may need protection from other inmates, a few need to be protected from themselves. Suicides have become more common since jails have held higher proportions of inmates with mental health and drug abuse problems. According to a national survey, the most common jail suicides are among pretrial inmates (National Center on Institutions and Alternatives [NCIA 1981]). Over one-quarter happen within three hours of admission and over one-half within twenty-four hours. The majority of suicides are booked on nonviolent charges but are under the influence of alcohol and/or drugs. Two-thirds of the suicides took place while the inmate was in an isolation cell. While this is far from the same as being in a single cell, some jailers do feel that single cells may contribute to the frequency of suicides.

This issue focuses on the degree of isolation that may be experienced by an inmate in a single cell and the opportunity for him to act without observation either by staff or other inmates. (It should be noted that feelings of isolation may be more prevalent in older single-cell jails, where long rows of cells face blank walls. Newer single cells that face a dayroom may not produce as extreme a sense of isolation.) In any case, it has been argued that in a multiple occupancy cell or dorm the inmate is in the company of others who may prevent or report the suicide attempt. It has also been argued to the contrary that the stresses on the inmate are higher in the multiple housing setting where he may be harrassed to the point of desperation.

If intake staff can properly identify inmates prone to suicide, and if housing staff can provide continuous surveillance of particular units of single cells, NCIA contends that it is better to place suicidal inmates in single-cell units rather than in multiple occupancy cells. But if adequate staff surveillance is absent, it appears that cellmates help provide safety for suicidal inmates because any human contact is better than none for them.

Inmate Personal Safety: Physical Assault

Single cells are widely favored as providing the greatest safety for inmates. If an inmate is confined within his own cell, other inmates cannot get at him to inflict harm. Time spent in dayrooms or other common areas is in larger groups and usually supervised by staff. Reports of physical and sexual assaults are much less common in single cells.

Research on Violence

As stated above, rather little data exists on violence as related to housing configuration. One study looked at rates of assault in various types of housing in the Florida prison system (Atlas 1982). The study compares violence of inmates housed in single cells, two-person cells, six-person cells, and twelve to eighty person dorms. Surprisingly, no clear relationships were found. However, these results are inconclusive, partly because the types of inmate and means of supervision vary considerably among the housing units chosen for study.

Other research is suggestive, but deals with more minor infractions than the violence studied above. McCain, Cox and Paulus (1980) found more rule infractions in dorms and multiple cells than in singles. Some of these would be altercations and fights, indicating that violence too would be higher. Megargee and Nacci (quoted in Thornberry et al. 1982) also found that rule infractions increase with density.

Other interesting research concerns the amount of space that violent and nonviolent individuals need around themselves in order to avoid feeling threatened. A study by Kinzel (1970) found that violent inmates' "body buffer zone" was four times larger than for nonviolent inmates (twenty-nine versus seven square feet). The zone behind the inmate was also held to be larger than the front for violent inmates. This may be at least part of the reason why violent inmates are less able to cope with sharing spaces with others.

Staff Safety

There is some evidence that newer, single cell jails are safer for staff. D'Atri (1981) was cited above as showing that inmates in dorms had more negative perceptions of guards than inmates in other housing types. This may translate into aggression and violence. For example, striking improvements in staff safety have been recorded in Ventura County's new jail in California (though many factors changed in comparison to the old jail, including greatly increased staffing). For the two years before the new jail opened, there were an average of 74 custody staff injury claims per year out of a population of 138 staff, a 57 percent injury rate. For the two years after the new facility opened, there were an average of 57 custody staff injury claims per year for 267 staff, a 21 percent injury rate (as reported to the California Board of Corrections).

Perception of Safety and Vandalism

In the jail situation, the **perception** of risk may be as important in generating fear and tension as the actual presence of risk. "As perceived control over risky situations decreases, so does the ability to find that risk acceptable" (Wener and Clark 1977, p. 16). At the Chicago MCC, staff's dependence on technological systems for basic services and support left them feeling "virtually helpless in the face of an equipment failure."

Similarly, the perception of vandalism can vary among users. At the New York MCC, inmates and staff concurred in the opinion that there is little vandalism or theft on the units as compared to other institutions. Administrators, however, seemed to feel that vandalism is rampant, perhaps because they see reports from all of the units. In following up on this issue, the researchers found that many of the cited incidents of damage were due to natural wear, poor equipment, or accidental breakage (Wener and Olsen 1980). If these results are valid, they suggest that the "normalized" atmosphere at the MCCs may indeed promote greater respect and care of the surroundings.

The Jail Image

People respond in complex ways to the physical appearance of a place—its size, shape, color, materials, signs and symbols. All these aspects add up to the total **image** the jail presents, the reaction to which will depend on a person's past experience and reason for being there. The image allows us to recognize what type of a place it is and sets up expectations for what will happen there and how we may be treated. The building, then, serves as a medium of communication between its owners or designers and its users.

The typical jail is easily recognizable—hard and impenetrable, with steel bars, sallyports, and barbed wire. The message is clear and may be received with dread, regret, or relief, depending on who is interpreting it.

A great deal has been written about the inappropriateness of the traditional jail image in the context of new attitudes toward the purpose of the jail (Moyer 1977; National Sheriffs' Association 1975; Sommer 1974). Bars represent a cagelike image that is out of keeping with the innocent-until-proven-guilty status of pretrial detainees or win a correctional approach to sentenced prisoners. Conflicting messages from the environment may inhibit the achievement of correctional objectives (Ricci 1971) or may simply be humorous. Herb Caen reports that "when you enter Santa Cruz County Jail, you come upon a barred door and a huge doormat reading 'We're Glad You're Here!'" (San Francisco **Chronicle,** 6 February 1979).

Research in settings that have eliminated the symbols of incarceration and attempted to achieve a more "normal" and humane (albeit institutional) environment has shown that this is effective in contributing to a variety of positive effects. The federal MCCs were programmed to reduce or eliminate symbols of incarceration in order to reduce their "institutional feel." They have exterior windows in bedrooms, no bars, and are decorated with carpeting, bright colors, and comfortable furniture to create a "soft environment" (Wener and Olsen 1978). It was expected that these features would reduce the "trauma" of incarceration and would "influence residents to take care of their immediate physical environment, thus reducing vandalism" (Wener and Clark 1977). As reported above, the MCCs appear to be successful in this regard, if not problem free.

A further aspect of normalization is that it should help to reduce barriers to community acceptance and participation in the jail (Moyer, 1977). On the other hand, a "new look" or cosmetic approach to deinstitutionalization will not change the nature of the jail.

Conclusion

A wide variety of ways in which the jail environment affects the attitudes and behavior of its users has been discussed and the findings of research studies in this area have been reviewed. While the amount of research done has been limited, the tenor of findings is consistent: the design of the jail environment is crucial to its operation and to the impact it has on the achievement of correctional goals for inmates, staff, and public users. However, the physical environment cannot guarantee or insure the achievement of these goals. It can only act in concert with administration, staffing, operations, program, and community support to help the jail become an effective institution serving society's ends.

References

American Correctional Association, Commission on Accreditation for Corrections. 1981. **Standards for Adult Local Detention Facilities.** 2nd ed. Rockville, MD: American Correctional Association.

American Foundation Institute of Corrections. 1968. **Philadelphia Detention Center: An Evaluation After Four Years Use.** Philadelphia: American Foundation Institute for Corrections.

Atlas, Randy. 1982. **"Violence in Prison: Architectural Determinism."** Ph.D. diss., Florida State University.

Benton, F. W. and Robert Obenland. 1973. **Prison and Jail Security.** National Clearinghouse for Criminal Justice Planning and Architecture. Urbana, IL: University of Illinois.

Bukstel, L., and P. Kilmann. 1980. "Psychological Effects of Imprisonment on Confined Individuals." **Psychological Bulletin** 88(2): 469-93.

Canter, D., I. Ambroso, J. Brown, M. Comber, and A. Hirsch. 1980. **Prison Design and Use: Final Report.** Surrey, England: University of Surrey.

Collins, Belinda L. 1975. **Windows and People: A Literature Survey.** A report prepared for the U.S. Department of Commerce.

Curran, Stephen, Robert Blatchley, and Thomas Hanlon. 1978. "The Relationship Between Body Buffer Zone and Violence as Perceived by Subjective and Objective Techniques." **Criminal Justice and Behavior** 5(1): 53-62.

d'Atri, D. A. 1975. "Psychophysiological Responses to Crowding." **Environment and Behavior** 7(2): 237-52.

————. 1981. "Measuring Stress in Prison." In **Confinement in Maximum Custody,** ed. David A. Ward and Kenneth F. Schoen. Lexington, MA: D. C. Heath and Co.

Dean, L. M., W. M. Pugh, and E. K. G. Gunderson. 1975. "Spatial and Perceptual Components of Crowding: Effects on Health and Satisfaction." **Environment and Behavior** 7: 225-36.

Evans, Robin. 1982. **The Fabrication of Virtue: English Prison Architecture, 1750-1840.** Cambridge, England: Cambridge University Press.

Fairweather, Leslie. 1977. "Evolution of the Prison." In **Prison Architecture,** ed. Giuseppe Di Gennara et al. Nichols, NY.

Farbstein, Jay. 1978. "A Juvenile Services Center Program." In **Facility Programming,** ed. Wolfgang Preiser. Stroudsburg, PA: Dowden, Hutchinson & Ross.

Farbstein, Jay, & Associates. 1983. **Housing Pretrial Inmates: The Costs and Benefits**

of Single Cells, Multiple Cells and Dormitories. Sacramento: California Board of Corrections.

Farbstein, Jay, and Richard Wener. 1982. "Evaluation of Correctional Environments." **Environment and Behavior** 14(6): 671-94.

Farbstein/Williams & Associates. 1981. **Corrections Planning Handbooks.** Sacramento: California Board of Corrections.

Fleising, Usher. 1973. "The Social and Spatial Dynamics of a Prison Tier: An Exploratory Study." **Man-Environment Systems** 3(3): 187-95.

Frazier, William. 1985. "A User-Based Evaluation of Contra Costa County's Main Detention Facility." Ph.D. diss., Golden Gate University.

Gersten, Raymond. n.d. **Noise in Jails: A Constitutional Issue.** Clearinghouse Transfer No. 19. National Clearinghouse for Criminal Justice Planning and Architecture, Urbana: University of Illinois.

Gilbert, Alfred. 1971. "Observations About Recent Correctional Architecture." **The Prison Journal** 51(1) 7-14.

Goldblatt, Lawrence. 1972. "Prisoners and Their Environment: A Study of Two Prisons for Youthful Offenders." Paper, North Carolina State University.

Greenfield, Larry. 1982. "Prison Population and Death Rates." Workshop presented at the 13th Annual Conference of the Environmental Design Research Association. College Park, MD.

Hahn, Robert S. 1973. "Behavioral Evaluation of a Juvenile Treatment Center." In **Environmental Design Research,** ed. Wolfgang Preiser. Vol. 1. Stroudsburg, PA: Dowden, Hutchinson & Ross.

Johnson, Carolyn, and Marjorie Kravitz. 1978. **Overcrowding in Correctional Institutions, A Selected Bibliography.** National Institute of Law Enforcement and Criminal Justice, LEAA.

Kinzel, Augustus F. 1970. "Body-Buffer Zone in Violent Prisoners." **American Journal of Psychiatry** 99-104.

Knight, Douglas. 1971. **Impact of Living Unit Size in Youth Training Schools.** A report prepared for the California Youth Authority, Division of Research and Development.

Leroy, Claude. 1977. "Space in the Prison." In **Prison Architecture,** ed. Giuseppe Di Gennaro, et al. Nichols, NY.

McCain, Garvin, Verne Cox, and Paul Paulus. 1980. **The Effect of Prison Crowding on Inmate Behavior.** A report prepared for LEAA.

McReynolds, Kenneth L. 1972. **Physical Components of Correctional Goals.** A report prepared for the Department of the Solicitor General, Ottawa, Canada.

McReynolds, K. L., and T. S. Palys. 1975. **A Proposal for a Spatial Assessment of the Maitoba Youth Centre.** Thornhill, Ontario, Canada.

Megaree, Edwin I. 1977. "The Association of Population Density, Reduced Space, and Uncomfortable Temperatures with Misconduct in a Prison Community." **The American Journal of Community Psychology** 5: 289-98.

Moore, Ernest. 1985. "Environmental Variables Affecting Prisoner Health Care Demands." In **Research and Design '85,** proceedings of the American Institute of Architects, Los Angeles.

Moos, Rudolph. 1975. **Evaluating Correctional and Community Settings.** Palo Alto, CA: Consulting Psychologists Press.

Moyer, Frederic D. 1977. "The Architecture of Closed Institutions." In **Prison Architecture,** ed. Giuseppe Di Gennaro, et al. Nichols, NY.

Moyer, Fred, Edith Flynn, Fred Powers, and Michael Plautz, 1971. **Guidelines for Planning and Design of Regional and Community Correctional Centers For Adults.** Urbana: Department of Architecture, University of Illinois.

Mullen, Joan, and Bradford Smith. 1980. **American Prisons and Jails, Volume III: Conditions and Costs of Confinement.** A paper prepared for the U.S. Department of Justice.

Nacci, Peter, Hugh Teitelbaum, and Jerry Prather. 1977. "Population Density and

Inmate Misconduct Rates in the Federal Prison System." **Federal Probation,** June 1977, pp. 26–31.

National Advisory Commission on Criminal Justice Standards and Goals. n.d. **Report of the Task Force on Corrections.** Washington, DC: Government Printing Office.

National Center on Institutions and Alternatives. 1981. **And Darkness Closes In; National Study of Jail Suicides.** Washington, DC: Government Printing Office.

National Sheriffs' Association. 1975. **A Handbook on Jail Architecture.** Washington, DC: Government Printing Office.

Nebraska State Bar Association, Committee on Correctional Law and Practice. 1977. **Jail Standards: Minimum Standards for Local Criminal Detention Facilities.**

Nelson, William (Ray). 1983. "New Generation Jails." **Corrections Today** 45: 108–12.

Paulus, Paul, Garvin McCain, and Verne Cox. 1978. "Death Rates, Psychiatric Commitments, Blood Pressure, and Perceived Crowding as a Function of Institutional Crowding." **Environmental Psychology and Non-Verbal Behavior** 3(2): 107–16.

Polson, Steven R. 1977. "Environmental Design Research within the Criminal Justice System." Paper presented at the Environmental Design Research Association Conference, May, Champaign, IL.

Prestholdt, Perry H., et al. 1976. "The Correctional Environment and Human Behavior: A Comparative Study of Two Prisons for Women." In **The Behavioral Basis of Design,** Proceedings of EDRA 7, vol. 1, ed. P. Suedfeld et al. Stroudsburg, PA: Dowden, Hutchinson & Ross.

Ray, D., D. Huntington, and A. Wandersman. 1979. "The Impact of Density in a Juvenile Correctional Institution: Effects, Recommendations and Policy Implications." Paper presented at the 10th Annual EDRA Conference, Buffalo, NY.

Reeves, I.S.K. 1985. "Color and Its Effect on Behavior Modification in Correctional/Detention Facilities." In **Research and Design '85,** Proceedings of the American Institute of Architects, Los Angeles.

Ricci, Kenneth. 1971. "Using the Building as a Therapeutic Tool in Youth Treatment." **The Prison Journal** 51(1): 22–32.

Silver, Paul. 1978. "New Directions in Correctional Design: Towards Humanization of Institutions." Paper presented at workshop at Environmental Design Research Association Conference, Tucson.

Sims, William R. 1976. "The Halfway House: A Diagnostic and Prescriptive Evaluation." In **The Behavioral Basis of Design,** Proceedings of EDRA 7, vol. 1, ed. P. Suedfeld et al. Stroudsburg, PA: Dowden, Hutchinson & Ross.

Sommer, Robert. 1975. **Tight Spaces: Hard Architecture and How to Humanize It.** Englewood Cliffs, NJ: Prentice-Hall.

————. 1971. "The Social Psychology of the Cell Environment." **The Prison Journal** 51(1): 15–21.

Srivastava, R. J. 1978. **Environmental Needs of Juvenile Group Homes.** Tucson, AZ: Environmental Research and Development Foundation.

Stokols, D., and D. G. Marrero. 1976. "The Effects of Environmental Intervention on Racial Polarization in a Youth Training School." In **The Behavioral Basis of Design,** Proceedings of EDRA 7, vol. 1, ed. P. Suedfeld et al. Book 1. Stroudsburg, PA: Dowden, Hutchinson & Ross.

Suedfeld, Peter, Carmenza Ramirez, John Deaton, and Gloria Baker-Brown. 1982. "Reactions and Attributes of Prisoners in Solitary COnfinement." **Criminal Justice and Behavior** 9(3): 303-40

Sweitzer, Susan. 1977. "Color Provides Milieu Enhancement Where Social Factors Are Regimented." **Architecture for Justice** (newsletter of the AIA Committee on Architecture for Justice). Sept., 4-5.

Sykes, Gresham. 1958. **The Society of Captives: A Study of a Maximum Security Prison.** Princeton, NJ: Princeton University Press.

Thornberry, T. P., et al. 1982. **Overcrowding in American Prisons: Policy Implications of Double-Bunking Single Cells.** National Institute of Corrections.

Toch, Hans. 1981. "Classification for Programming and Survival." In **Confinement in Maximum Custody,** ed. David A. Ward and Kenneth F. Schoen. Lexington, MA: D. C. Heath and Co.

Velde, Richard, ed. 1971. "New Environments for the Incarcerated." **The Prison Journal** 51(1).

Wener, Richard, and Nathan Clark. 1977. "A User-Based Evaluation of the Chicago Metropolitan Correctional Center: Final Report." A report to the U.S. Department of Justice, Bureau of Prisons.

Wener, Richard, William Frazier, and Jay Farbstein. 1985. "Three Generations of Evaluation and Design of Correctional Facilities." **Environment and Behavior** 17(1): 71–95.

Wener, Richard, and Christopher Keys. 1979. "The Effects of Changes in Population Density on Prisoners." Paper presented at the 87th Annual Convention of the American Psychological Association, San Francisco.

Wener, Richard, and Richard Olsen. 1980. "Innovative Correctional Environments: A User Assessment." **Environment and Behavior** 12(4): 478–94.

————. 1978. **User-Based Assessment of the Federal Metropolitan Correctional Centers: Final Report.** New York: Polytechnic Institute of New York.

32. Correctional Facility Programming

Who Will Use This Chapter

Primary Users
Project manager
Facility programming (and design) task force
Architect (if on board)

Secondary Users
Sheriff and corrections staff
Advisory committee

Introduction

What Is a Facility Program?

A facility program is a **statement of requirements for a building project.** These include objectives, issues, a description of what will happen in the building, user needs, and problems to be solved in the design.

The facility program is **not** the same as a "correctional program" (such as vocational education), although it will include a listing of all the programs to be offered in the jail. "The program," as used here without specifying "facility" program, has nothing to do with computers.

The program is a formal communication between the client (jail system or county) and its architect so that he or she can begin design.

The American Institute of Architects' standard contract between the owner and architect specifies that "the Architect shall review the program supplied by the Owner." Thus, unless arranged otherwise, the entire responsibility for producing the program rests with the owner (the jail or county). In most cases some consultant help is required, either from the architect (as an "extra" service) or from a programming specialist.

In the past the program was little more than a listing of the spaces to be included in the building. Now it is much more: a statement of intent for the facility, an exploration of values, needs, and requirements.

The Program Is a Link to Design

The new jail building will provide a framework for the people and activities it will contain. It can either allow and support its functions or it can inhibit them. Thus the architect must understand what the jail needs. Otherwise there is no possible way that he or she can design a building that responds to those needs.

Just as you would not have a tailor make a suit of clothes without measuring you first, the designer must have enough information about the jail system so that the building can fit it. An accurate, thorough, and clear program document prepares the architect to begin the design task.

In the absence of a program, the architect relies on other sources of information and considers only factors other than those that concern the future use of the jail, such as aesthetics, economics, or building codes. Decisions about how the facility is to be operated may end up being made on a drafting table in the architect's office.

In addition, the program document serves as a record of the needs and intentions of the jail system. This aids in making the design more accountable, since it can be judged in terms of its performance in satisfying stated and agreed-upon criteria. Statements that are recorded and published are less likely to be misunderstood.

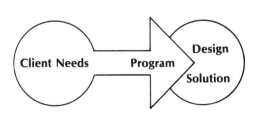

User-Oriented Programming

While there are many critical technical issues that must be dealt with in programming and design, the basis for making decisions on most issues seems to boil down to questions about how the resulting physical environment will affect its users.

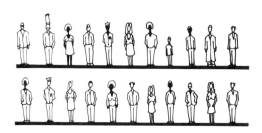

The people who will occupy and use the building know the most about their activities and needs. This is the rationale for involving them in programming and design. The programming process provides an orderly method for gathering people's input and communicating the result to the architect.

In addition, users who have been involved in the process are more likely to be satisfied with the resulting product—both because it is more suitable and simply because they have been involved. It has been said that "people support what they help to create." Thus a participatory task force approach to programming is proposed here.

The needs of all major users should be taken into account. Since there are many different types of users, this becomes a considerable task. At a minimum, consider the needs of inmates, staff, visitors, administration, law enforcement, and the public.

Functional and Architectural Programming

It is common, although not universal, to divide the program into two separate but related parts: functional and architectural programs.

The **functional** program describes the users of the building, what they will do there, and their needs.

The **architectural** program describes the performance required from the building or specifies what various aspects will be like.

Following a brief discussion of the programming process, the next sections will deal with these two aspects of the program.

The Programming Process

Before programming begins, it is assumed that needs assessment and feasibility studies for the jail will have already been carried out and will have clearly identified the need for renovation or new construction. (Refer to Parts 3 and 4.) Programming takes from two to six months and is to be carried out by the programming task force, probably in conjunction with a programming consultant or architect.

The Programming Task Force

A programming task force should be established, with a trusted coordinator (perhaps the project manager). The role of the team should be clear and understood by all task force members as well as by the authority that created it. This role includes advising, developing information, and reviewing consultants' work.

Representatives of **all** user groups should be included on the programming task force, since each group has knowledge to contribute and an interest in the outcome. Some of the represented interests should include: security, administration, programs, intake/release, food service, operations, and maintenance. Both male and female officers should be represented. Inmates should also have a voice, perhaps through a representative of the inmate council (if there is one) or by including an ex-offender. A religious counselor or inmate rights group member might also be called upon to speak for inmates. Jail volunteers, community support groups, or other concerned individuals or groups such as Legal Aid and ex-offenders or representatives of inmate groups should also be considered for inclusion. Law enforcement and the courts may also wish to be represented.

There must be open, effective communication channels within the task force and between its members and the groups or interests they represent. Some of the techniques that will prove helpful are covered in the chapters on problem identification (Chapter 9) and action planning (Chapter 11). Preparing and distributing agendas in advance of meetings, regularly reporting back to constituencies, and using group discussion techniques that respect individual contributions may all help.

This task force should continue in operation during the design phase to give input to the architects and to review the design. In addition, it may form the basis for the task force that will plan the transition into the new facility (see Chapter 36).

Use of Programming Consultants

Consideration should be given to the use of consultants during this phase. There are consultants who specialize in jail operations, architecture firms that offer or specialize in programming services, and planning/programming firms that specialize in justice facilities. It is possible to hire these consultants either to help the jail system complete its tasks or to contract for completion of the tasks themselves.

While the jail system could complete the functional program itself, it will need help with the architectural program. This might come from a member of the county's public works or building department staff or from a consultant. If contracted, the cost of programming and related services may run from one-quarter to one percent of estimated construction costs, depending on precisely which services are included and the size and complexity of the project.

There are pros and cons to having an architecture firm do the programming, either with its own staff or else with a programming consultant as part of its team. Favoring this arrangement is the fact that the architect will be familiar with the program requirements and not need a transition or communication period.

The drawback of having the architect do the programming is the potential for bias due to several factors. First, the architect is facility-oriented and may not give enough emphasis to functional issues or consider nonfacility solutions to issues that arise. Preconceptions about the final design have no place in programming. Second, if the architect's fees depends upon the final construction cost of the project and at the same time he or she is responsible for recommending its scope, there can be a built-in conflict of interest.

Functional Programming

Introduction

The functional program is a detailed description of what **should** and **will** happen in the new facility, not a description of what **does** happen in the existing one.

The understanding of what will happen in the new facility that develops during functional programming becomes the basis for determining how the building should be designed to **support** user needs during the architectural programming phase. Only with a clear statement of needs is it possible for the design to respond to those needs.

The burden is on the jail system, possibly with the help of a consultant, to define its future activities and needs.

The functional program is sometimes called the "operational", "service", or "correctional" program.

Its content typically includes the following topics, each of which will be discussed:

- Mission statement
- Policies and procedures
- Standards
- Programs and services
- Users
- Activities
- Circulation and sequences
- Psychological issues
- Operating costs
- Future trends

Mission Statement

The team should already have a basic mission statement for detention and corrections in the county (see Chapter 10). This should be reviewed and revised or fleshed out as necessary to apply to the facility in question. A useful elaboration is to look at the objectives that various user groups within the jail and the community hold for its function.

Policies and Procedures

Policies and procedures should **control** what happens in the jail; the jail's design should not dictate policy. Therefore policies and procedures should be defined for the new facility. This does not necessarily mean a complete revision of the policy and procedures manual at this time, but rather the development of an outline with some of the main points and intentions filled in. Detailed procedures should be developed as facility planning progresses, to the point that they are complete somewhat before construction is finished.

Standards

All relevant **standards, codes, and guidelines** that apply to the design or operation of the facility should be reviewed and a commitment made to the level of standards compliance that will be sought in the new facility. That is, will the jail system opt to go beyond state standards and strive for accreditation by complying with national standards? (Refer to Chapter 3.) In addition, a continuing liaison with periodic reviews should be maintained with agencies enforcing the standards or with regulatory or funding authorities.

Programs and Services

A listing of the programs and services offered or likely to be offered in the future should be developed. Alternatives to incarceration such as screening for pretrial release or work furlough programs should be considered in light of their impact on building staffing and function.

Users

Unless the programming team understands **who** will be in the facility, the program will not respond to their needs. Therefore a list of **all** the kinds of users of the jail should be developed. The list should include all types of inmates by offense, status, classification, kinds of behavior, or special needs, and socioeconomic descriptors such as age or sex. All types of staff, visitors, volunteers, servicing, and emergency personnel should also be listed. For a more detailed approach to estimating staff, see Chapter 33.

The anticipated **numbers** of each user type and their **time involvement** (length of time spent, time of day, etc.) should be projected. (Refer to Chapters 18 and 19 for analysis and projections of inmate types and numbers.)

Because it represents such a large portion of operating costs, staffing requirements must be given primary consideration during programming and design. While programming may begin with the preliminary staffing estimates developed in earlier phases (Chapter 19), these must be updated and refined as programming proceeds. An important consideration in programming proceeds. An important consideration in programming and design is ensuring that the building can be staffed efficiently. Detailed information on estimating staffing appears later in this chapter.

Activities

Activities consist of individual and group actions and patterns of action. They are the visible expression of users carrying out programs or making use of services. Activities are anything described by a verb of action: for example, walk, eat, sit, talk, or fight. The major activities for each user type or area in the building should be listed.

Circulation and Sequences of Events

The major linkages or flows between activities or areas should be listed. Flows of **people, information, and things** should be included. Characteristics of the flows that can be included are volume, frequency, and importance.

Also important is an understanding of the typical sequences of events or activities. Typical sequences include intake and booking, meal service, visiting, sick call, recreation, court transport, and release. The sequence should trace **who** is involved, **what** they do, and **where** they do it, from the beginning to the end of the event. Sequences are easier to understand if they are recorded as flow diagrams. Once developed, they should be reviewed and verified with building users for accuracy and used to explore options, problems, and issues that may affect the design. They can also be used to test the design at a later time.

Psychological Issues

In general, psychological issues involve the special needs, expectations, attitudes, beliefs, and behaviors of jail users, especially staff, administration, inmates, visitors, and the community. The purpose of exploring these issues is to identify those that result in special uses of, needs for, or demands on space.

For example, inmates and correctional officers have a particular range of attitudes toward each other and tend to interact in certain ways. There may be desired styles of interaction (such as respect and helpful communication) and undesirable

Example of Activity Sequence

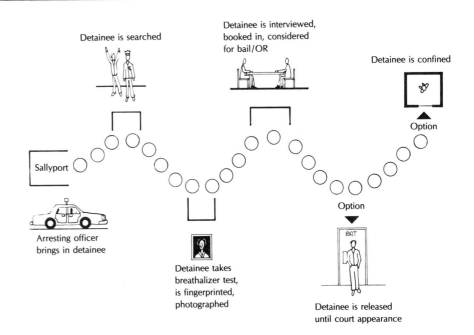

ones (such as belligerence or violence). In this section of the program, the team should consider administrative strategies and design arrangements (such as the placement of the control station, if any) that encourages desired patterns and discourage undesirable ones.

Operating Costs

Cost is usually one of the key determinants in facility programming and design. Over the life of the building, operating costs will account for higher expenditures than construction costs. Operating costs are greatly affected by facility planning, from the simple inclusion of new functions to the efficiency or effectiveness with which they are carried out. Therefore they should be examined as part of the programming process and used to help select among possible operational and design options.

Future Trends

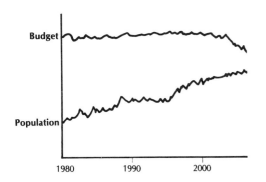

Consider and list those future events that would have significant impact on the jail: for instance, cause major changes in population (numbers or types), programs, staffing, or budgets. State the likelihood of the event occurring and its possible impact on the jail facility, such as expansion, contraction, or remodeling.

Topics worthy of consideration include future changes in law, correctional philosophy, programs, demography, and technology. While none of us can predict the future, it is worth thinking about and attempting to insure that the facility can respond to at least the most likely or pervasive trends.

Architectural Programming

Introduction

The architectural program develops information about how the building should perform in response to the requirements of the functional program. By **performance**, we mean that the program will state what the building should **do** rather than what is should be like. Stating performance requirements leaves the design team more room to find creative solutions than they would have if they were told precisely what the building should be like.

While functional programming can be done largely by the jail system itself, architectural programming demands the input of specialized knowledge, either from a consultant or the county public works or building department.

The level of programming described in the material that follows is very thorough and complete. While all of the issues that are discussed must be considered at some point in the design process, jail officials or architects may prefer to integrate some aspects of the process with design. This is entirely acceptable as long as key components are not thereby left out.

The kinds of information developed in the architectural program can be divided into that which applies to the building as a whole and that which applies to each type of space such as each office or single cell. Both types of information are briefly described below.

Information about the Facility as a Whole

A Design Objective

Objectives. There should be a statement of the design objectives for the building, considering its form, function, cost, energy efficiency, and time performance (useful life).

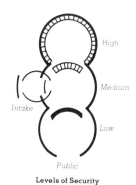

Levels of Security

Provide Levels of Security
Many detainees present little risk of escape, assault or vandalism, while a few present considerable risk. Therefore, provide progressive levels of security, starting with high security at intake (and for those who continue to require it) and moving to medium and lower levels as inmates show they warrant trust. Keep visitors, administration and supply/service functions outside of the secure perimeter and provide separate entrances.

Architectural character. Describe the desired image and appearance of the building.

Spaces. All indoor and outdoor spaces should be listed, including both net usable and gross square footage. Since jails are not very 'efficient," a ratio of 60 to 65 percent net usable area is acceptable.

A List of Spaces

RESIDENTIAL SPACES				
ROOM TYPE	CODE	USABLE AREA	NUMBER OF ROOMS	TOTAL AREA
Single Occupancy Rooms	SGRM	70	69	4,830
Maximum Secure Rooms	MAXRM	70	8	560
Segregation/ Isolation/Discipline Room	SIDR	70	3	210
Work Release Room	WRRM	70	20	1,400
Dayrooms	DYRM	35/bed	100 beds	3,500
Showers	SHWR	32	10	320
Work Release Toilet/Shower				
(Male)	WRBTH	108	2	216
(Female)	WRBTH	84	1	84
Shift Com. Off. (Mgr.)	SCOFF	100	1	100
Staff Work Area (Clerical)	STWRK	60	1	60
Clothing Storage	CLOTH	64	1	64
Staff Toilet	(None)	48	2	96
RESIDENTIAL SUBTOTAL (Usable area)				11,440

Linkages and separations. Describe the desired and required linkages or adjacencies between spaces. This is often expressed by a diagram. Undesirable or unacceptable proximities may also be noted.

An Adjacency Diagram

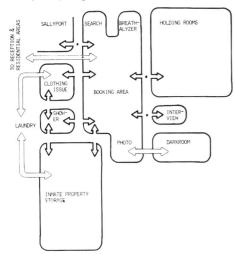

A Program Summary Sheet

Alternatives. A thorough program will initiate the study and evaluation of alternative physical design solutions to functional requirements.

Construction cost. On the basis of the list of spaces and other information, a preliminary estimate of construction costs can be developed. This is usually a per-square-foot cost. Total project cost may be even more useful at this time. Project costs include not only building, equipment, and site development costs, but also site acquisition, professional fees, administrative costs and contingencies (see Chapters 5 and 26).

Site criteria. A statement of site selection, if needed, and site development criteria should be developed (see Chapter 34). It may include issues such as space requirements, buildable area, open space needs, proximity to related services such as courts, acceptability of or to neighboring functions, transportation availability or cost, and utility provisions.

Linn County Corrections: Programs/Recreation	RWROF
RELEASE/WORK RELEASE OFFICE	**187 SF**

Behavioral Issues	Design Response
Creative thinking, self-expression, and diligent work should be encouraged. Having a dignified work environment can boost release and work release officers morale and productivity. Two occupants may desire and need some acoustical and visual separation from each other as well as from other spaces.	Should be pleasant and distraction free; provide no views of or sounds from active areas, sound barriers to adjoining spaces, warm colors and varied textures. Design space and choose furniture that allows several possible furniture arrangements. Spatial configuration should be conducive to having two clearly defined and separate work areas.

Users	Activities
Release officer Work release officer (may be, at first, same person as release officer) Inmates, families and friends of inmates Other agency personnel Other staff	Paperwork Telephoning Counseling Interviewing Confering Planning Reading Typing Investigating candidates for work release

Safety & Security	Ambient Conditions
Lockable file cabinet and desk drawer; provide secure vision panel in door and escape-proof, yet unobtrusively secure, windows. Avoid furniture with sharp edges or points. Provide partial (but non-obvious) visual accessibility from another work station and/or "help" buzzer.	HEAT/COOL: Maintain comfortable temperature VENT: Natural (window) ACOUSTICS: Provide sound baffles LIGHT/VIEW: Natural light with view. Moderate overall light; task light at work surface.

Materials	Code/Agency Reqts.
CEILING: Acoustic treatment WALLS: Vinyl covered or painted gypsum board, tackboard FLOOR: Commercial carpet	ACA, 5118, 5363, 5370: space is provided for conducting programs for inmates; when a pretrial intervention program or diversion program exists, provide sufficient space, staff and equipment for it; where statute permits, provide for work or study release programs.

Special Reqts. & Furnishings	Adjacencies
2 work stations, each with: Desk Desk chair 1-2 visitors' chairs File cabinet Phone Movable partition between work areas	Near secretarial/clerical area in administration Near building entry and waiting room Secure circulation from residential areas Near multi-purpose room

PROGRAM SUMMARY SHEET	Farbstein/Williams & Associates

Information about Each Type of Space

Users. List the primary users of the space, including an estimate of their numbers and perhaps the time pattern of their use.

Activities. List the major activities that are expected to occur in the space.

Objectives. Consider expected and desirable behaviors for the space, together with notions about how the design can encourage or support desirable behaviors and inhibit undesired ones.

Safety and security. Indicate specific users and conditions that generate concerns for safety and security along with the level of building performance necessary to respond to these concerns.

Linkages and separations. List required linkages or separations between this space and others, if not already developed above.

Ambient conditions. List environmental conditions required in each area including heat, ventilation, light, view, and acoustics.

Materials. Develop a statement of the performance required or of recommended choices for construction materials and surface finishes.

Furnishings. State the performance required from or recommended choices for furnishings.

Equipment. Consider special equipment needs, systems or services such as electrical, plumbing, security, communications, or computing.

Size. State the area in square feet and critical dimensions or shape of the space.

Other. List any additional or special requirements for the space such as adaptability, multiple/sequential use, and expandability.

This information is typically recorded on a program summary sheet for each area or functional unit.

Parking Requirements

Numerous factors influence how many parking spaces your county needs. The major ones are: number of staff, number of inmates and visiting policies and hours, access to and adequacy of public transportation, and what other departments, if any, are housed in the facility.

Number of staff. Many counties have planned their corrections facility's parking lots figuring that there should be enough staff parking spaces for the two largest consecutive shifts to park simultaneously. This is to facilitate one staff briefing the next and and to provide time for showering, changing clothes, and entering and exiting the facility. Consider projected numbers of staff and the quantity of county vehicles when calculating staff spaces. Count on some ride-sharing and use of alternative modes of transportation.

Number of inmates and visiting policies. The more inmates there are, the more visitors' parking spaces are needed. These are used by those picking up discharged inmates and those visiting inmates. Visitors include family, friends, officers of the court (e.g., probation and parole officers), lawyers, bondsmen. Generous visiting hours will tend to reduce the number of spaces required since all visitors will not have to be there at the same time. On the other hand, policies that enable frequent and/or long visits will increase the number of spaces required. As with staff, consider future capacity projections and visiting policies when figuring the number of spaces needed.

Adequacy of public transportation. If your county has frequent public transport between the facility site and areas where employees and inmates live, the number of parking spaces can be reduced somewhat. Bear in mind, however, that many of the facility users are not likely to use public transportation no matter how convenient or inexpensive it is.

Other departments. If the facility houses other functions, such as courts, probation, or sheriff's offices, substantially increase the number of staff and visitors' spaces to accommodate them. To do this, conduct a survey of all affected departments. For each department, obtain estimates of the number of employees and visitors that will drive to the facility.

Other. Provide parking spaces (and circulation) for trash and delivery trucks, court transport vehicles, patrol vehicles, bondsmen and, possibly, vehicles stolen or held as evidence.

Using the Program to Evaluate Design Proposals

It is critical that the program be **applied** by the design team. Therefore the issue of communication is paramount. The architect must fully understand the directions and requirements of the program. Even if the architect is part of the programming team, the program report should clearly state and, where helpful, illustrate its message. The programming team should conduct one or more meetings at the start of the design phase for the purpose of orienting the designers to the intent, organization, and contents of the program.

The program contains the criteria to which the design should respond. Or, in other words, it "states the problem" that the design should solve. The program is therefore a tool for the task force in judging conceptual or schematic designs proposed by your architect.

Review objectives and requirements stated in the program and have the architect show you—to your satisfaction—that the design responds to the stated needs.

The activity sequences are particularly useful tools for design review. Have your architect "walk you through" the design and demonstrate where various sequences take you.

As stated elsewhere, it is difficult for nonarchitects to understand plans. Therefore have your architect show you circulation paths, control points, sight lines, and so on. Even better, have the architect make a working model (the larger the scale, the better), which is much easier to visualize than a plan. Some architects make working models as part of their design process. These are very different from the slick presentation models that are sometimes commissioned. Often working models are rough and can be rather easily changed to try different arrangements. If not otherwise provided, you should include the preparation of a working model in the architects' contract.

Negotiating Trade-offs and Changes in the Program and Design

Any design does some things better than others; in fact, solving one problem in the design may actually cause other problems to appear! Since there are always "trade-offs" in design, you will have to establish your priorities. The more important criteria must be satisfied, sometimes at the expense of less important ones.

DUNAGIN'S PEOPLE by Ralph Dunagin © 1981 Field Enterprises, Inc.
Courtesy of Field Newspaper Syndicate

Trade-offs are a result of various constraints or limitations on the design. These include the budget, which necessitates deciding the most important ways to spend limited funds; the site, with existing buildings and circulation paths to relate to, sometimes with limited or oddly shaped buildable areas; the complexity of the functions to be accommodated; and sometimes the design itself, which may emphasize one function or set of values to the detriment or exclusion of others.

The program and its requirements should not be treated as totally fixed or unchangeable. While it represents the best idea of how things should be done at a certain point in time, new ideas or information may suggest—or require—changes.

More accurate pictures of cost, which are developed during design, may force trade-offs or compromises. These are acceptable as long as you are careful to insure that major objectives or functional criteria continue to be handled properly.

References

Benton, F. W. 1981. **Planning and Evaluating Prison and Jail Staffing Patterns.** Vol. 1. Washington, DC: National Institute of Corrections.

Palmer, Mickey A. 1981. **The Architect's Guide to Facility Programming.** New York: Architectural Record Books; Washington DC: American Institute of Architects. A comprehensive guide to facility programming that explains its function and process, describes techniques, and includes case studies. Can be valuable to clients as well as architects.

Peña, William M., William Caudill, and John Focke. 1977. **Problem Seeking.** Boston: Cahners Books. A very clearly presented approach to architectural programming. Popular with architects.

Preiser, Wolfgang F. E., ed. 1985. **Programming the Built Environment.** New York: Van Nostrand Reinhold Company. A book of varied programming case studies, all of which are oriented toward the building user.

Sanoff, Henry. 1977. **Methods of Architectural Programming.** Stroudsburg, PA: Dowden, Hutchinson & Ross. Surveys a wide range of activity and user-oriented programming methods. Also presents many ranking, rating, and trade-off methods.

33. Estimating Staffing Requirements

Who Will Use This Chapter

Primary Users
Project manager
Jail administration
Task forces

Secondary Users
Board of commissioners
Planning team
Advisory committee

Introduction

During the lifetime of a jail, staffing is the largest single cost of operation and exceeds many times over the cost of initial construction. Thus it is critical when designing a jail to consider the staffing needs imposed by any particular physical configuration. Different configurations may require substantially different numbers of staff while accommodating the same number of inmates.

Staffing levels are also affected by a jail's programs, by its inmate capacity, by its inmate population, by laws and court decisions, and by the jail's mode of operation. It is important, for example, that staffing needs be considered in terms of the quality of inmate care offered by the jail, and also in terms of the quality of work experience for the staff. Since staff typically spend more of their lives in jail than inmates, it is crucial that jails be designed to help staff do their jobs and receive satisfaction in the process.

This chapter explores the complicated question of staffing and its relationship to jail planning. In it we look at factors that affect the number of staff needed, the means of estimating the number of staff required for a particular jail, the staffing needs inherent in various types of inmate housing arrangements, and the effect of staffing requirements on life-cycle costs.

Staffing and the Planning Process

Staffing estimates should be prepared at each stage of the planning process. As soon as the number and type of inmates is determined, a preliminary estimate of staffing levels should be developed.

During the programming phase, it is necessary to refine the preliminary analysis and develop a more accurate picture of staffing requirements. Efficiency in staffing is one basis for evaluating proposed designs. These refinements can be used to estimate costs and test programming concepts for cost effectiveness.

As design begins and progresses, the method presented in this chapter should be used to further refine projections and test proposed designs. In fact, it is only when a schematic design proposal is developed that an informed determination can be made about where staff will be stationed, how many are needed to supervise an area, and how much movement will be required.

During the correctional planning process, the board of commissioners must be kept informed of projected changes in capacity or operations so that they can understand how many staff are needed and why. This is critical since the jail will almost certainly be asking for a large and costly increase in staff.

Factors That Affect Staffing Requirements

The population housed. Who the facility houses influences the quantity and types of staff needed. A pretrial facility, for instance, will require more intake staff and fewer program staff than a facility for sentenced inmates. And pretrial inmates who may be suicidal require more surveillance and interaction with staff than do minimum security sentenced inmates.

The number of inmates. Smaller facilities seem to require somewhat higher staff-to-inmate ratios than larger facilities. Sometimes this is because living units in smaller facilities are smaller and require a higher staff/inmate ratio. Also, larger facilities may be more conducive to certain economies of scale; for example, a cook who prepares food for twenty-five may also, with inmate help, prepare food for fifty inmates.

The responsibilities of staff. For example, a jail with ten female beds can be more staff-efficient if female officers have responsibilities in addition to simply staffing the women's unit. On the other hand, of course, staff should not be spread too thin.

The programs the jail will provide. When you developed your mission statement and goals (Chapter 10), you probably made commitments, directly or indirectly, to the quantity and/or categories of staff. For example, if rehabilitation is a part of your mission, program staff are needed. If frequent officer/inmate contact is desired, more correctional officers are needed.

The length of the program day. The time that inmates are out of their cells also influences the number of staff needed. If the program day includes two shifts rather than one, more residential, security, and program staff are required.

The location of program and recreation areas. Where these areas are located in relation to housing units influences staff numbers. If visiting and recreation areas are adjacent to housing (or if visitors or inmates do not need to be escorted), fewer staff may be needed than if correctional officers are required for escorting inmates to other parts of the jail.

The location of the jail. Where the jail is located has major effects on staffing for a pretrial detention facility. If transportation is required from jail to court, the longer it takes to get to court and the more presentenced inmates there are, the more staff are needed.

The use of trustees. Using such inmates may help reduce staff numbers. While ensuring that safety and security are maintained, it may be possible to have several inmate trustees take the place of a maintenance officer or a cook.

The "shift relief factor." When estimating staffing, remember jails are operated twenty-four hours a day, seven days a week. Many posts are continuously staffed; while some positions are staffed during one or two shifts either every day or just on weekdays. To determine your shift relief factor—the number of people needed to fill one post—refer to Table 33.1.

Table 33-1. How to Calculate Your Jail's Shift Relief Factor.

Step

1. Number of days per year that the jail is closed (that is, no services are offered; for jail, should be zero). _____ (a)
2. Number of work days per year equals 365-(a). _____ (b)
3. Number of regular days off per employee per year (Usually 52 weeks/yr x 2 days off/week = 104). _____ (c)
4. Number of vacation days off per employee per year. _____ (d)
5. Number of holiday days off per employee per year. _____ (e)
6. Number of sick days off per employee per year. _____ (f)
7. Number of other days off per employee per year. (This includes time off for injury on the job, union meetings, military leave, funeral leave, unexcused absences, disciplinary time off, special assignments, etc.*) _____ (g)
8. Number of training days per year. _____ (h)
9. Total number of days off per employee per year equals (c) + (d) + (e) + (f) + (g) + (h). _____ (i)
10. Number of actual work days per employee per year equals 365-(i). _____ (j)
11. Shift relief factor equals (b) ÷ (j). _____ (k)

*Another factor you might wish to include in Step 7 is the time it takes to fill a vacancy.

For a post that is continuously staffed (such as a control center) the shift relief factor is likely to be between 5.1 and 5.8; in other words, it will take between five and six staff members to fill it. As you will see, this calculation takes into consideration all shifts, time off, training, sick leave, and so forth. The shift relief factor, and hence the number of employees needed per post, is considerably smaller for jobs that are filled during one or two shifts on less than seven days of the week.

The design of the facility. The design should respond to your county's needs and desires regarding staffing. However, the reverse can also occur: design can dictate staffing needs. For example, a residential control room that, through location and equipment, enables two staff to manage one hundred inmates will require fewer staff than a scheme that has an officer assigned to each twenty-person dayroom. Similarly, a compact jail with corridors that can be controlled by stationary staff needs fewer staff to escort inmates than an elongated jail with "blind spots" and doors that cannot be electronically controlled.

The internal "patrol" or surveillance interval. The length of that interval, stipulated by the state, county, or jail administration, is often related to the type of housing. At night, inmates in multiple-occupancy cells might need to be observed every thirty minutes, while inmates in single cells could be observed considerably less frequently (perhaps every two hours), except for those who are suicide risks.

The type of supervision and surveillance in the housing units. The number of staff needed is affected by the extent to which the county wants staff to communicate with inmates, search inmates and their cells, find information for inmates, ensure that safety and security are maintained, and that rules are followed.

Standards, Laws, and Court Orders

There are numerous standards and guidelines that directly and indirectly affect staffing. The standards a county **must** follow are those mandated by the state and the county itself, or those imposed by a court order.

Some states review counties' staffing procedures on a regular basis. And many states must review and approve counties' plans for new jails, additions, and renovations—in part, to ensure that staffing plans are compatible with the design. Some state staffing requirements for county jails are more specific and comprehensive than others; Texas' **Jail Standards,** for example, says that at least one corrections officer is needed for every forty-five inmates.

There are several national standards that go beyond what is required by most states, and some counties elect to follow these. Although they are not universally accepted, the most highly regarded national jail standards are those of the American Correctional Association/Commission on the Accredition for Corrections (ACA/CAC). Their **Standards for Adult Local Detention Facilities** include several regulations that could affect the number of staff needed for various housing types. Around-the-clock supervision of inmates by trained personnel is required (2-5171), and every control station must be continuously staffed (2-5172). Other ACA/CAC regulations are more specific. First, correctional officer posts must be located immediately adjacent to inmate living areas to permit officers to hear and respond promptly to emergency situations (2-5173). Second, all high- and medium-security inmates are to be personally observed by a correctional officer at least every thirty minutes on an irregular schedule. More frequent observation is required for those inmates who are violent, suicidal, mentally disordered, or who demonstrate unusual or bizarre behavior (2-5174).

Another set of national standards that affects staffing is the American Public Health Association's **Standards for Health Services in Correctional Institutions.** These standards describe staff functions and the means of performing them, leaving it up to localities to interpret the standards for their particular situations. For example, they suggest that the health staff should be large enough to provide quality care to all prisoners. They warn against relying on formulas for determining numbers of health care staff because smaller institutions with high turnover rates and many substance abusers need more staff than larger facilities with more stable and healthy populations.

Means of Estimating Required Staff

The degree of accuracy in projecting staff needs depends on how detailed your information is concerning both operations and design. Estimates will be rough in the early planning stages and become more detailed as planning progresses. However, there are no easy formulas for estimating staffing requirements. Simple staff-to-inmate ratios are unreliable since good rules of thumb do not exist. Little guidance is available at this rough level as to what is adequate, inadequate, or overly generous, since too much depends on the nature of the prisoner population, the type of operation, the design of the facility, and the correctional programs offered.

Some facilities with large numbers of staff, many programs, and many security posts require about as many staff as there are inmates (staff to inmate ratio 1:1). Facilities with low staffing ratios may be in the range of 1:5 or 1:8, staff to inmates. These facilities would find it more difficult to support programs, would have little opportunity for other than purely routine staff-inmate contact, and achieve very easy—or, more likely, very little—direct visual surveillance. A better method is to examine each required staff position.

Staff Positions. Estimates are based upon consideration of each position required for each function and location in a proposed facility. In planning and programming phases, positions can be determined using the list of jail programs and services, together with an estimate of the number of housing units and control stations. In the design phase, estimates can be based upon actual locations and movement patterns of staff. A checklist of potential positions is included in Table 33-2.

Table 33-2. Potential Positions in Jail Staffing

To develop an estimate of the total staffing required in the jail, start by considering every function which staff must fulfill. Determine the number of staff needed for each function on each shift. If the position operates on a 3 shift per day, 7 day per week basis (such as Control Room Officer), multiply the number of separate posts times the relief factor to determine the number of positions required.

For example, if there are 3 residential control rooms, each operated by a single officer, and the relief factor is 5.8, multiply 3 times 5.8 to obtain the 17.4 required positions.

Description of Position	Number of Staff Per Shift			or	Number of 24 Hour Posts	x	Relief Factor (if applies)	=	Total Positions Required
	Shift 1	Shift 2	Shift 3						
Administration									
GENERAL:									
Jail Administrator									
Assistant Jail Administrator									
Administrative Assistant									
Public Information/Community Affairs									
Internal Affairs Officer									
PERSONNEL:									
Personnel Officer									
Training Officer									
Payroll Clerk									
BUSINESS:									
Business Manager									
Budget Officer									
Accountant/Accounting Clerk									
CLERICAL:									
Administrative Secretary									
Receptionist/Typists									
Record Clerks									
Clerk Typists									
Clerks									
Switchboard									
PLANNING AND RESEARCH:									
Director									
Research Assistant									
Research Secretary									
Planner/Analyst									
ADMINISTRATION SUBTOTAL:									

Table 33-2. Potential Positions in Jail Staffing, continued

Description of Position	Number of Staff Per Shift			or	Number of 24 Hour Posts	x	Relief Factor (if applies)	=	Total Positions Required
	Shift 1	Shift 2	Shift 3						
Security									
GENERAL:									
Supervisor									
Secretary									
Shift Supervisor									
Assistant Shift Supervisor									
AREA SUPERVISOR:									
Master Control Room Officer									
Control Room Officer									
INTAKE:									
Intake/Release Supervisor									
Intake/Release Officer									
Clothing/Property Officer									
(See programs for additional staffing)									
SPECIAL:									
Visitation Officer									
Dining Officer									
Tower Officer									
Gate Officer									
Reception Officer									
Internal Movement Officer									
Program Correctional Officer									
Shakedown Officer									
TRANSPORTATION:									
Transportation Supervisor									
Transportation Officer									
Courtroom Officer									
Hospital Duty									
Elevator Operator									
LIVING UNITS:									
Control Rooms									
Living Unit Officer									
Floor Control Officer									
SECURITY SUBTOTAL:									

Table 33-2. Potential Positions in Jail Staffing, continued

Description of Position	Number of Staff Per Shift			or	Number of 24 Hour Posts	x	Relief Factor (if applies)	=	Total Positions Required
	Shift 1	Shift 2	Shift 3						
Support Services Unit									
GENERAL:									
Unit Supervisor									
Secretary									
HEALTH SERVICES:									
Health Service Director									
Physician									
Nurse/Physicians Assistant/EMT									
Dentist									
Dental Technician									
Pharmacist									
Medical Consultant									
Orderly									
X-ray Technician									
Laboratory Technician									
DIAGNOSTIC PERSONNEL:									
Psychiatrist									
Clinical Psychologist									
Social Worker									
Psychiatric Social Worker									
FOOD SERVICE:									
Food Service Director									
Nutritionist									
Cook									
Food Service Assistant									
Baker									
PLANT MAINTENANCE:									
Building Supervisor									
Engineer									
Fireman									
Janitor									
Carpenter									
Plumber									
Painter									
Locksmith									
Electrician									
Computer Technician									
Groundskeeper									
Trustee Supervisor									
MISCELLANEOUS:									
Barber									
Commissary									
Property Clerk									
Storeroom Officer									
Purchasing Officer									
Safety Officer									
Mail									
Laundry									
SUPPORT SERVICE UNIT SUBTOTAL:									

Table 33-2. Potential Positions in Jail Staffing, continued

Description of Position	Number of Staff Per Shift			or	Number of 24 Hour Posts	x	Relief Factor (if applies)	=	Total Positions Required
	Shift 1	Shift 2	Shift 3						

Program Unit

GENERAL:
Unit Supervisor
Secretary
Volunteer Coordinator

TREATMENT:
Psychologist
Social Worker
Clergy
Counselor
Caseworker
Recreation
Librarian
Substance Abuse Counselor
Intern

EDUCATION:
Director
Vocational Trainer
Academic Instructor
Art/Craft/Music Instructor
Intern

WORK RELEASE:
Work Release Coordinator
Job Developer
Instructor
Caseworker/Followup

CLASSIFICATION/INTAKE:
Classification Officer
Intake Screening
Court Liaison

RECORDS:
Record Supervisor
Booking Clerk

MISCELLANEOUS:
Grievance Officer
Disciplinary Officer
Ombudsman
Movement Officer
Legal Services

PROGRAM UNIT SUBTOTAL:

GRAND TOTAL:

Other "methods" for estimating staffing include the following:

Outcome Analysis. External measurements, including the number of behavioral incidents, the quantity of overtime, and staff morale, may imply that more (or fewer) staff are needed. This approach, known as outcome analysis, tends to reward incompetence and guesses that the solution to many problems is more staff (Benton). On the other hand, responding to some problems, such as low morale, with more staff may be effective. Outcome analysis is the most typical method of staff analysis currently used in corrections.

Comparative Analysis. Comparative analysis involves matching your jail with jails that are operating with similar population sizes and types, goals, facilities, and programs. Identifying similar jails may be the most critical step of this process. Matching your jail with another that is similar except for one major difference, such as population types, can be dangerous and misleading.

For this method to be most useful, at least several similar facilities should be identified and the number of staff in various functional categories, such as those categories shown in Table 33-1 should be gathered.

Your county may reap two additional benefits by examining staffing patterns from other jails. It may learn about alternative approaches to functions, some of which may be suited to your situation. Also, other counties' figures may be helpful in justifying greater staffing levels to your own county's officials and the general public.

Acknowledgment: Material for this chapter is adapted from jail staffing forms developed by Dave Voorhis and John Milosovich for the National Institute of Corrections Jail Center.

References

Benton, F. W. 1981. **Planning and Evaluating Prison and Jail Staffing.** Vol 1. Washington, DC: National Institute of Corrections.

Benton, F. W., E. D. Rosen, and J.-L. Peters. 1980. **National Survey of Correctional Institution Employee Attrition Rates.** New York. John Jay College of Criminal Justice.

Jail Standards. A report prepared regularly for the Texas Commission on Jail Standards.

34. Site Analysis, Selection, and Planning

Who Will Use This Chapter

Primary Users
Site selection task force
Planning team
Project manager

Secondary Users
Advisory committee
Consultant

If the planning team chooses to appoint a task force for site selection, it should include the project manager; a representative from each agency to be housed in the new facilities; and county staff with expertise in planning, engineering, finance, and legal issues. In addition, it is desirable to have public representation and professional input from an architect, planner, or other consultant who can assist the group with technical issues.

The Site Selection and Planning Process

Site Alternatives

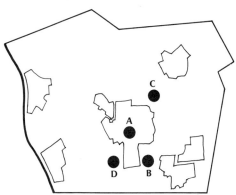

The site selection and planning process entails the following steps:

- Defining site needs and objectives.
- Identifying potential sites.
- Gathering information and analyzing each site.
- Evaluating the sites and selecting one.
- Acquiring the selected site (if not already county owned).
- Preparing an environmental impact report (if required).
- Preparing a site master plan.

To identify appropriate sites for consideration, the task force develops a list of site needs and objectives. These will include a definition of amount of buildable and open space needs, locational objectives, and any other key identifiable objectives. The task force then must identify potential sites, gather data on each one, and rank the best choices. Review the results with the advisory committee at this point, since site selection is among the most controversial of issues.

Once the site is chosen, the group may commission or direct the environmental impact assessment. It may be worthwhile conducting this before acquisition so that you will be aware of any serious and potentially costly environmental problems. Finally, a site master plan will be developed, taking into account objectives held for site design. Each of these topics is dealt with below.

Site Selection and Development Objectives

Site objectives describe the qualities necessary to support appropriately the activities that will occur on the site and the people who will use the site and its facilities. Express objectives in nontechnical terms that describe the community, governmental, or institutional expectations for the site or for any prospective location if a site has not yet been selected.

An effective way of generating these objectives is to "brainstorm" them, listing all suggestions and then discussing and refining them into a set of objectives for the site. (Refer to Chapters 9 and 11 for methods.) This should be done early in the process and reviewed by the advisory committee. The following are examples of site objectives that might be sought for correctional facilities.

- Site should be centrally located in community.
- Site should be open and approachable with "green" spaces for public use and a security perimeter.
- Site should be relatively level, for ease of development.
- Site should be close to other county agencies (particularly courts for a pre-sentence facility).
- Site should be easily accessible via public transportation.

Site Criteria

To ensure that the objectives established for the site are met, selection criteria should be developed and applied to each potential site. Meeting these criteria will help insure that objectives are attainable and that basic qualities or services can be provided at the site. You can use the checklist in Table 34-1 to determine whether you have addressed the criteria.

Locational Criteria

Locational criteria address qualities affected by where the site is and include access, the character of the neighborhood, and its zoning.

All types of users nd their vehicles should have access to the site. Specific types (or groupings) of facilities have specific access requirements, but the following issues should be reviewed for their relevance. Distances necessary for law enforcement agencies to travel to reach the site should be considered as well as distances to population centers of other areas of concentrated activity. Access to courts is always critical. If not immediately adjacent, the costs of transporting inmates to and from court must be considered along with means of transportation. The proximity of the site to county offices (such as probation, district attorney, or other service providers) is important as well as the relationship to private offices (such as attorneys). To facilitate visiting and release, the site should be close to public transportation.

The **character of the neighborhood** surrounding the site will undoubtedly affect the location of correctional facilities. Location in a residential area may raise community opposition or contradict zoning regulations. However, depending on the kind of facility, it may not be appropriate to locate it too remotely from the county seat, despite potential opposition.

The most appropriate sites are frequently those near the center of government. Typically these already have some justice-related functions and are quite accessible. Their use is accepted without being viewed as an infringement on other types of uses and occupants such as retail sales, multiple family housing, or commercial zones.

To a certain degree, the appropriate neighborhood character is determined by site objectives. Occasionally certain undesirable areas, such as industrial or landfill zones, are not excluded by the site objectives. In most cases, because of noise or unpleasant odors, these types of land use do not make good neighbors for justice facilities and should be discouraged.

Zoning restrictions will also have an impact on site selection and should be considered from the outset. In denser locations, the allowable floor-area-to-land-area ratio may prohibit a building tall enough to accommodate the required spaces. While current zoning patterns may or may not prohibit use of a site, the criteria should address future zoning changes and their influence upon city and county plans.

Legal Issues

To avoid potential problems, identify as early as possible such legal issues as site easements or required notifications, assessments, approval processes, and the like.

Physical Criteria

Physical characteristics of the site can have a major impact on its suitability for your purposes. Information on a wide range of site characteristics will need to be gathered and evaluated in terms of how they will affect your program or on construction costs.

The **area** of a site must be large enough to support the required building and outdoor activity spaces, as well as to allow for adequate parking and service space (operations, trash, recreation). It should also allow for future expansion. "Buildable area" is determined not only by physical size but also by the zoning restrictions, topography, and soil/geological conditions. This issue is critical, since it can affect the configuration and number of stories of the building.

The **soil** should have sufficient bearing value to support a building of the proposed size and type of construction without inordinately high foundation costs. It should also be free of drainage problems or a high water table. If the topography is too severe, the resulting slopes may prohibit building, make access difficult, or yield drainage and flooding problems.

Utilities, such as water, sewer, power, and gas, may or may not be easily provided or may not be available at all. If not immediately available, the costs of providing them at the site must be ascertained, since these costs can be significant enough to prohibit use of a location.

The **exposure and orientation** of the site will influence energy and operating costs. The substantial building mass typical of detention facilities provides opportunities for careful building orientation, solar heat gain, thermal insulation, and other elements of active and passive solar design.

The cost and character of the design are also influenced by other site qualities. These may include the nature of the appearance and approach to the facility, views (desirable or undesirable), noise sources in the vicinity, or other features that may not be compatible with residential and office functions within the facilities.

The **ecology** of a site will most likely be documented in the environmental impact assessment. Potential threats to fragile ecosystems may have to be minimized by sometimes costly methods. Since placement on the site will determine environmental impact to some degree, these threats may be handled in such a way as to mitigate their effect on environmentally sensitive features.

Acquisition Issues

A site must also be obtainable. If the county does not own the property, the ownership must be researched before negotiations can begin. Property ownership and tax records maintained by the county assessor and tax collector will provide this information.

Once ownership is determined, there are three highly critical aspects of acquisition.

- **Can the property be obtained** through negotiation or condemnation?

- **What are the costs** to acquire, develop, and operate at the site (for instance, transport of inmates)?

- **How much time is required** to acquire and develop the property? (For example, are zoning changes or other time-consuming permissions needed?)

Environmental Impact Report (EIR)

If your project is larger than a minor addition, determine the need for an environmental impact study. A "negative declaration" is a finding that the project would probably not have major environmental effects. In this case, no further study is needed. However, negative declarations are rarely adequate for jail construction.

In that case, your county (or a consultant) will have to study the potential impact of the project upon the site's vegetation, wildlife, and land use. It will also address the project's influence on the surrounding area in terms of water runoff, pollution, traffic, transportation, population, property values, social services, business, and industry. Any significant effects might require detailed study and the inclusion of so-called mitigation measures before a project can begin.

Public hearings to acquaint the community with the project and hear their concerns are part of the environmental impact process.

When the site is to be purchased, it is important to conduct a preliminary environmental investigation prior to acquisition. It is to be hoped that you can identify any major problems that might require not only a full EIR (which costs money and takes time), but expensive site development measures as well.

Site Master Planning

The selection of a site is also affected by factors concerning its future use. These include:

- Anticipated future expansion.
- Potential requirements for other facilities (in addition to the jail).
- Likelihood of removing facilities currently on the site.
- Potential for future reduction in operations or space needs of planned or existing facilities.

Such factors concerning the long-term development of a site are normally addressed in a site master plan. The plan controls where and how proposed facilities, roads, open spaces, landscaping, utilities, and the like will be located, expanded, or removed over a period of years. The plan usually shows the development in phases over time, with each phase representing the completion of a major change on the site. Or it may show how such changes can be accommodated without specifying when they will take place.

Site Master Plan

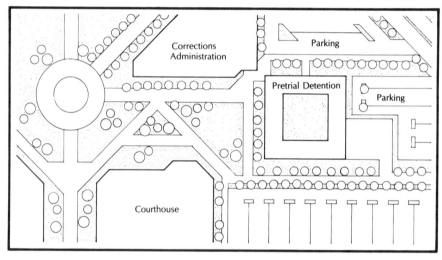

Before selecting a site, your county should consider its probable future needs. For example, will other county facilities such as additional correctional facilities or offices be needed in the future, and would it be best to locate them on the same site?

Considering your county's long-term needs will help you select a suitable site and plan the development of that site, whether for a jail, a justice complex, or a wide array of county facilities. The checklist shown in Table 34-1 may help you review the features of proposed sites. Table 34-2 provides an evaluation form for rating proposed sites once their numbers are narrowed down to major candidates.

The following checklist presents a set of criteria often used in assessing the suitability of potential sites.

Table 34-1. Site Analysis Checklist

1. Site Objectives

Image
Function
Economics
Timing

2. Locational Criteria

Access:
- ☐ For all users (depends on functions included)
- ☐ Law enforcement (routes and distances)
- ☐ Courts (if not on same site)
- ☐ Public (population centers, transport)
- ☐ Relation to county seat, other agencies

Neighborhood Character:
- ☐ Compatibility

☐ Local support/opposition
☐ Desirable/undesirable surrounding uses

Zoning:
☐ Allowable floor area ratio
☐ Current zoning classification
☐ Relation to city and county plans

3. Physical Criteria

Site area:
☐ Building area
☐ Parking area
☐ Outdoor activity areas (e.g., recreation)
☐ Open space, landscape, etc.
☐ Area for future expansion
☐ Total site area needed

Soil/Geology:
☐ Bearing value
☐ Drainage and water table

Topography:
☐ Slopes
☐ Buildability
☐ Drainage/flooding

Utilities:
☐ Availability and cost
☐ Sewer (sanitary and storm)
☐ Water
☐ Power
☐ Gas
☐ Phone
☐ Cable TV
☐ District heat (cogeneration?)
☐ Exposure/Orientation:
☐ Sun (light, solar energy source)
☐ Wind
☐ Views (desirable and undesirable)

Noise:
☐ Type, level, timing
☐ Impact on planned functions

Ecology:
☐ Indigenous flora and fauna
☐ Potential environmental impacts
☐ EIR requirements?

4. Acquisition Issues

Cost:
☐ Acquisition
☐ Site development
☐ Site-specific construction costs
☐ Operational costs (especially transportation)

Time:
☐ Time for acquisition and development

Ownership:
☐ County-owned land
☐ Other agency
☐ Private owner

Acquisition Method:
☐ Condemnation
☐ Negotiation
☐ Assessment

The following is an example of a form used to assess sites for a proposed justice center. One sheet is filled out for each site under consideration. A rating scale (1 = poor to 5 = excellent) evaluates each site on each point. Remember, however, that some criteria may be more important that others and that if a site is to be used for more than a jail, you must add factors which specifically relate to those facility types.

Table 34-2. Justice Center—Site Evaluation Form

Site Description

Site Code Number:

Assessor's Number:

Owner:

Area (acres):

Description of Property:

Estimated Cost:

Criteria	Comments	Ranking (1 = Poor, 5 = Excellent)
Access (Public, staff, law enforcement, etc.)		
Neighborhood Character		
Zoning		
Topography		
Utilities (water, sewer, power, etc.)		
Noise		
Other Comments:		

Developed by Linn County, Oregon, Sheriff's Department

References

Burchell, Robert W., and David Listokin. 1975. **The Environmental Impact Handbook.** New Brunswick, NJ: Center for Urban Policy Research, Rutgers—The State University. Presents an array of standardized approaches to EIR procedures and requirements.

Lynch, Kevin. 1975. **Site Planning.** 2nd ed., Cambridge, MA: The MIT Press. A comprehensive guide to both the issues and techniques of site planning. Widely used by design professionals since its first publication in 1962.

Office of Planning and Research. 1981. **CEQA: The California Environmental Quality Act: Law and Guidelines.** Sacramento: State of California.

Rubenstein, Harvey M. 1969. **A Guide to Site and Environmental Planning.** New York: John Wiley. A reference text, combining an introduction to site design with technical information necessary for site analysis and planning. Material covers site selection, analysis, land use, visual design factors, and landscaping details.

35. Ongoing Project Management

Who Will Use This Chapter

Primary Users
Project manager
Transition task force
Advisory committee

Secondary Users
Corrections/Sheriff
Board of commissioners

Introduction

Having devoted so much effort and care to the planning process up to the point of facility design, it is critical that the county maintain an organization that can monitor the project through completion of construction, movein, and operation.

Ongoing monitoring, evaluation, and planning functions will help corrections prepare for and implement programs, move into and operate facilities and continue (periodically) to update and review corrections and criminal justice systems data.

Through such ongoing management, potential problems can be anticipated or at least identified before they become unmanageable. The people or agencies in positions to solve them will already be mobilized.

Participants' Roles

As the facility moves into the construction phase, the project manager and planning team should begin preparations to move to the new facility. The programming and design task force should convert its function to that of the transition task force, perhaps adding certain other members.

The advisory committee's role, however, should be ongoing. It will support the transition process and monitor correctional system performance and programs as well as continue to coordinate with the rest of the criminal justice system.

Staff to the committee should continue gathering and analyzing data on system performance and evaluating the effectiveness of programs. Periodically reports should be presented, and policy and programs re-evaluated.

Staff Preparation for Moving into and Operating the New Facility

Opening a new facility requires a significant amount of preparatory planning. Often the new facility is physically very different from the existing one. New procedures and operations must be developed and, one hopes, the bugs worked out **before** the first inmates move in. The staff must understand the concepts behind the design in terms of the operational (and sometimes philosophical) assumptions built into the plan.

Run through procedures a number of times prior to the actual move so that each individual is aware of how to perform his or her part. This orientation should be carried out in conjunction with testing all equipment and systems to insure that they are performing properly and support staff actions.

To handle both planning and logistics of the move, organize a transition task force during the construction phase. This group should be drawn, at least in part, from the programming and design task force whose members are the people familiar with the building design and its intended operation. Functions of the transition task force include:

Updating the policy and procedures manual and developing detailed descriptions of procedures to be followed in the new facility.

Carrying out (or coordinating and reviewing) a "final" operational staffing analysis, including shift assignments.

Coordinating the hiring and training of new staff in all aspects of corrections.

County
Corrections
Policies &
Procedures

Correctional Officer	8-4	4-12	12-8	SWING
● JIM J.	✓			
BILL E.		✓		
JOHN F.			✓	
ART D.				✓
● JOE S.	✓			
JOHN B.		✓		
MIKE R.			✓	
BOB A.				✓
●				

This includes orienting existing staff to the building and training them in new procedures and use of new systems. The latter should not be done too early since staff members may forget what they have learned by the time of the move.

Placing of movable furniture and equipment.

Testing the performance of all systems and all new procedures.

Unit County Jail			
● System	Date	Performance	
ALARMS			
• SMOKE	3-16	O.K.	
● • DOORS	3-16	O.K.	
CCTV	3-17	NEEDS WORK	
AUTO · DOORS			
● RM - CELL C-1	3-17	A BIT STICKY	
RM - CELL C-2	3-17	O.K.	
RM - CELL C-3	3-17	O.K.	

Planning and overseeing the logistics of the move into the new facility (for instance, who will go where, and when.)

Conducting media and public relations efforts concerning the new facility. Organizing and conducting tours and perhaps overnight visits to the facility for staff, families, VIP's and the public. Speaking to school and public service or social clubs about the new facility.

Troubleshooting during and after movein.

The architectural consultant should orient staff to the building and train them in the operation and utilization of systems and equipment (in coordination with manufacturers). At that time, the facility users' manual should be delivered and explained along with the "as-built" drawings.

The transition task force may make good use of the National Institute of Corrections' program, "How to Open a New Institution," which covers many of the organizational and logistical aspects of such a move. (Contact NIC for information).

Ongoing Data Gathering and Analysis

To keep tabs on the ever-shifting demands placed on the jail, certain data gathered for the needs assessment should be reviewed periodically. These data are most useful when they go beyond the minimums that your state may require for its annual reporting.

Responsibility for these data collection and planning functions are delegated by the sheriff or jail administrator to a staff planner or a regional criminal justice planner. Ongoing data collection is much easier if the jail tailors its booking form to the data used in Part 3.

At least every year—perhaps every 3 to 6 months—the jail should review its capacity projections, updating them in light of intervening experience. The actual number of people in various categories who were booked and the length of time they spent in jail will form the basis for this analysis, together with revised county population projections.

Each year or two, the jail should carry out a smaller-scale version of the jail population profile as done in Chapter 14. In this way the jail can monitor changes in the composition of its population and identify shifting problems and needs.

In addition, newly instituted programs should be monitored to see how they are working. To do this, institute an orderly recordkeeping system at the start of the program. Otherwise the information will not be there when you want or need it. The next section discusses how that information is used to evaluate operations.

Monitoring, Evaluating, and Problem Solving

The staff responsible for gathering and analyzing jail population data should make periodic (monthly or quarterly) reports to the advisory committee.

Each six to twelve months, the performance of various correctional and jail-related programs should be reviewed. This review should be both **informal**, looking at peoples' impressions of how programs are working, and also formal, measuring program performance in relation to stated objectives.

At these periodic review sessions, problem identification techniques (such as those discussed in Chapter 9) may be used to uncover new or ongoing problems. Jail inspections and grand jury reports should also be reviewed.

Overcrowding ranks among the most persistent jail problems. One of the reasons that new jails built to twenty-year capacity projections fill up immediately on opening is that no effort is made to monitor and coordinate the justice programs that were anticipated during planning. Thus it is critical to scrutinize the performance of these programs carefully as the facility begins and continues operations.

Conclusion

We end **Correction Facility Planning and Design** with this chapter. While no treatment of corrections planning can be "complete," we have presented a great deal of information in a format that we hope will prove useful.

While corrections planning can be time-consuming and complex, the achievement of a responsive and effective corrections system is a source of pride for the community and professionals who bring it about.

References

Adams, Stuart, 1975. **Evaluative Research in Corrections: A Practical Guide**. A report prepared for the U.S. Department of Justice, National Institute of Law Enforcement and Criminal Justice. Reviews the status of corrections evaluation and provides a how-to guide for evaluating programs.

Farbstein, Jay, Richard Wener, and Patricia Gomez, 1979-80. **Evaluation of Correctional Environments**. San Luis Obispo, CA: Farbstein/Williams & Associates. A series of reports on how the jail environment affects inmates and staff, methods used to measure this impact, and result of jail case studies.

Klein, Malcolm, and Katherine Teilmann, eds. 1980. **Handbook of Criminal Justice**

Evaluation, Beverly Hills, CA: Sage Publications, A collection of rather technical papers on issues in criminal justice program evaluation.

Milosovich, John, and David Dupree. 1980. **Opening New Prisons, Jails and Community-based Centers.** College Park, MD: American Correctional Association. Presents information developed in NIC's "How to Open a New Institution" program.

Morris, Lynn Lyons, ed. 1978. **Program Evaluation Kit**. Beverly Hills, CA: Sage Publications. A series of eight step-by-step handbooks showing how to organize and conduct a program evaluation.

U.S. Department of Justice, Federal Prison System, Bureau of Prisons. n.d. **Activation Manual: Staff, Equipment, Inmates**. Washington, DC: Government Printing Office. While oriented toward prison facilities, this manual provides a model process for organizing the startup of a new facility. Contains many checklists and an over-all schedule.

Appendices

Appendix A:

Snapshot Profile Data Form

Last	First	Middle Initial

1. Inmate Name: _____

2. Local Identifying Number _____

3. State or Federal Identifying Number _____

4. Facility in Which
Inmate Housed: (B)
  1.) Assign number to
  2.) each detention
  3.) facility operated
  4.) by the county.
  5.)
    .)
    .)

☐ 1

Assign one number each to: other counties within state and out of state

9. Arresting Agency (B)
Assign number to each agency which arrests and books in local facilities.

☐ 8 ☐ 9

5. Sex: (B)
  1. = Male
  2. = Female

☐ 2

10. Type of Arrest (B)
  1. = On-view
  2. = Warrant
  3. = Enroute
  4. =) Add other arrest
  5. =) categories as
  .   ) desired.
  .   )
  .   )

☐ 10

6. Race: (B)
  1. = White
  2. = Black
  3. = Mexican-American
  4. = Japanese
  5. = Chinese
  6. = American Indian
  7. = Filipino
  8. = Pacific Islander
  9. = Other/Unknown

☐ 3

11. Length of Stay (hours) (B)
  1. = 0–1 hours
  2. = 1–4 hours
  3. = 5–9 hours
  4. = 10–24 hours
  5. = More than 24 hours

☐ 11

7. Age: (B)
(enter actual years)

☐ 4 ☐ 5

8. Place of Residence: (B)
Assign numbers to
each city in the
county to include one
number for county
unincorporated area.
If desired, assign
numbers to neighboring counties.

☐ 6 ☐ 7

12. Length of Stay (days) (B)
Enter actual number of days elapsed from date of booking to the date the profile is being taken.

☐ 12 ☐ 13 ☐ 14

13. Current Sentence (B)
(Enter actual sentence as noted by comparing release date and booking date noted in jail records).
Enter 0-0-0 if the inmate is unsentenced.

☐ 15 ☐ 16 ☐ 17

B = Basic   S = Secondary

14. Primary Charge: (B)

See offense grouping sheet for penal code violations related to the offense classes noted below. Included as Appendix F. You may wish to reorganize this list to reflect your state's penal code.

18 19

Felony

01. = Murder/related violent crime
02. = Other violent anti-person crime
03. = Violent crime involving police officer
04. = Family offense
05. = Sex offense
06. = Commerical sex offense
07. = Burglary
08. = Weapons
09. = Other property crimes
        (non-violent)
10. = Drug/prohibited substance—use
11. = Drug/prohibited substance—sale
12. = Automobile violations
13. = Probation violations
14. = Miscellaneous

Misdemeanor

15. = Violent offense—civilian
16. = Violent offense—police officer involved
17. = Burglary related
18. = Family violence
19. = Sex offense
20. = Commerical sex offense
21. = Weapons
22. = Non-violent/non-burglary property
        crime
23. = Nuisance
24. = Public inebriation
25. = Drug/prohibited substance—use
26. = Drug/prohibited substance—sale
27. = Probation violation
28. = Automobile offense—alcohol involved
29. = Automobile offense—non-alcohol related
30. = Miscellaneous

15. Number of Additional Felony Charges (B)

0 through 8, enter actual number;

9 or more, enter 9

20

16. Number of Additional Misdemeanor Charges (B)

0 through 8, enter actual number;

9 or more, enter 9

21

17. Bail Set on Current Arrest: (B)

0 = Bail Information Unavailable

1 = Less than $150

2 = $151 to $500

3 = $501 to $1000

4 = $1001 to $2000

5 = $2001 to $3000

6 = $3001 to $4000

7 = $4001 to $5000

8 = $5001 to $7500

9 = $7501 +

22

18. Wanted by Other Jurisdiction (B)

0. = No arrest warrant or parole hold

1. = Parole hold

2 = Arrest warrant by other county

3. = Arrest warrant by state agency

4. = Arrest warrant by federal agency

5. = Arrest warrant by local, in-county

6. = Probation Hold

7. = Unknown

23

19. Nature of Charges in Other Jurisdictions (B)

Enter most serious charge using categories listed under #14.

24 25

20. Total Outstanding Warrants and Holds: (B)

0 = None

1–8 = Actual number

9 = 9 or more

26

21. Bail Amount of Outstanding Warrants: (S)

0. = Information Not Available

1. = Less than $150

2. = $151 to $500

3. = $501 to $1000

4. = $1001 to $2000

5. = $2001 to $3000

6. = $3001 to $4000

7. = $4001 to $5000

8. = $5001 to $7500

9. = $7501 +

27

22. Number of Prior Felony Convictions: (B)

1–8 = Enter actual number

9 = 9 or more

0 = None

28

23. Most Serious Previous Felony Convictions (S)

See offense grouping sheet (Appendix F) for penal code violations related to the offense classes noted below.

☐ ☐
29 30

Felony

01. = Murder/related violent crime
02. = Other violent anti-person crime
03. = Violent crime involving police officer
04. = Family violence
05. = Sex offense
06. = Commerical sex offense
07. = Burglary
08. = Weapons
09. = Other property crimes (non-violent)
10. = Drug/prohibited substance—use
11. = Drug/prohibited substance—sale
12. = Automobile violations
13. = Probation violations
14. = Miscellaneous

24. Number of Previous Misdemeanor Convictions: (S)

1–8 = Enter actual number
9 = 9 or more
0 = None

☐
31

25. Most Serious Previous Misdemeanor Conviction (S)

See offense grouping sheet (Appendix F) for penal code violations related to the offense classes noted below (excluding warrant or hold information recorded in #16, above).

☐ ☐
32 33

Misdemeanor

15. = Violent offense—civilian
16. = Violent offense—police officer involved
17. = Burglary related
18. = Family violence
19. = Sex offense
20. = Commerical Sex Offense
21. = Weapons
22. = Non-violent/non-burglary property crime
23. = Nuisance
24. = Public inebriation
25. = Drug/prohibited substance—use
26. = Drug/prohibited substance—sale
27. = Probation violation
28. = Automobile offense—alcohol related
29. = Automobile offense—non-alcohol related
30. = Miscellaneous

26. Current Other Pending Cases (S)

1. = Yes
2. = No
3. = No information

☐
34

27. Past Bench Warrants for Failure to Appear (S)

1. = Yes
2. = No
3. = No information

☐
35

(Difficult to document in most jurisdictions. If available, should be collected).

28. Previous Incarceration History (S)

0. = No previous incarceration
1. = Previous time unsentenced in county system
2. = Previous sentenced time in county system
3. = Previous time in state facility

☐
36

29. Reason Misdemeanor Offenses Not Citable (B)

01. = Too intoxicated
02. = Required medical care
03. = Multiple VC 40302 violations
04. = Outstanding warrants
05. = Lack of personal identification information
06. = Jeopardize prosecution of case
07. = Safety of persons/property endangered
08. = Refused to sign citation waiver
09. = Warrant arrest
99. = Unknown

☐ ☐
37 38

30. Current Housing in Facility: (B)

Assign codes to the various potential housing situations in the jail facility/ other detention facility (e.g. single cell; dormitory; medical unit; etc.)

☐
39

31. Custody Problem(s) Determining Housing Requirement (B)

(a) First Problem

☐ ☐
40 41

(b) Second Problem

☐ ☐
42 43

(c) Third Problem

☐ ☐
44 45

00. = No custody problem
01. = Violent behavior
02. = Suicidal
03. = Escape history
04. = Mental problem—non-violent
05. = Mental problem—general population
06. = Medical problem—general population
07. = Medical problem—required observation
08. = Homosexual/transsexual
09. = Prison gang member
10.   Enemies in facility population
11.)   Add other relevant
12.)   characteristics
13.)   which impact housing
14.)   and/or consideration for pretrial release

32. Employment Status: (S)

0. = Currently unemployed
1. = Employed—full time job
2. = Employed—part time job
3. = School—full-time enrollment
4. = No information

46

33. Residence Pattern: (S)

0. = No residence pattern in local area
1. = Present residence in local area—last 4 months and/or 2 local residences last 6 months.
2. = Present residence in local area—last 6 months and/or present and prior resident —1 year.
3. = Present local residence—1 year or more
4. = No information

47

34. Family/Community Ties (S)

0. = No family ties
1. = Lives with non-family
2. = Lives with/has weekly contact with family

48

35. Alcohol/Drug Abuse/Mental Health Problems (B, if available)

(a) First Problem

49

(b) Second Problem

50

(c) Third Problem

51

0. = No problem
1. = Drug addiction—active at time of booking
2. = Drug addiction—past history
3. = Alcoholic
4. = Mental problems—on medication in facility
5. = Mental problems—out-patient at time of arrest.
6. = Mental problems—previous history of care but not under active care at time of arrest.

36. Marital Status (S)

1. = Married
2. = Single
3. = Divorced
4. = Separated
5. = Widowed
6. = Unknown

52

37. Adjudication Status of Unsentenced Inmates (S)

1. = Awaiting Municipal Court arraignment
2. = Arraigned at Municipal Court level, awaiting preliminary hearing
3. = Arraigned at Municipal Court level, awaiting Municipal Court trial.
4. = Arraigned at Superior Court level, awaiting trial.
5. = Completed preliminary hearing at Municipal Court level, awaiting Superior Court arraignment.
6. = Convicted at Municipal Court level, awaiting sentencing.
7. = Convicted at Superior Court level, awaiting sentencing.
8. = Sentenced at Superior Court level, awaiting transfer to state facility.
9. = Other sentenced inmate.

53

Appendix B:

Suggested Sources for Snapshot Profile Data

This appendix shows basic and alternative sources for the data elements in the snapshot profile. The alternative approach need only be used when the basic source is not available.

Data Element	Suggested Source (& Alternative)
4. Facility Where Inmate Housed	Booking sheet or jail roster (Alternative Source: Review list of inmates with jail commander at time profile constructed; note location of all inmates as of the time designated as the baseline for the snapshot.)
5. Sex 6. Race 7. Age 8. Place of Residence	Booking sheet or jail jacket/folder containing papers related to each inmate. Arrest report related to current offense also likely to contain required demographic data. (Alternative Source: Distribute simple demographic questionnaire to all inmates in custody at the time the profile is taken. Collect and transfer information to tally sheet. If questionnaire is necessary to collect required demographic data, consider distributing and collecting at the next meal following the cut-off hour established to construct the population profile. Distribute with meal and collect completed questionnaire upon completion of the meal. If questionnaire is used, audit sample to insure validity.)
9. Arresting Agency	Booking sheet or copy of arrest report contained in inmate's jail file.
10. Type of Arrest	Booking sheet or copy of arrest report contained in inmate's jail file.
11. Length of Stay (hours) 12. Length of Stay (days)	Booking sheet, jail ledger, or copy of arrest report contained in inmate's jail file. Release log. (Alternative Source: To facilitate computation and recording of length of stay data, construct simple reference table counting days which precede the profile date as shown in the example which follows)

Profile Date: 4-20-81

Date	Days	Date	Days
4–20	0	3–18	32
4–19	1	3–17	33
4–18	2	3–16	34
4–17	3	3–15	35
4–16	4	3–14	36
4–15	5		

Data Element	Suggested Source (& Alternative)
13. Current Sentence	Copy of court sentencing order contained in inmate's jail folder. Booking sheet.
14. Primary Charge 15. Additional Felony Charges 16. Additional Misdemeanor Charges	Booking Sheet—for both sentenced and unsentenced prisoners. Copy of court sentencing order contained in inmate's jail folder—for sentenced inmates. Copies of relevant court documents contained in inmate's jail folders—for unsentenced inmates. (Alternative Source: In constructing the profile, it is important that current charge status of each sentenced and unsentenced inmate is recorded. Care needs to be taken that the current charge (as opposed to arresting charge) is documented for those unsentenced inmates who have been arraigned and are still in custody. This differentiation is important because, often arraignment charges differ markedly, in terms of both seriousness and number, from charges at the time of arrest and booking. If current charge data is unavailable from jail documents, a list of inmates could be prepared and checked against court files to document charge status as of the date of profile construction. It should be noted that this could be a time consuming exercise and is probably better suited to a small sample size.)

Data Element	Suggested Source (& Alternative)
17. Bail Set on Current Arrest	Bail schedule adopted by county judges or bail documents contained in inmate jail files.
18. Wanted by Other Jurisdiction 19. Nature of Charges in Other Jurisdiction 20. Total Outstanding Warrants and Holds 21. Bail Amount of Outstanding Warrants	Wants and warrants information contained on booking sheet or noted in jail file of each inmate. Statewide/regional data system material inserted in jail folders. (Alternative Source: Have jail personnel conduct check for wants, warrants, holds, and transfer results to tally sheet.)
22. Number of Prior Felony Convictions 23. Most Serious Previous Felony Conviction 24. Number of Previous Misdemeanor Convictions 25. Most Serious Previous Misdemeanor Convictions	Rap sheets attached to booking sheet/inserted in jail inmate file or folder. In those counties with automated criminal justice information systems, conviction histories could be produced for each inmate, analyzed and transfered to the data/tally sheet. Interview forms completed by jail or other staff to collect information to support decisions related to releasing inmates on their own recognizance. (Alternative Sources: Two alternative sources exist: (1) through the sheriff's department, get criminal history summaries—use inmate name and number to collect statewide data; or (2) through department of justice, request criminal history listings for each inmate incarcerated at the time sample was taken. Both sources will provide statewide arrest and conviction history, to the extent they exist, for each incarcerated individual. Data will also include information on sentenced time served at state or local correctional facilities. It should be noted that arrest disposition data from some counties is underreported and the criminal history summaries noted above may be incomplete.)
26. Current Other Pending Cases	Notations on booking sheets or pretrial release interview forms. (Alternative Source: A list of inmates can be prepared and checked against court files to determine if inmates have multiple pending cases in local courts. It should be noted that this could be a time consuming exercise and is probably better suited to a relatively small sample.)
27. Past Bench Warrants for Failure to Appear	Notations on booking sheets or pretrial release interview forms. (Alternative Source: Difficult to construct if system has not been established to routinely record historical failure to appear information. Alternative approach could consist of checking list of names of incarcerated individuals against court records (alphabetic cross reference first and then, if FTA/disposition data are not recorded on the court's master index, check of each court file. It should be noted that this could be a time consuming exercise and is better suited to a small sample size.)
28. Previous Incarceration History	Data contained in jail/custody file of each inmate. Realistic source only if sheriff's record keeping practices include maintenance of a single, continuing custody file for inmates. Subject to limitation of providing local incarceration history only.
29. Reason Misdemeanor Offenses Not Cited	Arresting officer certification on arrest report. Check inmate custody file for arrest report and analyze information/extract data. (Alternative Source: Check inmates against the record files of the arresting agency; review relevant arrest/crime, incident report and note reason misdemeanor citation **not** granted on the tally sheet.
30. Current Housing in the Facility	At the time profile is taken, make copy of jail assigment/housing roster if housing location data are not noted on the booking sheet or in the custody file. (Alternative Source: Make list of all inmates in custody at time profile taken. Circulate list to facility commander(s) and request them to notate housing location as of that date/time for each inmate. (For accuracy, must be done same day as profile.) Transfer to tally sheet.)
31. Custody Problem(s) Determining Housing Requirements	Classification records maintained by jail. (Alternative Source: In absence of formal classification system and records, you will need to rely on knowledge and experience of jail custodial personnel. An alternative approach would be to review each inmate with a small group of line/command personnel and have them classify each inmate in terms of the custody and behavior characteristics listed on the tally sheet.)

Data Element	Suggested Source (& Alternative)
32. Employment Status	Pretrial release interview forms.
	(Alternative Source: If pretrial release program does not collect and verify this information as a continuing practice, alternative approach would be to expand inmate questionnaire/survey approach noted for demographic data elements (5, 6, 7, 8 above). In collecting these data through survey form or personal interview, care will need to be exercised to ensure accuracy in terms of response by inmates. This might include random verification of data recorded on inmate survey responses. While verification can be expected to improve the validity of questionnaire data, inmate releases authorizing verification of data will have to be obtained to ensure that inmate privacy rights are not violated.)
37. Adjudication Status of Unsentenced Inmates	Court status information noted on booking sheets or in inmate custody files.
	(Alternative Source: Prepare a list of all unsentenced inmates and check that list against court dockets to note status as of the profile date. It should be noted that this could be a time consuming exercise, depending on the structure of court records, and should be considered as a contributing factor in deciding whether to "sample" or to construct a 100% profile.)

Appendix C:

Sampling Guidelines

As noted in Step 1, if your facility has a large population, or if you wish to study releases over a long period, you may want to **sample** rather than study **all** of the people in the jail. The following paragraphs describe the advantages and disadvantages of sampling. They also discuss how to construct samples for either the snapshot or longitudinal profile.

Advantages of Sampling

"Sampling" requires less time for data collection.

When populations are relatively large, properly constructed samples can accurately portray relevant characteristics of total jail and other detention facility populations.

If data are not readily available to satisfy information requirements related to jail profile construction, sampling provides the opportunity to increase staff time to "search out" difficult data by reducing the number of inmates profiled.

Disadvantages of Sampling

In analyzing detention facility populations for facility planning purposes, it is frequently important to identify and isolate small population components to assess security, program, or other characteristics with relevance for facility planning purposes. When samples are drawn from relatively small populations (less than 1000), there is some danger that these sub-components of the general population might be obscured.

If findings from the profiling are controversial, it might be more politically defensible to have a 100% portrait of the facility's population upon which to base analyses and conclusions.

In selecting which approach to follow (sampling versus 100% study), consider the following decision criteria.

When to Sample

When population levels exceed 200 inmates.

When staff time available to conduct the needs assessment is limited.

When jail documents are limited in scope and content and "extra" work will be required to search out information.

When study results are unlikely to be subjected to major challenges by community groups.

When to Employ a 100% Study

When population levels fall below cut-offs shown below.

When jail documents contain most or all required data in a readily accessible form.

When profile results and their interpretation are likely to be subjected to a substantial amount of community controversy.

When data collection personnel have sufficient time to profile the entire population.

How to Construct a Sample for the Snapshot Profile

If sampling is selected as the desired approach, follow these steps to select and construct a study sample.

Task 1. Determine your preferred sample size. Use the table which follows for sampling guidelines.

Population	Sample Size
0–200	100%
201–300	200 plus 25% of population above 200.
301–400	225 plus 20% of population over 300.
over 400	240 plus 15% of population over 400.

Task 2. Make a comprehensive list of all individuals who are incarcerated at the time the profile is to be constructed. Use jail booking files or another list as your source to construct list.

Task 3. Give an identification code number to each of the names on the list, starting with 1 and numbering sequentially until each name on the list has been assigned a different number.

Task 4. Obtain a table of random numbers from a library, bookstore, or statistics textbook.

Task 5. Use the random number table to select which inmates to include in your analysis. This is done by going sequentially through the random numbers and including each inmate whose number appears, until you have a large enough sample. If each random number in the table is longer (more digits) than your identification code, treat your codes as three or four digit numbers (e.g., 1 would be 001 or 0001) and look only at the last three or four digits of the random number.

This procedure eliminates bias in selecting who to include in the study.

How to Construct a Sample for the Snapshot Release Study or the Longitudinal Profile

The following steps can be used to make sampling decisions for Part Two, Release Analysis of the snapshot profile, as well as the longitudinal profile.

Review jail records to determine the volume of releases on an annual basis over the last twelve months. Based on recent release volume, determine how many releases to include. Refer to the following table for the number of releases and method of selecting them.

Sampling Guidelines for Constructing a Longitudinal Profile

Annual Bookings/Releases	Volume to be Analyzed	Suggested Sampling Technique
Less than 3,500	500 or 3 months' releases, whichever is greater.	Pick calendar period. Study all releases.
3,501 to 7,300	750 or 10 percent of releases, whichever is greater.	Pick calendar period. Select every "n-th" release to include. "N" represents the interval necessary to create sample size.
7,301 to 14,500	1,000 or 10 percent of releases, whichever is greater.	Same as above.
14,501 to 29,500	1,500 or 10 percent of releases, whichever is greater.	Same as above.
29,501	1,500 or 5 percent of releases, whichever is greater.	Same as above.

Reference

Lakner, Edward, **A Manual of Statistical Sampling Methods for Corrections Planners,** National Clearinghouse for Criminal Justice Planning and Architecture, University of Illinois, Champaign, Il, 1976.

Appendix D:

Estimated Time Requirements for Snapshot Profile

		Data Collection Hours Per 100 Inmates *	
Data Element	**Source**	**If Data Are Centralized in Jail Files**	**If Some Data Must be Reconstructed**
1, 2, 3, 4, 5, 6, 7, 8, 9, 10, 11, 12, 13, 14, 15, 16, 17, 18, 19, 20, 21, 22, 23, 24, 25, 26, 27, 28, 29, 30	Booking Sheet/ Custody File	From 10 to 20 person hours required to build tally sheet for each 100 inmates assuming that all data elements are available from custody files or booking sheets available from central source in the jail	6 to 7 person hours to extract data from booking sheets
18, 19, 20, 21	Custody File/ Rap Sheet		12 to 18 person hours to request printouts; sort; transfer to tally sheet
22, 23, 24, 25	Custody File/ Rap Sheet		Included in staff hours noted above
26, 27, 37	Custody File Court Records		16 to 32 person hours to access court records and transfer data
28	Custody File Rap Sheet		Included in staff hours noted above related to accessing history records
29	Custody File Police Agency Records		16 to 24 person hours to access police agency records
31	Classification Records; Interview w/Jail Staff		10 person hours/100 inmates
32, 33, 34, 36	Pretrial Interview From Inmate Survey		24 to 40 person hours to develop
35	Classification Records; Interview Medical or Mental Health Staff		10 person hours/100 inmates
Total		10 to 20 person hours/100 inmates	94 to 141 person hours per 100 inmates

* The actual time required is dependent on data accessibility; estimates noted in the table can be used to develop staff commitment requirements given varying levels of data availability.

Appendix E:

Inmate Release Data Form

(Note: You may wish to alter this form if offense and type-of-release categories differ in your state.)

Inmate Number	Booking Charge	Type of Release	Booking and Release Dates and Times									Average Length of Stay	
			Booking Date and Time				Release Date and Time						
			Mo.	Day	Yr.	Time	Mo.	Day	Yr.	Time		Days	Hours

Felony

01 = Murder/related violent crime
02 = Other violent anti-person crime
03 = Violent crime involving police officer
04 = Family violence
05 = Sex offense
06 = Commerical sex offense
07 = Burglary
08 = Weapons
09 = Other property crimes (non-violent)
10 = Drug/prohibited substance—use
11 = Drug/prohibited substance—sale
12 = Automobile violations
13 = Probation violations
14 = Miscellaneous

Misdemeanor

15 = Violent offense/civilian
16 = Violent offense/police officer involved
17 = Burglary related
18 = Family violence
19 = Sex offense
20 = Commercial sex offense
21 = Weapons
22 = Non violent/non-burglary property crime
23 = Nuisance
24 = Public inebriation
25 = Drug/prohibited substance—use
26 = Drug/prohibited substance—sale
27 = Probation violation
28 = Automobile offense—alcohol related
29 = Automobile offense—non-alcohol related
30 = Miscellaneous

Type of Release

1 = Bail/Bail Bond
2 = 10% bail
3 = Own Recognizance (OR)
4 = Supervised Release (SOR)
5 = Misdemeanor Citation
6 = Transferred to other agency
7 = Diverted—Released
8 = Trial Complete/Case Disposed (note— please differentiate in those cases where people are held in custody until disposition and subsequently serve sentenced time without leaving custody)
9 = Case not prosecuted
10 = Transfer to alcohol program
11 = Transfer to drug program
12 = Completed sentence

Length of Stay

Enter the date and time of booking and release. These are not variables, but are used to compute Length of Stay.

Compute actual days between booking and release as extracted from booking files; ensure all spaces are filled—for example, if length of stay is one day—code it 001; if length of stay is 14 days, code it 014; and so on. If released on booking day, enter 000. If unknown, enter 999. If individual was sentenced and completed sentence, record elapsed time from appropriate entry date (booking date for those who were not released during pretrial period and commitment date for those sentenced people who were released pretrial.)

For lengths of stay less than one day, compute the hours spent in the jail. Code the result as follows:

1 = less than 4 hours
2 = 4–7 hours
3 = 8–11 hours
4 = 12–23 hours

Appendix F:

Suggested Offense Groupings of Penal Code Violations

(Note: Counties may wish to work out their own categories.)

Felony Classes

Profile
Code   Offense

01 Murder/Related Violent Crime

Murder
Manslaughter
Mayhem
Assault w/intent to commit murder
Assault w/intent to commit rape, etc.
Rape

02 Other Violent Anti-Person Crimes

Kidnap
Kidnap for ransom/robbery
Robbery
Assault w/intent to commit a felony
False Imprisonment
Assault w/a deadly weapon
Shooting at a dwelling

03 Violent Crime Involving a Police Officer

Assault on a Police Officer
Battery on a Police Officer
Assault w/a deadly weapon on a Police Officer

04 Family Violence

Child Beating
Child or Wife Beating

05 Sex Offenses

Incest
Lewd act with child
Perversion
Child molestation

06 Commercial Sex Offenses

Seduction for prostitution
Pimping/pandering
Obscene Material

07 Burglary

Burglary

08 Weapons

Prohibited weapon
Felon, addict w/weapon
Concealed weapon
Destructive device
Felon w/firearm

Profile
Code   Offense

09 Other Property Crimes (non-violent)

Bookmaking
Forgery of I.D.
Forgery of checks
Fictitious checks
Checks, insufficient funds
Theft of credit card
Grand Theft
Receiving stolen property
Malicious mischiefs/vandalism
Attempted crime
Petty theft w/prior conviction
Petty theft w/prior felony
Using minor as agent
Auto theft

10 Drug/Prohibited Substance-use

Possession of dangerous drugs
Forging prescriptions
Illegal possession
Forging presc. for narcotic
Possession w/o presc.
D.U.I., Drugs

11 Drug/Prohibited Substance-sale

Furnishing drugs w/o presc.
Possession for sale
Illegal transport, sale
Using minor in sale, transport
Sale to minor
Sale (falsely represented)
Cultivation of marijuana
Possession of marijuana for sale
Marijuana: transport, sale
Use of minor in sale, transport
Maintaining a place
Illegal possess., for sale
Illegal transport, sale
Inducing, violating, minor agent
Furnishing substance
Possess., intent to manufacture

12 Automobile Violations

Hit & run w/injury
D.U.I. w/injury

13 Probation Violation

Profile Code	Offense		Profile Code	Offense

14 Arson

Arson

15 Miscellaneous

Conspiracy
Non-support
Solicitation to commit murder

Misdemeanor Classes

16 Violent Offense-Civilian

Simple assault
Battery
Assault w/a deadly weapon
Shooting at a dwelling

17 Violent Offense-Police Off. Involved

Resisting a Police Off.
Assault on a Police Off.
Battery on a Police Off.

18 Burglary Related

Possession of Burglary related tools
Trespassing
Loitering on priv. prop.

19 Family Violence

Child Beating
Drunk in presence of a minor

20 Sex Offenses

Contributing to the delinq. of a minor
Perversion
Failure to register w/Sheriff
Indecent exposure
Soliciting to indulge in lewd conduct
Loitering in public toilet for lewd acts
Peeking into inhabited dwelling
Loitering where children congregate

21 Commercial Sex Offenses

Seduction for prostitution
Obscene matter
Prostitution

22 Weapons

Brandishing a weapon
Concealed switchblade
Felon with a gun
Carrying a concealed weapon
Carrying a loaded weapon
Possession of a gun
Felon with a gun

23 Non-violent/non-burglary property crime

Gaming
Bookmaking
Forgery
Insufficient funds—checks
Insufficient funds—checks
Petty theft
Theft of credit card
Use of credit card— knowing illegal
Petty theft
Shoplifting
Receiving stolen prop.
Taking vehicle temporarily
Defrauding innkeeper
Possess. of stolen articles
Malicious mischief

Soliciting crime
Attempted crime
Petty theft with prior misdemeanor
Petty theft with prior felony

24 Nuisance

Failure to provide
Riot
Incitement to riot
Riot
Unlawful assembly
Refusal to disperse
Disturbing the peace
Refusal to disperse
Impersonating a Police Off.
Damaging jail
Begging
Disorderly conduct
Outraging public decency
Harassing by telephone

25 Public Drinking

Under the influence of alc.

26 Drug Use

Possession of dang. drugs
/AC Possession: less than 1 oz of marijuana
Possession of a needle
Frequenting place of narcotics
Forging or altering presc.
Possess. of dang. drugs.

27 Drug Sale

Transport less than 1 oz of marijuana
Maintaining a place where drugs used
Furnishing substance

28 Probation Violation

Profile
Code   **Offense**

29   Automobile—Alcohol Related

Driving under the influence
of alcohol/drugs
Drinking in motor vehicle
Open alcoholic container
in vehicle

30   Automobile—Non-Alcohol Related

False statements/fict. names
Impersonating a CHP Officer
False information
False report of theft
Altering motor or other no.
Altering engine or serial no.
Tampering with auto
Driver must be licensed
License presented to officer on demand
Suspended or invoked license
Hit & run w/property damage
Reckless driving
Reckless driving (w/injury)
Driving under the influence of drugs
Speed contests
Vehicle on public paths/trails
Trespassing
Reckless driving, w/ORV
False signatures
Failure to appear to pay fine
Failure to attend driving school
Failure to observe signs, etc.

Appendix G:

Sample Inmate Needs Survey Form

"Hi, I'm _____. Thank you for coming. I hope you will be able to help me by answering a few questions. As you may know we are doing a survey to find out what people think about some of the jail programs and how they could be improved. We just want an overall picture—we will put all the information we get together and no one will know who said what. Because of this, the form we use to record your replies has no name on it. (Show questionnaire). We are just keeping this list of names (show interview schedule) so we know who we have seen and who we still have to see. No one outside our office will see the individual questionnaires. The information will be used to help plan improvements in the jail system.

"Now, as I said, we are interested in your opinions, but if you don't have any opinion on something, or don't know, or don't want to answer—that's OK. Just say so.

"Do you think you can help us?"

(Interviewer—answer any questions, clarify, etc. If respondent is unwilling to participate, thank him again and let him go.)

Respondent Number □ □ □

Interviewer Introduction

The first section is about procedures, rules and regulations. But first, in general, would you say that the jail system is—

- □ Very good
- □ Good
- □ Poor
- □ Very Poor
- □ Don't know/no opinion/refuse to answer

(Interviewer, if response is stilted, etc., insert reassurance on lines of Introduction. Attempt to establish rapport. Answer to this question not coded.)

Now, in detail; were there any particular procedures which caused you problems:
1. When you were arrested and booked?
   1. Took too long
   2. Difficulty in getting use of telephone
   3. Other (Specify)

2. How many hours did the arrest and booking take?____ hours.

(If your county has no own-recognizance release program, skip 3 through 7.)

3. Did you apply for OR?
   1. No
   2. Yes

   (If No)
4. Why didn't you apply for OR?
   1. Didn't want it
   2. Didn't know about it
   3. Didn't think I would get it (previous record, type of offense)
   4. Too much hassle
   5. Too many inquiries made
   6. Other (Specify)

(If Yes)
5. Were you interviewed for OR?
    1. No
    2. Yes

6. Did you get OR?
    1. No
    2. Yes

(If No)
7. Why do you think you didn't get OR?
    1. No family in area
    2. No job
    3. No local connections
    4. Outstanding warrant(s)
    5. Previous non-appearance
    6. Type of offense
    7. Previous absconding/escape
    8. Other (Specify)

(If No to Q 6)
8. Did you post bail?
    1. Relative posted bail
    2. Friend posted bail
    3. Bail bond from commerical company
    4. Other (Specify)

(If on OR)
9. Did you have any particular difficulties in relation to making arrangements for your trial while on OR?
    1. Difficulty in getting private attorney
    2. Difficulty in getting together with Public Defender
    3. Difficulty in getting practical help/advice from Probation Department
    4. Difficulty in getting practical help/advice from Public Defender Department Social Workers
    5. Other (Specify)

(If held in custody)
10. Did you have any particular difficulties in making arrangement for your trial while in jail?
    1. Difficulty in getting private attorney
    2. Difficulty in getting together with Public Defender
    3. Difficulty in getting practical help/advice from official agencies (e.g., probation)
    4. Difficulty in getting practical help/advice from Public Defender Department Social Workers
    5. Other (Specify)

11. For your trial did you have:
    1. Private attorney?
    2. Public Defender?
    3. Conducted own case?

(If private attorney)
12. How many discussions did you have with your private attorney before your trial?

(If Public Defender)
13. How many discussions did you have with your Public Defender before your trial?

14. Were discussions with your attorney
    1. Before day of trial?
    2. On day of your trial only?
    3. Both before and on day of trial?

    (Interviewer—If trial lasted more than one day, record position as at first day of trial)

15. After conviction but before sentence were you?
    1. Released on OR?
    2. Posted bail?
    3. Held in custody?

16. Before you went into the jail, did you know the procedure for getting onto work furlough?
    1. No
    2. Yes

    (If Yes)

17. Before you went into the jail, who told you about getting onto work furlough?
    1. Previous knowledge
    2. Private attorney
    3. Public Defender/Public Defender Social Worker
    4. Probation Department/Probation Officer
    5. Friend
    6. Other (Specify)

This section is about problems you may have had after being sentenced.

18. Did you apply for work furlough before you started serving time?
    1. No
    2. Yes

    (If No)

19. Why didn't you apply for work furlough?
    1. Didn't want it
    2. Didn't think I would get it
    3. Didn't have job arranged
    4. Too difficult to apply/too much hassle
    5. Rehab people unsympathetic/unpleasant etc.
    6. Other (Specify)

    (If Yes)

20. Did you get work furlough?
    1. No
    2. Yes

    (If No)

21. Why do you think you didn't get work furlough?
    1. Nature of offense
    2. Previous absconding/escape
    3. Rehab people said I was unsuitable for work furlough
    4. Didn't have job already arranged
    5. Rehab people vetoed job already arranged
    6. Rehab people couldn't find me a job
    7. Rehab people prejudiced/out to get me/play favorites, etc.
    8. Other (Specify)

(If Yes)
22. Were you in _____ (facility) when your work furlough was approved?
    1. No
    2. Yes

    (If Yes to Q 20)
23. How long were you in _____ (facility) before you started work furlough?
    ____ days

    (If Yes to Q 20)
24. How long did it take for your first pay check to reach you?
    ____ days from pay day

Now, this next section is about things here at the jail.

25. What programs and facilities are there to help you while you are here in the jail and when you get out?
(Interviewer—unaided recall—do not prompt)

	Unaided recall	Service used	Rating of service used	Impressions of other services

Alcohol and Drug program

Medical Services—
    Doctor
    Dentist
    Eye Doctor
    Nurse
    Other

Jail Counselors

Rehab Officers

Education/Teacher

Religious Programs/Clergy

26. Have you taken part in any of the programs or used any of the services?
(Interviewer—use list above and read out each item)

27. How would you rate each of the programs you used—on a scale:
    1. Don't know/no opinion/refused to answer
    2. Hindrance
    3. Not helpful
    4. Helpful
    5. Very helpful

(Interviewer—read out each service used by respondent and score above—e.g., Did you find ____ very helpful/
helpful/not helpful/hindrance)

28. What impressions do you have of the other services?
(Interviewer—read out services NOT used by respondent. Ask what is your impression of _____? Do you think it
is very helpful, etc.?)

29. If other programs were available would you PERSONALLY use any of the following:
(Interviewer—read list through and then repeat item by item. Explain if necessary)
1. Reading, writing, arithmetic classes?
2. Art, music?
3. Individual counseling?
4. Personal problems discussion groups?
5. Classes on how to apply for a job (e.g. act at interviews)?
6. Training in the jail for the kinds of job you might look for outside?
7. Hobbies classes—woodwork, crafts etc.?
8. Other (Specify)?

30. What other kinds of programs would you find useful?

31. Would you work inside the jail for a small wage?
1. No
2. Yes

(If Yes)
32. What would be the minimum wage you would be willing to work for?
1. 50 cents per hour
2. $1 per hour
3. $1.50 per hour
4. $2.00 per hour
5. $2.50 per hour
6. Minimum wage ($3.35 per hour)

This next section is about services from people outside the jail.

33. Have you been contacted by anyone from the Probation Department since you were arrested?
1. No
2. Yes

(If Yes)
34. When was this?
(mark as many as appropriate)
1. Between arrest and trial
2. For presentence report only
3. While convicted but unsentenced
4. While in jail sentenced

35. How many times have you talked with a probation officer about your affairs since you were arrested this time (i.e., since arrest on charge for which now serving sentence)?

36. Did you find your discussion(s) with the probation officer helpful?
1. No
2. Yes

37. Would you like more contact with a probation officer?
    1. No
    2. Yes

    (If Yes)
38. Why would you like more contact with a probation officer?
    1. For counseling/talking things over, etc.
    2. For practical help
    3. Other (Specify)

Now, could we talk about what you are going to do when you leave the jail?

39. What area are you going to live in?

40. Do you have somewhere to live immediately when you leave the jail?
    1. No
    2. Yes

41. Who will you live with immediately after you leave the jail?
    1. Nuclear family—if married, (including common-law) with wife and children if unmarried, with parents
    2. Extended family—including in-laws
    3. With others—including hostels, etc.
    4. Alone
    5. No fixed abode

42. Have you got a job to go to?
    1. No
    2. Yes
    (Interviewer—probe gently to see if this is realistic; e.g., "Gee, that's great, what is it?")

    (If No)
43. Will you look for a job?
    1. No
    2. Yes

44. What kind of job will you look for?

45. In looking for a job, what kinds of things would help you before leaving this jail?
    1. Employment counseling
    2. Information about job openings
    3. Information on job skills/training centers
    4. Information on placement services/centers
    5. Help in setting up interviews
    6. Release for interviews
    7. Other (Specify)

46. How are you going to look for a job when you leave?
    1. Employment Department
    2. Private employment agencies
    3. Newspaper
    4. Family or friends
    5. Other (Specify)

The next section is about money.

47. How much money do you think you will have when you leave the jail?

48. Will that be enough to get you to (destination)?
    1. No
    2. Yes

49. After getting to _____, how long do you think that money will last?
    _____ days

50. What will you do when you have spent the money you go out with?
    1. Use savings, sell or pawn something
    2. Borrow from family
    3. Borrow from friends
    4. Apply for Welfare
    5. Apply to private charitable organizations
    6. Creative financing/hustle
    7. Other (Specify)
(If answer is 4–6, Interviewer should probe gently to ascertain if respondent knows enough about system to be able to get money from source.)

51. How will you do that?
    1. Doesn't know enough
    2. Knows enough

52. Now, so far, is there anything we haven't covered that you think is important, or would like to add?

"Now, I wonder if you would mind giving me a little background information about yourself? This is just for statistical purposes and won't be used to identify any individual."

53. (Do not ask unless uncertain) Ethnic Group
    1. White   6. American Indian
    2. Black   7. Filipino
    3. Mexican-American   8. Pacific Islander
    4. Japanese   9. Other/Unknown
    5. Chinese

54. Could you tell me what age you were last birthday?
    ____ years

55. What is the highest grade of school or college you completed?
    1. Grade School
    2. High School
    3. High School Graduate
    4. Some College, Trade or Tech School
    5. College Graduate
    6. Postgraduate

56. How long is your sentence in the jail?
    _____ weeks

57. How long have you still to serve?
    _____ weeks

58. What was your conviction for?
    (Interviewer—circle this conviction)

Col 1	Col 2	Col 3	Col 4	Col 5	Col 6
Felony	No. of convs.	Place(s) sentence served	Misdemeanor	No. of convs.	Place(s) sentence served
Violent			Violent		
Sex			Property		
Burglary			Family		
Other Property			Sex		
Drug Use			Public Drunk		
Drug Sale			Drug Use		
Other			Drunk Driving		
			Other		

59. How many previous convictions do you have?

    (Interviewer—fill in columns 2 & 5 above for each category of offenses)

60. How many times have you been in jail or prison (sentenced) before this time?

61. Where was that?
    (Interviewer—write in table above places sentence served for each conviction)

    (If had previous sentence(s)
62. How long were you free between release from your last sentence and being arrested on the charge you are now serving
    time for?
    _____ weeks

63. How long have you been free during the last year?
    _____ weeks
    (Interviewer—help respondent define 1 year past)

64. Who were you living with during that time?
    1. Nuclear family—if married, with wife and children
                      if unmarried, with parents
    2. Extended family—including in-laws
    3. With others—including hostels, etc.
    4. Alone
    5. No fixed abode

65. Are you married?
    (Interviewer— prompt if answer is No)
    1. Single   4. Widowed
    2. Cohabiting   5. Separated
    3. Married   6. Divorced

66. Have you any children? How many?

67. Were you working immediately prior to coming into the jail?
    1. No
    2. Yes
    3. Sometimes/casual

    (If Sometimes/Yes)
68. What was your job?

69. Did it pay well? About how much per hour?
    $_____

70. How long had you had that job?
    _____ weeks

71. Did you lose this job when you were arrested?
    1. No
    2. Yes

72. How many jobs did you have in the last year?

73. What is the longest time you have ever been in any one job?
    _____ weeks

74. What is the longest time you have been in any one job in the last year?
    _____ weeks

"Well, that's the end. Thank you very much. Is there anything you would like to ask me about the survey?"

    (Interviewer—answer any questions as simply as possible)

"Well, thank you very much (name) for your help. We really appreciate it. I hope everthing goes well for you now."
Show respondent out.

Interviewer—check over questionnaire for blanks, etc. Now, before next interview.

Appendix H:

Projection Method Two

Projection Method Two: Project future trends based on average daily population and average length of stay

Task 1: Record Average Daily Population (ADP)

Document or compute average daily population in your county's detention facilities for the last 10 years or whatever period is available (preferably 5 years or more). Record separately for each facility.

Example of Historic Arrest Trends		Your Computation of Historical Arrest Trends	
Year	ADP	Year	ADP
1974	114	19	
1975	118	19	
1976	116	19	
1977	124	19	
1978	132	19	
1979	127	19	
1980	139	19	
1981	136	19	
1982	140	19	
1983	142	19	

Task 2: Record Average Daily Bookings (ADB)

Document average daily bookings in your county's detention facilities for the last 10 years or whatever period is available (preferably 5 years or more). Record separately for each facility.

Example of Average Daily Bookings		Your Computation of Average Daily Bookings	
Year	ADB	Year	ADB
1974	16	19	
1975	18	19	
1976	17	19	
1977	20	19	
1978	23	19	
1979	22	19	
1980	24	19	
1981	27	19	
1982	26	19	
1983	30	19	

Task 3: Compute Average Length of Stay (ALS)

Compute the average length of stay for each of the last ten years by dividing average daily population by average daily bookings. Repeat for each facility. (Average Daily Population **divided by** Average Daily Bookings **equals** Average Length of Stay in Days.)

Example of Average Length of Stay					Your Computation of Average Length of Stay				
Year	ADP	÷	ADB	= ALS	Year	ADP	÷	ADB	= ALS
1974	114		16	7.1	19				
1975	118		18	6.5	19				
1976	116		17	6.8	19				
1977	124		20	6.2	19				
1978	132		23	5.7	19				
1979	127		22	5.8	19				
1980	139		24	5.6	19				
1981	136		27	5.0	19				
1982	140		26	5.4	19				
1983	142		30	4.7	19				

Task 4: Study Trends in ADP and ALS

Observe and compute trends in average length of stay and average daily bookings for the last ten years. Use the data displayed in Task 3, totaling the average daily population and average lengths of stay and dividing by the number of years included (for 10 years of data, divide by 10). Display trends in graphic format by plotting your data for each year in the same manner as the illustrations.

Average Daily Bookings by Year

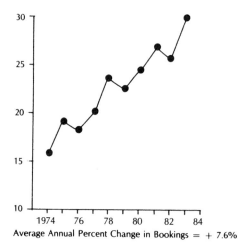

Average Annual Percent Change in Bookings = + 7.6%

Average Length of Stay by Year

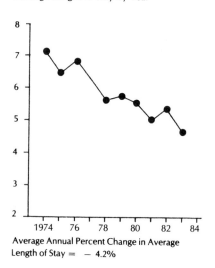

Average Annual Percent Change in Average Length of Stay = − 4.2%

Task 5: Make Projection Assumptions

Review past trends and consider what you've learned from your analysis of the criminal justice system in other steps of this process. For example, consider whether it is reasonable to expect continuing decreases in average length of stay, continuing increases in daily bookings and so forth. Based upon this review, state the assumptions which you feel will provide a reasonable basis for the projections.

Example of Assumptions

"Assume that bookings will continue to increase at the historically computed rate of 7.6 percent per year."

"Assume that Average Length of Stay will continue to decrease at same rate as observed for the last ten years (4.2 percent) for the next five years and then remain constant."

List of Your Assumptions

1. _____

2. _____

3. _____

4. _____

etc. _____

_____

_____

_____

_____

_____

_____

Task 6: Select Projection Technique

Select a mathematical technique for making the projections. Choose from among techniques such as straight line progression based on past trends, regression analysis, or other comparable projection techniques.

Task 7: Project Average Daily Bookings

Using the selected technique and based on your assumptions, project Average Daily Bookings for the 20-year planning period. Project yearly for the first ten years and in five-year increments thereafter. The following example uses a straight line projection that assumes a constant increase of 7.6 percent each year.

Example of Projected Average Daily Bookings

Projection Year	% Change	ADB
1984	–	30
1985	7.6	32
1986	7.6	35
1987	7.6	37
1988	7.6	40
1989	7.6	43
1990	7.6	47
1991	7.6	50
1992	7.6	54
1993	7.6	58
1994	7.6	62
1999	7.6	90
2004	7.6	130

Your Computation of Projected Daily Bookings

Projection Year	% Change	ADB
1st Year		
2nd Year		
3rd Year		
4th Year		
5th Year		
6th Year		
7th Year		
8th Year		
9th Year		
10th Year		
15th Year		
20th Year		

Task 8: Project Average Length of Stay

Project anticipated Average Length of Stay for the 20-year planning period. The following example uses a straight line method with a constant decrease of 4.2 percent each year for five years and then a leveling off.

Example of Projected Average Length of Stay

Year	% Change	ALS
1984	–	4.7
1985	−4.2%	4.5
1986	−4.2%	4.3
1987	−4.2%	4.1
1988	−4.2%	4.0
1989	−4.2%	3.8
1990	–	3.8
1991	–	3.8
1992	–	3.8
1993	–	3.8
1994	–	3.8
1999	–	3.8
2004	–	3.8

Your Computation of Projected Average Length of Stay

Year	% Change	ALS
1st Year		
2nd Year		
3rd Year		
4th Year		
5th Year		
6th Year		
7th Year		
8th Year		
9th Year		
10th Year		
15th Year		
20th Year		

Task 9: Project (Unadjusted) Average Daily Population

Convert Average Length of Stay and Average Daily Booking projections to Projected Average Daily Population for the planning period. This is accomplished by multiplying average daily bookings by average length of stay for each year over the planning period. The following formula is used:

$$\text{Projected Average Daily Population} = \text{Projected Daily Bookings} \times \text{Projected Average Length of Stay}$$

Example of Projected Average Daily Population

Year	ADB	×	ALS	=	ADP
1985	32	×	4.5	=	144
1986	35	×	4.3	=	150
1987	37	×	4.1	=	152
1988	40	×	4.0	=	160
1989	43	×	3.8	=	163
1990	47	×	3.8	=	179
1991	50	×	3.8	=	190
1992	54	×	3.8	=	205
1993	58	×	3.8	=	220
1994	62	×	3.8	=	236
1999	90	×	3.8	=	342
2004	130	×	3.8	=	494

Your Computation of Projected Average Daily Population

Year	ADB	×	ALS	=	ADP
1st Year					
2nd Year					
3rd Year					
4th Year					
5th Year					
6th Year					
7th Year					
8th Year					
9th Year					
10th Year					
15th Year					
20th Year					

Task 10: Develop Compensation Factor for Peak Population Times

Review daily population data for the last six to twelve months. Compute "average" high or peak population by noting high or peak population each month and dividing by the number of months. Compare to the average daily population for the same period.

Task 10.1: Compute Population Fluctuations

Example of Population Fluctuations

Month	ADP	Monthly High
Dec.	136	148
Jan.	135	149
Feb.	137	144
Mar.	138	150
Apr.	135	151
May	140	147
Total:	821	889
Div. by 6 =		
Average:	137	148

Your Computation of Population Fluctuations

Month	ADP	Monthly High
1st		
2nd		
3rd		
4th		
5th		
6th		
Total:		
Div. by 6 =		
Average:		

Task 10.2: Compute Adjustment Factor

The Adjustment Factor is computed as the percentage of the peaks over the average population.

$$\frac{\text{Difference}}{\text{Average Population}} + 1 = \text{Adjustment Factor}$$

Example of Computation of Adjustment Factor

High Population:	148
Average Population:	−137
Difference:	11

$$\frac{11}{137} + 1 = 1.08$$

Your Computation of Adjustment Factor

High Population:	_____
Average Population:	−_____
Difference:	_____

$$\frac{\text{Difference ( )}}{\text{Average Population ( )}} + 1 = \text{Adjustment Factor ( )}$$

Task 11: Project Required Capacity

Use the Adjustment Factor to convert Population Projections into needed projected capacity to accommodate projected peak population swings.

Example of Projected Capacity

Year	Projected ADP	×	Adjustment Factor	=	Projected Capacity
1985	144	×	1.08	=	155
1986	150	×	1.08	=	162
1987	152	×	1.08	=	164
1988	160	×	1.08	=	173
1989	163	×	1.08	=	176
1990	179	×	1.08	=	193
1991	190	×	1.08	=	205
1992	205	×	1.08	=	221
1993	220	×	1.08	=	238
1994	236	×	1.08	=	255
1999	342	×	1.08	=	369
2004	494	×	1.08	=	533

Your Computation of Projected Capacity

Proj. Year	Projected ADP	×	Adjustment Factor	=	Projected Capacity
1st					
2nd					
3rd					
4th					
5th					
6th					
7th					
8th					
9th					
10th					
15th					
20th					

Task 12: Divide Projected Population By Sentence Status and Sex

In this last task of Method Two, review data from past years and calculate proportions of the average daily sentenced population and unsentenced males and females (if both are to be included in the subject facility). Apply these percentages to projected total population. If such historical breakdowns are unavailable, use percentages developed from analysis of jail population profile data. If adequate data are available, the entire projection process can be based upon figures for sentenced and unsentenced populations.

Index